Y0-BER-871

ARGUMENTS ON AMERICAN POLITICS

ARGUMENTS ON AMERICAN POLITICS

John C. Shea
Editor
West Chester University of Pennsylvania

Brooks/Cole Publishing Company
Pacific Grove, California

HILBERT LIBRARY
FRESNO PACIFIC UNIV.-M. B. SEMINARY
FRESNO, CA 93702

Brooks/Cole Publishing Company
A Division of Wadsworth, Inc.

© 1991 by Wadsworth, Inc., Belmont, California 94002. All rights reserved. No part of this book may be reproduced, stored in a retrieval system, or transcribed, in any form or by any means—electronic, mechanical, photocopying, recording, or otherwise—without the prior written permission of the publisher, Brooks/Cole Publishing Company, Pacific Grove, California 93950, a division of Wadsworth, Inc.

Printed in the United States of America

10   9   8   7   6   5   4   3   2   1

Sponsoring Editor: *Cynthia C. Stormer*
Marketing Representative: *Ron Shelly*
Editorial Assistant: *Cathleen Sue Collins*
Production Editor: *Penelope Sky*
Manuscript Editor: *Betty G. Seaver*
Permissions Editor: *Carline Haga*
Interior and Cover Design: *Roy R. Neuhaus*
Cover Illustration: *Roy R. Neuhaus*
Art Coordinator: *Cloyce J. Wall*
Interior Illustration: *Cloyce J. Wall*
Index: *Do Mi Stauber*
Typesetting: *Kachina Typesetting, Inc.*
Cover Printing: *Phoenix Color Corporation*
Printing and Binding: *The Maple–Vail Book Manufacturing Group*

Library of Congress Cataloging-in-Publication Data

Arguments on American politics / John C. Shea, editor.
    p.   cm.
  Includes bibliographical references and index.
  ISBN 0-534-13890-X
  1. United States—Politics and government.
I. Shea, John C.
JK274.A79 1991
320.973—dc20   90-37797
                          CIP

HERKIMER LIBRARY
HERKIMER & KASPENED COMMUNITY COLLEGE
HERKIMER, NY 13350

FOR THE CHILDREN

Beth, John, Tom, Matt, Anne, Leah, Laura, Amy, John Michael, Karen, Jenny, Abby, Max, Nicky, Ken, Jennifer, B.J., Rachel, Paul, Heather, Rachel, Rebecca, Kristin, Duane, Monty, Scott, Tadd, Craig, Glenn, Nicole, Blaise, Michael, Graham, Annie, Ian, Colin, and Tony.

Preface

The American political system, with its constitutional provisions of federalism and separation of powers, is one of the most complex in the world. Even those who have devoted their professional lives to understanding it are challenged. New items always crowd the political agenda, but the perennial issues linked to the basic institutions of the republic are equally compelling.

Arguments on American Politics has a pro–con format, which helps students understand how people on opposing sides of a discussion organize and present their arguments. Several features are unique to this book, of which three

are most important. First, we have avoided the temptation simply to concentrate on current policy proposals. The issues we address were selected carefully to correspond to the outlines of most American government courses, which cover major governmental institutions and political processes. Second, all the essays were written specifically for this book, in response to specific questions. Finally, all the writers read the first drafts of the essays written from the opposite side of the question at hand, and could thus incorporate their responses in their own final essays. This approach is based on the Supreme Court practice in which the justices circulate draft opinions and are able to respond to the opposing arguments. Some of our essayists responded to their "opponents" by name; others chose simply to imply their knowledge of dissenting opinions; all took their opponents' arguments into account. The essays are focused on specific topics and questions, and tend to be equivalent in length.

It is important to note that our writers are arguing as advocates, seeking to make the strongest possible case for the side they have been asked to defend, without stretching the limits of credibility. In two cases, authors actually wrote for the side they disagreed with (initially, at least). As debaters know, there is no surer way to learn the strengths and weaknesses of an opponent's case than to try to make that case your own. There are some very robust exchanges, and arguments are developed that may anger many readers or make them feel uncomfortable. If we cause such reactions, we may inspire students to examine both sides of an issue: if we make readers think, we will have succeeded.

COVERAGE

Our first and last sets of essays are the exceptions to our pro–con format. The first section is about the role of the American government in the next century. Here, three authors were asked only to concentrate on domestic politics, but otherwise to develop their positions (liberal, conservative, and moderate) as strongly as they could. In the last section, on foreign policy, three essays provide very different outlooks on the international arena.

We begin, then, with an overall perspective on the role of American government in the next century. No one is able to predict the future with any certainty, and Professors Bosso, Allen, and Shea extrapolate from what each of them sees as the condition of the United States today. Although they reach very different conclusions, there is remarkable agreement on the problem of the declining sense of community.

In the second section, Professors Blessing and Saffell consider the desirability of adopting a parliamentary system for American government, as a way of examining the structure of the presidential system that features the separation of powers. For more than twenty years the president has confronted a Congress in which at least one, and usually both, houses have been controlled by the opposition party. But even when this has not been the case (during the Carter administration), no president has been able simply to command the fiercely independent members of Congress. We are not going to adopt the British parliamentary model in the foreseeable future, but there is no better way of understanding our system than to compare it to the alternative.

In our third section we ponder a question that is central to democracy: Does public opinion really affect the behavior of policy makers? The debate here centers on the role of elites in American society and government. Elitists hold that there is a small minority, whose members share the same values and hold key positions, that makes major decisions about allocating resources. This position is defended by Professor Margolis, who argues that public opinion has little effect on final choices. Professor McAdams argues the case for competing elites that do in fact respond to majority sentiment.

In our fourth section the question is whether interest groups or political parties provide the most effective vehicles for democratic representation. Professor Bosso holds that voters organize to combat relatively meaningless electoral choices; Professor Stone finds that parties are a more inclusive and thus democratic alternative.

In the fifth section we question whether television, which plays a key role in our political process, undermines our democratic institutions. Professor Hallum holds television responsible for declining levels of electoral participation, for citizens' alienation from politics and government, and for withholding information on major issues. The rejoinder is that television is fundamentally a messenger and that objective issues reported on television are more to blame.

In the sixth section we consider whether Congress should have a central role in the making of foreign policy. Professor Johnson argues that this is required by the Constitution; what has happened when Congress has been left out suggests that a larger legislative role is both necessary and desirable. Professor Oliver contends that the president, as recognized by the courts, has to assume overall direction to ensure national security, although there is a place in the process for Congress.

In the seventh section we ask whether our country is best served by a powerful presidency. Professor Milne argues that the system works well only when a strong and dynamic president runs the executive branch; that neither Congress nor the courts can fill this role. Professor Robertson is far less sanguine about the centralization of power in what he refers to as the "covert presidency."

In the eighth section we look at the Supreme Court, that unique American institution. Is it democratic for the power of judicial review to be possessed by nine judges who are appointed for life? Professor Urey argues that it is, if American democracy is properly understood. Professors Heck and Arledge contend that judicial government is fundamentally irreconcilable with the idea of majority rule.

In the ninth section we turn to civil rights and affirmative action, one of the most controversial of policies. Professors Lenz and Stetson see affirmative action as a legislative attempt to balance past wrongs inflicted on minorities and women; Professor Allen argues that affirmative action is simply reverse discrimination, requiring us to judge people not as individuals but as members of groups.

In the tenth section we ask whether the powerful American emphasis on individual rights threatens the freedom and well-being of ordinary citizens. Professor Scott argues that it does, and that a free press for pornographers, and an excessive zealousness in separating church from state, infringe on the rights of the vast majority of citizens. Professor Riley counters that respect for the rights of society's outcasts is in the interests of all.

Finally, in the eleventh section, we imagine the United States in the years ahead. Professor Johnson believes we need to improve our understanding of foreign places and people, and of the workings of government; to diminish our fear of the communist "threat"; and to require our leaders to be less eager to intervene in the affairs of other countries. Professor Mulcahy believes that our relations with the Soviet Union will continue to dominate our foreign policy, even though the nature of that relationship is changing and may well become less confrontational. He argues that the world will become multi-polar, and that we must adjust to a relationship with our allies that is based more on cooperation than on American leadership. Professor Garcia and Mr. Neagle have a very different emphasis, stressing the need for international cooperation in solving such global problems as ecological threats to the planet. They foresee that nation-states may play a diminished role and that international non-state actors may take a larger part.

TO THE INSTRUCTOR

Arguments on American Politics will be used primarily as a supplement in courses on politics, but it is just as suitable to courses on issues or public policy. The essays may be a source of discussion, starting points for student essays, or resources for small groups developing further analysis of particular issues. Student debates, of course, almost suggest themselves in conjunction with this text.

An instructor's manual contains twelve questions for each essay. Some of these require descriptive answers, some analytical. Some are comparative, referring to other essays, and some assume that students are familiar with related materials. For example, questions about the essays on interest groups versus parties, by Professors Bosso and Stone, might require that students understand basic aspects of these subjects. As explained in the manual, all such questions are coded as to the underlying assumptions. A final set of questions may be used in a comprehensive examination. The manual is a usable product, not the boilerplate too often associated with such efforts.

ACKNOWLEDGMENTS

Any attempt to thank the people involved in *Arguments on American Politics* inevitably errs in missing some. There would have been no book at all without the initial encouragement of Ron Shelly, and of Leo Wiegman, who decided it was worth the effort. Special thanks must be extended to Cindy Stormer, political science editor at Brooks/Cole, whose cheerful encouragement and suggestions played such a major role, and to Penelope Sky, production editor. Students often wonder why their teachers write so much better for publication than in the informal notes that adorn tests and term papers. The answer is that seldom-heralded but vital copy editors cheerfully (we hope) correct our most grievous mistakes. Our special thanks go to Betty G. Seaver for these efforts. Many embarrassing potential errors were avoided and strengths increased as a result of patient reviewing by our colleagues: Steve Kurvink, California State University at Fullerton; Brian Roberts, University of Texas at Austin; and Priscilla Southwell, University of Oregon at Eugene.

Many a spouse, secretary, friend, child, and colleague helped each of us improve our manuscript, suffered with us, and offered encouragement. To all of them we offer our appreciation, and I exercise an editor's prerogative in singling out my wife, Louise, as truly representative of the long suffering. It is customary for the editor to take responsibility for any remaining errors and to absolve all others; I choose to do nothing of the kind, but instead maintain the pretense that imperfections are deliberate devices to keep readers on their toes. Whether or not you are prepared to accept that proposition, instructors and students alike are invited to send corrections, comments, and suggestions for improvements in future editions to me in care of Brooks/Cole.

John C. Shea

To The Student

As you read the essays that follow, you will find that many of them are about the concept of democracy, a term that many of our writers found it necessary to define. This is not surprising, considering that they are examining American politics. Many words can be applied to our political system, including "presidential," "constitutional," and "federal," but "democracy" is the key. Democracy was the rallying cry of the students who were gunned down in Tiananmen Square; it is central to the demands for change that broke Eastern Europe out of forty years of Soviet repression; to restore a democratically elected government was among the Bush administration's justifications for the December, 1989 invasion of Panama. We like to believe that democracy is the essence of the American political system.

I urge you to think about the real meaning of democracy in the American context, as opposed to the way it is referred to in everyday argument and in the press: as an idealized symbol with little real content. What does democracy mean, and what are its limits, ideally and in practice? I also hope you are prepared to see relationships among the various topics addressed by our writers. For example, how is the argument about the influence of elites related to the role of parties and interest groups, or to such policies as affirmative action? How does the separation of powers in a presidential system influence foreign policy?

Learning requires an exposure not just to facts but to ideas; most important is your ability to master those facts and ideas and use them as the basis for your own ideas and conclusions. If this book contributes to that end, we will have satisfied our purpose. The essays you are about to read cover a wide range of questions, but only you can supply the "right" answer to many of the most basic ones.

The Editor

John C. Shea is Professor of political science at West Chester University, where he has served as department chair, academic dean, and chair of the curriculum committee. He is the author of *American Government and Politics, Second Edition,* published by St. Martin's Press in 1987. In the early 1960s, Shea served in the United States Foreign Service as Vice Counsel and Third Secretary at the U.S. embassy in Montevideo, Uruguay. He subsequently earned his Ph.D. at the University of Pittsburgh.

Shea has taught American government courses for 23 years, and believes that the principal challenge in this undertaking is winning students' interest.

"At West Chester, as at many schools, American government is a general education alternative, so most of the students are not majors. As with any liberal arts core requirement, we are trying to help students learn three things: to think analytically, to understand the paradigms of the discipline and, we hope, to become familiar with the subject matter. I believe it is always easier to accomplish these goals if students can see that American politics is just inherently exciting; if you can bring the conflicts that are so much a part of politics out into the open and encourage students to confront them and think them through. That's what inspired *Arguments on American Politics.*"

The Contributors

Wayne Allen is Assistant Professor of political science at Louisiana State University and assistant director of its Eric Vorgelin Institute for American Renaissance Studies. He has written on terrorism and the metaphysics of evil. A forthcoming work is "The Breakdown of Authority and the End of Community." His Ph.D. is from the University of California (Riverside).

Paula C. Arledge is Assistant Professor of political science at Northeastern Louisiana State University. She is the author of "John Paul Stevens: A Moderate Justice's Approach to the Constitution," *Whittier Law Review* (1989). Her Ph.D. is from the University of New Orleans.

James A. Blessing is Associate Professor of political science at Susquehanna University. He is the author of "The Suspension of Foreign Aid," *Polity* (Spring, 1981) and "It All Started with Swordfish," *Crescent* (Sept. – Oct. 1977). His Ph.D. is from the State University of New York (Albany).

Christopher J. Bosso is Assistant Professor of political science at Northeastern University. His publications include *Pesticides and Politics: The Life Cycle of a Public*

Issue (1987), which was co-winner of the award by the Policy Studies Organization for the best book in policy studies for the year. He also wrote "Mass Media and the Ethiopian Famine," in Margolis and Mauser, eds., *Manipulating Public Opinion* (1989). His Ph.D. is from the University of Pittsburgh.

José Z. Garcia is Associate Professor of political science at New Mexico State University. His article, "On Tragedy in El Salvador," appeared in *Current History* (January, 1990). During the 1989–90 academic year he was Visiting Professor at the U.S. Army School of the Americas, Fort Benning, Georgia. He received his Ph.D. from the University of New Mexico.

Anne Motley Hallum is Assistant Professor of political science at Stetson University. She is the author of "Presbyterians as Political Amateurs," in the *Congressional Quarterly Press*, 1988. She is currently preparing a publication on U.S. religious interests in Central America. Her Ph.D. is from Vanderbilt University.

Edward V. Heck is Professor of political science at San Diego State University. He is the author of "Changing Voting Patterns in the Warren and Burger Courts," *Judicial Conflict and Consensus* (1986), and co-author with Albert C. Ringelstein of "The Burger Court and the Primacy of Political Speech," *Western Political Quarterly* (1987). His Ph.D. is from Johns Hopkins University.

Loch K. Johnson is Regents Professor of political science at the University of Georgia. Among his publications are *America as a World Power* (1990), *America's Secret Power* (1989), and *A Season of Inquiry* (1988). His Ph.D. is from the University of California (Riverside).

Timothy O. Lenz is Assistant Professor of political science at Florida Atlantic University. He is the author of "Republican Virtue and the American Vigilante" *Legal Studies Forum*, (1988). His Ph.D. is from the University of Minnesota.

Michael Margolis is Professor and head of the department of political science at the University of Cincinnati. He is the author of *Political Stratification and Democracy* (1972), and *Viable Democracy* (1979), and with Gary A. Mauser co-edited *Manipulating Public Opinion* (1989). His Ph.D. is from the University of Michigan.

John McAdams is Associate Professor of political science at Marquette University. He has frequently published in journals, including the *American Political Science Review*, the *Journal of Politics*, and the *Sociological Quarterly*. His Ph.D. is from Harvard University.

Dorothy McBride Stetson is Professor and chair of political science at Florida Atlantic University. Her publications include *Women's Rights in France* (1987), and the forthcoming *Women's Rights in the USA*. Her Ph.D. is from Vanderbilt University.

James S. Milne is Professor of political science at West Chester University of Pennsylvania and director of its master's of science in administration program. A frequent consultant to government, he has written and spoken frequently on the presidency and American politics. His Ph.D. is from Temple University.

Kevin V. Mulcahy is Associate Professor of political science at Louisiana State University. He coauthored with Cecil V. Crabb Jr. *American National Security: A Presidential Perspective* (1990) and *Presidents and Foreign Policy: FDR to Reagan*

(1986). His Ph.D. is from Brown University.

John Neagle was a graduate student in political science at New Mexico State University when he wrote his contribution to this book.

James K. Oliver is Professor of political science and director of the international relations program at the University of Delaware. He is coauthor of *United States Foreign Policy and World Order* (1989), and *Foreign Policy Making and the American Political System* (1987). His Ph.D. is from American University.

Dennis D. Riley is Professor and chair of the department of political science at the University of Wisconsin at Stevens Point. He is the author of *Controlling the Federal Bureaucracy* (1987), "Excellence in Private High Schools: The Market Didn't Do it," in the *American Political Science Review,* (June, 1990), and "Issue Areas and Differentials in Agency Power (*American Political Science Review,* September, 1976). His Ph.D. is from the University of Michigan.

David Brian Robertson is Associate Professor of political science at the University of Missouri (St. Louis). With Dennis R. Judd he coauthored *The Development of American Public Policy: The Structure of Policy Restraint* (1989), and is the author

of "Governing and Jobs: America's Business-Centered Labor Market Policy," (*Polity,* Spring, 1988). His Ph.D. is from Indiana University.

David Saffell is Professor of political science and chair of the social science division at Ohio Northern University. He is the author of *State and Local Government* (4th ed., 1990), and *Essentials of American Government* (1989), and editor of *The State of the Union* (1990). His Ph.D. is from the University of Minnesota.

Jo Ann M. Scott is Assistant Professor of political science at Ohio Northern University, where she also serves as director of the criminal justice program. Her Ph.D. is from the University of California (Riverside).

Walter J. Stone is Associate Professor of political science at the University of Colorado at Boulder. His publications include *Republic at Risk: Self Interest in American Politics* (1990), and "The Carryover Effect in Presidential Elections," *American Political Science Review* (March, 1986). His Ph.D. is from the University of Michigan.

Gene R. Urey is Professor and chair of political science at Susquehanna University, where he also serves as coordinator of the legal studies program. His Ph.D. is from Syracuse University.

Contents

ARGUMENTS ON
AMERICAN POLITICS

I

INTRODUCTION

What Will Be the Proper Role of Government in the Next Century?

In the first three essays, unlike those that follow, our authors were free to roam the political landscape, their sole restriction being to concentrate on the domestic side of U.S. politics. Each prepared a first draft without any consultation as to what the others might decide to emphasize. When the three papers were exchanged, there was a striking point of agreement among them. The authors see major problems in the years ahead but, from individually very different perspectives, they all believe the major source of difficulties is a declining sense of community.

It is not surprising that the writers are deeply troubled by the current state of American society. Such concern probably "goes with the territory" of being social scientists, and especially of being political scientists. We are expected to take a longer view than do politicians, who often are unable to look past the next election. We can, we hope, be more dispassionate and disinterested than those whose jobs depend on the approval of the voters.

The concept of community has to do with beliefs that bind members of a society together, that cause them to think of themselves as one, as sharing in the experience of being a people. Sebastian De-Grazia put it this way years ago:

> The Great Community, as the ancient Greeks understood well, the community which embraces all other communities, is the political community. Holding it together are systems of beliefs, flexible bands, weaving through and around each member of the community, compacting it, allowing some stress at times, coiling like a steel spring at others. The basic denominator of citizens is these belief systems which express their ideas concerning their relationships to one another, and to their rulers. Without them, without this fundament of commonness, no political community can be said to exist. [De-Grazia, *The Political Community: A Study in Anomie*, 1948.]

A nation that does not have this sense of commonality is one whose members are less likely to be willing to make sacrifices in the common interest, less willing to extend to one another the hand of compassion or, indeed, even the ordinary courtesies modern life demands so that we may live together peaceably while getting on with our private lives.

What are the causes of this declining sense of community and what are its possible cures? Here our writers exhibit sharp philosophical differences.

Wayne Allen and Christopher Bosso place the loss of a sense of community most centrally in their essays; they also have the sharpest difference as to its roots and rectification. Allen sees the problem as one of the abandonment of traditional values and a rising effort to ascribe "goodness" to government. Although justice may occasionally require governmental action, for the most part

government shows its goodness (its regard for the community) negatively, by refraining from injustices. He clearly believes that restitution of a sense of community will have to take place outside government, cannot be engineered by it, and demands a return to traditional religiously based ideals that emphasize the role of the individual.

Bosso agrees that government cannot find the corrective to a declining sense of community for us, that solutions do not come from the top down. But, contrary to Allen, he very strongly holds that vigorous governmental action is needed. The world is too complex and interdependent to allow people to function as essentially isolated individuals. For government to respond only minimally to major societal failings, in Bosso's view, only serves to perpetuate them. Further, he stresses the need to find more forms of citizen involvement and therein shares with Allen an aversion to decision making from on high. Where Allen sees an excess of democracy (through misunderstanding of the concept), Bosso sees too little.

John Shea's essay is more eclectic, detailing many of the problems besetting our society. Without stressing the forms of renewed citizen involvement, he shares with Bosso the view that our present institutions are not working. He does not speak to solutions.

In reading these essays, you the student need to be aware of and search for other points of agreement and their underlying different assumptions. The sharp clashes over philosophy of government among our essayists occur, most importantly, in connection with fundamental notions about the proper place of government in society and government's relationship to citizens, both collectively and individually. These essays invite you to examine, in the broadest perspective, your own beliefs about our society and politics. More specifically, three questions are suggested. First, what are the major problems confronting the United States today? Second, what are their origins, and what responsibility does government hold for their creation? Third, what, if any, should be government's part in their resolution? The answer to the last question depends heavily on the answers to the first two.

Government and Democratic Governance into the Twenty-First Century

Christopher J. Bosso
Northeastern University

The United States no longer is an innocent youth. It certainly is not so old as England or China, yet it is a more *mature* place, blessed by whatever advantages accrue from age but anxiously aware that its often rambunctious adolescence is a fond memory. And, as with any passage into reluctant adulthood, the United States is forced to shed its childlike ways and act its age. To resist is to suffer that grand illusion of perpetual youth, a mirage dangerous to so powerful and volatile a nation.

A society is, or should be, a special organism, one that conjures images of family, partnership, and community. Be it for reasons of kinship, race, creed, or national identity, a society embraces a people into a single and identifiable entity. That whole—the society—is by definition and necessity greater than the sum of its parts. You cannot describe a society of perfectly unattached and uncooperative individuals and make any real sense; the very concept has no meaning unless there exists a web of connections and obligations among those included in the community. It has nothing to do with actually liking one another—though that probably would not hurt. We as Americans form a society simply because we are all citizens of a legal construction called the United States.

This idea of community is central to any discussion about the proper role of government. We are by nature social beings, and inevitably will design for ourselves rules for interacting with one another in stable and predictable ways. Such are the origins of government, a device we create ultimately to enforce our own rules and to protect us from one another or from outsiders. Be they in the form of the Ten Commandments, the judgments of tribal elders, or statutes made by a legislature, rules do exist and are enforced by some authority. Otherwise, relations among us ultimately degenerate into brute survival of the strongest. Those who assert that government is unnecessary in this age of enlightenment and rationality are utopians; let *them* live in contemporary society without it, for even rational people can do great evil. Government in some form is necessary, but what *is* worth serious debate is what we ultimately should want from that government, and what should properly be delivered.

It is illogical to assume that societies and their governments are static, like statues in a museum. Nothing in this universe is unchangeable: whole continents have been created and destroyed simply because volcanoes erupt or mountain ranges shift; leviathan stars have flared out as their base elements dissipated; entire animal and plant species have become extinct because they failed to adapt to changing climatic conditions or proved unable to ward off voracious predators. So it is with human societies, which too decay if they do not adapt to shifts in their economic, cultural, technological, or political environments. Human history is strewn with the remnants of once-proud civilizations that died out, in some

instances as precipitously as the dinosaurs.

Unlike the Aztecs, the Assyrians, or the Khmer, some societies manage to survive, though not necessarily in the same form, level of power, or degree of sophistication. The Chinese, to use one example, have retained a great deal of their identity despite centuries of often tumultuous change. The cost often has been high because to adapt is inevitably to shed some traditions or long-accepted norms, but the Chinese remain demonstrably Chinese. The Amish in North America, to use a different sort of example, have survived thus far by adopting selected new technologies and altering some cherished ways of life in the face of powerful external cultural and social forces. But the Amish, like the Chinese, probably are a bit less unique than they once were, in no small way because adapting has stripped away some of their insularity and forced them into a great deal more interaction with outsiders. Whether the tiny Amish society in the United States can survive *and* retain its special identity is uncertain—the impact of change is particularly devastating for smaller societies—but the alternative is even less palatable. The Shakers, for example, once flourished as a religious community of thousands, but the decades have reduced them to a pitiful remnant of aged adherents because their own rules, such as total celibacy, did not allow for adaptation. The choice exemplified by the Amish and the Shakers is clear: adapt and *be changed*, or simply cease to exist.

The United States, despite our frequent illusions of somehow being special, is no exception. Indeed, our society today is nothing like that rather isolated agrarian land of our forebears, so it is improbable that our ways of behaving or the manner by which we govern ourselves has remained unaltered. Those words chiseled into the Constitution of 1787 may look pretty much the same on paper, but their intrinsic meaning, and the expectations we as citizens hold about the proper role of government, would completely mystify James Madison and the other founders of this political system. After all, this is not the society of the self-sufficient farmer, the small merchant, the seafaring trader, or the hardy pioneer that spawned this system of government over two hundred years ago. This no longer is a land of vast and untapped resources, of open and relatively uninhabited spaces, all of it there for the taking. It no longer is that relatively small and almost totally homogeneous world of white, Anglo-Saxon Protestants seeking a living in the New World detached from the strictures of the Old.

It is, instead, a huge and richly diverse society, a powerful and wealthy nation of every type of ethnicity, racial origin, and creed imaginable. It is, instead, a largely inhabited and tamed land, one facing resource scarcity and common problems on a level of severity not witnessed in our past. It is, instead, a responsible world leader, no longer that isolated and somewhat eccentric republic of its rebellious youth. It *all* has changed on a staggering scale, and, as a result, so must our inherent beliefs about how we as a people, and how our government as our surrogate, should act. Two words that long have dominated our political discourse—*liberal* and *conservative*—may remain, but they either will be altered in their intrinsic meaning or will wither into irrelevancy. Ideas, and ideologies, too must change.

If the United States no longer is that innocent and experimental society of its eighteenth-century youth, then our very understanding of this society and of the proper responsibilities of the government

must be refurbished to meet the needs of our twenty-first-century adulthood. Such changes cannot simply be at the margins—an institutional adjustment here, a procedural reform there—but must reside at the very core of our public philosophy. It is we, the American people, who first and foremost must change in our hearts and in our minds, for it is our very national culture that will direct our future as a people and a place.

THE INDIVIDUAL RECONSIDERED

Our orthodox national creed has at its heart the glorification of the rugged individual, the independent, plainspoken, virtuous, and tough risk taker who blazed new trails, conquered a continent, challenged the conventional wisdom of the less heroic, and succeeded often on little more than smarts and grit. The ideal of the strong individual permeates our popular renditions of history (Daniel Boone), our contemporary mass culture (Clint Eastwood), and our political life. The presidency, for example, today is an office of almost deistic proportions, in which sits an elected demigod who we voters demand stare down our enemies, battle a weak-willed and recalcitrant Congress (which, it should be noted, we also elect), and prevail time and again over hordes of gray-suited bureaucratic drones. In any case, the great leader prevails or is judged a failure, even when "failure" results from conditions or events arguably beyond the control of one individual.

Or the creed is the mythology of the intrepid entrepreneur, the bold samurai warrior of the free market whom we average folk elevate to the pantheon of heroes for his battles with entrenched corporate interests, intrusive government, or other nations' bureaucrats. It is, above all, the language and mythology of Horatio Alger, those rags-to-riches yarns that still shape our aspirations. It is the yearning to believe that, as the sagas say, anyone can be president, anyone can make it with hard work, anyone can realize the American dream. If none of these things comes true for us, that's all right; something *will* for our children.

All this homage to the individual is fine to a point. Nobody wants to dampen the entrepreneurial spirit and ethic of hard work that make this a dynamic society. The starkest alternative is social regimentation and stagnation, traits that the Soviet Union and other centrally planned societies see increasingly as corrosive to national survival, much less economic or technological progress. Governments that seek social control above all other values eventually implode from internal rigidity, or decay from the pervasive apathy of their dissatisfied peoples.

But before you lapse into satisfied nationalistic self-righteousness, look around for a moment. What you may see is a United States where the icon of the individual no longer makes much *practical* (as opposed to ideological) sense. Instead of the isolated rough-hewn homestead and the sod-busting pioneer farmer we have the rigorously planned condominium village and the white-collar professional sitting before a computer display terminal in some regional office of some multinational corporation. Instead of the solitary inventor toiling long hours in some dimly lit garage, we have teams of scientists and engineers collaborating in huge aseptic laboratories to produce new and ever more sophisticated technologies. Few of us today really lead truly independent lives; we instead work and live together in increasingly complex and interconnected communities, the "anti-city" of the suburban executive office parks and residential developments that sprawls across the landscape. We provide for ourselves not with plow or hunting rifle but with the automatic teller banking card in yet another shopping mall, followed by dinner at the latest theme franchise restaurant or a movie at the local octaplex. We no longer are so isolated by distance but are linked together ever more closely by telephone, satellite, and airplane. We are, more and more, a truly national community, less regional in flavor and more firmly part of an even more encompassing global village of nations, corporations, and international organizations.

We also face an array of common problems that defy the individualistic solutions of our past. Once upon a time in our country, so the story goes, it was relatively easy to get up and leave your troubles behind, to move on to newer and always greener pastures, to blaze new trails. If the local economy was stagnant, or its employers discriminated against you for reasons of race or ethnicity, you could migrate to the newly emerging farmlands and towns of the frontier. If you felt stifled by the values or norms of your neighbors, you could go to where "civilization" had yet to take complete root. If the local factory spewed forth noxious pollution, you could move to where the air was fresh and the water sweet. There always was someplace to go in our American fable: more virgin land, more unspoiled nature, more unexplored territories, more golden opportunities to shuck the past and start over. It is the imagery of Huckleberry Finn, bemoaning the prospects of schooling and telling Jim: "But I reckon I got to light out for the Territory ahead of the rest, because Aunt Sally she's going to adopt me and sivilize me and I can't stand it. I been there before."[1] It is, above all, the mythology of a still slightly wild youth.

At risk of bursting this dream of perpetual renewal, we must acknowledge that those days have changed dramatically, and it is time for this society to grow up and meet the challenges of our age head on instead of always seeking to "move away." If we are burdened by environmental problems produced by urban industrial society, such as acid rain or the greenhouse effect, we no longer can simply escape them. There is no place left to go. If communities suffer from economic woes, it no longer simply is a matter of "voting with your feet" to sunnier climes: our national economy is meshed increasingly with those of other nations, conditions that defy purely localized solutions. The hard truth of the next century is that *our problems will be common problems*, national and international problems, requiring communal solutions on a scale and duration that Americans in peacetime are neither accustomed to nor comfortable with.

This is not to suggest that little room remains for the innovator, the entrepreneur, the true nonconformist seeking the less traveled road. Hardly. Society today seems far more indulgent than ever about diversity in individual tastes and styles, be it in the arts, business, or even politics. The breakdown during the past three decades of some of the more suffocating strains of conformity typical of midcentury industrial society has made this society more heterogeneous, more vibrant, and more accommodating. Most of us no longer spend our entire lives in one workplace or residence but experience a diversity of jobs and communities unmatched in human history. Part of this is by choice—we Americans seem viscerally uncomfortable with locking ourselves into one situation for life—but much of it is by necessity, as the national economy has evolved from its more stable industrial base reminiscent of the 1950s to the more wide open and ever-changing "postindustrial" foundations of today.

It is, in many ways, a more open and liberating place. We are a freer people in the sense that the older and more rigid hierarchies of industrial corporatism, the local community, or society in general have been loosened by the needs and dynamics of the current age. We are exposed more readily to other races, creeds, and cultures than our predecessors might imagine, far less closed and homogeneous in our communities, lifestyles, and beliefs. We probably know more about the world, enjoying the benefits of instantaneous global communications and the ease of travel to once exotic locales. Although our technology provides the opportunity for some to rein in our freedoms—the specter of Big Brother looking into our private lives probably is more real today than ever—we also have greater opportunities to work and live in ways far removed from the company town. We are more educated, more mobile, more adaptable, wanting greater flexibility, attached to one another less by residence than by interests and issues.

These realities show up on a global scale as well. The "American Century," those few decades after World War II when the United States went it alone and dominated the world in virtually every manner, is long over—except, perhaps, for a popular culture whose freewheeling zaniness seems endlessly appealing. That era of unchallenged power fell victim not to traitors and incompetents from within—though we spent a lot of time and effort trying to expose them—but to dramatic and irresistible changes in the world about us. No longer is this society a self-contained economic juggernaut, capable of perpetually producing and consuming for itself while almost totally divorced from conditions elsewhere. Instead, American businesses and workers compete worldwide with companies and workers of equal or greater capabilities, with peoples intent on realizing much the same dreams we hold. In fact, the very notion of an "American" company is fast becoming obsolete, done in by the complete blurring of the lines of corporate ownership and control, product differentiation, work forces, and even customers. Japanese automakers retail cars here using parts made in Mexico and assembled in Ohio or Tennessee, while American companies operate factories in Malaysia and Brazil or engage in cooperative ventures with any number of Japanese, Korean, German, or Italian firms. An American may occupy a high position in a Swiss firm, a citizen of Ireland may run an American company, and in both cases the corporations themselves may be owned by stockholders the world over. The edges of the domestic economy grow ever fuzzier, with the movement of capital as fluid as is the flow of manufactured goods or information and entertainment, all caring little for time zones or national boundaries. The vaunted notion of a truly free market is dead everywhere but in too many American minds, as governments the world over help their companies and workers develop new products and markets. And, within it all, Americans realize increasingly that going it alone no longer makes practical or ideological sense.

THE ENGAGED CITIZEN

It is hard to imagine a more immense gap than that between our contemporary world and the ethos of government that so long has guided our beliefs. It is an ethos dedicated to an eighteenth-century proposition that government simply is a

necessary evil and should be kept as minimal and controlled as possible. Without abandoning the healthier aspects of that ethos—we always should be wary of ceding to government too much power over our private lives—it is nonetheless time to rethink government's proper role in our economy and society. Some roles probably will endure—such as law enforcement, national defense, and management of the currency—but others must change as we confront the realities of our future.

The proper role for *democratic* government in the twenty-first century is to act as a partner, a broker, and a coordinator as citizens strive for common solutions to common problems. It is not for government to stand idly by with its hands off, for that stance is no solution at all and ultimately serves only to perpetuate the inequities and inefficiencies plaguing contemporary U.S. public policy-making. Minimalist government may have suited the era of the self-sufficient farmer and the frontier (even then more as myth than as reality), but those days are over.

It also is true that governing elites alone cannot solve our problems for us, a lesson we learned the hard way in decades past. Nor should we in a democratic society *want* it that way. We as citizens in a free land should never wish to have decisions made purely from the top down, forged in the closed rooms of corporate boards or bureaucratic committees. We instead should demand that as citizens we have a say in the direction of this nation beyond simply electing people to office every so often or protesting when decisions made by elites rub us the wrong way. The ultimate purpose of government in a democratic society is to give *all* citizens a chance to be heard and to participate meaningfully, not just through the ballot box but on the shop floor, in local planning boards, in the city halls. It is not just political equality that must be stressed, but equality of voice, of opportunity to be involved, of the right to be consulted.

If government is to serve our needs well, more emphasis must be placed on designing institutions and processes that make it easier for citizens to achieve common goals and avoid outcomes that rob one side to pay another. But, to make this all work, citizens also must begin to think not as individuals in the jungle but as partners in a true community. We are a people whose destiny increasingly is tied not to the heroic actions of a few great leaders but to the everyday actions of average citizens in support of a common good. We see, and may even reluctantly accept, this reality, for it is in many ways no longer a time where individualistic solutions to or escapes from common problems will suffice. We no longer can afford a mentality of "I got mine, you get yours" because that ethos is obsolete and ultimately destructive in a world where everyone loses if the problems we face are not solved through the careful building of consensus. A society is in many ways a fragile being, and the ethos of unchecked private gain at the expense of the public good is counterproductive in the end.

The proper role of democratic government is to promote true representation and consensus-building. This sounds rather archaic because the writers of the Constitution had many of these same ideas in mind, but somewhere along the way between then and now those ideals were bastardized by gradual solidification in the power of economic, political, and technocratic elites and the concomitant surrender by citizens of their rights and roles in decision making. This shift was not simply the product of outright villainy by elites or of any innate laziness on the part of the mass public.

Rather, it came about with the stunning evolution of a localized agrarian society into one first national and industrial, and then postindustrial and international. It also came about with the movement of the United States from national isolation to world leadership and all the national security needs such a role dictates. Whatever the case, the net effect during the twentieth century has been to shift effective (as opposed to symbolic) decision-making power from the citizenry to the elite.

It is high time that a democratic citizenry reclaim its proper power and reimpose its views on how a society is to allocate its riches and its burdens. Some might argue vehemently that the pressures and demands of the next century will be so stupendous and so complex that only the most expert and well positioned can be allowed to make public policy. The lament is heard everywhere that the average citizen is too uninformed, too passive, too easily swayed by illogical and momentary passions to govern responsibly or well. This is the same hue and cry raised in the 1780s by people like Alexander Hamilton, whose stark fear of the common people ("the mob") drove him to call originally for a monarchical presidency and for far greater power in the hands of the "natural aristocracy" of learned affluent men.

Such elite biases have coexisted uneasily with Americans' innate populism for over two centuries, and our history occasionally has exhibited sharp swings between extremes. But government by elite is proving increasingly dangerous to the health of a democratic body politic because of the greater array of powerful tools available to those who govern. From television to computers, satellites to high-tech weaponry, the elites of the twenty-first century will have at their disposal instruments for mass influence and control far beyond the wildest dreams of Stalin or the worst nightmares of George Orwell.

But, say some, *enlightened* elites would not use such instruments except in dire emergencies. After all, they too believe in fundamental American values and would never usurp the ultimate right of the people to govern. The real problem is not those who govern, goes this line of argument, but that the people are too many and too diverse to govern wisely or well in this complex and fast-paced world. It is the responsibility of those at the top, those trained to govern, to steer the nation through the tricky shoals of the next century. The alternative is anarchy and national decline. This is outrageous.

If we but look back through American history, what is striking is how many failures in democratic governance can be laid at the feet of irresolute elites, not stupid or lazy citizens. Those who "lead" have been the problem, for if citizens are intolerant or selfish, it is because Americans, like all people, tend to respond to cues or directives transmitted by those in positions of authority. Leaders who blithely dismiss the citizen as inept or apathetic have only themselves to blame, for to suggest that the citizen is the weak link in democratic government is a savage indictment of both our history and ourselves.

It seems eminently reasonable to charge instead that any weaknesses in democracy are due to the failure of governing elites to present to average citizens real opportunities for participation in public policy-making. If citizens have not acted as hoped, it is equally reasonable to suggest that elites, for their part, simply have failed to lead responsibly or well. It is small wonder that Americans vote in ever decreasing proportions but at the same time organize themselves into ever more numerous associations and lobbies. Voting is seen increasingly as of little relevance or utility, while more direct forms of participation fulfill both immediate needs and citizens' belief in their capacity to know their own interests. Elections and politicians are empty promises, and the citizen instead opts for direct and more easily controlled ways for influencing public policy.

The United States is not, never has been, and never will be ruled by the "people." It is both an impossible and unfair standard by which to judge, for classical democracy is not doable in anything but the smallest of societies. We almost always select surrogates to act on our behalf because our society is too big for everybody to participate directly in all decisions, but we reserve for ourselves the ultimate right to intervene in policy-making or replace those who apparently violate our trust. The few *always* rule, supposedly in the name of all, so it is insulting to always ascribe the failings of representative government to the people.

The real problem is that average people get remarkably few *valid* opportunities to have their voices heard, to exercise their roles as citizens. Why, for example, do local zoning boards convene meetings in private when making controversial decisions, only to be chastened and resentful when irate homeowners react passionately afterward? The images are commonplace: upset residents yelling at local officials while the television cameras record a scene of bitter accusations and near hysteria. Substitute for the zoning board the local town council, the state legislature, or some national regulatory agency, and the same imagery emerges: the people are too irrational to govern.

This is patent nonsense. These people are frustrated because they never had a real chance early on in the decision-making process to have their say. What is shown by the cameras is anger at being left out, at being "consulted" only after the options had been whittled down for them to a pitiful few by governing elites acting on behalf of their own agendas and interests. What is seen is a people who were not given a chance to exercise their citizenship.

The proper and essential role for government in a democratic society is to avoid this sort of result, which is bad both for policy-making and for democratic values. Too often public officials meet some precise letter of a law mandating public notification of meetings by tacking up short memos on some hidden-away town bulletin board or in some incomprehensible ad in the town newspaper. The problem gets worse the higher up you go, to the point where most Americans haven't got the slightest idea what their national government is up to on 99 percent of the decisions being made. Is this because citizens are lazy, or is it because we make it too difficult for anybody but public policy professionals or political junkies to get information? The answer is obvious. It also is wrong.

Those in authority have a simple responsibility to get out of their offices and contact those citizens who are affected, to engage more energetically in getting the public involved in making public decisions. The proper role of government is to ensure valid and sustained democratic representation. This is not only good politics—people are more likely to accept decisions that they feel were made fairly—but also good policy-making. Too many policies are made by government elites with little or no early citizen input only to be blocked or heavily revised when public outrage erupts, which suggests that elites have no locks on reason or knowledge.

This standard may seem trivial, over-

ly concerned with process, as opposed to the substance of what government should do. It is neither when we consider the very nature of the problems we will face in the next century. If our problems are increasingly problems of the common, problems of the whole, then our decision-making processes must more diligently involve the whole community from the very start. For example, obviously nobody wants waste disposal sites or prisons or halfway houses in his or her neighborhood, but these public facilities must go *somewhere*. Too often in our past we have "solved" such problems either by walking away from them—out of sight, out of mind—or by dumping them onto communities too poor or too weak (usually both) to withstand the power of their more organized and affluent neighbors. The first response no longer is practical, as seems increasingly manifest, and the second violates every norm of equity that supports democratic government. By placing the common burden so unfairly on a few, we perpetuate a belief that in the end only money and power matter.

The only way to ensure that common problems are decided both fairly and well is to ensure that as many affected citizens as possible are brought into decision-making processes early on. This standard requires that elites reach out, that they sacrifice some of their precious authority for the sake of real representation. If the problem is regional waste disposal, the first item on the agenda must be to gauge public attitudes about the *problem*, not simply their reactions to proposed "solutions" made by some interdepartmental planning group. It might mean some delay at the beginning, to be sure, but the end might well be a decision that meets not with screaming residents but with an agreement that all interests and all views were considered fairly.

We have learned these lessons the hard way too often in the past, and have witnessed too many failed projects and too many disillusioned Americans for our efforts. Democracy is not particularly efficient, but it is not sheer anarchy. When it works as best as it can, it provides for fairer and more enlightened government. Fairness is the keystone of democratic government, and to sacrifice this good for the sake of some marginal efficiency is ultimately to sever the very fibers that knit this society together. Rather an extra year to deliberate local transportation needs than a superhighway that tragically divides a community in half, literally and figuratively. Rather heated debate and bruised egos than unfair burdens and scuttled projects that are necessary to address common needs. Rather elites that must reach out than a public disaffected and cynical about government. Life might well be made more difficult for those who govern, but the alternative threatens the very foundations of a healthy democracy.

COMMUNITY AND RECIPROCITY

In return for more central governing responsibilities, citizens must begin to think and act more cooperatively than perhaps they have been accustomed to in the past. We cannot solve common problems any longer by palming them off on others, for if we are to enjoy the benefits of contemporary life, we all must share in the burdens that maintaining the quality of that life will entail. This means ultimately that a sense of reciprocity must be cultivated in the American ethos, that unadulterated individualism must be tempered by a greater sense of community and sharing.

It also means an end to that pernicious myth perpetrated in our lifetimes that we as citizens somehow are "entitled" by law to certain individualistic benefits, that we have a basic right to some chunk of the public good. This is not only nonsensical but dangerous ultimately to the community's very health and moral fiber. The citizen in this society has basic and inalienable *political* rights, but no more has a "right" to a pension, free health care, or subsidized education than General Motors has to tax breaks or U.S. Steel (now USX) has to pollute the atmosphere. We *do*, however, have the right as citizens to press for these benefits if we want them. That is the democratic principle at work.

If we do want these benefits, however, we must reimburse something of ourselves to the community, for the common pot is not bottomless. It must be replenished constantly, and the mythology that we are "entitled" to some good only reinforces the notion that the free lunch is the guiding principle of American life. If a student deserves free medical school training, we should provide it, but only if the new doctor reciprocates by serving for a while in a poor or isolated area. If someone needs welfare, we should grant it, but only if the recipient performs some service to the community (such as on public works projects) and undergoes job training. If the elderly want their pensions, younger generations should not balk, but those on Social Security have a reciprocal duty to support education for the young so that the nation can produce new generations of citizens capable of supporting the old. If an affluent suburb does *not* want to get stuck with some public facility, it should pay a disproportionate share of the costs, monies that would go to the locality that accepts the waste plant or prison.

In short, as we receive, we also shall give. We cannot have benefits without reciprocity, cannot have entitlements without returning something of ourselves to our community. This rule must apply not only to those in dire need but to all, for to apply it only to the poor or old is unfair and disruptive of the common good. The free-lunch mentality so typical of our past can no longer be our operating ethos, for it is dangerous and divisive for a nation seeking to solve its common problems and striving to maintain democracy in more ways than just on paper.

Thus, the proper role of government is to draw upon the innate values and talents of its people, which are considerable. The proper role is to promote a sense of community, inclusion, and reciprocity, without which truly democratic government cannot endure. This is not some mushy-headed do-goodism at work but hardheaded, practical, and responsible answers to nagging governing and representative dilemmas. Government by elites, whether they be liberal or conservative, Democrats or Republicans, might survive for a while, but it will be a hollow shell, existing primarily for the profit of the few. Societies where the senses of community and reciprocity erode cannot survive, and will degenerate into lethargy, greed, and cynicism. Such are not the roots of healthy democratic governance, and the proper role of government is to enable citizens *to act as citizens,* and to promote in them a national creed that we are indeed each other's keepers.

NOTE

1. Mark Twain, *The Adventures of Huckleberry Finn,* in *The Unabridged Mark Twain,* ed. Lawrence Teacher (Philadelphia: Running Press, 1976), 1:956.

SUGGESTED READINGS

FALLOWS, JAMES. *More Like Us: Making America Great Again.* Boston: Houghton Mifflin, 1989. A challenge to the wave of literature that emerged in the late 1980s urging Americans to be "more like the Japanese" (see, for example, Reich, *Tales of a New America,* below). Fallows argues simply that Americans cannot and should not want to be more like the Japanese, largely because both peoples and their societies are anchored in entirely unique and irreproducible cultures, one based on the individual, the other on the group. Americans can and should *learn* from other peoples, if only to moderate our renowned insularity, but we should be wary of undermining the very values upon which this society and nation have flourished.

LUOV, RICHARD. *America II.* New York: Penguin Books, 1983. A fascinating examination of "postindustrial America." It is, on one hand, a country of small-scale entrepreneurs, high-tech industries, planned condominium communities, and decentralized patterns of work and habitation. On the other hand, it is a country in which smokestack industries are in decline, older urban areas are allowed to decay and, perhaps most troubling, the poor and unskilled increasingly are stranded on the outside looking in. "America II" is a far different place than the post-World War II industrial United States. Whether it is a *better* place is up for debate.

REICH, ROBERT. *Tales of a New America: The Anxious Liberal's Guide to the Future.*

New York: Random House, 1987. An avowed liberal student of public policy looks at other nations (and, particularly, Japan) and in the process takes on many of the powerful myths that have driven Americans on over the past century. Reich discusses how those myths central to American political culture (for example, the triumphant individual) may or may not offer a functional guide to the next several decades. In short, Reich seeks to redefine those myths. Worthwhile reading in conjunction with Fallows, *More Like Us*.

The Ideology of Happiness: The Rise of American Decline

Wayne Allen

Louisiana State University

When contemplating the future of the United States, one cannot but think of the words of a former secretary of state, Henry Kissinger: "When we do not know where we are going, any number of paths will get us there." The future points in many directions, and the direction we take is in good measure the result of where we have been, and how we define ourselves as a people. But there are forces at work now corrupting the American self-definition. Although the world is not ours to covet or control, our course into the next century will finally be decided by our moral worth as a people.

In this era of diminishing expectations, with its restraints on resources, dangerous population growth, deterioration of law, and expansive government, we will have to set limits to our appetites, personal and national. The problems we face are indissolubly human, hence moral. They defy remedy by government and solutions through legislation. We must fall back on ourselves. Since the 1960s there has been an increasing personalization of politics to satisfy individual private happiness. Politically speaking, not much could be worse. We reversed three thousand years of political history and now see in government not the plague of mankind, but its salvation. And it began with our increased idealization of democracy.

Government is a form of organization to maintain order among people. Democracy is one variant. The contribution of liberalism to democracy was to overcome one weakness of this form. Too much liberalism leads to tyranny by law and those who dispense it. Yet too much democracy leads to an idolization of *"the people"* and the destruction of majoritarian politics; hence the consensus that is the heart of democracy.

Democracy has come to be understood as nothing more than a smorgasbord of concepts, ideas, even feelings. The desire to incorporate all things into democracy springs from the purely modern belief that the cure for all of people's problems is located in government. Behind this belief stands the illusion that a properly constituted government—one that includes all things, especially power—can render human beings rational, reasonable, and of course happy. It is the dangerous belief that government makes man. This follows the growth of humanism and relativism, with their secularization of God and deification of man. This has succeeded only in taking man's mind off the transcendent by placing it on himself. Democracy is particularly well-suited to this egoistic self-glorification. But this was not always the case.

The ancient Greeks who gave us democracy were well aware of its tendency to degenerate into a type of "massocracy," or mob rule. Socrates preached against democracy. Plato tried to overcome it. Aristotle cautioned against its excesses. Rather than expand its meaning, these wise men contrived ways to constrain it: Socrates by warning about the passions of the masses, Plato by introducing the laws as a standard of ethical conduct, and Aristotle by recommending an elite (aristocracy) to guide it.

We moderns have gone the other way, and we think the more we add to democracy the more we can expect from it. Today freedom is detached from restraint, rights are disconnected from responsibilities, authority no longer guides opinion but springs from it, law is disembodied from morality, and the individual is no longer a member of the community but confronts it as an adversary. Our obsession with equality has prompted a leveling of excellence to the lowest common denominator. Those we used to praise and reward as the best among us are now viewed with suspicion. Where the Greeks turned to the best men to guide their democracies, we turn to those who flatter us with likenesses of ourselves. Equality today has been translated into a mechanism to reduce individuals, who are unequal by nature, to economic subparts of a government whose sole purpose is to lubricate the mechanism. Thus, we get policies like affirmative action that impose "equality" downward through the coercive power of government.

This modern reinterpretation of democracy is accompanied by the deformation of ideas originally intended to ensure its survival. Authority has disappeared as a source of inspiration for the individual and an adhesive for the community. The erosion of the public good has been followed by some vague ideal of "social justice," which turns out to be self-interest inscribed into government policy. The constitutionalism of early liberalism, with its former regard for majority rule, has been jettisoned in favor of minority tyranny. Law is no longer an ethical minimum, but an instrument for achieving maximal economic results for the group. Rights are disconnected from responsibilities, the duties that go with good citizenship, and have become claims against the community. Rights were once a claim of freedom against government for the sake of community; they have become the corrosive of community for the sake of the individual.

THE FOUNDERS AND THE PUBLIC GOOD

The American community once represented a vision of goodness held valid by its members. The sharing of the vision formed the "glue" of living together. The vision, as it was augmented by succeeding generations, formed an *ethos*, or ethic, for living one's life. In other words, one's conduct was derived from and helped shape this ethic. Each individual thus shared in the moral authority of the community. We retain this understanding today. It is evident in such statements as "What will the community think?" Or, "How will the community respond?" What is being asked is, "What does the community hold dear?" The value at issue is a portion of the moral fabric of the community and suggests good conduct among men. Communication (from the same root as for our word *community*) is the transmission of good conduct *for* the community, for the sake of those who live in it.

This was the understanding of our Founding Fathers. They preferred the older, Aristotelian notion of public good. It was not government they sanctified and founded but a vision of public life whose end government was to serve. That is, the institutions we constituted were to serve an ethic, a morality we found essential to public life. This is precisely why our government was emasculated by having its powers divided so it could not act contrary to public goodness. Government was the means, goodness the end. In *Federalist* 10, for instance, "justice" or "private rights" is the essential end of government. In *Federalist*

45, also by James Madison, we see that the public good, the real welfare of the great body of the people, is the supreme object to be pursued, and "no form of government whatever has any other value than as it may be fitted for the attainment of this object."

Yet, Madison in *Federalist* 51 also tells us that "justice" is to be subsumed in the public good as the "supreme object to be pursued." In other words, the individual for whom justice is sought is the first consideration of government, and the public good (morality) is the prime concern of the people. Government then protects rights; the people, goodness. "Justice," or "private rights," is thus subordinate to public goodness. As understood by our Founders, justice means the protection of each person's faculties (private rights), the minimum one expects when choosing civil society. Of course, choosing entails consent, which is the essence of community. Consent, in turn, is the constraining force on all others who have also chosen; it allows for public life.

This forms the compact, or contract, of U.S. public life. When we choose something, in the Founders' case not only a form of government but a public ethic, we consent to the things that likely flow from our choice. By contracting for a public good, we necessarily consent to the limitations this good imposes on us. Madison noted how "all power in just and free governments is derived from compact." John Adams, in the Massachusetts Bill of Rights, went even further: "The body politic is . . . a social compact by which the whole people covenants with each citizen and each citizen with the whole people that all shall be governed by certain laws for the common good. . . ." The law is then an instrument of morality.

This is why Bosso's confusion of society, community, and government is misleading, even dangerous. In fact, a society that lacks community is going to need a strong, perhaps tyrannical, government precisely because there is no ethic, no community, that serves as a foundation for good conduct. Such a society needs government, with its coercive institutions, to impose decisions on the people rather than being guided by them. Nor is the United States a mere "legalism" that requires law rather than moral sense to keep citizens from one another's throats. Law inhibits, restrains, and threatens; it does not unite. Indeed, the more dependent on law we become, the less we have in common. Look at the correlation between the increasing numbers of lawyers and the extremity and frequency of violence.

Viewed from the perspective of the individual, the object of justice *must* be in harmony with civil society; that is, the vision of public goodness that formed the founding of the body politic in the first place. This serves as a restraint on the individual, who benefits from community; it is a restraint on government as well. The public good, the "supreme object to be pursued," is the real object of government because only a good government may superintend a good public. A good government must then secure the faculties of all of its citizens as an ethical minimum of government. Equally, however, any majority (in the process of democracy) must always aim at the public good (community), thereby assuring protection for, but not the wishes of, the minority.

The idea of good government, one guided by the community's notion of goodness, was stated by Madison in the *Federalist Papers*. He likened good government to republicanism because "no other form would be reconcilable with the genius of the people of America; with the fundamental principles of the revolution.

. . ." Principles preceded government. Republicanism, he argued, would suggest the "capacity" for good government and was contingent on "honorable determination" toward public aspiration, a vision of the public good. This was clearly echoing Plato's belief that good government is not possible without a standard of goodness. It also establishes the Constitution as an embodiment of moral sentiment. In the Founders' minds, the possibility of good government, a republican idea, was tempered by the skepticism of government to bring about that good—an *early* liberal idea.

Justice may sometimes require an active government. But for the most part government shows its goodness (its regard for community) negatively, by refraining from injustices on the part of selfish rulers, belligerent majorities, or aggressive minorities. It shows its goodness positively by serving the public good, that is, by promoting the majority sentiment of the community. This is clear in the Preamble to the Constitution: Although justice is to be established, the "general welfare" (goodness) is to be promoted.

This was not optimistic moralizing on the part of the Founders. Their reading of history informed them of the urge for power by individuals, groups, and especially government. This is exactly why the first political freedom has always been freedom from government. It corresponds to the people's wish to be left alone. Goodness sustains community and restrains government; it leads to stability, duration through time—tradition. This is also why the Constitution was made difficult to change.

It is mistaken to believe that the Constitution is a mere "legalism," a parchment adaptable to the times. It is, instead, a restraint on the people precisely because the future is unknown. Alexander Hamilton warned in *Federalist* 34 that the nation's future can largely be understood in terms of the past:

> We must bear in mind that we are not to confine our view to the present period, but to look forward to remote futurity. Constitutions of civil government are not to be framed upon the calculation of existing exigencies, but upon a combination of these with the probable exigencies of ages, according to the natural and tried course of human affairs.

Bosso's recommendations for change and adaptation hence defy not only the Founders but political history as well. He confuses innovations in technology and science with culture and morality. The Constitution is a result, an outcome, "an ordered scheme of liberty," based on tried principles of good conduct. It was meant as a standard, an anchor, to secure the American people in the face of change. This is what prompted Madison's injunction in *Federalist* 63: A "sense of community ought . . . in all free government, ultimately prevail over the view of its rulers. . . ." Clearly, the intention was that the goodness of the people, their moral sense, would shape the institutions and policies of government. This is democracy!

Historically, democracies have proven to be the most unstable of all forms of government, and our Founders knew this. The Constitution was meant to resist the all-too-human passion to alter government and community according to mood or caprice. Whatever alteration is made must conform to those principles of community that brought the Constitution into existence in the first place. So, Bosso errs badly when he says Madison would be mystified by the United States of today. Hardly! The only thing that would

mystify him would be the power we have given government over our lives.

Government must be energetic enough, and only energetic enough, to prevent the injustices that it itself is denied by the people and their vision of the public good. Should government seek to *do* good rather than *be* good, it would impinge on the people by robbing from them the very reason they chose civil society: their vision of public goodness.

The inherent danger in establishing ends for government is that government and individuals have different ends. By its nature government requires uniformity; it must impose a unity on the variety of its citizens. The fact that these ends are to be decided by individuals and not government is unarguably clear in the rough draft of the Declaration of Independence. Jefferson recognized the "ends" of men who are "created equal and independent" as "truths" that are "sacred and undeniable." To "secure these ends, governments are instituted among men. . . ." Jefferson here identified individual ends as the ethical minimum for choosing and consenting to government. These individual ends are "sacred" because they are endowed "by their Creator" (bestowed by God), and they are "undeniable" (inalienable) because they are the minimum for which a free individual would give up a portion of personal freedom to the community. This is perfectly consistent with Jefferson's reading of the English philosopher John Locke. It was Locke who said of free men, "secure to them the ends for which government was first erected." At the same time it is the public good that keeps equally created but "independent" individuals from allowing their faculties (rights) to collide and destabilize the community. This is in keeping with Jefferson's reading of Montesquieu, who said that the first principle of a republic is virtue.

American decline really began with the first serious effort to ascribe goodness to government; to believe that government has ends beneficial to the people, who are, themselves, the shapers of goodness. Such a belief destroys community and turns democracy upside down. Lincoln's formula, "government of the people, by the people," is then replaced by the antidemocratic formula "people by the government and for the government." Rather than seeing government as the protector of our rights, as did the Founders, we now see it as the source of them. Our happiness appears to be something bestowed by government.

THE DISTORTION OF DEMOCRACY

The breakdown of law and the loss of moral sense have led to the erosion of authority and corruption of the American *ethos*. Prior to the twentieth century, the morality that gave the nation a sense of self was derived from God. This is clearly evident in the earliest pronouncements of the first English settlers. The intimacy between God and politics was established by the Pilgrims in the Mayflower Compact (1620). It expresses the sentiment of a people who, "by these presents, solemnly and mutually, in the presence of God and one another, covenant and combine ourselves together into a civil body politick, for our better ordering and preservation and furtherance of the ends aforesaid. . . ." This "covenant" or contract formed the foundation of the American community. The foundation was more than a religious-based faith; it was a God-derived source of good conduct.

Another early expression of moral authority appeared in two of John Winthrop's sermons: "A Modell of Christian Charity" (1630) and "Speech to the General Court" (1645). Winthrop invoked the ideas of love and grace as transcendent religious values whose "proper end and object of authority" is God's "love and mercy." They would counter the forces of "natural liberty" (what we call personal freedom) by cementing the ties of community. Winthrop made his appeal to the mind, not the body, to transcendent ideas, not bodily passions. His hope was assent by conviction, not coercion. Obedience could then be attained by the dignity conferred on those who submitted.

The ultimate rejection of Winthrop's proposals is visible in the increasing secularization of American life. As the United States retreated from God-based law, wrongdoing was explained away with theories of social causation. The most vicious criminals were soon identified not as evildoers but as victims of an uncaring society. Social causation soon obliterated common moral sense. Secularization further undermined traditional liberalism, which was so dependent on the values of Judeo-Christian morality, as the basis for community. The question never asked by twentieth-century liberalism was decisive in its later degeneration: If the source of authority is located in God's commands and is manifest only in the community with shared values, what then happens to authority when God disappears as an agency and community collapses as a reality? With the collapse of community we are left with competing theories of social causation, none of which has proved adequate as a restraint on human conduct.

The degeneration of any community to a mere "legalism" effectively destroys its authoritative beliefs and eventuates in the pitting of one individual against all others. Without authoritative beliefs there is no reason an individual should suffer a hardship just for the sake of the law. The law tells us what is wrong, not what is good. The American *ethos*, formerly derived from God's will, served as the bond between the individual and the community. As this bond eroded, there was nothing left upon which to build authority. Severed from God and community, the individual is left chartless and adrift in a darkness with no community beacons to serve as guides for life.

The relationship between the individual and community is more fragile and intimate than one might suspect. The loss of community puts the individual at risk. Richard Friedman, for instance, notes that a government has authority and is legitimate only so long as it embodies and promotes the shared values of the community:

> Although a common set of authoritative beliefs is constitutive of the social order, the weakening or dissolution of those beliefs is bound to generate destructive acts directed against the values and practices of the established social order and even ultimately against the self, e.g., suicide, madness.[1]

Taking this argument one step further, we can say that personal deviancy, criminality, and even suicide follow the collapse of community. This is certainly a powerful partial explanation for the drug culture and the high rate of teenage suicide. The destruction of the family at the hands of New Left rhetoric and policies of the 1960s, coupled to the breakdown of community, has thrown the individual into a void. He is not only alone, he is lonely.

The further equalization of American life, now so firmly rooted in the atomized notions of humanism and relativism, finally degraded authority to mean no more than what others think. This reduces authority to a fashion defined by the czars of the media. Fame is confused with celebrity; popularity is mistaken for greatness. The collapse of moral authority eventually prompted an effort to locate authority in an institution of government. People began to rely on government where earlier they relied on themselves, the community. The American people's persistent disenchantment with the legislative branch shifted their attention to the Supreme Court. In the absence of morality there was a turn toward law. But by the middle of the century this, too, proved a disappointment. And it would have come as no surprise to our Founders.

Contrary to popular belief, our Founders realized the hopelessness of trying to locate authority in an institution that is not sanctioned by something outside and superior to itself. It was Alexander Hamilton who insisted that "the majesty of national authority" should rest on an independent judiciary. But he also knew that the Supreme Court had neither the "force nor will" to effect decisions. The Founders had succeeded in separating power from authority, popular passions from judicial wisdom, but they consigned to the Court the role of judging law without a moral foundation for making it. The United States was left with an institution of authority with no appeal to anything beyond itself. There was command, but no source from which to inspire obedience. The Court could appeal to nothing but self-interest. By the twentieth century judicial review on matters of morals and public policy undermined the authority of the Court entirely.

During the 1950s the Supreme Court began to assert itself, not as an arbiter of law but as chief engineer of a social policy bereft of any moral foundation whatsoever. The Court was the last institutional effort to give guidance to a people in search of themselves. Indeed, the Court represented the most recent governmental desire to extend itself *over* the people without a moral justification for doing so. This gave birth to the interventionist state in America and with it the ambition of certain men to make their ideas the standard for humans living together. Only this time democracy and majority rule would be set aside.

The idea of an activist or interventionist state derives largely from the conceit born during the French Revolution (1789). The French made the individual the centerpiece of their ideology (Jacobin liberalism). For the first time they saw in man an essential and natural goodness and perfectability. This view defies the Judeo-Christian belief that man is born into corruption: a sin that only the individual in moral community can overcome with God's grace. Instead, the Jacobins turned from God and toward the state.

With natural goodness and human perfectability as operating assumptions, the Jacobin liberals believed that social harmony and integration could be achieved through the coercive power of law and state regulation of education. According to this view, man no longer has to wait on the inscrutable will of God for happiness. Through government, a man-made institution, man can shape himself in his own best image. This self-flattery began the arrogance known as French humanism. The two great spokesmen for humanism, Helvetius and Holbach, argued, "Men have in their own hands the instrument of their greatness and their felicity, and . . . to be happy and powerful nothing more is requisite than to perfect the science of education."[2] The implications are purely totalitarian. Once government controls education, it

can control man and thereby direct him toward governmentally defined ends. Education, seen as "science," can mean only a regimented, massified diet of stale social bromides served up by teachers who are themselves instruments of government policy. We are "educated" to believe the state makes us happy, and accept it unflinchingly only because the "educators" have been at it for so long. Of course, the fallacy in this thinking is that individuals, even if similarly educated, are moved by different motors, and that morality (not training) is what drives these motors. But state activists demand control of education so they can control the "science" that produces like-minded individuals.

With increasing centralization of private functions under the state, what the French call *etatism*, men supposedly will be made happy through state functions. Thus, under the coercive powers of government, education is secretly made the vehicle for transporting someone else's values. Is it any wonder, then, that education has become the battlefield in the struggle for men's souls? This is why parents in ever-increasing numbers are selecting private schools that transmit the values *they* wish *their* children to have. This only hints at the corruption of the public philosophy.

Among the other ideas to emerge from the period around the French Revolution were a boundless belief in Reason and a reverence for Progress. Reason and Progress were accorded the status of absolutes, replacing God. Supposedly, progress would be made, and enlightenment proclaimed, through a human construction, government. Abandoning the traditional Western belief that "reasoning" (as a faculty) and "reasonableness" (a character trait) were attributable to individual talent or family upbringing, the Jacobins imposed their idea of reason on people with the expectation that it would improve society. Thus, the state became the highest good and society was supposed to "progress" as the result of state-controlled agencies. The fact that this belief ended in the infamous French Reign of Terror only renewed the Jacobin argument that the failure was due to a weak state, not the illusion of their theory of education or their reverence for reason. The Jacobins soon redoubled their efforts to strengthen government. Although their success was short-lived, it served as a precedent for the Western world. It resulted in increasing democratization and the effort by government to justify all acts, including the worst crimes, in the name of the people.

The rise of democracy to near-universal assent was coupled to its expanding meaning. Increasingly did politicians speak to larger numbers of people, more diverse in taste, education, and sophistication. Government soon enjoyed and even demanded greater benefits from this expansion. The French legacy of *etatism* soon meant not only a centralization of private functions but domination by government in order to make people happy. This began the personalization of politics, the effort to transform government into an instrument to satisfy personal wants.

Government in this way became connected to the masses by way of an abstraction: The People. Every dictator and totalitarian now seeks approval of atrocities committed by invoking the name of the people. Ironically enough, democracy has become the instrument of popular oppression. Nearly three thousand years after its origin in ancient Greece, democracy has come to mean little more than a demagogic assertion of popular support. It did not start off that way.

The root *cracy* (rule by), when coupled to *demes* (or *demos*, people), has come to mean popular government. Yet as the Greeks understood it, democracy was considered a regime fraught with danger. The Greeks viewed the *demos* as a mass or mob of essentially uneducated people who sought public support for their private wants. The *demos* wanted to extend their private, self-interests into the public realm. This is how politics acquired its negative image. In other words, self-interest, not the public good, was multiplied endlessly until one interest prevailed in combat over all others. Without a vision of public goodness, democracy degenerates into a battlefield of self-interest.

The famous French observer of life in the United States in the 1820s, Alexis de Tocqueville, connected democracy to the lower stratum of society precisely for this reason. This is why he felt public opinion was emerging as the source of authority. Public opinion is the source of dangerous passions (today too easily exploited by unscrupulous media). Forty years later, at Gettysburg, Abraham Lincoln spoke of government of and by the people while referring to no single stratum. Instead, his understanding of "the people" was not as a means to justify government but an aggregate of individuals, a community, which defines government. He was not speaking to the common citizen but to what is common in people, the public good.

In the name of democracy certain principles that seem related to it have been badly inflated or misshapen. Liberty, equality, justice, even education are assumed to be so fundamental to democracy that we dare not think of it without them. But today these principles have taken on a new meaning and thereby distort democracy itself.

Since the French Revolution there has been a concerted effort to oversimplify democracy. The idolization of the masses for the first time allowed a government to murder tens of thousands of persons in the name of a romantic illusion, The People. Instead of government's being seen for what it is, an instrument to serve public goodness, people were used as instruments by government for a larger political project, "public welfare." In other words, The People were seen as a vehicle to reach the ends of government.

One of the problems faced by the United States today is both the overwhelming support of democracy and a general ignorance of what it means. In the broadest sense, being democratic means that those things that are done reflect democracy. But democracy, like The People, has been transformed into an ideal, one attainable through neither Greek theory nor contemporary practice. As a consequence, more is expected from democracy than it can deliver.

Theoretically, participation, not equality, is the hallmark of democracy. Taken to its logical extreme, the more participation, the more democracy. But this extreme was never reached in Greece; it was limited by talent and seriousness. This is exactly how nineteenth-century liberalism saved modern democracy: by restricting suffrage to responsible participants, that is, by making citizenship meaningful. The argument was that politics is a solemn enterprise and should be open only to those who take it seriously. The increasing urbanity of women, made possible by developments in technology, succeeded in securing their politicization in 1920. Yet, the glorification of democracy led to a reduced age for voting (eighteen) at the very time education in the United States was coming into disrepute. The removal of literacy requirements for voting further devalued the democratic process. The decline of edu-

cated skills among Americans degrades democracy into a politics of emotion, the grist of demagogues.

The basic reasoning in favor of political participation (note Plato's *Republic*) has always been that a person takes public life more seriously than private life. One may harm oneself in private but many others in public. The maxim for participation has been to put one's community ahead of oneself. But the rise of the masses to power has resulted in the expansion of government for satisfaction of private wants. And it is private wants rather than public goodness that identify members of the masses.

If Professor Bosso is to be taken seriously on this count, then he surely realizes that participation is enhanced at the local level: the states and communities. This is where people have direct control over their fate, and where the gap between leaders and led is narrowed. True democracy takes place in the meeting hall, not the halls of Congress. Participation is blunted by distance; it is frustrated by administration and representation. In face-to-face community, people *know* who is the best among them.

When scholars of democratic theory ask serious questions about democracy in practice, the inquiry always turns on consent. Logically, it is obvious that a majority of people is preferable to a minority. The more people who consent to government, the closer we come to democracy as a practicable form of governing. And the only real boon to democracy was the modification *early* liberalism made by incorporating *serious* participants into the consensus-building process. This was done through the very technique that made liberalism what it was: a guarantee of popular government through constitutional restraint, the restraint on human passions.

Restraint on human passions appeared in the mechanical principle of majority rule, modified by protection of the vulnerable minority. The English philosopher John Locke, the earliest exponent of liberal democracy, knew that majority politics was immune from abuse only as the minority approaches zero. Because this never happens in a mass society, Locke wished to make sure the minority was never eliminated. Early liberalism, then, restrained the majority—hence democracy itself—only by assuring the survival of the minority.

Because majority rule means rule over and against a minority, and because democracy also means rule by the people, constitutional restraints on the majority set restrictions on democracy. This is consistent with democracy as a process, but the process must not be confused with government, the institutions set to work by democracy. The people are the end in this process precisely because their participation has as its object their betterment, the public good. The formation of a majority, the consensus building that makes for a majority, is what tells government how to act. If the vote is taken seriously, by thinking participants in the process, the majority becomes an aggregate of people that tells government what to do.

Because democracy can be seen only as a process by virtue of the mechanical need to "count noses" in order to make it effective, it is overturned by the present trend toward minority tyranny. Under the *early* liberal restraint on democracy, majority rule subsumed minority survival, not its sovereignty. The rise of minority rulership, so clearly visible in affirmative action and other group programs, does not suspend democracy, it nullifies it entirely. This repositioning of power elevates government over democracy and annuls the power of the majority. This effectively transforms government into an instrument of popular oppression.

LIBERALISM, SECULARISM, AND THE LAW

The corruption of liberalism in the latter half of the twentieth century is manifest in its effort to establish ends for government. This necessarily reduces people to a means, an instrument. As originally conceived, liberalism was a set of ideas (not ideals) and constitutional limitations on the excesses of democracy for the sake of the individual in aggregate. The early liberal proponents (Locke, Montesquieu, Smith, Kant, Jefferson) believed individuals were sufficiently distinct that each one should be able to pursue personal ends (happiness) within an "ordered scheme of liberty." This was in keeping with Kant's maxim to treat people as ends, never as means. At the same time, the individual was restrained by order within a scheme of liberty for the sake of the public good, community. The old liberal idea was that individuals were unique enough to have different ends, but alike enough to want to pursue their ends within a commonly created world. Liberalism today, however, uses uniqueness to uproot and shatter the community. Without limits set to distinctness by common convictions, the "glue" of community decomposes into an atomized, individualized society; this is anarchy.

The new, deformed liberalism has thus negated morality in favor of an idealization of individual "choices," not between good and evil but between alternatives provided by society. Yet there is no standard of good to mediate between these alternatives. Choice is now based on individual preference, which means the satisfaction of bodily wants regardless of who gets hurt (in abortion, as an example). A society that lacks the capacity to regulate its pleasures finally succumbs to human appetites. This explains the growth of pornography, for instance, which, according to the new criteria, cannot be condemned as wrong against a standard of goodness. Instead, it is reduced to the "freedom" of choice to see or not to see it.

Whatever else might be said of pleasures, the one unassailable fact is that they do not make for community. This prompted the politically brilliant insight of the famous Nobel laureate Aleksandr Solzhenitsyn. He warned the United States that when liberty degenerates into simply "unlimited freedom in the choice of pleasures," it becomes impossible to answer the question, "Why and for the sake of what should one risk one's precious life in defense of the common good?" Indeed, if choices are not mediated or restrained by the common good, there is no community at all because nothing makes for community, least of all widely shared pleasures. Nowhere is this more evident than in the current effort to transform choices into "rights" and thereby pretend some approval for them. This effort extends to perversions that stand outside not only the American community but Western civilization as a whole.

The current attack on morality, with its intention to reduce everything to mere choice, has concluded by granting protection to homosexuals through politics rather than science. By a 58 percent membership vote (rather than scientific analysis) of the American Psychiatric Association (APA) our judgment of homosexuality, both religious and moral, was supposed to shift from tolerance (of a disorder) to approval (of a choice). Using tactics of intimidation and violence to threaten delegates at the early-1970s APA meetings, the "gay rights" activists were able to challenge the larger heterosexual population with notions of "sexual preference" supposedly equal to that of the community as a whole.

The corrosive effect that approval of homosexuality has on the family and the community is plain. Rooted firmly in the tradition of Judeo-Christian morality, the family is now redefined around the fickleness of personal choice. No longer seen in terms of moral, genetic, or generational bonding, the family is degraded into a series of personal choices based on often aberrational sexual preference. That this aberration confronts the community as an adversary is obvious in the current AIDS epidemic.

Shea's identification of AIDS as a major future problem is correct, but the problematic nature of AIDS is political and moral rather than medical. This is painfully obvious in the homosexuals' assertion of their private (sexual) right not to be tested for the virus, which confronts the community's fear of transmission of the disease primarily through homosexual promiscuity. Echoing a number of recent studies, Dr. Marjorie Rosenberg notes that promiscuity is so great among male homosexuals that five hundred different sexual contacts by the age of thirty-seven is not unusual.[3] Thus the normal bonds that connect individual to family and family to community are severed in favor of unrestricted personal appetites.

The political success of this adversarial attack on the community reached its high point in 1984. During the Democratic convention the "gay rights" activists demanded and received a designated seat on the Platform Committee. Still, the disintegrative character of the battle between homosexuals and the community is given the gloss of respectability in social science circles today by pushing the relativist argument that neither nature,

God, nor community is decisive in shaping one's sexual life. Yet another Greek lesson is thereby lost on us today: to be free from one's pleasures requires the avoidance of slavery to one's appetites.

This same relativism, with its rejection of God, nature, and community, is employed by feminists, who assert boldly that "nature is not destiny!" They, too, disconnect themselves as individuals from community, only this time it's in behalf of gender. Although they demand rights for women, they explicitly renounce the gender responsibilities consigned to women by nature and community. Seeing themselves as economic subordinates of a larger *material* order (a Marxist proposition), they *choose* economic opportunity over maternal designations (nature) and familial responsibility (community). They see an unborn child (which they define as fetal "tissue") as an economic obstruction to their mobility in the marketplace. Of course, this degrades maternal and family sentiment into obstacles in the path of personal self-fulfillment. Abortion is then seen by feminists as economic liberation from the bonds of matrimony and the commitment to others. The execution of an unborn child and the refusal to accept the consequences for one's own acts that issued in that child are *chosen* over economic self-restraint and devotion to others. This further diminishes community through a vulgar selfishness (masked as opportunity) that confronts all others as economic competitors.

Formerly a pluralistic society held together by moral sentiment, the United States is coming apart as the results of intergroup combat. The authority of the moral community, which served as a limitation on all members of the community, individuals as well as groups, is eroding under the weight of those who choose to confront the community as adversaries. Politically speaking, not much could be worse. The noted philosopher Alasdair MacIntyre relates the disappearance of moral authority directly to relativism and increasing secularization. In *Secularization and Moral Change* he writes:

> In our society the notion of moral authority is no longer a viable one. For the notion of authority can only find application in a community and in areas of life in which there is an agreed way of doing things according to accepted rules. . . . Unless there is an established and right way of doing things, so that we have social agreement on how to follow the rules and how to legislate about them, the notion of authority in morals is empty.[4]

Community decay bodes ill for the future of the nation. Each self-defining group (homosexuals as family "partners," for example) that asserts its choices are equal to any other choices rejects the body of Judeo-Christian morality—the Puritan ethic—which for over two hundred years has held us together as a people. Contrary to contemporary secularists, it is precisely *because* of this morality that the United States could tolerate so much diversity—but only to a point. We have yet to learn that not all things are tolerable.

Since the Reformation of Luther and the republicanism of John Locke, liberalism has degenerated from this standard of public goodness into some vague notion of public welfare. The public good entails judgments of right and wrong conduct, a definition of the moral community. It is a public philosophy whose heart is a standard of goodness. But "welfare" is oblique, implying a measure of health. The current concern to control AIDS by condoms rather than conduct is an example. But "welfare" is not derived from God or nature. Instead, it derives from purely functional claims of preferences arbitrated by an abstraction called government. By using the term *welfare* social "scientists" hope to avoid moral language. Note the current effort to reduce everything to a psychological problem.

Yet if freedom is seen as an absolute, one outside the context of community, this implies the ability (indeed, the choice) to do evil as well as good. Government activists take this to mean that society must be reformed so "welfare" will result. Although these activists do not see the state as good, they do see it as an instrument, with its coercive laws and violence, for shaping the public welfare, described today as "social justice."

Furthermore, liberalism's degeneration into an activist government mentality predictably entailed the decomposition of Western law. Originally conceived as an ethical minimum (the maximum was set by the community), law under early liberalism was intended to secure individual claims of freedom against government. It was *not* an instrument for expanding rights beyond community. The source for this early liberalism was the English Revolution of 1688, the time of Locke. The French Revolution is the source of current liberalism. Law was employed by the French to reshape man, hence its brutality.

The freeing of legislation from law by transforming it into an instrument of social welfare succeeded only in destroying the essential adhesive of law necessary for community. The turning over of traditional and natural law to politicians ended by reducing government to an instrument of men, men whose passions rage in different directions, carrying the law along. Legislators are unrestrained in their desire for reelection and in consequence make laws to satisfy the tempo-rary whims of the populace, not to uphold ethical standards.

Yet early liberals recognized that positive (written) law is no better than an ethical minimum, and is alterable by legislators seeking popular approval. Neither government nor law, they argued, could satisfy the insatiable appetites of the masses. Instead, they believed that society should conform to law, and law to morality. Indeed, the importance of morality to early liberal theory is obvious in the history of liberalism provided by the famous philosopher George Sabine. In *A History of Political Theory* Sabine identifies the two "assumptions" or axioms of liberalism: "individualism," and the fact that "relationships between individuals in a community are irreducible moral relations."

The individual of early liberalism was defined in terms of the "moral relations" of the community. Freedom, then, was seen as an idea, not an ideal that confronts the community. Whether self-imposed (through moral training) or imposed by government, freedom was constrained through an elaborate moral order. Grounding freedom in the individual, not government, early liberals saw the individual as a moral agent; he was responsible for *his* acts. They believed morality should be the basis of law rather than what it is today: an antagonist of law.

The convergence of secularism and its belief in science with liberalism and its belief in the science of education is the result of the vain belief that all human problems are soluble through institutions devised by humans—a Jacobin idea. The new secular liberalism must now oppose religion as a countervailing set of beliefs that threaten worship of the state. And for a very simple reason: religion diminishes the importance of what the state can or cannot do.

The government that recognizes religious liberty as the first freedom thereby admits (knowingly or not) the limits on its own political rule. This is why one of the first oppressions by a new Marxist dictatorship is religion. Marxism claims an earthly transcendence, a heaven on earth in which all the cares and woes of the world will be overcome. Religion, however, calls for a self-transcendence, a subordination of politics for the sake of the soul.

State activists demand primary loyalty. The more intensely people turn to the state, the more control the activists have over their lives. It is a human weakness to be controlled by the *things* we want most. And the state is clearly in charge of things. If our passions can be shaped and satisfied by the state, then we concede an awesome power to it. This is why politicians, the real beneficiaries of state power, try to contain the potentially subversive power of religious institutions. this also explains the current effort by secular liberals to purge prayer from schools. And they are demanding the elimination of *all* religious symbols from the classroom, including the Ten Commandments. Indeed, the hostility of the American Civil Liberties Union (ACLU) to religion is so intense that its policy 99 declares that no "public area of any facility built or maintained with public resources [may] contain any recognizable built-in religious symbol." This is the same ACLU that promotes homosexual marriages (policy 264) and defends child pornography (policy 4).

It is deceitful to assert that religious and political mingling violates the principle of separation of church and state. *Absolutely* no such principle exists, or was ever intended by our Founders to exist. The "wall of separation" between church and state is a bogieman. Jefferson wrote this now overworked phrase in a letter to a small Baptist congregation—not as a policy recommendation—eleven years after ratification of the First Amendment. Indeed, he was not even in the country during the debate on the "establishment-of-religion" clause. This is also the same Jefferson who invoked man's "Creator," "nature's God," "Laws of Nature," and the "Supreme Judge of the World" as the foundation for declaring the independence of the colonies. The fear of religious bigotry that secularists say they feel is actually a ruse to conceal their fear of secular bigotry. It's simple: state worshippers do not like God worshippers. And the law, formerly grounded in "nature's God," is the prime instrument for uprooting the moral and religious sentiment of the community. This explains the secularist's turn to the courts and judicial policy-making in order to control the United States.

The willingness of the American people to turn their political fate over to the Supreme Court rests partially on the misguided notion that the law is separate (and separable) from moral considerations, a dangerous illusion at best and a clear abdication of democratic responsibility at worst. Neither judges nor lawyers are equipped by education or enlightenment to claim sovereignty as the best or wisest articulators of political values. But this has not stopped the state activists on the Court, or their supporters in the legal profession.

Abram Chayes, a Harvard law professor, arrogantly asserts that the judicial process is superior in every way to the present democratic process. The reason? He argues that the judicial process is governed by lawyers, and lawyers are governed by "professional ideals of reflective and dispassionate analysis of the problem before [them] and [are] likely to have some experience in putting this ideal into practice."[5] He further asserts that the

Court is insulated from "narrow political pressures." Yet the Court today is under siege precisely because it has yielded to "narrow political pressures."

According to Chayes and his activist allies on the Court the Founders were remiss in failing to see the advantages of ignoring Congress, the president, and the people entirely. Why engage in the clumsy process of democracy when we can have government by the judiciary? This is elitism with a new sordid twist. It was precisely this legal arrogance and the fear of an imperial judiciary that prompted Alexander Hamilton to declare in *Federalist* 78, "The fabric of American empire ought to rest on the solid basis of The Consent of the People." Even Hamilton's political opponent, Thomas Jefferson, cautioned that "to consider the judges the ultimate arbiters of all Constitutional questions is a very dangerous doctrine indeed, and one which would place us under the despotism of an oligarchy."

State activists, whether on the Court, in the legislature, or in the academy, are more concerned to smuggle in their own ideology of an activist government that bypasses democracy than to accept a vision of public goodness esteemed by a majority of citizens. Yet the primacy of *early* liberalism over democracy—that is, the concern to restrict government before advancing rights—is evident in the adoption of the Constitution before establishing the Bill of Rights. But recently, the Court has made such an effort to deny democracy by prolifically granting "rights" that it appears as though we owe our rights to government. At the same time, the struggle over rights has eclipsed the vision of public goodness and undermined the very foundation of community.

THE ASCENDANCY OF RIGHTS

Perhaps the only thing that unites the political Left and Right in the United States is agreement on the bursting of the social bond. All parties concur that there is no *sensus communis*, no sense of community. But the Left fails to recognize that the sense of community is derived from a *theologica civilis*. A society reduced merely to its separate components, individuals, lacks community because it lacks a vision that would unite the individuals.

One hardly need invoke the name of Aristotle to understand that when a community has no sense of itself, social life is impossible, even dangerous. A community is held together by belief. Whether an African tribe, Greek *polis*, Tartar village, or modern industrial state, every political association requires some belief, myth, or faith to which its peoples can together adhere. This is imperative in the United States, with its diverse population. Without this belief, myth, or faith, the community comes unglued; it degenerates into clusters of isolated individuals who confront one another as adversaries.

Diversity invites comparison and breeds suspicion. Without a sense of community, whose source must lie outside or beyond the society itself, society is reduced to tiny clusters of solitary individuals. These clusters form organizations in neoprimitive warfare, each one struggling for the resources of society. In the modern industrial network we call the United States, isolation has become a mass phenomenon. Without a communal bond individuals are attracted to the most bizarre and preposterous notions as guides for life: astrology, the occult, the drug culture, satanism. The community has collapsed; in the rubble one finds atomized individuals, alone and frightened.

In the United States the Left blames capitalism for the disintegration of communal life, as it does for all evils of the world. Christopher Lasch, for instance, maintains that the individualism of our market economy has produced a culture of narcissism.[6] Lasch ignores the fact that the hedonistic, self-indulgent principles of the 1960s, "If it feels good, do it" and "Do your own thing," were mouthed by the enemies of capitalism. This was the ethic of the drug culture, whose narcissistic impulses are doubted by no one. Of course, these bromides for living (and dying) are utterly incapable of replacing the Puritan ethic, and could hardly unite a people economically, let alone politically. Such views are not new, nor are they confined to popular writers of the 1960s and 1970s. The surge of moral and cultural relativisms, with their focus on the individual and their attack on absolutes, has undermined morality and transformed everything into an economic argument.

Yet, the search for communal decay in economic systems (a hidden Marxist assumption) would certainly have located this degeneration in the 1930s when economic deprivation was at its worst. But crime, especially violent crime, was considerably less then than during the 1960s and 1970s, when the Left called into question the very foundation of the American *ethos*. Simultaneously, the warring tribes of relativism and humanism sabotaged the absolutes of the Puritan ethic and elevated economics over moral and spiritual matters as guides for life. Americans were thus left nothing but economics to believe in.

The attack on the moral standard that stood above and beyond man was predictably followed by the disintegration of the community. The other-directedness provided by God was inverted; it was turned toward man. Responsibilities to others were soon inverted toward rights for oneself. Self-discipline gave way to self-expression. The individualism that had underwritten capitalism required ambition and hard work for achievement. But this achievement could be granted only through recognition and prestige bestowed by others who live in a common world, a world made common by others. The commonality of the United States was prescribed by the Puritan ethic; its values set limits to achievement and thus restraints on conduct. This has been turned upside-down today, morally and legally. Rights have replaced responsibilities, and this reflects the deformation of community into a society of isolated persons. The law has degenerated into an arbiter of rights, and morality no longer speaks to goodness but appears to favor the winner in a confrontation of rights against rights.

The sociopolitical implications of this legal and moral battle are obvious. Professor William Donohue notes how "rights are directed inwards, i.e., they serve the interests of those who exercise them. Responsibilities are directed outwards, i.e., they serve the interests of others. Rights liberate; responsibilities constrict."[7] In a society that increasingly defines freedom as absence of restraint ("Do your own thing") and rejects discipline in favor of self-expression, the other-directedness required for community is obliterated.

Traditionally, rights were proscribed by one's immediate relations, family, friends, community, country. They were derived from the community, its vision of good, and were intended to assure the individual a place in it. But for each right there was an equal and corresponding responsibility, what the Greeks called duty. *Both*, not one, identified the individual as an integral part of the larger whole, family, and community. Responsibilities personalized the impersonal community. But the "rights revolution" ended the only way it could: in a confrontation between individuals that could be settled only in court. The Supreme Court was now ready to replace the people as the determiner of public goodness.

At this point the individual, while asserting the many rights granted by the Court, is held above the very community that is the source of the rights the individual claims. The logical outcome, of course, is a struggle between the individual and the community, self-assertion versus public goodness. Rights are now elevated above community and confront it as an adversary.

This adversarial relationship was born in the Marxist critique of the United States during the 1960s. "We are all victims" of the harsh realities of capitalism, we were told. To seek "remedy," we have to turn to that great body of moral inspiration, the Supreme Court. But with nothing beyond its own political agenda to turn to for an appeal, the Court is left the task of arbitrating between competing claims of rights. As a consequence, individuals who were once members of the community have been reduced to combatants in a war of rights. Equally, the traditions of republican government, what we call democracy, have been crushed under a body of litigation that can no longer justify itself morally.

A mass society does not have to be an undifferentiated society. The United States could withstand diversity only because the diversity ranged within limits set by public goodness. That is, the authority of the community was accepted by all in the public realm, men as citizens, regardless of the uniqueness of individual private lives. Indeed, it is critical in our community to distinguish between the things that belong in private, which should be hidden from public view, and the things essential to public goodness. To carry private vices into public places only corrupts the public good. Of course, goodness cannot be deformed to mean relativism—relative to what? If goodness is misshapened by its proximity to others, then so is evil, and the distinction between the two is soon lost.

The fascination with cultural diversity, the ongoing search for one's roots, one's own kind, is the latest and most obvious assault on the United States, not merely its laws but its *ethos* as well. And it is no coincidence that this assault is carried out by the relativists who are secular in belief, partly because of their idealization of Marx. They want to deculturize the nation to bring an end to the *American century*.

The *American century* is a conclusion, a consequence of the American community. It is not the result of natural resources; these were abundant in other lands. Nor is it due to industrialization, an activity open to all who chose to participate. Indeed, it is the result of a people bounded on the one side by republican principles and the other by God. The former opened the New World to diverse peoples; the latter protected it by faith. The American community is a symbolization of a politically free people that, in order to assure this freedom, set limits to conduct under the principles of Judeo-Christian theology. But if these limits are diluted or restrained by nothing but "choice," then the only thing that separates good from evil is mere preference, private passions—the appetites of the brute.

Our community is both wider and deeper than other communities. It is wide enough to accept peoples of diverse ancestry; only this nation has set in place a statue that beckons the dispossessed. It is deeper in that the only requirement for shelter is that such persons subordinate this diversity for the sake of the community. To give in to the present demands for racial and cultural particularity is to revert to the tribalism of the Old World, the very forces that brought people to the New World. To yield to the peculiarities of human appetites is to succumb to the savagery that slumbers beneath all civilizations.

NOTES

1. "On the Concept of Authority in Political Philosophy," in *Concepts in Social and Political Philosophy,* ed. Richard Flathman (New York: Macmillan, 1973), p. 123.
2. J. L. Talmon, *The Origins of Totalitarian Democracy* (New York: Norton, 1970), p. 34.
3. See her article for a wonderfully concise history of the homosexual movement in the United States. *Commentary* 84 (December 1987).
4. The Riddell Memorial Lectures, 1964 (London, 1967), p. 53.
5. In Walter Berns, *Taking the Constitution Seriously* (New York: Simon & Schuster, 1987), p. 219.
6. *The Culture of Narcissism.* (New York: Norton, 1978).
7. William Donohue, "The Social Consequences of the Rights Revolution," *Intercollegiate Review* 22 (Spring 1987): 41–42.

SUGGESTED READINGS

BERNS, WALTER. *Taking the Constitution Seriously.* New York: Simon & Schuster, 1987. A historical study of constitutional development and the recent effort by the judiciary to usurp the powers of democracy.

DIAMOND, MARTIN. *The Founding of the Democratic Republic.* Itasca, Ill.: F. E. Peacock, 1981. An examination of the founding of the United States and of the particular moral and political principles at the core of the founding.

DIGGINS, JOHN P. *The Lost Soul of American Politics.* Chicago: University of Chicago Press, 1984. One of the most thorough analyses of American intellectual and moral history ever written. The author focuses on virtue as the adhesive for the endurance of the regime.

Among the Problems Facing American Government: The Ability to Govern

John C. Shea

West Chester University of Pennsylvania

The general question for this set of essays invites philosophical speculation. What is meant by government's "proper role"? Is *proper role* a judgmental term, suggesting some presumed normative standard? Or should our inquiry be more analytical, extrapolating from current trends and attempting to predict the preoccupations of political authorities as we face the twenty-first century? I believe both philosophical speculation and analysis are necessary. No matter what standards are used to define government's place, the civil authority must be made relevant to the existing world. Normative judgments are as old as Plato's assumption that philosophers make the best rulers, and as new as the prescriptions for betterment offered by the candidates in the latest political campaign. Plato also gave us the observation that the first reason for the state was the need for cooperation in satisfying the goals of human beings.[1]

Some scholars have suggested narrower, less enlightened but perhaps more accurate explanations as to what rulers see as the real mission of government. In *The Prince,* for example, Niccolò Machiavelli (1469–1527)—acknowledged for centuries as a shrewd student of statecraft—saw the job of the ruler as perpetuating himself in power. Of the cynical dicta of Machiavelli-like observers of politics, Robert MacIver wrote, "Most of these precepts are concerned not with the larger issues of government but with the much narrower question of how a ruler or a ruling group can gain or retain power. . . ."[2]

The idea that the function of government is simply to enable the power holders to hold onto power is not particularly inspiring, although it may be an accurate depiction of the realities of politics. As the Watergate noose tightened, Nixon desperately maneuvered to stay in the White House even as he asserted that he was motivated by the desire to protect the institution of the presidency. He was simply more flagrant in doing what all chief executives are apt to do when in trouble.[3] Rulers have often acted against the interest of the governed so as to preserve or expand their own power. Stalin crushed the Ukrainian peasants and caused the death of millions of enemies, real and imagined, to ensure his near-total control of the Soviet Union.

Recognizing that rulers sometimes comport themselves in this fashion, we still may safely conclude that such behavior is contrary to the "proper role" of government. The quotation from MacIver begun earlier continues: "We cannot reduce the vast business of government to a few precarious techniques for holding onto office. The tasks of government are manifold and comprehensive, emerging from complicated and ever changing conditions."[4]

The truth is that different societies have different expectations as to the "proper role" of government and governors. In some, a division between the religious authority and secular authority would be unthinkable; in others (such as the USSR), values about common property have caused the state to become involved in the prosecution of a whole range of economic "crimes"—the sorts of things that people become rich, famous, and much admired for doing in the United States today.

So, to understand the "proper role" of government, we must first understand that there are principles, differing from case to case, that underlie each society. They are accepted by the vast majority of any given population as "truths" that few question or even think about. Ordinarily, these truths are not examined and one should not expect them to be, except in the most extraordinary circumstances. Americans, for example, believe in such ideas as majority rule, separation of church and state, freedom of expression (in general), the strength and worthiness of the U.S. constitutional system (even while viewing many of the officeholders under the system as unredeemed charlatans), and are taught to admire and be grateful for the sacrifices made to "secure our freedoms" by our forefathers in defense of "our way of life."[5] All societies in fact operate on the basis of such undebated, or seldom debated, and consensual givens. It has to be so, for without widespread agreement on principles and heroes, nations simply cannot function—people will not accept the legitimacy of the government nor of the decisions it makes. As Roberta Sigel put it, for newly independent states, "the first order of business . . . often is the creation of a sense of we-ness, national loyalty and consensus. . . ."[6] The givens that define the political universe are not necessarily rational or correct. Often they are not ideas at all but more in the nature of allegorical tales about traditional heroes whose exploits we are invited to honor and, perhaps, to emulate. In the case of Americans, we learn about a galaxy of founding fathers (George Washington, Benjamin Franklin, Thomas Jefferson, and others, plus Abraham Lincoln). The shared legends help to hold us together as a nation. Some have obvious political points, such as Patrick Henry's stirring "Give Me Liberty or Give Me Death" oration to the Virginia House of Burgesses. Others teach such entrepreneurial values as inventiveness (Franklin's experiment with the kite and electricity). Still others are simply facts that by retelling have been invested with an aura of special significance (say, that George Washington lived in Mount Vernon; he was traditionally identified as a surveyor, only more recently as a slave owner).

The values and ideas that underlie our political society and form our political culture have paradoxically been in place for a long time and are constantly, although slowly, changing. They are essential for defining our view of the "proper role" of government. One of the quintessential American values is a pragmatic approach to problem solving, often referred to as the "can-do" approach, the idea that for every problem there is a solution, if it can just be identified. This is a way of saying that if one wishes to understand the role of the U.S. government in the 1990s, one must begin by identifying society's major problems.

The proper role of government in the twenty-first century, as in every period of history, is to anticipate and meet the major challenges to the well-being of the constituent population. The difficulties in doing so are three: first, defining what well-being includes; second, determining what the threats to that well-being are; and third, deciding upon a course of action most likely to inhibit the threats and promote the desired ends. The last step may prove especially troublesome. Often Americans have been politically paralyzed because of deep divisions about how to deal with particular problems (energy, trade deficits, ecology, to name several) and as a result take no action at all. Some (usually referred to as "conservatives" in political shorthand), like Allen, may well see as the principal threat to societal well-being a proposed expansion of the role of government in the life of society. The traditional liberal might argue that a healthy society demands greatly expanded social programs for the less well off. Or, again, conservatives would rely on the private sector and the workings of the marketplace to make the United States more competitive. Liberals might be more likely to be concerned with the social costs imposed by the "invisible hand" of capitalism.

How does one begin to compile a list of present and potential U.S. problems? The drawbacks in such an undertaking are evidenced by a problem that now would be at or near the top of every such list: AIDS. Yet a list of problems on the horizon ten years ago would not have carried even a hint of that outbreak.

Looking into the future has always been a chancy enterprise. History is littered with predictions of cataclysms and disasters that never occurred. Nevertheless, undaunted by a whole history of such failures, this author will attempt to name the major problems apt to beset the nation in the next decade.

Before doing so, however, let me establish a taxonomy of problems based heavily on the four categories developed by Richard Scammon and Benjamin Wattenberg in another context.

Category one is national security problems, including foreign relations and defense issues.

Some disagreement exists on whether the Soviets will continue to be at the top of our international concerns. Might they be replaced by, say, international terrorism, or perhaps a fear of Japan?

There are, of course, a multitude of potential international crises that could occupy the time and energies of Americans. It is certain that the poverty, drought, war, and starvation that plague much of the less developed world will continue unabated. Blood will go on flowing in South Africa. Turmoil in the Middle East and revolution in the Caribbean and Central America will persist. Castro, Khaddafi, or some similar notable may make a move that by our lights is irresponsible and fraught with dire consequences for the United States and/or the world.

The death of this or that world leader, the fall from power of leaders in China or the Soviet Union—any of these events could cause a major refocusing of our attention and international concern. It is, however, my judgment that three major international problems will command our attention as the 1990s wind down. The first is a return of the "energy crisis," a special legacy from the Reagan administration, of which more later. The second problem is the growing dominance of Japan in world markets, and the intensifying American perception of Japan as a threat to our world leadership; relations will, at best, be cool. The third and by far the most severe foreign policy problem will be relations with Mexico.

In the early 1970s Hans Morganthau predicted that within fifteen years Americans would identify not the Soviet Union but Mexico as their number-one foreign policy concern. He may have been a little off on the timing, but essentially he had it right. The United States is the only country of the First World that borders on a Third World country. And Mexico is not simply a Third World country. It is a country with a rapidly increasing population: in 1990 about 83 million, and doubling approximately every twenty-five years. It exhibits the most revolutionary of conditions: a declining standard of living, a large (for the Third World) and

relatively radicalized intelligentsia, and a history of animosity toward the United States. Mexicans can stand on the banks of the Rio Grande and look northward at the allure of modern society. Moreover, Mexico borders on not only the United States but on Central American countries even less affluent than itself—and whose poor are often inspired to make the overland trek to the North.

There has been considerable dispute as to the impact of Latin immigration on the United States up to this point, but there is no question that some time soon the United States will confront social and economic (and perhaps political) revolution on its southern border. It also seems a virtual certainty that "Anglo" (and very likely black) Americans will demand that the Mexican border be closed and more tightly controlled than has been our practice. Further restrictions on immigration would, in effect, be punitive steps against Mexico and will have grave consequences. All this makes it inevitable that Mexican relations will loom larger in U.S. foreign policy and domestic politics than has been true since the time of the Mexican Revolution.

Category two problems have to do with energy and environmental issues. I have already played Cassandra by predicting a return of the oil shortage. Environmental considerations will complicate the matter. Ecological worries have ruled out greater utilization of coal, the fossil fuel the United States has in abundance, as an acceptable substitute for oil. The unpopularity of expanded dependence on nuclear power need hardly be discussed. And other alternatives are not readily apparent. Two things, however, are predictable in this connection: Americans will not be willing to live with a lowered standard of living, and the process of getting from the present fossil-fuel-dependent economy to the next stage, whatever it is, will be economically and politically very stressful.

Even apart from energy there is a full menu of environmental issues. Whatever strides have been made in cleaning up rivers, the air, and to a lesser extent the land in the United States and in the nations of Western Europe, they have been more than matched by the deteriorating environmental conditions in much of the Third World. It is certain that amelioration and correction will require an unparalleled degree of international cooperation. Indeed, General Secretary Gorbachev has expressed the hope that U.S.-Soviet combined efforts in this area will help to bring the two superpowers closer together.

Two environmental problems that stand out are the hole in the ozone layer and the dangers of a greenhouse effect's causing a warming of the earth's atmosphere. I have no more scientific knowledge about these matters than do many of my readers (and undoubtedly less than many), but as a reasonably close reader of the reports in the popular press, I believe it is safe to say that they will be moving toward the top of government agendas in the years ahead.

The implications of the ecological and environmental crisis are staggering. We are conceivably talking about major reductions in manufacturing in order to ensure the survivability of the planet. We are possibly facing basic alterations in the life-styles of the majority of humankind. Even should it turn out that the reports of the imminence of the death of Earth are somewhat premature and exaggerated, it is certain that we will need to consider monumental changes in energy usage and waste disposal.

One additional ecological/environmental disaster may occupy the U.S. government. The big California earthquake may take place (or, more recently seismologists tell us that a temblor of significant magnitude may occur along the Mississippi or the East Coast). The point here is that the nature of "natural" disasters is such that we cannot forecast what is coming or when, nor to what degree it will occupy policy-makers. Nature has its own agenda; witness how the great drought of 1988 brought into question decades of thinking about farm surpluses.

Category three comprises economic problems, about which we will say the least. Part of the reason is that the trade and federal deficits are the most-discussed problems at the moment and therefore the most apt to be addressed in some fashion. Also, it often happens that issues that are the most talked about are not in fact as important as they seem to be. By the time you read this essay, it may be that inflation or unemployment or both will again be taking a turn in the limelight.

Category four constitutes social issues. Despite the seriousness and intractability of some of the problems mentioned earlier we believe these problems are even more severe. Social issues include drugs; crime; matters that engage many political action groups and newspaper writers (prayer in the schools, education, abortion, gay rights, women's rights); and the sort of very profound issues that Senator Patrick Daniel Moynihan has focused on: welfare and the disintegration of the family to the extent that one-third of all children are born into single-parent families.[7] Such family issues have heretofore been confined principally to what has been termed the American underclass and have not threatened the stability of society. But although the beleaguered family may be more obvious among minorities, no stratum of society is untouched.

All the critical social issues become manifest in increasing illiteracy (and its negative results for U.S. productivity), vandalism and abuse of public facilities, a rising level of uncivil behavior in public (perhaps most indulged in at sporting events—hardly a uniquely American phenomenon) and, in general, what might be called the decline in a sense of community. A society in which people shoot randomly at passing motorists or indulge in drive-by killings is not in good health.

I concur with Bosso and Allen on the importance of the decline in the sense of community. It stems from many causes and in many ways is not new. It is doubtful that blacks felt themselves to be more a part of society in the 1940s, but the stark fact is that they then had little political power and their alienation was neither as visible nor as potent. It is now truer than ever before that there are major black ghettos where most whites would not think of traveling, especially on foot or after dark. And there are white areas where any black presence immediately becomes a subject of interest to the police, no matter what guidelines the courts establish.

The increasingly vocal alienation of groups that feel themselves to be consistent losers in the political game is, as political scientists expect, producing people who no longer feel bound by the rules and are willing to go beyond them to achieve their ends. The most visible evidence of this is crime.

Moreover, there appears to be a decline in a sense of morality in high places. In the business world the biggest rewards seem to go to "raiders," whose principal contribution to the commonweal is the eviscerating of corporations for their own gain. Throughout the country developers rip up cities without thought to the poor, who are displaced, and multiply suburban housing tracts and shopping malls in a manner that despoils the ecological and social environment.

A sense of community is a society's greatest strength. Ironically, in many ways the Japanese attack on Pearl Harbor led to a greater sense of community in the United States and hastened victory in World War II. It put to rest the divisiveness of the isolationists and caused Americans to act as one in pursuit of the war. Although it is sophisticated these days to downplay what the United States did in that war—as if 300,000 battle deaths should simply be overlooked—the truth is that victory required enormous sacrifices and great changes for millions in their way of life to produce the incredible outpouring of war materials that fueled the Allied effort. It was possible only because there was a sense of oneness among the people, a belief in the purpose of a greater community that does not exist today. One wonders if even an event like the attack on Pearl Harbor could produce such a commonality of purpose in the 1990s.

There are many social changes taking place in the United States that clearly have not been adequately addressed. The evolving status of women in the workplace and in the home has not found suitable response from the political system. What is to be done about children whose parents work? There is no systematic day care program, and even if there were, no real consideration has been given to the long-term sociological implications of having whole generations of children raised by strangers in even the best of circumstances (which all too often are not what prevail). Allen's apparent desire to return women to the home in fulfillment of what, in his view, nature decrees, ignores the reality that for many American families a second breadwinner is not a philosophical choice but an economic necessity.

A sort of moral anarchy seems to have struck the populace. President Carter has often been criticized for his "national malaise" address. What has been forgotten is that his words were well received because they struck a responsive chord. The public turned on him only when he immediately followed it up by dismissing four members of his cabinet.[8] During the Reagan administration the "sleaze factor" became almost an accepted part of government; greed was in. It has been pointed out that in the 1930s and 1940s those who betrayed the United States to the USSR did so out of ideological conviction; today they do it for money. High-ranking Pentagon officials have sold classified bidding information to defense contractors without regard to any interest but their own. In 1988 then-speaker of the House James Wright "published" a ghostwritten book, bought by the thousands by those who wanted not to read his thoughts but to influence his behavior, and he reaped royalties so high as to make the whole process patently dishonest. What Walter Lippmann referred to as the public interest seems to have disappeared as a consideration of high officials.[9]

SUMMING UP

The foregoing is a considerable litany of the problems facing the U.S. government in the future. What do they have to do with the role of the government in the years ahead? I return to my earlier point that the purpose of government is to secure the maximum well-being of the people being governed. This is, of course, as Lasswell would tell us, the stuff of politics rather than political science.[10] I have no intention here of prescribing answers, something political scientists seem to be no better at than politicians.[11] I do contend, however, that identifying the salient problems of society is a necessary part of political analysis and the essential first step in their resolution.

The crucial argument of this essay is that Americans will come up against a crisis in the next several years greater than all the problems outlined above, and directly resultant from them: it is that the U.S. political system is ill-suited to deal with these challenges. We have just come through an orgy of self-congratulation, beginning in 1976 and continuing through the bicentennial of Washington's inauguration in 1989, celebrating the successes of the political system. Any serious student of the economy will tell you that one of the great strengths of the country has been the rock-solid popular support for our political system. It is hardly any secret that Saudi princes (to use a stereotype) make investments in the United States because they believe the U.S. political system, with its strong emphasis on private ownership, renders such investments safer than anywhere else in the world from the threat of nationalization.

In the pre-Reagan years political science was seized with analysis of the U.S. system of government based on the idea of institutional paralysis: So many interests had become involved in the process that government, the decision maker, was unable to resolve conflict in a way that allowed the system to work. Important problems could not be resolved; they simply dragged on. Then along came Ronald Reagan, and for a few years the decision-making apparatus worked. His entourage of skilled manipulators were able to work the levers of power in such a way as to force through the administration's policy positions. Although his second term saw a rapid falloff in his ability to move his radical agenda along, he still finished his time in office with higher approval ratings than any president in the past forty years.[12] It is an important point to keep in mind.

One must be cautious in sounding too gloomy about the ability of the political system to respond to pressing problems. But the prolonged, orchestrated celebration of U.S. democracy in itself may be a sign of some trouble. As Lasswell put it, "A well established ideology perpetuates itself with little planned propaganda by those whom it benefits most. When thought is taken about ways and means of sowing conviction, conviction already has languished; the basic outlook of society has decayed, or a new triumphant outlook has not yet . . . [emerged]."[13]

What the Reagan administration basically succeeded at (with greater or lesser help from events, depending on one's ideology) was dealing with the twin monsters of inflation and unemployment that had gripped the Carter administration. By the shrewd manipulation of symbols, the Reaganites at least temporarily restored national pride. Inflation and unemployment did, indeed, hold the potential of wreaking havoc upon the system had they not been addressed, and the economic ones were. But the American sense of well-being may have been only temporarily improved. As the Reagan years waned, public opinion polls showed increasing doubts about the long-term outlook.[14] Meanwhile and far more seriously, the twin deficits in trade and the budget steadily ballooned.

It is the totality of sobering problems, problems that threaten the sense of security of Americans individually and collectively, that is worrisome. And the problems coincide with a fragility in the commitment to the political system. Americans still vigorously express support for the ideals of the Constitution, U.S. democracy, and the heroes and traditions that bind us together as a people. But enthusiasm for political leaders certainly has cooled, as has that for many of the major institutions.[15]

Further, it is obvious that in many ways we are more than ever a polyglot society. Hispanic Americans in many areas of the country are able to function without English-language skills; there is growing separation of black and white Americans; and the alienation of those who have never been reconciled to the fundamental changes in social mores identified with the 1960s persists.

The destruction of the lives of many Americans through technological unemployment or changing world conditions—farmers, steelworkers, miners—has not been suitably addressed. Their contempt for the people they see as running (and ruining) the United States from Washington and Wall Street is not likely to produce a reservoir of support for the system.

Now let us turn to the system itself. The constitutional structure erected in Philadelphia in 1789 has served us well. It is complex and resistant to change even in the best of circumstances. In the spirit of the fathers of the Constitution, and going far beyond the original design, we Americans have produced a system of government wherein power is deliberately divided in complex ways. It is spread among the various branches and agencies of the federal government and between the states and federal government, and a great deal is reserved for the private sector.

Two factors made this system work. Most commonly cited is the traditional role of political parties. A president could call on the partisan loyalty of members of Congress, governors, mayors, and thousands of other officials to help him accomplish his political agenda. Especially in Congress the leadership could usually rely on the strength of party ties in lining up votes. Today the vast majority of members of Congress are elected as the result of their own efforts or through the efforts of political action committees. The partisan glue that held the process together is simply gone.

The other strength of the system was the great commonality of values discussed at the beginning of this essay. Americans shared values that defined us as a people, values about our heroes, the high and noble nature of our system of government, and about our own special sense of oneness. The growing divisions among us when confronted with the pressures of today put all that in jeopardy.

What is the proper role of U.S. government in the next century? To find a way to allow the political process to work; to find a way whereby Americans will again have enough of a sense of a shared stake in the outcome of major disputes to allow decision making to go forward.

What will be the nature of the resolution of the problem? It is good to be able to avoid answering that question on the grounds that the answer is truly political philosophy and not political science. In the following essays, several authors address problems of our political system ranging from the roles of parties and interest groups to the proper functioning of Congress, the presidency, and the courts. In the very next section, the merits of a parliamentary alternative to our separation of powers is ably examined by Professors Blessing and Saffell. But whatever the institutional answers (which are critical), I, along with my colleagues Bosso and Allen, remain convinced Americans will not be able, as a society, to make them work without finding a renewed sense of community to underlie the whole.

It is not my desire to end this essay on a pessimistic note. Politicians often comment, truthfully, that Americans have measured up to daunting challenges in the past and will do so again. But surely no useful political nor educational purpose is served by failing to face the enormousness of the challenges facing us in the coming decade.

NOTES

1. Plato, *Republic* 2, cited by William Archibald Dunning in *A History of Political Philosophy*, vol. 1, "Ancient and Medieval" (New York: Macmillan, 1930), p. 28.

2. Robert MacIver, *The Web of Government*, 2d ed. (New York: Free Press, 1947), pp. 7–8.

3. There are many books and studies that make this point about final days of the Nixon administration; see, for example, Dan Rather and Gary Paul Gates, *The Palace Guard* (New York: Harper & Row, 1974), pp. 309–11.

4. MacIver, *Web of Government*, pp. 7–8.

5. See, for example, Donald J. Devine, *The Political Culture of the United States* (Boston: Little, Brown, 1972), especially pp. 179–230.

6. Roberta S. Sigel, "Introduction," in *Learning About Politics: A Reader in Political Socialization*, ed. Roberta S. Sigel (New York: Random House, 1970), p. xi.

7. *New York Times*, June 22, 1988, p. 1.

8. Joseph A. Califano, *Governing America* (New York: Simon & Schuster, 1981), pp. 428–40.

9. Walter Lippmann, *The Public Philosophy* (Boston: Little, Brown, 1955), pp. 41–46.

10. Harold D. Lasswell and Abraham Kaplan, *Power and Society: A Framework for Political Inquiry* (New Haven: Yale University Press, 1950), pp. xiii–xiv.

11. James Anderson, *Public Policy Making* (New York: Holt, Rinehart & Winston, 1979), pp. 6ff.

12. *New York Times*, January 18, 1989, p. 1.

13. Harold Lasswell, *Politics: Who Gets What, When and How* (New York: Whittlesey House, 1936), pp. 29–30.

14. *Washington Post*, June 29, 1988, p. A4.

15. For an excellent summary of polls showing the decline of confidence in our institutions, see James L. Sundquist, "The Crisis of Competence in Our National Government," *Political Science Quarterly* 92 (Summer 1980): 183–208.

SUGGESTED READINGS

DE BEUS, J. G.   *Shall We Make the Year 2000?* London: Sidgwick & Jackson, 1985. A British publication that is a little difficult to find in this country but worth the effort. Written by a former Dutch ambassador to the Soviet Union, it concentrates on political challenges, especially that of nuclear war.

BROWN, LESTER R., ET AL., EDS.   *State of the World.* New York: Norton, annual. A review of many problems, from population explosion to agriculture. Very thorough, very gloomy, very important.

PRESIDENTIAL STUDIES QUARTERLY.   18 (Summer 1988). The special issue, "Bicentennial and Quadrennial Considerations," includes thoughtful articles on the problems of our system of government by David Gergen, Lloyd Cutler, and Hedrick Smith, among others.

II

SEPARATION OF POWERS

Would a Parliamentary System Be Better Suited to Modern American Society Than Our Presidential One?

In what is probably the most often quoted statement from the *Federalist Papers*, James Madison said,

> If angels were to govern men, neither external nor internal controls on government would be necessary. In framing a government which is to be administered by men over men, the great difficulty lies in this: You must first enable the government to control the governed; and in the next place, oblige it to control itself (No. 51, February 6, 1788).

Madison's solution: a government wherein power is divided between the states and the national government and among the executive, legislative, and judicial branches of the national government. Indeed, it is further divided between the House and the Senate—a necessary added precaution in Madison's view because "in republican government, the legislative authority, necessarily, predominates."

There can be little argument that for over two hundred years the constitutional system established in Philadelphia in 1789 has served us well. But that does not mean it has been static. We have amended the Constitution twenty-six times, and we have also altered the system by judicial decision and by custom and usage. Nowhere in the Constitution, for example, is mention made of national nominating conventions, the way the electoral college actually works, or the enormous changes in the workings of the executive and legislative branches. Certainly one reason our system has survived for more than two centuries is its adaptability.

Professor Blessing, in "The Separation of Powers: An Idea Past Its Prime," declares that a major transformation is needed: the replacement of the presidential system with a parliamentary system. He sketches many of the recent problems confronting the American national government that were considered in the previous section and goes on to argue it is separation of powers that makes it difficult to deal with problems in an effective way. Blessing's argument is one for the rationalization of U.S. government. Under a parliamentary system there would be every incentive for cooperation between a fused executive and legislative branch and less possibility of avoiding responsibility for policy failures.

Professor Saffell's emphasis in defending the present structure is more on process than problems. He reasons in "Why the United States Should Not Change to a Parliamentary System of Government" that the present system can be made to work and that parties are not as irresponsible as Blessing would have us believe. Moreover, he argues that the British model of the parliamentary system (the example most frequently cited by both authors) creates as many problems as it solves; in fact, he points out that British reformers frequently look to the U.S. separation of powers for ideas on how to improve their government. Saffell also speaks in praise of the function of U.S. legislators as service-oriented representatives of their constituents as well as participants in the policy-making process.

The arguments made in the two essays go to the core of the institutional system of American national government. There is no denying that it is more difficult for an American president to get a program enacted into law than it is for a British prime minister with a solid parliamentary majority to do so. In many ways the question is what value we should place on efficiency, and whether the price of our fundamentally slow-to-respond separation-of-powers system is not too high.

Americans have often been slow in their politics to meet problems head-on, seemingly preferring to wait for them to go away or to deal with them piecemeal. Sometimes they do go away; at other times they build to a crisis that demands response. It is unlikely that Blessing's scheme will become a part of our constitutional system in the near future. He invites us to address, however, whether such a far-reaching change ought at least to be given serious consideration: Is the system broken and in need of major repair?

In reading these examinations of one of the crucial institutional foundations of our constitutional system, students might ask themselves what they consider to be the essential features of that system. The answer might in turn depend on two further queries. If a parliamentary system were to be adopted, would it be more efficient? If so, would the resulting sacrifice in leverage provided to political minorities to prevent enactment of legislation they oppose make the system more or less democratic?

The Separation of Powers: An Idea Past Its Prime

James A. Blessing
Susquehanna University

Government in the United States today does not work to great advantage. There is consensus that the American system of government is ineffective and that this has much to do with the relationship between Congress and the presidency. Just turn on the national television news for a week and note how frequently our political leaders, news commentators, and business leaders bemoan the failure of the government to arrive at an effective policy toward long-term health care, balancing the budget, poverty, and on and on. And also note how often this failure is placed in the context of conflict between the executive and legislative branches.

All sorts of words and phrases are used to describe this situation, with *deadlock, gridlock, stalemate,* and *lack of balance* being four of the more popular. But whichever terms are used, the point remains the same: The struggle between Congress and the presidency is unduly hindering effective policy and something needs to be done to improve the situation. James Reston wrote in the *New York Times,* "The leaders of both parties agree that the present gridlock between the Executive and Legislative branches cannot continue."[1] Perhaps the best evidence of the problem is presented by Professor Saffell in the opposing article when he applauds the fact that "in 1988 the Democratically controlled Congress succeeded for the first time since 1976 in approving all spending bills before the new fiscal year began. . . ." Saffell may be satisfied with *one success in twelve years* but many others are not.

That presidential–congressional relations are a problem is amply evidenced by the attention paid to them. The Founding Fathers and the anti-Federalist opposition hotly debated the issue at the Constitutional Convention in 1787 and in the press during the debates over ratification. Woodrow Wilson was concerned about the issue when he wrote *Congressional Government* and *Constitutional Government in the United States*. The issue is a continuing concern of most textbooks on U.S. government, and on the presidency and Congress. It is a principal theme in the journal *Presidential Studies Quarterly*. It was a central issue when the Center for the Study of Democratic Institutions published the Tugwell Constitution in 1970, and when Lloyd N. Cutler proposed significant structural changes in 1980.[2] And during the bicentennial period, studies and symposia repeatedly addressed the topic.[3] The list could go on and on, but the point is obvious: concern about presidential–congressional relations and their effect on public policy has been and still is a matter of primacy to political leaders, academicians, and the public. To borrow an old colloquialism, where there is smoke, there must be fire.

The fire in this instance is the effect presidential–congressional struggles have on governmental policy-making, an effect that is customarily viewed as debilitating. To quote one expert on the presidency, "Congress–President relations in general have long been a realm of difficulty—too much deadlock, too much delay and watering down of policies. . . ."[4] One need only look at the stupendous growth in the national budget deficit, cumulative debt, and the trade imbalances that have resulted in our becoming a debtor nation for the first time in the twentieth century to observe a lack of effective government policy. (We have now joined Mexico, Brazil, India, and others in this ranking, while West Germany and Japan, for instance, remain creditor nations.) As many have commented, the refusal or inability of the president and Congress to make or agree upon difficult decisions regarding the balance between spending (which everyone favors in some areas) and "revenue enhancers" (what most of us call taxes) has resulted in the mortgaging of the future. You and your children and grandchildren will bear the burden for current failures of the president and Congress to balance the books. The burden will be higher taxes, fewer benefits, and very possibly a lower standard of living within the next twenty-five years.

There are numerous other examples that can be cited to illustrate the inability of the president (whoever he has been) and Congress (no matter which political party has been in the majority in either or both houses) to come to terms in regard to important domestic policies. For instance, whatever happened to the long-range energy policy that almost everyone said was needed to avoid a repeat of the 1973 and 1979 oil crises (those were the days when you could purchase gasoline only every other day, and even then you may have waited in line for an hour or more)? The most obvious results of that policy are the more than half-empty oil reserves in old salt caverns (they were never filled) and the now-idle ethanol plants in Louisiana.

Even better examples are the struggles between the president and Congress over foreign policy and the problems that ensue. One recent, well-publicized instance: U.S. policy toward Nicaragua. In regard to the Sandinista government in Nicaragua and the Contra rebels, Republican President Ronald Reagan favored aiding (overtly or covertly) the Contras in their armed struggle against the Sandinistas, while a primarily Democrat majority in Congress publicly and officially opposed such military aid.

Whether you agreed with President Reagan or with the congressional majority, the end result of this conflict over policy was the same: lack of a coordinated, unified, consistent foreign policy. If you were a member of the Sandinistas or the Contras, which position would you have believed to be the basis of U.S. foreign policy? In reality, the United States had two diverging policies toward Nicaragua. Not an effective way to conduct foreign policy, the president trying to go in one direction and Congress trying to go in another. The headline of an article by two U.S. senators, one a Republican and one a Democrat, both experts on foreign policy, tells it all: "Why This Country Can't Lead: Torn between a freebooting executive and 535 secretaries of state."[5]

Other examples could be given of similar negative effects on domestic and foreign policy stemming directly or indirectly from conflict between the legislative and executive branches, but there is little purpose in further belaboring the obvious. The real issue is whether or not the current system provides a policy-making process that results in effective policies. Experts on Congress, experts on

the presidency, and leading political figures agree that it does not.

THE LEGISLATIVE AND EXECUTIVE BRANCHES IN CONFLICT

Even if there is consensus that conflict between the president and Congress ends in stalemate and ineffective policies, who or what is to blame? Some scholars, such as Arthur Schlesinger in *The Imperial Presidency*, tend to say a too-strong presidency: the president and the executive bureaucracy have too much power and cannot effectively be controlled; thus, the president often implements policies that go against the will of the majority in Congress and the populace. Some, harking back to the concerns of Woodrow Wilson in *Congressional Government*, blame Congress: Congress has too much power; it cannot speak with a unified voice; it is dominated by special interests rather than the national or majority's interest; and it tries, unsuccessfully, to micromanage both foreign and domestic policy, thereby usurping executive authority. Similarly, others contend that the president has too little power, especially over foreign policy, as a result of congressional intrusion. Often cited to illustrate both views are the various Boland amendments passed by Congress in an effort to restrict presidential discretion in connection with the Contras in Nicaragua.

Still other commentators fault the political parties, arguing that the lack of disciplined parties brings about a lack of unity within Congress and/or between a political party in Congress and the president—even if of the same party—which in turn leads to differences between the two. And yet another group believes that there are too many or ill-timed elections for the House, Senate, and the presidency. Their frequency and timing, especially in nonpresidential election years, hinders obtaining or retaining a common majority in all three, thereby creating splits and positions resistant to reconciliation. And, when all else fails to be convincing, the blame is placed on the people in office: they do not have leadership skills, management skills (Reagan), and political knowledge of how Washington works (Jimmy Carter); they are too little concerned with details (Reagan) or they are too engineering-minded and too involved in details (Carter); they are too uncompromising and heavy-handed (former Speaker of the House James Wright in 1988); they are unethical (Richard Nixon and Watergate); or they are more concerned about reelection than making important policy decisions (everybody).

Just as there is much disagreement over who or what is responsible for the situation, so there is a corresponding variety of suggestions about how to fix the system. For those who argue that the presidency is too strong and/or out of control (or that Congress is too weak), the general remedy usually offered is to reduce the powers of the presidency and the executive branch, thereby bringing both under more control—usually by Congress. There are numerous examples of attempts to do so. In terms of domestic policy, for instance, Congress has established the Congressional Budget Office to offset the executive's Office of Management and Budget in an effort to have a greater role in preparation of the budget. During the Nixon presidency, Congress passed legislation to compel the president to spend funds appropriated by Congress (when Nixon tried to impound funds and prohibit their expenditure). In regard to foreign policy, recent similar examples are the Boland amendments restricting the type of assistance Reagan could give the Contras, and the War Powers Act limiting the president's ability to commit armed forces abroad when and where hostilities are imminent.

In contrast, for those who declare that the problem is a result of Congress's being too strong and/or too involved in executive matters (or that the presidency is too weak), the common recommendation is to reassert the power of the presidency and reduce congressional interference. This position is illustrated by the argument that the War Powers Act and the Boland amendments are unconstitutional restraints on the president's authority over foreign policy and that Congress should cease its attempts at micromanaging policy. And perhaps one of the more often repeated recommendations to increase presidential control is to provide the president with an item veto. Another notion is that the key to improving the system is to reform the political parties, especially within Congress, and to reform the body itself to offset the lack of unity within it and between it and the presidency. Those who take this stance typically call for increased party discipline and perhaps a revival of some sort of seniority system within Congress to bring about more effective leadership and internal workings. Congress could then better deal with the president, and in turn it would be a more cohesive body with which the president could cooperate.

There also are those who declare that the key to improving relations between Congress and the president and in that way improving policy-making is to reform the election system. Their recommendations include changing the term of the presidency to six years or changing the terms of the House of Representatives and/or the Senate, scheduling all these terms to coincide, and other similar ideas. All have in common the goal of reducing the time devoted to campaigning, and hence decreasing partisan wrangling over policy for election purposes, and of increasing the probability that the same majority (or party) would hold both the presidency and Congress.

And, finally, persons who lay both the splits between Congress and the presidency and the absence of effective policy-making at the door of poor leadership tend to focus on ways of improving the selection of those who rise to positions of leadership. In regard to the presidency, the most usual suggestion is to reform the primary and convention systems in ways that would decrease the impact of special interests, finances, and popularity contests and increase the probability that proven, experienced leaders would rise to the top. In regard to Congress, proposed reforms entail various ways of providing its leaders with more influence or control over the rest of Congress rather than ways to select people with better leadership qualities. In both instances, the dual theme is not only achieving better leadership but also promoting better relations between the branches, and, in consequence, more effective, timely policy decisions by overcoming the built-in conflicts between the two branches.

Try as Professor Saffell might to cast a positive light on the status quo by such things as disguising special-interest and PAC influence as constituency-interest representation, by praising undisciplined parties as being more representative, and by alluding to the balancing effects of off-year elections, the weight of the evidence is that the disadvantages of the separation-of-powers system outweigh the alleged advantages. The system, therefore, ought to be changed in one or more ways as outlined above.

What have been the purposes of the foregoing summary of views and recommendations concerning governmental policy-making, Congress, and the presidency, and the relationships among them? One, to show that there exists a consensus that policy-making is much too often ineffective; Saffell's stance that all is well ignores reality and diverts attention from the real problem. Two, to show that there is general agreement that conflict between the Congress and the presidency is at the root of the problem. Saffell's contention that Americans are happy with the system and don't wish to change it is contradicted by all the evidence to the contrary. Americans may be attached to the concept of the separation of powers, but they consistently condemn its results. Three, and perhaps most significant, to show that there is a *common thread* running through most of the seemingly contradictory recommendations for how best to remedy what is wrong. That common thread is the necessity to bring about more cooperation and unity of purpose between the president and Congress, whether that is accomplished by the foregoing suggestions or by creating a legislative–executive council, scheduling congressional elections in presidential election years, requiring consultation between congressional leaders and the White House before policy proposals are made, or permitting members of Congress to serve on the president's cabinet.[6] What a multitude of proposals have all said is that some kind of effort to overcome the conflict inherent in the separation of powers between the presidency and Congress must be made. In essence, they seek to one degree or another to make the relationship between the two branches more parliamentary in operation while retaining the formal notion of a separation of powers.

Why treat the symptoms rather than the disease itself? It is the constitutional separation of powers between Congress and the presidency that stalemates governance and gives us ineffective and watered-down policies. Rather than suggesting, as do most critics, that the separation be made less distinct and less antagonistic by grafting onto the system aspects of a parliamentary relationship, why not eliminate the root problem? *The United States should replace the existing separation-of-powers arrangement between Congress and the presidency with a parliamentary system that fuses rather than separates the legislative and executive offices.* The key principle of a parliamentary system is that the chief executive is a prime minister elected by the majority in the legislature and who can be removed from office by the legislature (vote of no confidence). This rather than having a president elected directly and separately by voters and who has powers independent or separate from those of the legislature (the separation of powers).

In adopting a parliamentary system, we should not copy all aspects of one country's model, as Saffell implies with his negative emphasis on particular aspects of the British version. For example, whether one or both houses of the legislature participate in the selection of the prime minister is a matter of choice, though most commonly the lower house has this power. In Italy, both houses share this power. Likewise, whether the prime minister and cabinet must be members of the legislature also is a matter of choice. In Britain they must; in France, if cabinet ministers are selected from the legislature, they must resign their seats (the incompatibility rule); and in West Germany they need not be (for example, Chancellor Willy Brandt's background was as mayor of West Berlin; Chancellor Helmut Kohl came out of

state government). Thus, Saffell's argument that a parliamentary system would prevent the rise to national leadership of another Franklin Roosevelt or Reagan is incorrect. We should adopt desirable parliamentary variations and avoid particular characteristics that appear to be undesirable.

BENEFITS OF A PARLIAMENTARY SYSTEM

What is to be gained from adopting a parliamentary system of government in the United States? By fusing rather than separating the legislative and executive powers, cooperation would be encouraged, not discouraged. Coordinated policies would be facilitated, not hindered. Both the legislature and the executive would have more to gain by cooperating with rather than opposing each other because the two would be interdependent and would share responsibility for policies and, most important, for retaining office. Under the current separation of powers, each often has more to gain from opposition than cooperation. Each can point the finger at the other for the failure in policy implementation. For example, Reagan blamed Congress for the deficits because it would not reduce domestic spending, and Congress blamed him for the deficits because he would not reduce defense spending or raise taxes. The result? The deficits continued and the national debt grew. Neither branch alone was clearly responsible, but they had not been able to agree on a policy response.

Infighting and lack of appropriate policy-making are not unique to the 1980s. They are ongoing, built into the system by the separation of powers. When, for example, President Harry Truman ran for reelection in 1948, his main campaign theme was that a vote for him was a vote against a "do-nothing Congress." Yet, unless the voters elect a president and a majority in both houses of Congress from the same political party, conflict automatically follows. Separate and off-year elections make this almost inevitable. The same political party controlled both the presidency and a majority in the House and the Senate in less than one-half of the years between 1948 and 1988. This divided control is illustrated by the 1988 elections, with Republican candidate George Bush winning while Democrats increased their control of both the House and the Senate. Saffell's argument that this is what the American voters desire is contradicted by evidence that most voters make their choices for president and Congress independently, with incumbency, not party or presidential preference, being the dominant factor influencing their vote for senators and, especially, members of the House.

In contrast, a parliamentary model by its very nature tends to assure that the majority that controls the legislature controls the executive because the legislature technically elects the prime minister. (The reality is that when elections are held, voters are marking their ballots not just for a candidate for the legislature but also for the candidate's party and for the party's identified nominee or candidate for prime minister.) Assuming a two-party dominant system as exists in the United States, the parliamentary model would tend to assure that the same party controlled both the legislature and the executive. This in itself would facilitate cooperation on policies rather than the conflict encouraged by the separation-of-powers model. A parliamentary system, further, would integrate the legislative and executive offices by making them dependent on each other. The chief executive or prime minister would be dependent on majority support in the legislature for retaining office, but with the executive's power of dissolution, the legislature in turn would be dependent on the executive for retaining office. To use the jargon of political science, each would be accountable to the other. The parliamentary relationship would therefore encourage cooperation between the two rather than conflict as is the case with the existing separation-of-powers model.

In addition to overcoming what many consider to be a major drawback of the American system of government, the inherent structural conflict, a parliamentary model would have secondary benefits. It would encourage party discipline on votes within the legislature because party members would realize that their political careers are closely tied to that of their party, the party's leader or prime minister, and to their policy positions and performance. After all, if one is in the majority that has selected the prime minister, one is clearly identified as being responsible for the policies of the government. If the policies succeed, credit follows; if not, blame. Responsibility is clearly allocated, and thus the legislators and the parliamentary executive are more likely to be responsive to the interests of the majority of voters. In contrast to our system, there is little room for blaming someone else.

Conversely, under a parliamentary system, the minority's or opposition's best chance of becoming the majority and controlling both the legislature and the executive is to propose policies that are clear alternatives to those of the party in power. The parliamentary system has the added benefit in this way of encouraging clearer policy positions by those competing for power. Accordingly, it affords the electorate a clearer choice of whom and what to vote for. Ballots are cast not only for a legislator but simultaneously for a party, a prime minister, and policies. The parliamentary system facilitates the ability of the majority to rule. In summary, if you want a government that is *more likely* to avoid standoffs, is more likely to pass and implement coordinated policies, that is, one in which responsibility is clearly identifiable, and that is more likely to represent the wishes of the majority of the people rather than those of special interests, then replace our separation-of-powers system with a parliamentary system that fuses the legislative and executive offices.

WHAT A U.S. PARLIAMENTARY SYSTEM WOULD DO

Can we guarantee that a parliamentary system would solve the many problems within U.S. government and solve the many problems confronting our society? Of course not. No system of government can guarantee that. Furthermore, I do not wish to suggest that. Rather, I am suggesting that a parliamentary system would eliminate not all conflict but much of the conflict that derives from our separation-of-powers system. And as I pointed out previously, almost all serious students of government agree that such conflict is the single most important aspect of government that hinders effective policymaking.

But, would replacing the separation-of-powers system remove all checks and balances and thereby open the door to tyranny? The prevention of tyranny was one of the major reasons for establishing separation of powers in the first place— as argued in the *Federalist Papers*. It is such an eventuality that Saffell suggests with his listing of the independent power of the British prime minister to make foreign policy, declare war, and withhold information from Parliament and the public under the Official Secrets Act. The quick and easy answer is no, replacement would not have that effect. First, a parliamentary system does *not* eliminate separation of powers *in toto*. The United States would still have a written constitution, a bill of rights, and a separate supreme court, which, through judicial review, would still be able to act as a check upon the parliamentary legislative–executive majority. There is no need, contrary to what Saffell argues, to adopt the British practice of parliamentary sovereignty with its relative lack of constitutional and judicial restraints. Rather, we should adopt variations upon the West German, French, and Canadian systems, which constitutionally spell out constraints, much as we do now.

Second, even within a parliamentary legislative–executive relationship, there would still exist checks and balances within the legislature and between the legislature and the prime minister or executive. Contrary to Saffell's contention that one house of the legislature must be dominant, as is the case with the British House of Commons, we could follow the Italian model, wherein both houses are equal in power, thus retaining that internal check. Furthermore, the minority or opposition in the legislature is able to challenge the majority, and both the minority and the majority in the legislature can, if necessary, challenge and even topple the executive government by a vote of no confidence. Conversely, the executive is able to check or restrain the legislature, if necessary, by dissolving it and calling new elections. Even though Saffell cites the United Kingdom as an example of the failure to bring governments down by a vote of no confidence, note that in a different context he cites France and Italy, where no-confidence votes have succeeded in toppling prime ministers. And, as the 1989 resignation of Prime Minister Takeshita in Japan shows, the extreme of a vote of no confidence is not always necessary.

The above characteristics of a parliamentary system would serve just as effectively as the current separation-of-powers system to prevent tyranny. Great Britain, Canada, Australia, the Scandinavian countries, and the Federal Republic of Germany, to mention a few, are not tyrannies, and all have parliamentary systems. Also, countries such as Argentina, Brazil, Chile, and the Philippines all have presidential systems modeled on the U.S. separation-of-powers system, and over the past ten to fifteen years each has experienced a dictatorship—military or civilian. In fact, the most useful preventive against tyranny has little to do with whether the government is presidential or parliamentary; rather, it appears to be the people's cultural, legal, and constitutional ethic.

If a presidential separation-of-powers system in itself is protection against tyranny, moreover, why did the United States help create parliamentary systems for Japan and the Federal Republic of Germany? When General Douglas MacArthur headed the U.S. occupation of Japan after World War II, the Americans designed what was known as the "MacArthur constitution," and it is still Japan's constitution. One of its primary goals was to prevent a rebirth of the tyranny that had existed during World War II. The same is true for the Basic Law (constitution) of the Federal Republic of Germany. The United States, along with Great Britain and France, had a major influence on its design after World War II; one of the primary goals was to prevent the rise of another Hitler. Yet there, again, the United States helped create a parliamentary system.

Still, as Saffell argues, are not parliamentary systems much more unstable than the U.S. presidential system? He cites Italy and the French Fourth Republic as evidence. The examples are good ones; by most criteria, these systems were unstable. But one should not commit the logical fallacy of inferring a universal absolute from a few cases. For example, Australia, Canada, the Federal Republic of Germany, Norway, Sweden, and the United Kingdom also have parliamentary systems; yet all are well known for their political and governmental stability.[7] Contrariwise, Argentina and Brazil have not been known for political stability, let alone democracy, during much of the previous four decades, and both have presidential separation-of-powers systems. Hence, logically and empirically, stability is related to factors other than whether the government is parliamentary or presidential in nature.

And yet, as Saffell asks, don't parliamentary systems encourage multiparty systems, which at least make instability more likely? The answer is not necessarily. Multiparty systems are more a result of a proportional representation (multimember district) election arrangement instead of a single-member district, winner-take-all election arrangement, such as exists in the United States and Great Britain.[8] And both the United States and Britain have two-party dominant systems (though each also has other minor political parties). But even multiparty systems and coalition governments do not necessarily result in governmental instability, as Saffell says. He ignores Australia, Canada, Japan, Sweden, and West Germany, which also have multiparty systems—and very often, in the cases of Sweden and West Germany, coalition governments—yet all are known widely for their governmental stability.

In a similar vein, Saffell criticizes the existence of third parties for making possible a government selected by a minority of the popular vote. Yes, that sometimes occurs, just as in the United States a president sometimes is elected with a minority of the popular vote: Nixon received 43.4 percent of the popular vote in 1968; John Kennedy, 49.7 percent in 1960; Truman, 49.5 percent in 1948; and Woodrow Wilson, 41.8 percent in 1912. And let us not forget Samuel Tilden and Grover Cleveland, each of whom won the popular vote but lost the presidential election.

What about Saffell's reasoning that a separation-of-powers system with undisciplined parties is more representative of constituent and local interests than is a parliamentary system? This is probably true—in the sense that parties and the government are more susceptible to minority and particular or special interests than to the majority or general or national interest. What Saffell is, in effect, arguing for without saying so is a system that represents the lowest common denominator and a system that promotes the old-fashioned pork barrel. The delegate theory of representation, a part of the U.S. mythology, promotes just that. What is needed is an educational effort to change that attitude and convince people (1) that a trustee theory of representation and government is better suited to meeting the challenges of the twenty-first century, and (2) that a parliamentary system would facilitate the ability of the majority to control government and to develop better policies. It would, to use some contemporary jargon, enable government to be proactive, not just reactive.

Nevertheless, you might believe, as does Saffell, that we should not change the separation-of-powers system created by the Founding Fathers. It works fairly well and has endured for two hundred years. True, but one of the reasons it has endured is because it has been changed by amendments and by interpretation through judicial review. The changes were made to address problems and concerns not foreseen by the Founding Fathers, whether it be the right of blacks and women to vote, the number of terms a president may hold office, or how the Senate is selected.

Is it not time once again to make a change in regard to a major problem and concern? As has been shown, there is consensus that government today is not very effective in addressing issues and problems. There is general agreement that conflict between the presidency and Congress is the cause, and, as has been shown, the conflict is inherent in the constitutional separation of powers between the president and Congress. Removing the source of conflict by doing away with the system in place and setting up a parliamentary system would pave the way for more cooperation and make more effective government more likely. Separation of powers is an idea past its prime; it is a hindrance. To rephrase Saffell's conclusion, the system is broken and we should fix it.

NOTES

1. James Reston, "Howard Baker as Veep," *New York Times*, June 19, 1988, p. E27.
2. The September/October 1970 issue of *The Center Magazine* is devoted to the Tugwell constitution. See also Lloyd N. Cutler, "To Form a Government," *Foreign Affairs*, Fall 1980, pp. 126–43.

3. For example, see "Polity Forum: Should the Separation of Powers Be Changed?" *Polity*, Summer 1987, pp. 660–77.

4. Thomas E. Cronin, "A Conversation-Interview on the American Presidency with Louis W. Koenig," *Presidential Studies Quarterly*, Fall 1986, p. 768.

5. *Washington Post*, December 1, 1987, p. A21.

6. Edward S. Corwin and Louis W. Koenig, *The Presidency Today* (New York: New York University Press, 1956); the Committee on the Constitutional System, cited in Raymond A. Moore, "The Constitution, the Presidency, and 1988," *Presidential Studies Quarterly*, Winter 1988, p. 56; David L. Boren and John C. Danforth, "Why This Country Can't Lead," *Washington Post*, December 1, 1987, p. A21; Donald L. Robinson, "Adjustments Are Needed in the System of Checks and Balances," *Polity*, Summer 1987, pp. 663–64.

7. To enhance governmental stability, the West German principle of a "constructive vote of no confidence" should be adopted. This requires the legislature (Bundestag) to have a positive majority in support of a new prime minister (chancellor) before it may topple a government.

8. A common practice used in parliamentary systems to restrict the proliferation of minor parties that can result from proportional representation is requiring some minimum percentage of the votes nationwide (usually 5 percent) before a party is eligible to obtain seats in the legislature.

SUGGESTED READINGS

GREGORY S. MAHLER. "Parliament and Congress: Is the Grass Greener on the Other Side?" *Canadian Parliamentary Review*, Winter 1985–1986, pp. 19–21. Reprinted in *Comparative Politics 88/89* (Guilford, Conn.: Dushkin Publishing Group, 1988), pp. 98–100. A comparison and contrast of the perceived strengths and weaknesses of the Canadian parliamentary system and the U.S. separation-of-powers system.

THOMAS KONDA, DONALD L. ROBINSON, AND JEFFREY LEIGH SEDGWICK. "Polity Forum: Should the Separation of Powers Be Changed?" *Polity*, Summer 1987, pp. 660–77. Robinson argues for parliamentary-type reforms; Sedgwick argues for the benefits of conflict between president and Congress; and Konda takes a "position sort of in between and off to the side" of the other two.

HOWARD A. SCARROW. "Parliamentary and Presidential Government Compared." *Current History*, June 1974. A classic, brief article comparing the two types of governments.

Why the United States Should Not Change to a Parliamentary System of Government

David C. Saffell
Ohio Northern University

Some political scientists and other commentators on American government long have contended that the British parliamentary system would be preferable to the system of government established in the U.S. Constitution. This paper will argue that such sentiments are based on an idealized version of the British system. It will be contended not only that it is highly unrealistic to suppose that we could change to a parliamentary system but that such a change would be undesirable, even assuming that a structural change were possible.

The parliamentary model tends to appeal to those who want government to be *efficient* and *accountable*. Parliamentary government is efficient because power is centralized in the hands of a prime minister and a cabinet. The prime minister is selected by the majority party in parliament and the cabinet is selected by the prime minister. Unlike in the U.S. system, all top government executives come from the legislature, in which they hold seats, and the chief executive almost always has a majority of his or her party members in the legislature. The parliamentary system assures that leaders have had extensive experience in the national legislature. It is believed to be more efficient than the presidential model because experienced leaders know how to deal with the legislature and because policies supported by the cabinet are virtually assured of being approved by the parliament. This is so because the prime minister represents the parliament's majority party, whose members are likely to be in ideological agreement with the cabinet. Unlike the situation in the United States, in Britain, which has a parliamentary system, there cannot be divided party control of government. Parliament's defeat of a proposal of the prime minister could lead to dissolution of the government and new elections. Most members of the prime minister's party do not wish to face new elections, especially because there are no primary elections in Britain and dissident members (MPs) might not be renominated by their party.

Parliamentary government is accountable because what a party promises in a campaign can be delivered in legislation. Party discipline is strong and the prime minister's party virtually can guarantee voters that its platform will be enacted. This is in contrast to the U.S. presidential system, wherein party discipline is weak and party control of government may be divided between the House and Senate or between Congress and the president.

Although the advantages of the parliamentary model are substantial—it is not easy to argue against efficient and accountable government—there are elements of these advantages that would pose major problems for the United States. Of course, there also is an inevitable gap between theory and practice. In many ways the current British and Canadian parliamentary systems do not operate as the model suggests. In addition, there are other aspects of parliamentary systems that would present substantial disadvantages if implemented in the United States.

The concentration of power in the office of the prime minister may enhance

efficiency, but it comes with a heavy price. The price is that it produces an executive that overwhelmingly dominates the legislature. In Britain the prime minister appoints people to office without confirmation by Parliament; makes foreign policy, including declarations of war, without parliamentary authorization; determines the budget without parliamentary approval; and may withhold information sought by Parliament. Moreover, there is no supreme court to check executive abuse.

As recent U.S. experience has shown, even with separation of powers (or, more precisely, separate institutions sharing power) it is difficult for Congress to control executive abuse. Still, congressional investigations of Watergate, the Iranian arms-for-hostages deal, and the Reagan nomination of Supreme Court justices show us that legislative checks can effectively hold the president publicly accountable for his actions. Other recent legislation, including the War Powers Act, the Budget and Impoundment Control Act of 1974, and the Freedom of Information Act are further evidence of a relative balance of power between legislators and the chief executive.

Professor Blessing argues that "government in the United States today does not work effectively," and he quotes James Reston to the effect that there is "gridlock" between Congress and the president. This clearly overstates the degree of contemporary legislative–executive conflict. For example, in 1988 the Democratically controlled Congress succeeded for the first time since 1976 in approving all spending bills before the new fiscal year began on October 1. As a case in point for gridlock Blessing suggests that we have had two conflicting policies toward Nicaragua: a presidential policy favoring aid to the Contras and a congressional policy opposing aid. In fact, the congressional policy has been the official policy, and this accurately reflects the unwillingness of the public to support greater U.S. military involvement in Central America. Under a more "efficient" parliamentary system we would run a greater risk of presidential domination without effective legislative checks.

Although U.S. political parties may not be as accountable as their British counterparts, this does not mean that they do not deliver on their platform promises. They have a much better record of performance than is generally believed; for example, the Republican party in 1980 promised to cut taxes, increase defense spending, and oppose the Equal Rights Amendment. Although our congressional parties lack the formal discipline of British parties, party identification continues to be the most important single predictor of how members of Congress will vote. For example, the *Congressional Quarterly* reports that in 1989 Democrats in Congress voted with their party on 81 percent of the party unity votes, and Republicans voted together on 73 percent of the party unity votes. (*Party unity* refers to those occasions when a majority of Democrats opposed a majority of Republicans.)

Although the parliamentary model assures that cabinet members (the political heads of major administrative departments) have had parliamentary experience, it also serves to keep other well-qualified persons out of government service. Those with tested administrative experience in large, complex private businesses would no longer be available to manage gigantic government bureaucracies. Instead, members of Congress who may never have managed anything larger than their office staffs would be placed in charge. Also excluded would be persons such as George Schultz and Elliot Richardson, who have managed several major government administrative departments but have never served in Congress. Members of parliament may have sharpened their debating skills during a lifetime of service, but they are not necessarily well prepared to be administrators. British cabinet secretaries overcome this problem by leaving day-to-day administrative management to a permanent corps of civil service personnel. The United States does not have such a corps and probably would not accept its existence.

Of course, the process by which the prime minister is selected also places outsiders at a great disadvantage. MPs who are not in the mainstream of their party will not be chosen, nor will persons not in Parliament be able to serve as prime minister. Throughout U.S. history, presidents have come to office with a variety of experiences outside Congress. Who could say that Dwight Eisenhower's leadership experiences in World War II did not prepare him well for the presidency? Several of the best presidents of this century, including Woodrow Wilson, Franklin D. Roosevelt, and Ronald Reagan, came to the presidency after serving as state governors.

Parliamentary accountability is based on strong, disciplined political parties. Even without advocating establishment of a parliamentary system in the United States, many critics of the inability of U.S political parties to govern have argued that we should move to party government or party responsibility.[1] These critics are dissatisfied with the issuelessness of the Democratic and Republican parties and their tendency to take similar positions on policy matters. To have strong, positive government, it is contended that we need a strong executive who is supported by cohesive political parties.

Responsible political parties (and

British parties are held up as the nearly ideal type) are characterized as presenting clear programs that outline what they will seek to accomplish if they gain control of government. In turn, these political parties will nominate candidates who are pledged to support the party's policy goals if they are elected. As a result, election campaigns focus on issues about which there are clear differences between the major political parties. Once the candidates have gained public office, voters can evaluate how well individual officeholders and their party have put into practice what they promised in the campaign. As a result, they can be held accountable in the next election for any shortcomings. Such a system of government is issue-oriented and its goals are to enact a definite set of public policies.

Despite the attractiveness of party responsibility, many U.S. political scientists have argued that it is unrealistic to suppose that it could be put into practice in the United States and, at any rate, it is not a desirable outcome.[2] As Sorauf and Beck note, responsible parties are highly unlikely to develop in the United States because most voters here are not sufficiently aware of political issues to allow them to evaluate the positions taken by parties. Americans are notoriously unconcerned about many issues or they take very inconsistent positions on a variety of public policies. That is, they are not consistently liberal or conservative on issues ranging from defense spending to abortion to economic protectionism. In turn, it is contended that the Democratic and Republican parties are too decentralized and too internally divided to be able to stake out clear policy positions.

The barriers to change that we have discussed deal basically with political attitudes and traditions. Even if these could be changed (and there is some evidence that the Republican party in the

Reagan era became more ideological), there are some basic structures of government that also would need to be changed if responsible parties were to exist. Most fundamentally, contrary to Blessing's contention that we could have a parliamentary system while retaining the formal notion of separation of powers, our system of separation of powers between the legislative and executive branches would have to be abolished. In addition, the two bodies of Congress (the House of Representatives and the Senate) would have to merge, or one would play a largely symbolic role, as does the House of Lords in Britain. As we have noted, the current system permits one party to control Congress (or one house of the Congress) and the other party to elect the president. At best, it is difficult to amend the Constitution, and we have never made a basic structural change in our national government.

There is substantial evidence that Americans like the idea of divided government. Since World War II one party has controlled the presidency and the other party has controlled at least one house of Congress about half the time. We like the checks and balances that separate congressional and presidential elections provide. Especially since the 1970s Americans have seen divided government as a desirable way to limit the growing power of the president. When asked in a Harris poll, a majority of Americans in 1984 said they would vote for Reagan but they preferred that the Republican party would not control both House and Senate. In 1988 Americans elected George Bush president with 54 percent of the vote, while Democrats gained seats in the House and Senate. It was the first time in twenty-eight years that the party winning the presidency lost seats in the House. Commenting on the results, Michael Dukakis suggested they showed that Americans want activist government as well as "continuity" in the White House.

Despite Blessing's assurance that one-party control of Congress and the presidency would facilitate cooperation rather than conflict, recent experience raises some doubts. For example, President Jimmy Carter (1977–1980) enjoyed Democratic majorities in the House and Senate, yet Congress defeated several of his major legislative initiatives. When Eisenhower was president (1953–1961) there often was greater legislative–executive cooperation when Congress was controlled by Democrats (1955–1960) than when Congress was under Republican control during his first two years in office (1953–1955). These examples show us that the cause of much legislative–executive conflict is a lack of unity among members of the president's own political party in Congress.

Voting patterns in the past twenty-five years present another major barrier to establishing responsible parties and ultimately creating a parliamentary system in the United States. Divided party control of government means that American voters increasingly have split their tickets and voted for Republican and Democratic candidates in the same election year. This contrasts with the situation before 1960, when most Americans voted a straight party ticket for all Democrats or Republicans in a given election. The independence of voters makes it unlikely that they would move to a system that does not allow them to split their tickets between parties.

It also is unrealistic to expect a switch to responsible parties because under the British system political party organizations select candidates; there are no primary elections. In fact, even the ordinary members of the party in government are excluded from the nomination process.

Since their inception near the beginning of this century, primary elections in the United States have become firmly established at all levels of government and they are a central part of the presidential selection process. We continue to have a profound distrust of party decisions made in "smoke-filled rooms." In a very real sense primaries allow political outsiders to compete for nominations and they open the selection process to all voters. For example, without primary elections in 1960 John F. Kennedy probably would not have been nominated for president.

The British system also strengthens the power of the party organization and weakens the link between constituents and their representatives by a system in which MPs often do not live in the district from which they are elected. Rather, the party decides the districts in which they will run for election and it is thereby able to place its top members in very safe electoral districts. Americans value the representational function of their legislators and expect them to provide a wide range of constituency services. It seems unthinkable that we would sever this connection.

We have touched on some of the undesirable effects of having a system of responsible parties. In a more fundamental way, it is argued that such a system would create a situation in which politics would become much more intense.[3] Each party would take increasingly dogmatic positions on public issues and the two parties might be unwilling to compromise their positions. In the U.S. system a premium has been placed on flexibility, compromise, and the ability to build coalitions across party lines in order to pass legislation. In a responsible-party system the legislature might cease to be a deliberative body because members would be committed to prearranged party positions. By focusing on political parties as the only means of political representation, interest groups would not have a major role to play and we would lose much of the richness and diversity of representation that has existed in the American system.

Responsible-party and parliamentary systems have a strong tendency to lead to a multiparty system. This is so because it is virtually impossible for only two parties to represent the specific interests of a complex society. Several parliamentary systems, such as those of Israel, Italy, and the Fourth Republic in France, have had a dozen or more parties running candidates in elections and a rapid succession of governments. Multipartyism also is encouraged by the way in which the prime minister is selected. If one party does not gain a majority of seats in the parliament, then a coalition government is formed by two or more parties. Relatively small parties can gain substantial political power by being part of the coalition. The great disadvantage of coalition governments is that they are highly unstable. If the prime minister cannot hold the members of the parliament together on major policy issues, then the government falls and new elections are held. In Britain a government may survive defeat on important issues in the House of Commons if the votes are not defined explicitly as votes of confidence. This happened repeatedly in the 1970s. In addition, party leaders may free members of Parliament to vote as they wish on some issues that are not crucial to the government. In some extreme circumstances, such as in Italy, governments may last only a few months. Of course, it is very difficult to run administrative departments or to accomplish policy goals in such a situation.

Although it is true, as Blessing notes, that parliamentary systems do not necessarily lead to multiparty systems, several extreme-case examples of multipartyism have been noted. Britain and the United States have had two-party dominant systems, but Britain has had more influential third parties than has the United States. The British Liberal party was one of the two major parties in the nineteenth century. After its eclipse by the Labour party following World War I, it has continued to be stronger than any U.S. third party in the same time period. The Social Democratic party (SDP), established in 1981, formed an alliance with the Liberal party. The alliance won 25.4 percent of the vote in the 1983 parliamentary elections and 22 percent of the vote in the 1987 elections. In 1988 the SDP dismembered itself and most members voted to merge with the larger Liberal party to form a new party, the Social and Liberal Democrats (SLD). This type of political activity is encouraged by a parliamentary system, and the SLD could become a strong third force in the middle of the political spectrum that would create instability in British government.

The mischief caused by a relatively strong third party also can be seen in the 1988 parliamentary elections in Canada. The popular vote broke down to about 43 percent for the Conservatives, 32 percent for the Liberals, 20 percent for the New Democrats, and 5 percent for other minority parties. In Canada's three-party dominant system, a minority of votes gave Prime Minister Brian Mulroney's Conservative party a majority of seats in Parliament because the Liberals and New Democrats split the opposition vote. In some instances the Conservatives won seats with less than 40 percent of the vote. In another parliamentary election held at about the same time in Pakistan, Benazir Bhutto claimed a victory even though her Pakistan People's party won only 92 seats in a 237-seat national legislature.

Other aspects of the British model that run counter to U.S. experience include the fact that there is not a fixed term for the prime minister. In Britain elections must be held at least every five years, but the prime minister is free to determine when there will be an election. Thus, an election may come in three or four years, when the government feels it is in the strongest position to retain power. As we have noted, elections may also occur when the government loses a vote of confidence and Parliament is dissolved. A fixed term of four years gives the United States president independence from Congress that allows him to make unpopular decisions without fear of having his government fall. Such bold (and unpopular) actions as Harry Truman's firing of General Douglas MacArthur in 1950 could be accomplished to best serve the interests of the country.

Several features of the British parliamentary system that have a strong appeal to American reformers seem to be based on misconceptions about how the British government has functioned throughout most of this century. We have discussed the ability of legislators to check the power of the prime minister by threatening to defeat a government proposal, thus causing dissolution of Parliament and new elections. Although threat of a vote of no confidence may have brought about some changes in British government personnel in 1940 and 1956, no government in this century has lost a vote of no confidence as a result of dissent by its own supporters.[4] In 1924 a minority Labour party government fell when it lost support from the Liberal party in a coalition government, and in 1979 the loss of Nationalist support deprived the Labour party of a majority on a vote of confidence. The fact is that MPs do not want to risk their seats in a new election.

At the time of Watergate there was speculation that such an incident in Britain would have brought about a vote of no confidence and the fall of the government. It is possible that had Richard Nixon been prime minister, he would have been forced out of office more quickly. After all, the impeachment process is very slow and, of course, no U.S. president has been impeached and removed from office. Even had that happened, there would not have been a legislative investigation and little might have been learned about the actions of Nixon administration officials. On the other hand, many believe that in Britain the government would not have been forced to turn over information and the press would have been blocked from having access to sensitive materials. In that case Prime Minister Nixon might have continued in office. Here the threat of impeachment forced the president to resign.

The U.S. president may be more effectively checked by midterm elections in which all seats in the House and one-third of the seats in the Senate are up for election. The president's party has lost seats in Congress in all but one off-year election (1934) in this century. For example, Democrats lost forty-eight seats in the House in 1966 as voters sent a message to Lyndon Johnson in the White House, and on the heels of Watergate, Republicans lost forty-eight seats in 1974. In parliamentary systems this midterm check does not exist. The only opportunity British voters have to express themselves is in by-elections after a member of Parliament dies or resigns.

Another feature of parliamentary government that often is cited by U.S. reformers is the theory of collective responsibility for government decisions. In an ideal system the prime minister is careful to consult with the cabinet before decisions are made, and once agreement has been reached, all members are bound publicly to support the policy. In practice, at least since World War II, decisions in Britain have been made by the prime minister and a small inner circle of advisers. Cabinet government has not served as an effective check on the power of the prime minister.

Finally, one of the most romanticized aspects of parliamentary government is the Question Hour, in which Cabinet members appear regularly for a grilling by members of Parliament. Although the current British prime minister, Margaret Thatcher, generally is present during the Question Hour, she prefers that her ministers answer the questions. U.S. cabinet secretaries often appear before congressional committees to answer questions, but the process is not nearly as dramatic as in parliamentary systems. In fact, ministers are adept at evading questions and seldom reveal any substantive information. Of the process in Canada, former MP James Gillies commented, "Anyone who has participated in question period knows its main purposes are to embarrass the government, to amuse the tourists and TV audiences, and to make life easier for reporters. It is a totally ineffective way to elicit significant information."[5]

In arguing against imposition of a parliamentary system in the United States, historian Arthur M. Schlesinger notes that for many British reformers the model government is that of separation of powers in the United States.[6] They want to give Parliament more power and they want to give members more independence in their voting. British reformers would like to establish an agency similar to the General Accounting Office that would monitor government spending, and they would like to have better

control over intelligence agencies. Indeed, several recent developments in Britain represent a move in the U.S. direction. Schlesinger notes the spread of "cross-voting" (voting against issues supported by the member's party), the establishment in 1979 of watchdog committees to oversee major administrative departments, and the demand by Parliament to initiate legislation. Few Americans want to grant such extensive power to the executive, nor do they want to turn back the clock on a series of reforms in the 1970s (the War Powers Act, the Budget and Impoundment Control Act) that enhanced the power of Congress.

The British parliamentary model places strong emphasis on centralization of control. In the United States, government is characterized by decentralization and fragmentation. We are most comfortable with multiple centers of power that tend to prevent any one group from gaining power at all levels and permit greater access by citizens to decision makers.

Why have the British people been willing to accept strong direction from London? In his classic study of the British constitution Walter Bagehot focused on the nature of British political culture to explain their deference to authority.[7] In a society with a definite class structure there is a willingness to accept the idea that those in the upper social classes should rule. Because the United States has stressed the concept of an egalitarian society, we have been much less willing to accept this kind of control. A geographically large country with diverse regional interests, we are more suited to a bargaining model of policy-making than to the kind of comprehensive policy that is needed in the responsible-party model.[8] Contrary to the beliefs of Blessing, there is little reason to believe that U.S. political culture has changed to the point where we would want to establish a vastly different system of government that puts a premium on centralization of authority and strongly ideological political parties. Besides, we tend to follow the maxim, "If it ain't broke don't fix it."

Blessing states that we could incorporate only those "particular variations" of parliamentary systems that have proven to be effective in other countries. This suggests (erroneously, I believe) that we could take a piece here and there and create an effective (and unique) hybrid system. It also erroneously leads us to believe that what works in other cultures will work here.

Of course we have political problems, but to suggest, as Blessing does, that poverty, the trade imbalance, and even AIDS would be dealt with better if we scrapped our separation-of-powers system is naive. Most of the social and economic problems he mentions are just as severe in Britain as in the United States. We need more effective political leaders, not a new political system.

NOTES

1. See Committee on Political Parties of the American Political Science Association, *Toward a More Responsible Two-Party System* (New York: Rinehart, 1950), and Austin Ranney, *The Doctrine of Responsible Party Government* (Urbana: University of Illinois Press, 1962).
2. Frank J. Sorauf and Paul Allen Beck, *Party Politics in America*, 6th ed. (Glenview, Ill.: Scott, Foresman, 1988), pp. 453–54.
3. Ibid., p. 453.

4. Philip Norton, *The British Polity* (New York: Longman, 1984), p. 71.
5. Quoted in Arthur M. Schlesinger, Jr., *The Cycles of American History* (Boston: Houghton Mifflin, 1986), p. 307.
6. Ibid., pp. 307–9.
7. See Walter Bagehot, *The English Constitution and Other Political Essays* (New York: Appleton, 1877).
8. Richard L. Kolbe, *American Political Parties: An Uncertain Future* (New York: Harper & Row, 1985), p. 43.

SUGGESTED READINGS

CROSSMAN, R. H. S. *The Myths of Cabinet Government.* Cambridge: Harvard University Press, 1972. Argues that such practices as the question period and collective decision making no longer operate in their traditional manner in the British parliamentary system.

KOENIG, LOUIS W., *The Chief Executive*, 5th ed. New York: Harcourt Brace Jovanovich, 1986. Pp. 398–405. Outlines the functioning of the British parliamentary system, compares it with our presidential system, and concludes that a parliamentary system carries major weaknesses.

SCHLESINGER, ARTHUR M., JR. "Parliamentary Government." *New Republic*, August 31, 1974. Opposes the executive domination of the legislature in a parliamentary system. Concludes that as a means of containing an imperial executive the full parliamentary solution is "absurd."

III

PUBLIC OPINION

Does Public Opinion Effectively Check the Behavior of American Policymakers?

In the most simplistic possible meaning of *democratic governance*, the people who make the laws (for example, members of Congress) and those in executive positions (the president) simply try to make sure they know what the people want and do it. No one over the age of twelve believes that this is the case in the United States, and very few would argue that it should be. Many policy decisions are made in congressional committees, in bureaucracies, and throughout all levels of government with the people not even being aware of what is happening, let alone having opinions on the matters. The real question is whether, within broad limits, decisions of policymakers are responsive to an amorphous idea called "public opinion."

Political scientists and other scholars have written volumes trying to define *public opinion,* an effort we will not attempt to duplicate here. Suffice it to say that public opinion is not a simple concept. On many questions of policy, the vast majority of people have no opinion; on other questions, opinions change easily and in response to single clues from the media and opinion leaders. Some issues arouse the interest of particular segments of the public that display no interest in other issues, suggesting the concept of alternate and various publics. We chose to avoid such matters by asking if public opinion is a check on policymakers. But, in essence, any question concerning public opinion necessarily becomes a question about the real nature of democratic governance.

Professor McAdams, in his essay "Public Opinion as a Constraint on Political Elites," answers our question in the affirmative. His argument is that in broad outline the electoral choices presented to Americans reflect the realities of U.S. political life; parties outside the mainstream do not do well because there is no support for their positions. Members of Congress in the main reflect the ideological convictions of their districts, and perhaps most important, believe they must stay in contact with the sentiments of their constituencies to be reelected. If both parties are of the center, well, that is where the votes are. He offers a more sophisticated understanding of democracy than the simplistic one we started with: Competing elites must find majority support among the electorate to win power.

Professor Margolis, in "Government by Elites in the Name of All," argues that our electoral rules—written by the major parties—effectively preclude representatives of electoral choice outside the elite consensus. Further, the major decisions regarding matters of economic choice are not made in the public arena at all but in the private sector. Neither Democrats nor Republicans advocate public ownership of the major means of production and distribution, and those who might offer such an alternative have no way of being heard or chosen.

Neither author argues the simplistic middle-school-civics version of democracy. For both, reality is far more complex than that. They accept that there are some areas of public life in which public opinion exercises control, and agree that elites are important in our political life. The question for you, the student, is what is the role of the elites? Is it, as Margolis suggests, the essence of our political process? Or do elites give a new life to democratic governance, even if a more sophisticated understanding of that concept is necessary?

Public Opinion as a Constraint on Political Elites

John McAdams

Marquette University

To say that elites make policy may strike the reader as a terrible thing to say about a government that is supposed to be a democracy. After all, isn't the point of democracy that the people rule? To a political scientist, however, the notion that it is elites who make policy is almost a tautology. We, after all, have a very large government with a multitude of policies. The people don't have the slightest chance to exercise any kind of effective oversight over the vast majority of these policies because they don't *know* about the vast majority.

The size of the modern nation-state and the rise of big government (consist-ing of enormous military and social welfare bureaucracies) make the problem worse. It is not practical for the mass of citizens to come together and vote on policy. Given the number and complexity of government policies, most decisions will be made by bureaucrats. Where decisions are made by elected officials, most of their actions will be out of the public eye. How many Americans, for example, keep close watch on the House Judiciary Committee's Subcommittee on Courts, Intellectual Property and the Administration of Justice?

Given that elites make policy, is it ever reasonable to say that any political

71

system is ever democratic? The answer is yes, *provided* (1) there are multiple competing elites within the political system, and (2) the public plays a key role in deciding *which* elite (or coalition of elites) gets to govern.

Where elites are excessively unified, it becomes unlikely that the public will be given any real policy alternatives. It is, after all, elites that generate policy proposals, even in the most democratic of societies. If there were no elites with a desire to move policy to the left or to the right, it is unlikely that the public would ever be presented with policies differing from the status quo. Seldom would such policies be advocated in the media. Never would such policies appear on the ballot during state referenda, and never would candidates run for office advocating such policies. If elites are excessively unified, the public has little chance of hearing two sides on any issue. Rather, the approved elite opinion dominates public discussion.

Of course, it is hardly necessary or even desirable that elites disagree about *everything*. For example, respect for the democratic "rules of the game" is certainly something we want elites to be unified on. If the Democrats had no compunctions about putting Republicans in jail whenever they could, and the Republicans reciprocated whenever *they* happened to gain power, democracy could hardly operate. Likewise, it is no great loss to the U.S. political system that neither the Communist party nor the Nazi party is a major political force. Both are, in their core beliefs, so far removed from the vast majority of Americans that they don't represent viable vehicles for a protest vote.

The important thing is not that competing elites actually *espouse* conflicting views, but that they *want to*. Quite often, elites refrain from advocating a policy precisely because they know that the public rejects it and would wreak vengeance on a party or candidate that did advocate it. Many conservative Republicans would, in their heart of hearts, like to cut Social Security payments; it is very hard to find a Republican candidate advocating such a policy.

Of course, the failure of elites to take contrasting positions on such issues has its costs; public discourse might be better served if unpopular positions were to get wider hearing. Yet, such failure is most certainly democratic, involving the masses controlling elites rather than elites controlling the masses. Further, if public opinion were to shift—if the public decided that old people were prospering at the expense of needy younger people—elites would be quick to exploit the shift by appealing to the newly articulated consensus.

When we talk of competing elites, the activists and officeholders of the political parties come immediately to mind. Parties are the organizations that actually compete for political office. They also attempt to control the governmental apparatus (as opposed to interest groups, which merely want to influence policy in one or a few areas).

Some democracies have what amounts to a two-party system (although, generally, minor or third parties are perfectly legal); others have a multiparty system. It might seem, at first glance, that a multiparty system is better: it gives each voter a much larger range of choice. Thus, if one wants to vote Socialist, or Libertarian, or for Prohibition, there is a party espousing the position one favors. Most political scientists are quite unenthusiastic about multiparty systems. It is very likely, under such systems, that no single party will get a majority of the vote. The government must then be formed out of a coalition of parties, some of them very small. For example, in late 1988 and again in 1990, the government of Israel was paralyzed because no one was able to put together a stable majority coalition in parliament. In such political systems, the voter has the luxury of voting for a party close to his or her preferred position, but has little way of knowing what sort of government is going to emerge after the election. In two-party systems, by way of contrast, the necessary compromises and coalition formation are done before the election. The coalitions then run, in the American case, as the Democratic party and the Republican party.

One can, of course, imagine a system with competing elites where the people at large have little say in how they are ruled. There are plenty of historical cases of "banana republics" where one military faction staged an uprising and displaced another. Likewise, in communist states one faction in a ruling politburo may get enough power to purge the government: it happened to Khrushchev in the Soviet Union and to the "Gang of Four" in China.

COMPETING ELITES NEED POPULAR APPROVAL

The whole point of democracy, however, is that rival elites must appeal to the people for the mandate to rule. Elections are the process by which this appeal is institutionalized. We quite clearly *have* elections in this country. People who don't like the U.S. political system must justify their dislike by arguing either that (1) no "real alternatives" are offered to the people, or (2) the people are unable to exercise their choice in an intelligent, responsible way. We will take these propositions one at a time.

Scholars who have studied the attitudes of U.S. political elites have found *some* powerful and important political elites positioned to the left of public opinion, and *other* powerful and important elites positioned to the right. Figure 1 summarizes a large array of studies. On the political right we find those whose privileges are associated with private business. Top corporate executives are heavily Republican, as are owners of large amounts of property. Also on the right, allied with the elite of the business class, are Republican party activists (the sort of people who hold party offices and are delegates to the presidential nominating convention), and top military officers.[1] On the political left we find an array of elites that are collectively referred to as the "New Class."[2] *Their* privileges (and they are most certainly privileged) derive from politics and the expansion of government. These elites include labor union leaders, black leaders, feminist leaders, academics and intellectuals, and the people who staff

Labor unions
Blacks
Feminists
Academics and intellectuals
Media
Democratic political activists
Public interest activists

Private business
Republican party activists
Top military officers

Left

Right

FIGURE 1 The structure of elite attitudes

media organizations, including *both* the news media and entertainment media. Democratic political activists are heavily recruited from, and represent, the New Class. Likewise, public interest activists represent the same sort of views (while often being radically at odds with the actual public).

It is important to stress that figure 1 charts the opinions of political elites, *not* the opinions of various groups in the population. Elites' attitudes are more extreme and more polarized than the attitudes of the general public. Consider black leaders, for example. They are close to unanimous in favoring busing for purposes of racial balance. Not only do Americans as a whole oppose busing, the best polls of U.S. blacks show the black community split down the middle, with about as many blacks opposing busing as favoring it.[3] Likewise, union leaders are overwhelmingly liberal and Democratic, but union rank and file are only a few percentage points more Democratic in their voting than are other Americans. In 1988, for example, 41 percent of voters in union households (as opposed to 53 percent of all Americans) voted for George Bush.[4] One could continue at some length on this point. Feminists, for example, are quite far to the left, but the gender gap in voting data is quite small (6 or 8 percentage points, typically). More striking, polls consistently show women to be *a little more conservative than men* on "women's issues."[5] On the other side of the spectrum, business managers generally lean Republican, but not as monolithically Republican as the chief executive officers of top ("Fortune 500") corporations.

Some of the elites of the New Class are not merely to the left of public opinion but are fairly radical. Lichter and Rothman, for example, found that 34 percent of their sample of staff people for public interest lobbying groups held a favorable view of Fidel Castro. Only 5 percent of the same sample had a favorable view of Ronald Reagan! Kadushin found that about half of his sample of "top intellectuals" favored the nationalization of basic industries—that is to say, about half were socialists. The *Washington Post* found only slightly lower levels of socialist sentiment among black leaders and feminist leaders.[6]

The distribution of elite attitudes across the ideological spectrum is important in evaluating charges that the U.S. public has been manipulated into believing certain things. One has to ask, manipulated by *whom?* By the liberal New Class or by the conservative business class? Certainly, both elites try to manipulate attitudes.

The rhetoric of a conservative president certainly aims to persuade the public to support him. During the administration of Ronald Reagan (dubbed "The Great Communicator") liberals were quick to point to the president's high approval ratings as evidence that presidential rhetoric had bamboozled the people into giving their approval to a chief executive who was "obviously" (the liberals assumed) an outrageous failure. A less biased examination of public approval of the president yields a very different conclusion. During Reagan's first term, there was an overwhelming correlation between the state of the economy and his approval ratings. When the economy was deeply mired in a recession, presidential approval was likewise mired in the 40–45 percent range. As the economy recovered, so did the public's assessment of the administration.[7] During Reagan's second term, the Iran-Contra scandal knocked the bottom out of the president's ratings; however, the INF treaty and the continued stability of the economy eventually restored them. If Reagan had such an ability to bamboozle the public, why did the ability twice fail so mysteriously during the recession (1982) and during Iran-Contra (1986–1987)?

Conservatives have often pointed to the liberalism of media people, and have drawn the inference that it has biased public opinion to the left. This line of argument asserts two quite distinct propositions: (1) the liberal attitudes of media people shape their coverage of important political issues, and (2) biased media coverage of politics affects the attitudes of people exposed to it.

Quite often, conservatives' charges of a liberal bias in the *coverage* the media give to political events are well founded. This bias is evident in the media's use of labels. In the controversy over abortion, for example, the media have labeled supporters with their own favorite euphemism: "pro-choice," but have refused to label antiabortion forces "pro-life."[8] Media interpretation of news events consistently favors liberals and Democrats. For example, the ethical problems of House Speaker James Wright were portrayed in the context of a partisan "ethics war" on Capitol Hill. Much was made of the partisanship of Republicans who accused Wright of wrongdoing. However, ethics charges against Ed Meese were interpreted as an example of the "sleaze factor" in the Reagan administration. The media said almost nothing about the partisan motivations of people bringing accusations against Republican officials.[9]

Consider, in this context, the 1988 presidential election campaign. The media groused continually about how "negative" and "dirty" and "mean spirited" the campaign had become. These charges were made *after* Bush attacked Michael Dukakis with a now celebrated series of campaign commercials on issues such as the Pledge of Allegiance and the Massachusetts prison furlough program, and on his performance (or lack thereof)

in cleaning up Boston Harbor. The media had very little to say about negativism, however, when Bush was attacked in highly derogatory (and highly *personal*) terms at the Democratic Convention.[10] The media echoed Democratic charges that the Bush campaign was racist to raise the furlough issue, but found nothing objectionable about Dukakis's charging that Bush was on the side of the rich, not on the side of ordinary Americans. Media charges of negativism, in other words, showed a double standard.

Did the media's liberal bias manipulate public opinion? It would be foolish to deny that it had any effect, but it is certainly pertinent to observe that the media's favorite candidate lost. The same observation could be made about several recent presidential elections. In 1984, for example, network news coverage toward Reagan was heavily negative. Among stories that had a discernible "spin" one way or the other, anti-Reagan stories consumed about *ten times* as much airtime as pro-Reagan stories. Stories about Walter Mondale were much more favorable; the "spin ratio" was about 1.3 to 1 in his favor.[11] The key point here is that manipulation is difficult in a society with multiple, competing elites. Presidential rhetoric is ineffective when the media are free to bring the bad news about the economy or Iran/Contra to the people. Likewise, liberal media bias is far from fearsome when a conservative Republican president or a conservative Republican candidate is free to carry messages directly to the people.[12]

To say that the media have a liberal bias might suggest that the political Left would be happy with the media, even if the political Right were not. It is not quite so simple, for although the media are left of center, there are people to the left of the media. This should not be surprising. There have often been, at the other extreme of the ideological spectrum, people who felt that the Republican party is much too moderate. The John Birch Society, for example, attained notoriety when its leader proclaimed that President Dwight Eisenhower was "a dedicated, conscious agent of the Communist conspiracy."[13]

Some on the left point to the fact that virtually all the major media outlets in this country are owned by capitalist corporations, and infer that the media will have a capitalist bias. This sounds plausible, but it is in fact grossly simplistic. In the first place, the capitalists who own the media may be quite far to the left of capitalists generally. For example, it is clear that the people who own the *New York Times*, the *Washington Post*, the *Los Angeles Times*, and a number of other media outlets are liberal Democrats, not conservative Republicans.

Second, if the capitalists who own the media really act like capitalists, that is to say, if they are mainly concerned with profits, it is hard to see why they would object to having liberals run their new organizations, provided those liberals managed to keep circulation (in the print media) and viewership (in the electronic media) up. Given the liberalism of journalists, staffing a news organization with conservatives would be difficult to do (and doubtless expensive because one would have to offer high salaries to induce conservative journalists to leave their present positions).

So it is that even quite conservative news outlets are often staffed by liberals and occasional radicals, whose ideology shows in their reporting. One particularly interesting recent case involves a University of California, Berkeley, journalism professor who once worked for the *Wall Street Journal*. A self-professed radical, he asserts, "Karl Marx [is] my all-time favorite journalist." He went to the *Wall Street Journal* directly from writing free-lance pieces for radical left outlets, including the Communist *Daily World*! More important was the fact that he managed to get favorable articles on several radical economists and their economic ideas into the (supposedly capitalist) *Journal* itself.[14] Conservative publishers are very far from enforcing a "party line" throughout their organizations.

Readers who happen to be college students will have little trouble seeing how such a thing could happen. First ask, "What sort of people make up this university's Board of Trustees?" The answer, quite typically, will be "wealthy business people." The next question would be, "Does the content of my courses have a conservative Republican bias, or does it seem to have a liberal Democratic bias?" The answer, for the vast majority of students in the majority of colleges, is the latter. This demonstrates an important reality of large bureaucratic organizations: the people at the top—those supposedly running things—often have only the most dubious and marginal control over those—supposedly subordinates—at the bottom.

Radicals, however, insist that the majority of journalists have a pro-capitalist bias. After all, journalists are, in the majority, liberals not radicals, and they often report unfavorably on communist regimes. At this point the reader must ask himself or herself, "If the media often portray communist regimes rather unfavorably, is it because reporters are lackeys doing the bidding of their capitalist masters or is it because *the reality* of communist regimes is in fact pretty grim?"

The argument made by the radicals seems almost bizarre in light of the growing willingness of people in communist countries (including people among the ruling elites of communist countries) to admit that their system (including both its economic and its political components) is a failure.[15] Indeed, one of my colleagues once quipped that we are fast approaching the point where there are more Marxists in the universities of capitalist countries than in the governments of communist ones!

The truth is that media liberals have historically shown considerable sympathy toward communist movements and governments. Communists have usually had the benefit of the doubt from liberals in the media. Thus, if the media often make communist governments look bad, it is because reality has shocked media liberals into understanding the nasty truth. The *New York Times* provides the classic case. In the 1930s, *Times* correspondent Walter Duranty filed reports from Moscow that almost unfailingly followed the Moscow propaganda line. He ignored widespread famine in the Ukraine (a famine caused by Stalin's policies), and reported the Soviet version of the "purge trials." The trials involved many old Bolshevik revolutionaries who were eliminated by Stalin by being framed, tortured until they confessed a variety of "crimes against the revolution," and executed.[16] In the 1950s Herbert Mathews of the *Times* portrayed Fidel Castro in a highly favorable light, presenting him as someone who would bring liberal democracy to Cuba. As Castro began to impose a communist dictatorship, the *Times* was extremely slow to admit what was happening.[17] During the Cultural Revolution in China, in the early 1970s, *New York Times* columnist James Reston toured the country and gushed about how the Chinese were "engaged in one vast cooperative barn-raising."[18] In all these cases, the *Times* was merely typical of the liberal media generally.[19]

Of course, reality eventually breaks through. Consider the case of China. The first U.S. correspondent actually to live in the Peoples' Republic after normalization of relations in the late 1970s was *New York Times* correspondent Fox Butterfield. He wrote a candid memoir titled *China: Alive in the Bitter Sea.* Two of the best recent books on Russia have been written by *Times* reporters: Hedrick Smith (who served in Moscow during the early 1970s) and David Shipler (who had the same assignment in the late 1970s and early 1980s). As for Cuba: the *Times* editorial marking the thirtieth anniversary of Castro's revolution showed few illusions about the society communism has created on the island.[20] Is the *New York Times* anticommunist? Yes. Does the *Times* have a bias against communist regimes? No; it historically has treated them more favorably than they deserved.

THE VOTERS MAKE MEANINGFUL CHOICES

American citizens are confronted with a system of competing elites. The Democratic party represents the New Class, and espouses policy positions popular in academia, among media people, and among some types of political activists (feminist, public-interest, and civil-rights activists, for example). In some instances these positions are the same ones that poor people take: support for more social welfare programs, for example. In other instances, the Democratic position is radically at odds with the outlook of Americans, including especially poor Americans. Examples include Democratic support for busing, opposition to school prayer, and a lenient attitude toward criminals. The Republican party represents the business class. It espouses policy positions popular in business (particularly among executives). As is the case with the Democrats, sometimes the Republican party is fairly well in tune with the majority of Americans (including poor Americans) and sometimes it is quite out of touch.

So American citizens have a choice. How do they exercise that choice?

Certainly, if one starts with an excessively idealistic notion of how public opinion and elections operate, the actual functioning of any democratic government will be found wanting. What would such an idealistic notion look like? The following might be the key elements:

1. Most people have opinions on most important public issues; the opinions are reasonably well-considered and stable.
2. Most people know where political candidates stand on most issues.
3. Candidates offer a clear choice on most major issues.
4. Most people vote on the basis of issues.
5. Voters are forward looking, judging what government will do for them (or for the nation) in the future.
6. Public officials conscientiously try to make policy consistent with public opinion, either because they fear electoral retribution if they don't, or because they *believe* policy should reflect public opinion.

It is easy enough to demonstrate that most of these conditions don't hold. Consider public opinion: the answers people give public opinion pollsters are notoriously dependent on how a question is asked. For example, Seymour Martin Lipset reports that 63 percent of Americans have a "great deal of confidence" in the "Army, Navy, and Air Force"; only 48 percent have a great deal of confidence in "the military"; and a minority of 21 percent have a great deal of confidence in "military leaders."[21] On the issue of abortion, polls have shown support for the proposition that any woman should be

able to get an abortion if she wants it ranging from a low of 23 percent (in a Gallup poll) to a high of 67 percent (in a *New York Times* poll).[22] It is also well known among social scientists that people's expressed opinions are highly unstable over time. Interview someone, and then come back two months or two years later and ask him or her the same question. Very often there will be an entirely different answer. Typically, over half the respondents in such a panel survey (the same people are questioned several times) seem to be answering at random.[23]

The reason for opinion instability is quite simple: On most issues, most of the time, most Americans don't actually have an opinion.[24] In the interview situation, however, people don't like appearing ignorant. Political scientist George Bishop, for example, found that fully a third of the people in his survey offered an opinion on the "1975 Public Affairs Act." A third may not sound like many people until one realizes that there was no such thing as the "1975 Public Affairs Act"![25] For the most part, it is not that people consciously lie about having an opinion (although there is certainly some of that) but, rather, that people readily latch onto something in the question wording or context to allow them to give a sincere but superficial response.

The other elements of the idealistic theory of U.S. government fare almost equally badly. Quite often, most citizens don't know where candidates stand on specific issues. In 1976, for example, only 38.9 percent of Americans believed that Jimmy Carter was more liberal than Gerald Ford on whether "government should see to it that everyone has a job and a decent standard of living." The rest either saw Ford as more liberal, saw no difference, or had no opinion themselves. On whether "government should aid minority groups," public perceptions were even less clear; only 29.2 percent saw Carter as more liberal.[26]

The problem is even worse in races for the House of Representatives because the level of media exposure is much lower. Hurley and Hill found only a very slight correlation between house members' positions on any of several important national issues and the public's *perception* of where incumbents stood.[27] Even when people can say where a candidate stands on an issue, what they say is often the result of "projection." Projection occurs when people misperceive the position of a candidate they like in order to bring the perceived candidate position more into line with their own views. A strong Democrat who is opposed to busing, for example, is likely to misperceive a pro-busing Democrat as being moderate or even conservative on the busing issue.[28]

Quite frequently, differences between candidates are muted. We have discussed the fact that Democratic and Republican party activists stand far apart ideologically, and we have also discussed that fact that the desire to win elections may cause elites to mute ideological differences and appeal to the political center. Presidential elections, such as those in 1956, 1960, and 1976, fielded quite moderate candidates. Naturally, citizens did not clearly perceive differences between them, nor did they vote issues to a large degree. One of the most significant cases of muted differences occurred in 1968, during the height of the Vietnam War. Richard Nixon and Hubert Humphrey were seen by the public as standing very close together near the middle of the hawk–dove spectrum, and thus voters unhappy with current policy simply had no clear way of expressing their discontent.[29] Even when issue differences between the candidates are large, as they were in 1964, 1972, 1984, and 1988, people are more likely to vote on the basis of party identification than on the basis of issues.

The realistic version of how U.S. government operates understands the reality of all these forces that militate against accountability of officeholders to the general public. Nonetheless, it sees reasonable grounds for a generally positive assessment of our democracy. The chief tenets of a realistic version are as follows:

1. There is often a clear thrust to public opinion. When there is, it powerfully affects elections and public policy.
2. A *substantial number* of citizens correctly perceive the positions of candidates on important issues, or they at least have reasonable means of *inferring* where the candidates stand.
3. Candidates often differ on important national issues, but when they do not, it is because they have chosen to accommodate public opinion by moving to the middle, where most Americans are.
4. Enough Americans vote on the basis of issues to force candidates to be very careful about where they stand; a wrong stand could cost votes.
5. Voters are often backward looking, judging the results of past policies and rewarding success and punishing failure.
6. Public officials often fear electoral retribution for taking unpopular stands; even when they feel free to do what *they* want to do, their decisions will not differ radically from public opinion because their values and attitudes are very similar to those of the American people.

Political scientist Everett Carll Ladd has observed that "public opinion . . . *symbolically articulates general values*, rather than responding literally to specific issues. In a basic sense, opinion is more poetry than prose."[30] For example, the public is strongly anticommunist and distrusts the Soviet Union, yet people yearn for peaceful cooperation rather than a costly and dangerous rivalry between the two superpowers. Likewise, where abortion is concerned, the public is both disquieted about the taking of a human life and very reluctant about imposing an involuntary pregnancy on a woman. There is a strong tension (although no logical contradiction) between these conflicting attitudes, and most Americans haven't worked out how they feel about specific policies.

Where relations with the Soviet Union are concerned, Americans will give the president some latitude, going along with either a major arms buildup or a major arms control treaty. (During the Reagan administration, the public went along with both.) Should the public believe that a president is weak and vacillating in the face of aggressive Soviet behavior, however, or (contrariwise) that a president or presidential candidate is too ready to fight and too little concerned about peace, punishment will follow. Carter is an example of the former. After coming into office promising to cut the defense budget, he said that "we are now free of [our] inordinate fear of Communism."[31] During the Carter years, however, the Soviets continued with a military buildup (putting SS-20 missiles in Eastern Europe, for example), continued to abuse human rights (expelling Solzhenitsyn, for one), and invaded Afghanistan. Carter finally proposed increases in the defense budget, supported the introduction of intermediate-range nuclear missiles to counter the Soviet SS-20s, and said, following the invasion of Afghanistan, "My opinion of the Russians has changed more drastically in the last week than even the previous two

and a half years."[32] Too late. Reagan, running as a forthright anticommunist, defeated Carter in 1980. Political scientists who have studied the election have found that perceptions of weakness and vacillation hurt the Carter candidacy. Kagey and Caldera, for example, estimated that a Republican advantage in attitudes on foreign policy give Reagan between 2 and 3 percent of the vote. And Miller and Shanks found that preferences for conservative policy change, including especially more defense spending, translated into a substantial Reagan advantage.[33]

Of course, bellicosity also can run afoul of public sentiment. In 1964 Republican candidate Barry Goldwater made some casual remarks about using nuclear weapons in Vietnam and generally seemed like the sort of person who was much too willing to go to war. Political scientists who have studied that election believe Goldwater suffered major electoral damage because of his excessive hawkishness.[34]

Another area where Americans' attitudes can be described as "poetry," but poetry with a clear message, is social welfare policy. Regarding poverty measures, the public has mixed feelings. Spending more for poor people is heavily approved, but spending on welfare or social programs is much less attractive. The ambivalence is reasonable enough: People want to help the poor but believe that many recipients exploit the welfare system and that many social programs haven't really helped things.

One clear message comes through, however, when we compare attitudes toward programs for the poor (such as welfare, Medicaid, food stamps, and so on) with attitudes toward programs that primarily benefit the middle class (Social Security, Medicare, veterans' benefits, and the like): Middle-class programs are vastly more popular. These attitudes shape public policy. This nation spends quite a lot of money on the poor. In 1986, for example, over $103 billion was spent on programs falling under the heading "public aid," which includes virtually all the programs targeted toward poverty. Yet over $398 billion was spent on "social insurance" programs (including Social Security and Medicare), and another $27 billion on veterans' programs.[35] The Reagan administration found out that it is possible to cut programs for poor people (although the cuts were in fact very modest and quickly offset by increases after the first Reagan budget) but middle-class programs are sacrosanct.

As discussed, the percentage of Americans who have a reasonably good understanding of where candidates stand in presidential elections is not large. The relevant question here, though, is whether *enough* Americans know where the candidates stand so that the candidates will be forced to moderate their positions to accommodate public opinion or risk losing an election. Among presidential elections since 1960, three have been cliffhangers (1960, 1968, 1976), and the three landslides (1964, 1972, 1984) have been won by around 20 percent of the vote. If about 10 percent of the electorate had changed their minds, even these landslide elections would have gone the other way. More important is the fact that no candidate can count on the next election's being a landslide.

Certainly, when candidates offer voters sharply contrasting positions, there is a substantial increase in the clarity of voters' perceptions. For example, in 1976 only 29.2 percent of a national sample was able to place Carter to the left of Ford on the issue of aid to minorities; in 1984

fully 47.3 percent saw Mondale as more liberal than Reagan on the same issue. On the issues of government job guarantees, 51 percent saw Mondale as being on the liberal side of Reagan.[36] When voters can see differences, substantial numbers vote on the basis of the differences.

To get some idea of what "substantial numbers" means, let us look at figure 2, which presents data from the 1984 National Election Study of the University of Michigan. Voters are categorized according to self-identification as Democrats, independents, and Republicans. Within those categories they are categorized as liberal, moderate, and conservative on the basis of their expressed opinions on a variety of political issues (abortion, government jobs, social welfare spending, school prayer). Party identification is clearly an important factor determining people's votes. Even among people who are conservative in their policy preferences, only 51 percent of the Democrats voted for Reagan, but 98 percent of the Republicans did. However, positions on issues also had a powerful effect. Among Democrats, for example, 8 percent of the liberals voted for Reagan, but (as we have seen) 51 percent of the conservatives. Issue voting was particularly important among independents, and less important among Republicans (who were pretty solidly Reagan voters).

Two moderate candidates make issue voting difficult because it is hard for voters to see any difference. *Both* candidates are near the center (where most voters are) and both are relatively acceptable. The presidential elections of 1956, 1960, 1968, and 1976 are cases in point. The Democrat was just a little to the left of public opinion, and the Republican just a little to the right. This was so even on the Vietnam issue in 1968; there was little

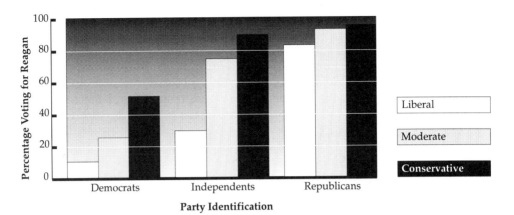

FIGURE 2 Voting and attitudes, 1984

difference between Humphrey and Nixon, and the average voter was situated between the two. There was no majority either for a more "dovish" immediate withdrawal, or for a "hawkish" escalation.[37]

Of course, national presidential elections are an extreme case where issue voting is concerned. What about less visible political contexts? My colleague Jack Johannes and I have studied voter behavior in elections for the U.S. House of Representatives, and we have found that voters are surprisingly capable of making rational voting choices based on issue positions of the candidates. Although the vast majority of voters know little about the specific issue stands of an incumbent representative, many voters have an overall idea where he or she stands in general ideological terms. Incumbents who are too far out of line do noticeably worse at the polls than those who are closer to the sentiments of a district.[38] Other scholars have found the same thing.[39] Further, voters seem to *assume* that a Democrat in Congress is likely to be a liberal and a Republican is likely to be a conservative. Thus, liberal voters are more likely to vote for a Democratic candidate, quite aside from whether they also happen to be Democrats. This as-

sumption—that Republican incumbents are conservative and Democratic incumbents liberal—is in fact quite reasonable. Exceptions are rare (especially outside the South).[40]

The notion that incumbent congressmen have something to fear at the polls seems to run contrary to the fact that they rarely fail to be reelected when they run. Usually, over 90 percent of incumbent candidates retain their seats. If an incumbent member takes a *career* perspective, however, he or she has much more to worry about. About one-third of congressmen who leave the House do so by losing an election, only two-thirds retire, and some of those retirees may have been motivated by an impending tough election battle.[41] More important, perhaps, is the fact that incumbents *see themselves* as beleaguered by potential electoral trouble. Richard Fenno, Jr., who spent a great deal of time traveling with congressmen to their home districts, concluded: "One of the dominant impressions of my travels is the terrific sense of *uncertainty* which animates these congressmen. They perceive electoral troubles where the most imaginative outside observer could not possibly perceive, conjure up or hallucinate them."[42] Thus, whatever the statistics show, congressmen have every reason to fear electoral reprisal if they fail to heed the wishes of their districts.

REWARD-AND-PUNISH VOTING

In the ideal world, voters would evaluate presidential candidates according to what they think alternative administrations (Democratic or Republican) might achieve during the next four years. Why not let bygones be bygones and vote in a way that might make things better in the future? In fact, voters are often backward looking, rewarding or punishing an administration on the basis of what has happened in the past. For example, the state of the economy has a clear effect on elections. When the economy is doing well, an incumbent president will do better than he would otherwise. Similarly, congressional candidates or other candidates of the incumbent's party will do better. Figure 3 shows something about how the process works. Again, we have controlled for the party identification of the voters. People whose personal finances had improved during the year prior to the 1984 election were more likely to vote for Reagan than people whose personal finances had gotten worse. The

difference was especially large for voters who were independents (43 percent versus 79 percent).

Figure 4 shows a further sort of retrospective voting. The question here is whether a voter felt that the nation's economy had gotten better, stayed the same, or gotten worse. Those who believed it had improved were much more likely to vote for Reagan than those who believed it had worsened.

We should also consider the "continuing election" represented by Gallup poll presidential approval ratings. In this connection, too, the state of the economy matters. As discussed, Reagan's first-term approval ratings were almost perfectly correlated with the state of the economy: very low when the economy was doing badly and better when the economy picked up. Although the evidence isn't perfectly consistent, it seems that presidents are *generally* rewarded for a healthy economy and punished for a downturn.[43]

This sort of reward-and-punish voting may have its problems. For example, it might not be the president's *fault* that the economy is faltering, and a member of the president's party in Congress probably has little say regarding economic policy. However, there is also

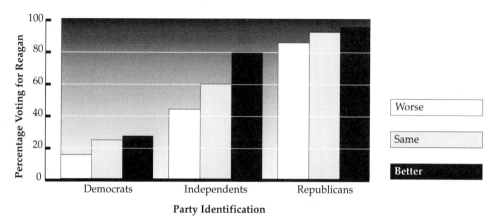

FIGURE 3 Voting and personal finances

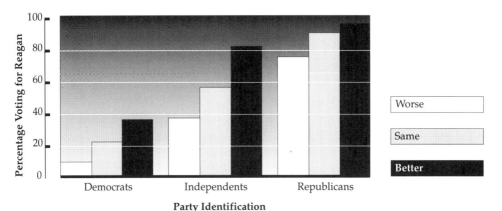

FIGURE 4 Voting and economic perceptions

much to be said for reward-and-punish voting. There is a robust sort of no-nonsense virtue in the fact that voters do not accept excuses or vacuous promises for the future; if things are going awry now, the people in power must pay.

We might also ask whether the public has the competence to pass judgment on, say, matters of macroeconomic policy. Can the average voter reasonably be certain whether he or she wants a monetarist, a Keynesian, or a supply-sider in office for the next four years? Certainly not. The details of policy are necessarily going to be handled by elites. The key question is, are elites going to be held to account for the results of their policies? There is much to be said for a system in which elites have some room to use their superior expertise in the specifics of policy, *provided* that the superior expertise produces policy that works, with the public getting to decide what "works" means.

Retrospective voting goes far beyond economic policy. A major scandal can have an effect. Watergate, for example, hurt Republican House candidates in the 1974 elections.[44] Foreign policy is an arena where retrospective voting is especially important. V. O. Key, for example, has shown that the dragging on of the Korean War hurt the Democrats in 1952. Specifically, voters who had voted for Harry Truman (the Democrat) in 1948 and who thought getting into the Korean War had been a "mistake" were especially likely to defect and vote for Eisenhower (the Republican) in 1952.[45]

Presidential approval ratings also reflect the effects of foreign policy failure. Note that *initially* a foreign policy crisis usually helps the president's standing with the voters—something political scientists call the "rally 'round the flag" effect.[46] This is true even of foreign policy fiascos, such as the Bay of Pigs invasion in 1961 or the seizure of U.S. hostages by Iranian militants in 1979.[47] However, if a crisis is protracted, if U.S. soldiers are dying for no especially good reason, or if the president seems powerless to defend the nation's interests, his standing will decline. This happened to Truman during the Korean War, to Lyndon Johnson during the Vietnam War, and to Carter during the Iranian hostage crisis.[48] Fear that it would happen to Reagan was a powerful factor in forcing the administration to withdraw U.S. marines from Beirut in 1984.

PARALLEL OPINIONS,
OFFICEHOLDERS AND PUBLIC

It is possible to have a functioning democracy in which officeholders are either far to the left or far to the right of the public. Such a system might produce perfectly democratic outcomes *if* the officeholders felt constrained to ignore their own opinions and give the public the policies it wanted. Still, most of us would be uneasy with such a system. The most dependable way of seeing to it that the public gets what it wants is to have officeholders who, in at least a broad way, hold about the same attitudes as the public.

Political scientists have done numerous polls of officeholders. Although the results vary, generally people who hold high level elective or appointive office show about the same liberal–conservative balance on most issues as the general public. CBS News, in 1970, 1978, and 1982, surveyed members of Congress and the general public, asking both groups about the same issues. The U.S. House was quite close to the populace in all three surveys. The Senate was more liberal than the public, although the 1980 election (which brought the defeat of several liberal senators) apparently brought the Senate closer to public opinion.[49]

Other surveys of elected officials have produced similar results. A 1972 survey by Louis Harris for a congressional subcommittee polled a broad range of elected officials (not just members of Congress) and likewise found them very close to a representative sample of all Americans. Finally, Uslaner and Weber polled a large national sample of state legislators, and again found that their opinions matched public opinion quite closely.[50] Such polls are misleading

in one sense. Political elites (such as members of Congress or other officeholders) are more extreme and opinionated than members of the general public. So the surveys compare rather "mushy" and equivocal opinions in the mass public with firmly (and sometimes emphatically) held opinions of the elites. The point, however, is that the liberal–conservative balance is usually very similar. There doesn't seem to be a systematic tendency for officeholders to be either more liberal or more conservative than the general public.

Of course, instead of looking at elite groups in the aggregate, and asking, "What do members of the House (or the bureaucracy, or the state legislature) believe?" we might look at variations in attitudes. For example, there are both liberal and conservative members of the U.S. House of Representatives. Do the liberal members come mostly from liberal districts, and do conservative members come mostly from conservative districts? Figure 5 shows some evidence on this question by means of the roll-call liberalism score of incumbents against the 1984 Reagan vote of the districts.[51] As we can see, there is a strong relationship. Districts that voted heavily for Reagan have representatives that are generally conservative. Districts that favored Mondale, on the other hand, have liberal-voting congressmen. It is difficult to explain the vast differences in roll-call voting without concluding that this particular elite, House members, are responsive to district opinion. People who assert that elites manipulate public opinion might assert that in different districts different elites manipulate public opinion in different directions (sometimes liberal, sometimes conservative). Given that the congressman is part of this elite, opinion will come to correspond to what the con-

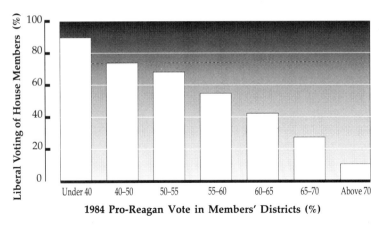

FIGURE 5   Liberal voting scores of House members compared to the pro-Reagan vote
in their districts

gressman wants. This argument flies in
the face of the fact that most of the forces
that might be able to manipulate opinion
(the media; highly visible officials, such
as the president) are national in scope.
More important, the argument *concedes*
that there is a system of competing elites
in the United States, with liberal elites
prevailing in some localities, and conservative elites in others.

If it is not a matter of manipulation,
then how does this strong correlation between district opinion and House members' votes come about? One possibility is
that incumbents, regardless of their personal beliefs, find it necessary to accommodate the opinions of the electorate.
There is certainly some of this going on,
although it is impressive that the liberalism score plotted on the graph includes
not merely a few highly publicized House
roll calls likely to be heard about back
in the district but also a cross-section.[52]
The majority of the correlation, however, is probably the result of conservative
districts electing conservative representatives and liberal districts doing
likewise. We know this because the few
studies of elected representatives that

have looked at their personal opinions
(as expressed in questionnaires) have
shown them to be strongly correlated
with opinions in the constituency.[53]

PUBLIC OPINION AND
PUBLIC POLICIES

In answering the question of whether
public opinion constrains policymakers,
direct evidence can be found by comparing public opinion with public policy.
Where liberal opinions prevail, do liberal
policies also prevail, and vice versa? We
have already discussed social welfare
spending and the fact that the general
shape of public opinion (which likes middle-class programs) accords rather closely
with the general shape of government
spending. There are, of course, coun-
terexamples. Liberals lament the lack of
stronger gun-control laws, a situation
that exists in spite of public attitudes supportive of such laws. Conservatives object to federal court decisions requiring
busing and the outlawing of school
prayer: in both cases, the public differs
with the judges quite strongly.

Some scholars have investigated a possible correlation between public opinion and policy. One approach was to look at variations in policy across states. Do states with relatively liberal populations have public policies that are more liberal than states with conservative populations? The answer is clearly *yes*. Hence, there is a strong correlation between a broad range of state policies and public opinion in the states. The relationship holds regardless of whether one defines *public opinion* in terms of the state's vote in the 1972 presidential election or in terms of whether the state's voters label themselves liberal or conservative.[54]

Another approach is to look not at variation in attitudes across states but at variations across time within the entire nation. Put more simply, when attitudes move in a liberal or conservative direction, does policy follow suit? Two major studies have concluded that this is precisely what happens. Page and Shapiro, for example, studied over 300 instances where national opinion (measured by opinion polls) changed between 1935 and 1979. In 231 of these cases, policy also changed, and two-thirds of the policy changes were in the direction favored by the public.[55]

Alan Monroe categorized a large number of polls taken between 1960 and 1974 according to whether the public favored the status quo or change. In 59 percent of the cases where the public indicated a preference for change, policy changed. In only 24 percent of the cases where the public indicated a preference for the status quo did change take place.[56] These numbers are impressive when one remembers how often the public gives frivolous or superficial answers to public opinion polls. If somehow the data used by Monroe and by Page and Shapiro could be culled to include only polls that represented "real opinion," the relationships would doubtless be even stronger.

SUMMING UP

Elites could escape the democratic dynamic if they could manipulate public opinion and condition it to accept whatever policies the elites wanted to hand out. But in the U.S. system the traditional business class and the New Class must *compete* in attempts to influence public opinion. The latter wants the public to prefer liberal Democratic policies; the former, conservative Republican policies. The public is in the middle. Elections allow the public to choose.

Although most citizens are not highly politicized and not especially well informed, they know when one elite gets too far out of line and espouses policies at odds with fundamental public values. They are content to allow the officeholders to handle the details of policy, but expect policy to work to produce peace and prosperity. Being skeptical both of politicians and of the media, citizens are difficult to manipulate. Thus, elites in our system of government cannot do anything that they please. There are many things that they cannot do because the repercussions of going against public opinion would be large enough to matter. They cannot do anything they want to do because, even in areas where the public has no preference for any particular policy, policies that produce bad results would damage incumbent politicians electorally.

The system could certainly operate more democratically, and there is plenty of room for discussion as to how it could be made to do so. But one warning is in order: Much of the discontent with the system comes not from people who want it to operate more democratically but from people who believe that *they* (and their friends) ought to have more of a free hand to implement *their* favored policies, regardless of the desires of the people.

NOTES

1. Barry Sussman, *Elites in America*, reprint of five articles in the *Washington Post*, September 26–30, 1976; Allen H. Barton, "Consensus and Conflict among American Leaders," *Public Opinion Quarterly*, 1974/1975, pp. 507–30; S. Robert Lichter, Stanley Rothman, and Linda S. Lichter, *The Media Elite* (Bethesda, Md.: Adler and Adler, 1986); S. Robert Lichter and Stanley Rothman, "What Interests the Public and What Interests the Public Interests," *Public Opinion*, April/May 1983; Jeane Kirkpatrick, *The New Presidential Elite* (New York: Russell Sage Foundation and Twentieth Century Fund, 1976); Everett C. Ladd, Jr., and Seymour Martin Lipset, *The Divided Academy* (New York: McGraw-Hill, 1975); *Newsweek*, "Can We Fight a Modern War?" July 9, 1984.

2. B. Bruce-Briggs, ed., *The New Class* (New York: McGraw-Hill, 1979).

3. Linda S. Lichter, "Who Speaks for Black America?" *Public Opinion*, August/September 1985; *Newsweek*, "The Black Conservatives," March 9, 1981.

4. *New York Times*, November 10, 1988, p. 18.

5. Robert Erikson, Norman Luttbeg, and Kent Tedin, *American Public Opinion*, 3d ed. (New York: Macmillan, 1988), pp. 199–203.

6. Lichter and Rothman, "What Interests the Public and What Interests the Public Interests"; Barton, "Consensus and Conflict among American Leaders," p. 517; Sussman, *Elites in America*.

7. Scott Keeter, "Public Opinion in 1984," in *The Election of 1984*, ed. Gerald Pomper (Chatham, N.J.: Chatham House, 1985).

8. See *MediaWatch*, January 1989, pp. 7–8. Media liberals insist that anti-abortionists should not be called pro-life because on other issues (capital punishment, for example) they often do not take the pro-life side. However, people who are pro-choice on abortion are quite often antichoice in other areas. Liberals generally believe that people should not be free to choose not to sell their homes to blacks, and many liberals support mandatory seat-belt laws, an antichoice position.

9. "No Single Standard for Sleaze," *MediaWatch*, July 1989, pp. 6–7.

10. Democratic speaker Ann Richards accused Bush of being "born with a silver foot in his mouth."

11. Maura Clancey and Michael J. Robinson, "The Media in Campaign '84: General Election Coverage: Part I," *Public Opinion*, December/January 1985.

12. News organizations' unhappiness over paid campaign media can best be understood in this framework. The Bush campaign used paid advertisements to bypass liberal elites within the media establishment and carry his message directly to the people. The refusal of the networks, on two occasions, to allow Reagan to address the American people is cause for concern; the networks would not carry his appeals for Contra aid, and

for the confirmation of Robert Bork. Apparently, the networks opposed Reagan on these issues and feared he would be able to sway public opinion to his side.

13. Gerald Schomp, *Birchism Was My Business* (London: Macmillan, 1970), pp. 36–37.

14. A. Kent MacDougall, "Boring from Within: The Bourgeois Press: Part One," *Monthly Review,* November 1988; A. Kent MacDougall, "Boring from Within: The Bourgeois Press: Part Two," *Monthly Review,* December 1988.

15. See for example Seweryn Bialer, "Central and Eastern Europe, Perestroika, and the Future of the Cold War," in *Central and Eastern Europe: The Opening Curtain?,* ed. William E. Griffith (Westport, Conn.: Westview Press, forthcoming).

16. Malcolm Muggeridge, *Chronicles of Wasted Time: The Green Stick* (New York: Morrow, 1973), chap. 5; Eugene Lyons, *The Red Decade* (New Rochelle: Arlington House, 1970); David Caute, *The Fellow Travellers* (New York: Macmillan, 1973). All of these works discuss the favorable view of the Stalinist USSR that prevailed among intellectuals generally, as well as in the reporting of Walter Duranty.

17. "The *Times* and Cuba," *Time,* July 29, 1959, p. 47; "Only Man in Step," *Newsweek,* October 2, 1961; "Fidelity to Fidel," *Time,* October 6, 1961.

18. *New York Times,* August 18, 1971. See also Reston's column in the *Times* of July 28, 1971, and the account of a CBS television interview in the *Times* of September 1, 1971.

19. Paul Hollander, *Ideological Pilgrims* (New York: Harper, 1981); Pascal Bruckner, *The Tears of the White Man: Compassion as Contempt,* trans. William R. Beer (New York: Free Press, 1986).

20. Fox Butterfield, *China: Alive in the Bitter Sea* (New York: Times Books, 1982); Hedrick Smith, *The Russians* (New York: Quadrangle, 1976); David K. Shipler, *Russia: Broken Idols, Solemn Dreams* (New York: Times Books, 1983). On Castro's Cuba, see the *New York Times* editorial, January 2, 1989.

21. Seymour Martin Lipset, "The Wavering Polls," *Public Interest,* Spring 1976.

22. The *New York Times* poll was reported in the *Times* on February 13, 1976; the Gallup poll was conducted in June 1983.

23. Philip E. Converse, "Attitudes and Non-Attitudes: Continuation of a Dialogue," in *The Quantitative Analysis of Social Problems,* ed. Edward R. Tufte (New York: Addison-Wesley, 1970).

24. Lipset, "The Wavering Polls," p. 89.

25. George F. Bishop, Robert W. Oldendick, Alfred J. Tuchfarber, and Stephen E. Bennett, "Pseudo-Opinions on Public Affairs," *Public Opinion Quarterly,* 1980, pp. 198–209.

26. Tabulations by the author from data supplied by the Interuniversity Consortium for Political and Social Research.

27. Patricia A. Hurley and Kim Quaille Hill, "The Prospects for Issue Voting in Contemporary Congressional Elections: An Assessment of Citizen Awareness and Representation," in *Public Opinion and Public Policy,* ed. Norman R. Luttbeg, 3d ed. (Itasca, Ill.: Peacock, 1981).

28. Michael King, "Assimilation and Contrast of Presidential Candidates' Issue Positions, 1972," *Public Opinion Quarterly,* 1977–1978, pp. 515–22.

29. Benjamin I. Page and Richard A.

Brody, "Policy Voting and the Electoral Process: The Vietnam War Issue," *American Political Science Review*, 1972, pp. 979–95.

30. *Christian Science Monitor*, September 21, 1988. Emphasis in original.

31. The statement was made in a speech on May 22, 1977, at Notre Dame University.

32. *Facts on File*, December 31, 1979, p. 974.

33. Herbert B. Asher, *Presidential Elections and American Politics*, 4th ed. (Chicago: Dorsey Press, 1988), p. 185; Warren E. Miller and J. Merrill Shanks, "Policy Directions and Presidential Leadership: Alternative Interpretations of the 1980 Presidential Election," *British Journal of Political Science*, July 1982.

34. Philip Converse, Aage R. Clausen, and Warren E. Miller, "Electoral Myth and Reality: The 1984 Election," *American Political Science Review*, June 1965, pp. 331–32.

35. These figures include spending at the federal, state, and local levels. See *Statistical Abstract of the United States, 1989*, p. 347.

36. See note 26.

37. Page and Brody, "Policy Voting and the Electoral Process."

38. John R. Johannes and John C. McAdams, "The Congressional Incumbency Effect: Is It Casework, Policy Compatibility, or Something Else?" *American Journal of Political Science*, August 1981, pp. 512–42; John C. McAdams and John R. Johannes, "Congressmen, Perquisites, and Elections," *Journal of Politics*, May 1988, pp. 412–39.

39. Robert S. Erikson and Gerald C. Wright, Jr., "Policy Representation of Constituency Interests," *Political Behavior*, Spring 1980, pp. 91–106.

40. Johannes and McAdams, "The Congressional Incumbency Effect"; McAdams and Johannes, "Congressmen, Perquisites, and Elections."

41. Robert S. Erikson, "Is There Such a Thing as a Safe Seat?" *Polity*, Summer 1976, pp. 623–32.

42. David R. Mayhew, *Congress: The Electoral Connection* (New Haven: Yale University Press, 1974), p. 35.

43. See Kristen R. Monroe, " 'God of Vengeance and of Reward'? The Economy and Presidential Popularity," *Political Behavior*, Winter 1979.

44. Eric M. Uslaner and M. Margaret Conway, "The Responsible Congressional Electorate: Watergate, the Economy, and Vote Choice in 1974," *American Political Science Review*, September 1985, pp. 788–803.

45. V. O. Key, Jr., *The Responsible Electorate* (Cambridge: Harvard University Press, 1966), p. 75.

46. John E. Mueller, *War, Presidents and Public Opinion* (New York: Wiley, 1973).

47. James Q. Wilson, *American Government*, 4th ed. (Lexington, Mass.: Heath, 1988), p. 553.

48. Social scientists who have studied presidential popularity have come to rather mixed conclusions about whether wars hurt a president's popularity, perhaps because they have typically used overly elaborate statistical models. See, for example, Douglas A. Hibbs, Jr., "Problems of Statistical Estimation and Causal Inference in Time-Series Regression Models," *Sociological Methodology*, 1973–1974.

49. Erikson, Luttbeg, and Tedin, *American Public Opinion*, p. 284.

50. Congress, Subcommittee on Intergovernmental Relations, *Confidence and Concern: Citizens View American Government, Part 1*, 93d Cong., 1st sess., December 3, 1973; Eric M. Uslaner and Ronald E. Weber, "Poli-

cy Congruence and American State Elites: Descriptive Representation versus Electoral Accountability," *Journal of Politics*, February 1983.

51. The liberalism score is that of the Americans for Democratic Action, based on roll-call votes during 1983.

52. Of course, *any vote*, contrary to the interests or views of the district, even one that seems "obscure," might be publicized by an opponent during an incumbent's reelection campaign. Well-run campaigns, in fact, have people whose job it is to pore over the record of the opponent looking for embarrassing statements, positions, or votes.

53. Gerald C. Wright, Jr., and Michael B. Berkman, "Candidates and Policy in United States Senate Elections,"

American Political Science Review, June 1986, pp. 567–88.

54. David C. Nice, "Representation in the States: Policymaking and Ideology," *Social Science Quarterly*, June 1983, pp. 404–11; Gerald C. Wright, Jr., Robert S. Erikson, and John P. McIver, "Public Opinion and Policy Liberalism in the American States," *American Journal of Political Science*, November 1987.

55. Benjamin I. Page and Robert Y. Shapiro, "Effects of Public Opinion on Policy," *American Political Science Review*, March 1983, pp. 175–90.

56. Alan D. Monroe, "Consistency between Public Preferences and National Policy Decisions," *American Politics Quarterly*, January 1979.

SUGGESTED READINGS

BRUCE-BRIGGS, B., ED. *The New Class?* New York: McGraw-Hill, 1979. A collection of articles about the liberal elite, arguing that certain growing sectors of modern societies are inclined by their class interests toward politics of the left.

ERIKSON, ROBERT S., NORMAN LUTTBERG, AND KENT L. TEDIN. *American Public Opinion.* New York: Macmillan, 1988. An excellent overview of public opinion and the process that translates public opinion into public policy.

LICHTER, S. ROBERT, STANLEY ROTHMAN, AND LINDA LICHTER. *The Media Elite.* Bethesda, Md.: Adler and Adler, 1986. Outlines the distinctive world view of the people who control the American media.

Government by Elites in the Name of All

Michael Margolis
University of Cincinnati

Rule by the common people is the essence of democratic governance. Although the arrangements may vary, all democratic governments assert that public policy flows from or is severely constrained by the wishes of ordinary citizens. Public opinion is the collective expression of these wishes regarding matters of popular concern. Even though public opinion in the United States is often identified with answers to public opinion polls or with the results of elections, it is also expressed through communications with policymakers, actions by groups of citizens, and information related in the mass media. Such communications and actions may vary from sending letters and telegrams, petitioning or telephoning, to lobbying, demonstrating, or even rioting. In the United States, as in all countries that proclaim themselves democratic, it is expected that policymakers will heed these expressions of public opinion.

The importance of public opinion is not limited to democratic governments. Indeed, the stability and legitimacy of all governments, from the most dictatorial to the most democratic, ultimately rest upon the goodwill or favorable public opinion of the masses. Public resistance to or outright overthrow of governments in Afghanistan, Burma, Israel, Mexico, the Philippines, South Africa, South Korea, and obviously most of Eastern Europe in the late 1980s serves to illustrate this statement. At the outset, therefore, let me concede that no government can long afford to repress the wishes and aspirations of substantial portions of its population.[1] In fact, let me concede the truth of an even stronger statement: no authority, public or private, can function effectively over time without the acquiescence of the great bulk of the population over which it rules. Students need only think of their own college or university: How many rules and regulations could the faculty or administration enforce if the majority of students decided to resist? Or think of a large public or private enterprise: Could management enforce its rules and regulations without the cooperation of the bulk of its employees?

It is one thing to state that virtually all authority rests upon the good opinion of relevant publics. It is quite another to contend that the behavior of public or private policymakers is *effectively checked* by the need to maintain such favorable public opinion. True, in the United States and other purportedly democratic countries, authorities cannot murder and pillage at will, nor can they forcibly separate parents from children, nor even forbid televising football on weekend afternoons.[2] But within broad boundaries policymakers normally can decide as they please, confident that their decisions will gain public cooperation or support, or at worst, public compliance or indifference. Put simply, the argument here is that notwithstanding the ultimate need for public compliance or support, the constraints placed on American policymakers—both public and private—are not very strong. Indeed, the control American public opinion exerts over policymakers resembles the "control"

student opinion exerts over faculty and administration more closely than it resembles popular models of democratic self-governance.

In contrast to their perceptions of their roles as students (or workers), however, Americans, in their roles as citizens, tend to think they exercise effective control over policymakers. But the key question here must be, over what policy matters do Americans exert effective control? As Andrew Hacker observes:

> America has been and continues to be one of the world's most democratic nations. Here, far more so than elsewhere, the public is allowed to participate widely in the making of social and political policy. The public is not unaware of its power, and the ordinary American tends to be rather arrogant about his right and competence to participate. . . . The people think they know what they want and are in no mood to be led to greener pastures. This is why we have driver-education courses in the high schools, lowbrow comedy on television, public loyalty investigations, and de facto racial segregation. These conditions persist because they have the wholehearted backing of local and national majorities. Policy-makers know that in a democracy public sentiment must be accommodated.[3]

Hacker goes on to point out that although Americans may control the sorts of policies listed above, they don't control many of the policies that affect their lives most directly. Consider, for instance, the question of employment. Job-related activities fill the largest single portion of the average adult's waking hours. In the United States the managers and directors of large corporations—not the people or their elected representatives—decide what kinds of jobs will be available, where they will be located, and how many there will be. Americans must adjust their lives in order to qualify for the jobs; those who cannot make the necessary adjustments find themselves out of work, not to mention out of luck.

Most Americans have a general aversion to anything that smacks of socialism. They behave as though it is perfectly democratic for their life chances to be governed by policies determined by various unelected corporate planners. Indeed, most believe that it is none of the government's business—or rather, none of the people's business, for democracy is government by the people—to tell private corporations what to do regarding jobs and investment. *Are there injurious or unhealthful consequences that arise from the practices of private enterprise?* The popular view, as President Ronald Reagan observed, is that governmental regulation of the economy—let alone planning or public ownership—is part of the problem, not the solution. Private enterprise will regulate itself. And this is not all. Most Americans also accept the notion that government really has no direct responsibility to provide for citizens' basic needs. Food, clothing, shelter, and medical care, in addition to employment, are provided for largely by private enterprise. Government need only assure that citizens receive opportunities for basic education, training, and investment.[4]

Such views, of course, are part of a larger picture, which for better or for worse, supports a liberal individualism that emphasizes self-reliance and downgrades the role of government in altering the domestic social and economic order. Not surprisingly, these views tend to reinforce values and institutions congenial to those who benefit the most from policies favoring private enterprise. In general, Americans whose income and status are above average express less support than others for government policies that distribute benefits like health care or social services or opportunities like job guarantees to the less well off. Moreover, those who don't do very well economically tend to place the blame for their failures on themselves rather than upon any flaws in the economic system.[5]

From early childhood most Americans are socialized to develop attitudes highly supportive of the political system. There is a presumption of the naturalness and benevolence of the political institutions and the economic order of the United States, and a corresponding disdain for foreign institutions and cultures. Americans not only are proud of their political institutions but also tend to equate democracy with a presidential system tempered by constitutionally recognized separation of powers, checks and balances, and independent state governments. They find nothing peculiar in the fact that the same two parties, both devoted to fostering private enterprise, have dominated government for the past 130 years. Nor do they consider themselves or their leaders arrogant for acting as though the aims of U.S. foreign policies are the expressions of God's will on earth.[6]

Opposition to foreign policy is permitted, but barely tolerated. As the style of the 1988 Bush–Dukakis presidential contest illustrated, authorities tend to question the patriotism of foreign policy critics, not the substance of their criticism. "America, love it or leave it!" is often the cry. In times of crisis, most Americans are happy to give the president and other policymakers the benefit of the doubt. Time and again public opinion polls have shown an immediate swelling of support for governmental actions in foreign policy crises, regardless of the success or failure of those actions.

And while decision makers do not enjoy such strongly supportive tendencies regarding domestic policies, the range of acceptable criticisms tends to be narrowly focused upon differences of opinion that stay within the mainstream policies of the Democratic and Republican parties. Yet these organizations are noted as much for their broad range of agreement as for their differences.[7]

In the sections below, readers will be asked to consider some alternative interpretations of values and institutions different from those that most Americans seem to take for granted. I will argue that the American two-party system limits the range of meaningful choices; that the values of liberal individualism presume an entrepreneurial society that no longer exists; that today such values tend to favor the interests of the very rich; that the mass media reinforce the worldviews of their owners even as they inform the general public; that public opinion polling structures the expression of public demands in manners congenial to the interests of those who sponsor such polls; and finally, that the limitations of acceptable opinions are so firmly entrenched that expression of opinions outside the boundaries set by the owners of popular media is severely sanctioned.

Before reviewing the evidence for the above assertions, I must add some qualifying remarks. To argue that the U.S. political system is considerably less democratic than is popularly maintained is not to argue that the government of the United States is no different from governments like those of the Soviet Union (at least prior to the 1990s), the Republic of South Africa (RSA), or the Islamic Republic of Iran. One can readily discern that formal political processes are less democratic in any of those countries than in the United States. The comparison to keep in mind, however, is the contrast between the United States as an exemplar of democratic governance and a realistic model of democratic governance. To assert that governance in the United States is more democratic than that in some nondemocratic country hardly proves that it is properly democratic. After all, the governance of the USSR, the RSA, and Iran is certainly more democratic than was governance in Nazi Germany under Hitler, yet none of these governments could be called a liberal democracy. Being more democratic than a dictatorship is hardly cause for celebration.

THE TWO-PARTY SYSTEM AND CHOICE

It may surprise some readers to learn that in the 1988 election there were more than a dozen candidates running for president. If you talked with friends, read the daily papers, or followed the news on radio or television, most of these candidates were hardly mentioned at all. Practically all the coverage of the presidential election was devoted to George Bush, Michael Dukakis, and their vice-presidential running mates. Even if you scrutinized the ballot, chances are that most of the other candidates were not listed. If you looked carefully, there was probably a place on the ballot where you could write in their names; the ballot booth may have contained a writing instrument for that purpose; and with luck, the local precinct officials might even have been diligent enough to tally such a write-in.

Once upon a time it was not so difficult for candidates from parties other than the Democratic or Republican to get their names before the public. For approximately the first hundred years of the republic, the parties, rather than the government, actually printed the ballots.

Any party that could gain access to a printing press could offer the voters its slate of candidates. Voters could decide which ballot or combination of ballots to mark and place in the ballot box. The ballot itself was not very secret: each party might use a distinctive color to distinguish its slate of candidates from the others, the better to guarantee delivery of votes bought and paid for. But the process certainly was democratic. Voters flocked to the polls, and some, especially in big cities, were so enthusiastic they voted several times. The average turnout has never been so high as it was in the last decades of the nineteenth century.[8]

By modern standards, of course, this sort of voting system was excessively democratic, for it was subject to all sorts of obvious abuses. The progressive reforms of the late nineteenth century and early twentieth were designed to curb these abuses. They introduced such innovations as registration lists to prevent multiple voting and the Australian ballot to prevent ballot box stuffing and to assure the secrecy of each voter's choice. But there was also a price to pay: If the state prints the ballot and keeps track of who is eligible to vote, then there must be rules to determine which party slates get on the ballot and which voters get included on the lists. Inevitably, this makes it harder for new parties to be included on the ballot, and for some new voters to become eligible. Moreover, because Democratic and Republican legislators write the laws, there is a natural tendency to favor the established parties. It is common practice, for instance, automatically to include only the candidates from parties that received a certain share of the vote in the previous election. New parties normally must present a petition with a large number of names, often equal to the minimal proportion necessary to qualify for automatic inclusion.[9]

The rules restricting access to the ballot, combined with an electoral system in which most officials need only a plurality of votes to win, as opposed to a fixed proportion or a majority of votes, serve to enhance the prominence of the Democratic and Republican parties. The overall effect of this is to restrict severely the electorate's real choice. The simple fact is that despite the celebrated diversity of their supporters, the Democratic and Republican parties agree on most major issues. Which party, for instance, advocates a positive role for government as an active participant in the economy? (Various socialist parties, not the Democratic or the Republican.) Which opts for virtually no active role at all for government to play in regulating either the economic activities or the voluntary social behaviors of the citizenry? (The Libertarian party, not the Democratic or the Republican.) Which party seeks to outlaw the manufacture and sale of the most dangerous widely used drugs? (The Prohibition party, which recognizes alcoholic beverages for the killers they are.) The Democratic and Republican parties are both for peace, prosperity, and a strong defense. They both stand for law, order, and family values. They're for fighting drugs, except for acceptable ones like alcohol and tobacco. Is it any wonder that nearly half the American voters cannot tell the parties apart when asked to distinguish them on the public issues the voters consider most important? Is it surprising that barely half the eligible electorate even bothers to vote in presidential elections? What real choice do the elections offer?[10]

THE VALUES OF INDIVIDUALISM TODAY

Carl Sandburg, the poet and biographer, used to relate a story about two maggots born in the same nest. The first had the good fortune of falling into a pile of manure; the second slipped into a crack in the sidewalk. The first maggot found that food was plentiful and life was easy. He grew strong and plump. The second had a tougher time. Food was scarce down in that crack in the sidewalk, and life was a struggle. One day the scrawny little sidewalk maggot managed to crawl out of his crack. He looked up and saw his well-fed brother sitting atop the pile of manure. "Hey brother," he called, "you're looking good. You're strong, healthy, and prosperous. I'm weak, sickly, and poor. Tell me, how do you account for the shape you're in? How did you rise to the top of the heap?" "Simple," replied the other. "Brains and personality!"[11]

The story is quintessentially American. It aptly sums up the self-congratulatory myth of the "self-made man" that permeates American culture. Even though the large majority of working adults are now wage earners or salaried employees of large private firms or public institutions, the popular values reflect those of a nation of small self-employed farmers and entrepreneurs. Americans admire successful individuals, and they tend to equate economic success with just deserts. Wealth and honor result from hard work, individual effort, and the willingness to seize opportunities when they arise—pluck and luck, in the words of Horatio Alger, whose boys' novels served to inspire and perpetuate the myth in the latter half of the nineteenth century.

Of course, it was during the latter half of the nineteenth century that the American frontier closed, and the industrial revolution set in motion the transformation of the U.S. economy from a nation of independent farmers and entrepreneurs to one of employees and wage earners. And throughout the first half of the twentieth century the United States gradually took on the features that characterize modern industrial nations: urbanization, bureaucratization, secularization, cosmopolitanism, and an increasingly complex division of labor. But popular ideals regarding social organization never caught up with actual social change.

Even today, when nearly 80 percent of the population lives in metropolitan areas and the majority of two-parent families have both parents employed outside the household, the virtues of small-town America—a dominant ethnic or religious group that sets social norms to which friends and neighbors conform; locally owned businesses that employ local residents and rely on community custom for their income; two-parent households with additional relatives living within or nearby; a father who earns the principal income and a mother who manages the household and volunteers for community service—are still the stereotypic ideals. These stereotypes pervade the commercials on major radio and television networks; they are reflected in reruns of programs like "Happy Days" and "The Brady Bunch"; and they are lauded by religious leaders like Jerry Falwell and political leaders like Ronald Reagan. Significantly, their relevance and applicability to real life in this country in the last decade of the twentieth century are rarely challenged by either the popular media or prominent public leaders.[12]

Most Americans work in large public or private bureaucracies, but only the former are popularly acknowledged. Public bureaucracies are typically characterized as unwieldy and inefficient; their existence is generally deplored. In contrast, large private enterprises are typically depicted as streamlined and efficient; their existence as bureaucracies is generally ignored. The fact of the matter is that the operational efficiencies of public and private bureaucracies resemble one another, and so do their leaders. The myth of entrepreneurial success suggests that every young person can get ahead on the basis of his or her talent, but the recruitment to top positions in both public and private bureaucracies is rather narrow:

> Individuals at the top are overwhelmingly upper- and upper-middle-class in social origin. Even those who have climbed the institutional ladder to high position generally started with the advantages of middle-class upbringing. . . . Elites are notably "Ivy League": 54 percent of top corporate leaders and 42 percent of top government leaders are alumni of just 12 well-known private universities. Moreover, a substantial portion of corporate and government leaders attended one of just 30 private "name" prep schools.[13]

Far from being an economy typified by competition among individual entrepreneurs, the U.S. economy is dominated by oligopolies of huge corporations that engage in limited competition among themselves. Just 100 of the 200,000 industrial corporations in the United States control approximately 60 percent of all industrial assets, and this percentage is growing, not shrinking. The concentration of assets in transportation, communications, and utilities is even greater than among industrial corporations, despite the breakup of American Telephone and Telegraph (AT&T). Before its breakup in 1984, AT&T controlled nearly as many assets as the next 49 largest companies combined. Even after its breakup, AT&T remains the largest company, and the seven new regional telephone companies created by the breakup rank third through ninth. Other sectors are similarly concentrated: the 50 largest (of over 14,500) commercial banks control approximately two-thirds of all banking assets; and the 50 largest (of over 2,000) insurance companies control over four-fifths. Moreover, the directorates of these companies have many overlaps. The company directors are not only drawn disproportionately from a restricted list of schools but belong to the same private clubs, and they tend to share the same lifestyles and values. Even though only about 15 percent hold two or more top positions on corporate directorates simultaneously, most assume a number of top positions in various corporate, civic, cultural, educational, and governmental institutions over the course of their careers. Finally, there is a pattern of interlocking memberships among the directorates of corporations by geographic region, and most interlocks are dominated by directors of the large commercial banks.[14]

As we have seen, popular portrayals of the U.S. economy generally emphasize the individual achievements of private entrepreneurs and generally ignore the concentrations of authority and power among the corporate bureaucracies. At the same time they generally deplore intervention by governmental bureaucracies into the private economy. *To whose advantage are such portrayals?* Principally, they are advantageous to those who already hold positions of economic power. The popular portrayals ignore the power of oligopolies to control many sectors of the market, and they presume that those in power have earned their positions by having outdone their competition in the free market. Conversely, they imply that those who have failed to get ahead have only themselves to blame for having lost the competition. And last, they disparage any attempts by government bureaucracies to intervene in the economy through regulation, planning, ownership, or even implementation of policies that redistribute resources from "winners" to "losers."

THE MEDIA: CONSOLIDATED AND CONTROLLING

In addition to the innovative entrepreneurs who lead private corporations, the popular image of U.S. society includes the courageous editors and reporters who constitute the corps of the free press. And in recent years, as Americans have come to rely most upon television news as the primary source of information about public affairs, the image of the free press has been expanded to include broadcast journalism. Americans believe broadcast and newspaper journalists, editors, and reporters are more honest and trustworthy than politicians, lawyers, salespeople, labor leaders, and business executives of all types except bankers. Only the police, the clergy, and those associated with the medical, educational, and engineering professions are thought to be more honest and trustworthy.[15] Who has not heard of the importance of the free press in checking the excesses of government and industry? All praise to the First Amendment guarantees of free speech and a free press.

The U.S. press is made up almost exclusively of privately owned, business-managed, profit-making enterprises. The overriding concern of those who own the press and broadcast networks is, by and large, making money, not exercising

their First Amendment rights. In line with this overriding concern, we have witnessed an enormous consolidation of ownership of the newspapers over the past thirty years. Nor is this all: There has been growth and consolidation of the magazine and book publishing, motion picture, and radio industries. And despite the advent of cable and satellite capacities, there has been relatively little growth in the area of public affairs broadcasting.

Over 70 percent of the 1,678 daily newspapers published in 1985 were owned by newspaper chains, a percentage that has been increasing annually for the past several decades. Fewer than twenty companies control over half the daily circulation; the top eight control over one-third. Barely 2 percent of the dailies face competition from another local daily in their market. Nor is the newspaper market unique; a comparable pattern of consolidation and control is found in other media as well:

> In 1981 twenty corporations controlled most of the business of the country's 11,000 magazines, but only five years later that number had shrunk to six corporations.
>
> Today, despite 25,000 media outlets in the United States, twenty-nine corporations control most of the business in daily newspapers, magazines, television, books, and motion pictures.[16]

The popular image of the openness of the press, like that of the openness of the political party system and of private enterprise, comports more with the United States of the 1890s than with the United States of today. In the 1890s, just as the legal requirements to establish ballot position for a political party were less onerous, so too it required less capital to start and maintain a newspaper, magazine, or publishing house. In 1900 there were 2,042 daily newspapers with 2,023 separate owners, and even though commercial radio, television, and motion pictures did not exist, many more magazine and book publishers held significant shares of the market independently than are held today. Moreover, journalism had not yet adopted the modern professional norms of neutrality. Major newspapers often supported particular political parties, and interpretive journalism was not confined to the editorial and op-ed pages. Although this meant that not all the "facts" would be reported objectively, it also meant that reporters were not shy about using their own experience, knowledge, or expertise to interject comments on events about which they were reporting. When a George Bush declared himself strong on the environment, or a Michael Dukakis declared himself strong on defense, reporters who wrote the "hard" news story might actually comment on the men's records rather than merely report their remarks.

The media of today are largely part of the corporate establishment. As such, they tend to reflect and in turn to propagate a conservative ideology. The railings of the far right notwithstanding, the mainstream news media present a picture of reality that supports powerful groups and established causes. Whites, males, management, and officialdom are favored over blacks, females, labor, and dissidents. Private enterprise, capitalism, national chauvinism, and militarism get mostly positive coverage; socialism, communism, internationalism, and disarmament get mostly contempt. The internal contradictions of dominant political and economic institutions, coupled with the need to maintain credibility as the peo-

ple's watchdog, force the news media to criticize government and industry from time to time, but the general thrust of the coverage is highly supportive of the established order.[17]

THE NATURE OF PUBLIC OPINION POLLING

Research on public opinion has expanded greatly since World War II. The establishment of national polling organizations and the advent of modern computers have enabled researchers to solicit, collect, and analyze the opinions of representative samples of American adults on vast numbers of issues of public concern. These developments, combined with popular notions of liberal democracy, have led some commentators to treat the results of public opinion surveys not merely as data that help inform policymakers, but as mandates, violations of which required explanation and justification. Some have even suggested that a high correspondence between changes in popular opinion and changes in public policy is the mark of a successful democracy.[18]

The underlying premise here is that responses to such polls represent valid expressions of what democratic theorists have defined as public opinion. Yet consider the sources of most of the public opinion polls: they are commissioned by leaders in private industry and government, by educational institutions whose boards of directors are dominated by such leaders, or by the mass media that publish the results. *Are the questions fair and comprehensive or do they tend to represent an agenda favored by established groups?*

A perusal of archives of public opinion polls taken in the United States turns up bundles of questions about policies and issues of the day, but few about "nonissues," that is, plausible alternative policies that never seem to reach the public agenda. *Is the economy in trouble?* There are lots of questions about tariffs, import quotas, government loans, and labor costs; there are few that solicit opinions about socialist alternatives. *Is there a government scandal?* We find many questions about the honesty and integrity of politicians, but hardly any about the extent to which the political and economic systems encourage selfishness and greed. *Is there poverty at home and abroad?* Polls are replete with questions about industrialization, productivity, job training, birth control, and abortion, but there's hardly a whisper about the fairness of capitalism or the redistribution of wealth.[19]

The above circumstances suggest that public opinion polling serves as much to manage popular attitudes as it does inform policymakers of the wishes of the people. It there were no polls, policymakers would have to rely more heavily on communications and behaviors of organized groups, or sometimes even of mobs, in order to gauge public opinion. Instead, polls tend to transform the expression of opinion from a voluntary group behavior into a manageable individual response. In essence, polling domesticates opinion by shifting responsibility for raising issues from the mass public to the policymakers who formulate the questions. Moreover, polling can serve to undermine the credibility of dissident elites. *Do union leaders say that health and safety procedures are inadequate in certain manufacturing units? Does the NAACP say there is invidious discrimination regarding housing or employment?* Polls may show that the rank and file don't know much or don't feel strongly about

these issues. If so, policymakers can ignore these issues yet still proclaim themselves democrats whose only aims are to follow public opinion.[20]

SUMMING UP

To recapitulate: I contend that the institutional arrangements and the values of modern U.S. society make it nearly impossible for public opinion to form an effective check upon the behavior of policymakers. Although policymakers are constrained to maintain the general goodwill of the public, the latitude allowed them is very broad. The Democratic and Republican parties legitimate the alternatives defined by those in power and limit dissent to choices within a predetermined range. These alternatives discourage socialistic policies that involve government in the economy, and they largely exclude policies that challenge the economic values of corporate bureaucracies that dominate most sectors of the market. The policymakers themselves tend to come from similar middle- to upper-class backgrounds; approximately half the top government and corporate officials are drawn from only a dozen leading institutions of higher learning.[21] The mass media, which are themselves part of the corporate economy, reinforce liberal individualistic values and nationalistic worldviews that are congenial to those in positions of power. By formulating the questions that go into most public opinion polls, policymakers in government, industry, educational institutions, and the media control much of what is declared to be public opinion.

For policymakers, the beauty of the whole situation is that the American people generally believe they are the authors of the decisions that policymakers wanted in first place. Most people accept the notion that the differences between the Democratic and Republican party candidates pretty much represent the full range of viable alternatives that could be considered. Few lament the lack of either a powerful socialist alternative or of a genuine party of the religious right. The minority parties that do exist are hardly heard from at all.

Beneath the seeming contentment, however, there lies a certain amount of fear. Despite each American's celebrated rights to free speech and assembly, certain opinions may be too dangerous to utter, certain groups too dangerous to join. For most people, communism is such an idea, and the Communist party is such a group. Even though communism has never been a very popular cause in the United States, as of this writing there is nothing illegal about declaring oneself a communist supporter or, for that matter, joining the Communist party. But consider the following experiment: The next time the Communist party runs an advertisement in the *New York Times* soliciting donations or memberships, suppose you send the party a personal check for one dollar. Now, most people wouldn't choose to do that simply because they don't like what the party stands for. *But is that the only reason?* Sending the party a personal check for a dollar leaves a written record. If they found out you support the Communist party, landlords might not rent to you; businesses might not deal with you; employers might decide not to hire you. *And they probably would find out, wouldn't they?*

The fact of the matter is that even in the United States the limitations of acceptable opinions are so firmly entrenched that expression of ideas that transgress the boundaries is severely sanctioned. In countries like the USSR the government punishes those who express the wrong opinions. In the United States the government leaves that up to private enterprise. In either case policymakers rather than ordinary citizens have the dominant role in setting the boundaries of public choice.

NOTES

1. See David Hume, *David Hume's Political Essays* (Indianapolis: Bobbs-Merrill, 1953), pp. 24ff.
2. As of this writing (November 1988), the question of whether or not football (soccer) games shall be played at all, let alone televised, on Saturday (sabbath) afternoons is a bone of contention surrounding the formation of the next government of Israel.
3. Andrew Hacker, "Power to Do What?" in *The Bias of Pluralism*, ed. William E. Connolly (New York: Atherton Press, 1969), p. 68.
4. See Gallup survey 255G, 6/7–10/85: "Which is biggest threat to nation: big business, big labor, or big government?" Also trend on question 1959–1983. *The Gallup Poll: Public Opinion, 1985* (Wilmington, Del.: Scholarly Resources, 1986; Robert Y. Shapiro et al., "The Polls—Employment and Social Welfare," *Public Opinion Quarterly* 51 (1987):268–81.
5. On class attitudes, see Robert S. Erikson, Norman R. Luttbeg, and Kent L. Tedin, *American Public Opinion: Its Origins, Content, and Impact*, 3d ed. (New York: Macmillan, 1988), pp. 170–72; on employment opportunities, see Robert Lane, *Political Ideology* (New York: Free Press, 1962), pp.

242–46; Kay Schlozman and Sidney Verba, *Injury to Insult: Unemployment, Class and Political Response* (Cambridge: Harvard University Press, 1979), pp. 138ff.

6. See Harry Holloway and John George, *Public Opinion: Coalitions, Elites and Masses,* 2d ed. (New York: St. Martin's Press, 1986), chap. 5; Gabriel Almond and Sidney Verba, *The Civic Culture* (Boston: Little, Brown, 1965), chap. 3; Gallup polls 6/9–16/86 on pride in the United States and survey 168G, March 1987, on relevance and importance of religion in *The Gallup Poll: Public Opinion, 1986 and 1987.*

7. See John Mueller, *War, Presidents, and Public Opinion* (New York: Wiley, 1973); Samuel Kernell, *Going Public* (Washington, D.C.: Congressional Quarterly Press 1986), pp. 148ff.; Herbert Asher, *Presidential Elections,* 4th ed. (Chicago: Dorsey Press, 1988), table 4.3.

8. See W. Dean Burnham, *Critical Elections and the Mainsprings of American Politics* (New York: Norton, 1970), chap. 4.

9. By the late 1960s the rules were often written so as to disadvantage third parties so unfairly that the courts eventually forced several states to ease their requirements. Ironically, it was George Wallace's presidential run in 1968 as the law-and-order cum racist candidate of the American Independent Party that brought suit to democratize the rules for ballot eligibility.

10. See Asher, *Presidential Elections,* chaps. 1, 4. Also W. D. Burnham, *The Current Crisis in American Politics* (New York: Oxford University Press, 1982), chap. 4.

11. The author had the pleasure of hearing Sandburg tell the story at "An Evening with Carl Sandburg," in Finney Chapel at Oberlin College in the early 1960s.

12. See Alan Wolfe, "Cultural Sources of the Reagan Revolution: The Antimodern Legacy," in *The Reagan Revolution?,* ed. B. B. Kymlicka and Jean W. Matthews (Chicago: Dorsey Press, 1988), pp. 65–81.

13. Thomas R. Dye, *Who's Running America? The Conservative Years,* 4th ed. (Englewood Cliffs, N.J.: Prentice-Hall, 1986), p. 278. Dye's findings are based on a systematic study of 7,314 leaders who occupy positions of authority within major public and private institutions. See pp. 9–13 for an explicit description of this elite.

14. The above discussion is based on data presented in Dye, *Who's Running America?,* chaps. 2, 6.

15. Thomas Dye and Harmon Zeigler, *American Politics in the Media Age,* 2d ed. (Pacific Grove, Calif.: Brooks/Cole, 1986), chap. 5.

16. Ben Bagdikian, *The Media Monopoly* (Boston: Beacon Press, 1987), p. 4; see also *Editor & Publisher Yearbook* (annual volumes).

17. See Michael Parenti, *Inventing Reality: The Politics of the Mass Media* (New York: St. Martin's Press, 1986); W. Lance Bennett, *News: The Politics of Illusion,* 2d ed. (New York: Longmans, 1987).

18. George Gallup, *Public Opinion in a Democracy,* Stafford Little Lectures (Princeton: Princeton University Press, 1939); Alan Monroe, "Consistency between Public Preferences and National Policy Decisions," *American Politics Quarterly* 7 (1979):3–19; Paul A. Burstein, "Public Opinion, Demonstrations, and the Passage of Anti-Discrimination Legislation," *Public Opinion Quarterly* 43 (Summer 1979):157–72.

19. On "nonissues," see Peter Bachrach and Morton Baratz, "Two Faces of Power," *American Political Science Review* 56 (December 1962):947–52, and "Decisions and Non-Decisions: An Analytical Framework," *American Political Science Review* 57 (September 1963):632–42. For public opinion questions, see *The Gallup Poll* (annual volumes).

20. Benjamin Ginsberg, "How Polling Transforms Public Opinion," in *Manipulating Public Opinion: Essays on Public Opinion as a Dependent Variable*, ed. Michael Margolis and Gary A. Mauser (Pacific Grove, Calif.: Brooks/Cole, 1989), chap. 13.

21. Dye, *Who's Running America?*, pp. 190–91.

SUGGESTED READINGS

DYE, THOMAS R. *Who's Running America? The Conservative Years.* 4th ed. Englewood Cliffs, N.J.: Prentice-Hall, 1986. Taking "the inevitability of elites" in any society as his starting point, Dye examines the socioeconomic characteristics of leaders in twelve sectors: industrial corporations; utilities, transportation and communication; banking; insurance; investments; mass media; law; education; foundations; civic and cultural organizations; government; and the military. He culls information about 7,314 individuals who occupy formal positions of authority in major organizations or institutions in each of these areas. Although some may quibble with the exact listing of leaders, those included control over half the nation's assets in industry, communication, transportation, utilities, banking, and private university endowments. They control over two-thirds of the insurance assets, and nearly 40 percent of the assets of private foundations. Combined with control of the major news agencies, newspaper chains, television networks, and the top executive, legislative, judicial, and military positions, they are indeed a formidable national elite. Dye demonstrates the relative narrowness of the social backgrounds and interactions of members of this elite, but he avoids theorizing about "elitism and hierarchy in American society." Dye leaves it to his readers to relate his data "to their own theories of power in society," an exercise in which the author of this chapter has liberally engaged.

ERIKSON, ROBERT S., NORMAN E. LUTTBEG, AND KENT L. TEDIN. *American Public Opinion: Its Origins, Content, and Impact.* 3d ed. New York: Macmillan, 1988. This book presents a broad introduction to research in the field of public opinion, covering both substance and methods of study. The authors cover questions regarding public opinion and the importance of partisanship and ideology, the impact of the mass media, and the influence of parties, elections, and interest groups. Their discussion focuses upon the role of public opinion in democratic societies and assesses its impact on the formulation of public policy in the United States. Even though greater citizen participation in policymaking is a democratic desideratum, the authors find that many citizens lack interest in and awareness of public affairs. This raises doubts about the practicality and wisdom of providing opportunities for such greater citizen participation, and the authors remain skeptical about whether or not such increased participation would produce better public policies.

MARGOLIS, MICHAEL, AND GARY A. MAU-

SER, EDS. *Manipulating Public Opinion: Essays on Public Opinion as a Dependent Variable*. Pacific Grove, Calif.": Brooks/ Cole, 1989. The sixteen original essays in this book argue that the initiatives of political elites are generally more important than those of mass publics for determining public policy outcomes. The essays emphasize the importance of mass media in linking the opinions of elites to those of ordinary citizens. The book integrates concerns about influencing opinions in elections, in public policy struggles, and over the long term through political socialization and education. The introductory essay sets forth the expected advantages of studying public opinion as a dependent variable, together with the normative implications of this perspective. The substantive chapters employ the perspective in a variety of electoral, policy, and long-term contexts. In the concluding essay the editors provide an empirical and normative assessment of the results, and they outline a theory of the role of public opinion in modern democracies.

IV

INTEREST GROUPS AND POLITICAL PARTIES

Which Provides the Most Effective Vehicle for Democratic Representation: Interest Groups or Political Parties?

The ideal of democratic government is supported by nearly all Americans, including the authors of these essays. The question explored in this section is which of two institutions is most suitable for making government truly responsive to the needs of the people as a whole.

In his essay "Interest Groups and Democratic Representation" Professor Bosso argues that our electoral system provides too limited a choice—between only two parties—and the losers, even though they may be almost as numerous as the winners, are totally shut out. Fortunately, in his view, there is the alternative for the losers: the interest-group process.

For years commentators have bemoaned the relatively low (and declining) rates of participation in our elections, as well as the growing presence of interest groups and their influence on public policy. Bosso declares that the voters are not fools; they know that electoral participation has little direct influence on the policies that officeholders adopt. The choice between the Democratic and Republican parties (which he compares to a choice between vanilla and French vanilla) is not terribly meaningful. Moreover, our constitutional systems and laws are structured to perpetuate this state of affairs. We shut out of electoral politics those who speak for interests not near the center because a winner-take-all electoral system allows only the moderate parties to win office. Nevertheless, the American people know that by organizing for specific purposes, they can make themselves felt and persuade their elected representatives to respond.

Walter Stone does not find our parties perfect nor interest groups without merit. Rather, he argues in his essay, "The Parties and Electoral Democracy," that on the whole our political parties provide the more democratic and realistic vehicles for popular control. He says that we must accept people as they are and not as we might like them to be in some idealized version of democracy. Voters do not and will not, in fact, devote most of their waking hours to careful study of the philosophies of the parties but will judge the parties by the results they produce. If the Republicans are in power and are seen as doing a good job, the voters will reelect them; if not, they will "switch brands," just as an auto buyer will not repurchase a make that has failed to perform properly. Further, Stone finds that the most effective groups are those that represent the well-off; groups that respond to and represent business and commercial interests have far and away the most influence in government. Only elections allow all to participate on an equal footing; to rely on group politics for democratic governance is to grant unequal influence to the most powerful among us.

The reader might ask, does it matter at what level a group operates or the kind of issue it addresses? Is it conceivable that groups organized around local issues are more representative than those that operate in Washington? Is it possible that grass roots groups involved with specific issues are more effective than those meant to address a broad spectrum of issues, which perhaps are better addressed by the parties?

It is also reasonable to begin to raise questions linking these essays with earlier ones. What is the connection, for example, between the criticisms Bosso levels at our institutions and those discussed by Blessing in his proposal supporting a parliamentary system? Does Stone's contention that the parties are broadly effective reinforce McAdams's argument that public opinion is a check on policymakers?

Interest Groups and Democratic Representation

Christopher J. Bosso
Northeastern University

We Americans are ill-served by our political parties. They never have worked particularly well, even during their supposed glory days in the nineteenth century, and we are doomed to perpetual disappointment if we look today to our parties to reflect accurately the sheer diversity of this vast land and its many peoples. Not only do the parties not mirror the vibrancy of this society, they *cannot* do so.

This sad reality exists not because the parties are run by small-minded political hacks—though they sometimes are—but simply because the framers of the Constitution created a political system that does not allow parties to fulfill their democratic purpose. The same document that we revere as the supreme example of the power of enlightened thought nowhere even mentions parties specifically, an omission that speaks volumes about the founders' intentions. By extension, any parties that do emerge are woefully inadequate means for linking citizens with those who govern.

Voters seem to have absorbed the message that their party system fails to guarantee democratic representation. The percentage of Americans who consider themselves strong Democrats or strong Republicans has eroded badly during the past thirty years. Fewer voters swear any consistent allegiance to a party; instead, many base their electoral choices primarily on pet issues or the characteristics of individual candidates. What is more, ever lower percentages of those eligible to vote are turning out come election day, indicating at a minimum that great segments of the public regard elections as hollow exercises.

Compare, however, this dismal state of affairs to what is happening elsewhere on the political landscape. More citizens than ever organize or belong to interest groups at all levels of the political system. Thousands of organizations, ranging from business associations to welfare rights groups, proliferate in both Washington and the state capitals. Grass roots political activism continues to surge, as it has consistently since the early 1960s. Citizen groups push ever more ballot initiatives to bypass elected officials and imprint the public's will directly on government policy. It indeed is a far more vibrant scene, a picture of a citizenry confident in its political efficacy and determined to shape its future with its own hands.

This tale of two types of political organizations argues emphatically that interest groups, not parties, more directly and more accurately serve the public good. Interest groups are the present and future of democratic representation in the United States; political parties are the always inadequate past. Our task as a people thus is both to remove societal and legal obstacles to interest group formation for any part of this society and to ensure that the structures of government decision making are open to as many voices as possible. If we do so, the natural proclivity of Americans to rouse themselves to defend their needs and demands will take over. Interest groups may not serve the public good per-

fectly, but they certainly are more effective vehicles for democratic representation than any political party can be under our Constitution.

PARTIES AND WINNER-TAKE-ALL ELECTIONS

Interest groups and political parties do not exist in separate worlds. There is only so much "space" in any political system, so interest groups and parties jostle with one another for advantage, or even dominance. But that space is not some open plain, free of barriers or boundaries. It is, instead, a maze constructed by the Constitution and embedded with rules of the game by which all players must abide. And, upon examination, the rules of the game erode the capacity of political parties to do anything but compete in election contests, which, despite anything Professor Stone claims, themselves are increasingly suspect mechanisms for linking citizen opinions to public policy.

Parties in the United States always have existed for one simple purpose—to win elections—a reality that colors everything about them, their very size and breadth, their structures and internal dynamics. The Constitution makes it so, and what the constitutionally created election system mandates is that candidates from two political parties—Democrats and Republicans—*alone* have any credible chance to win any given election contest at any given level of government at any given time. Think about this for a moment: a nation of almost 250 million people, a citizenry characterized by virtually every type of race, ethnic, and religious background, occupation, and substantive interest, has but two political parties that are worth anything in the practical sense! Two, and no more. If the political realm can be likened to a marketplace, as Stone suggests, then the party system must be ripe for antitrust action.

This stunning reality has little to do with some quaint tradition or with some odd wrinkle in our national temperament predisposing us only to these two ancient behemoths. After all, we have plenty of third parties, a term that itself says a lot about how the two major parties dominate both our political agenda and our terminology. Our electoral choices are distilled to but two options because our Constitution and two centuries of biased statutory tinkering have constructed a formal system of elections that eventually sluices all voters into but two big camps.

To be precise, U.S. political parties are the creatures of an election system based on the simple principle that only one candidate in any contest can win. Everybody else simply loses because the winner-take-all system allows for no partial victories. Combine this with the plurality rule, by which the winner is determined simply by who gets the most votes, and the picture gets a bit clearer. For example, if Smith gets 45 percent of the vote in a senatorial contest and Martignetti gets 46 percent, Smith loses simply because another candidate got more votes. Smith did pretty well—45 percent of the total vote is nothing to be embarrassed about—but that is of small consolation: Smith *still* lost. Martignetti goes to the Senate; Smith goes home. There is no middle ground.

Those who supported Smith for all intents and purposes *also* have lost because their candidate, a person backed for ardent issue or ideological reasons, has come up short. What is more, Smith's supporters may not feel that Martignetti will adequately represent their interests once in office. This perception rings especially true when the constituency in question is divided sharply by race, class, or ideology, where the winners differ distinctly from the losers. Suppose a race for the U.S. House of Representatives has two contenders, one white and one black. Suppose also that the House district in question is exactly 51 percent white and 49 percent black. If all whites back the white candidate and all blacks support the black contender— not a totally hypothetical scenario if U.S. political history is any guide—it is obvious that almost half of the electorate will feel left out after election day.

If this happens repeatedly, and if the white incumbent feels no need to reach out to black voters (perhaps out of fear of a white backlash), it also is likely that blacks will feel progressively disenfranchised from the political system. They probably will stop voting, thus ensuring that a large chunk of the electorate will not have its voice heard. That the percentage of Americans who vote regularly has dropped dramatically during the past three decades suggests just how alienated many citizens have come to feel about an election system that apparently fails to suit their needs. It no longer is just a hypothetical case.

PARTIES AND PROPORTIONAL REPRESENTATION

Whatever the ramifications for voter turnout, the premium for candidates and their parties in the U.S. system is to win; coming in second is worthless. This brutal reality determines why the United States has only two political parties capable of winning elections. A small party (the Citizens' party, for example) may be able to harvest 10 percent of the vote in some contest, but probably will get naught for all of its efforts. That is fine so long as party loyalists care more about ideology or issue positions than about winning, but most people in politics eventually *do* want to win, do want at least to get the chance to put their views to the test. To do this, they must essentially subordinate themselves to some larger and more encompassing organization, an entity capable of victory in a winner-take-all election. What inevitably results is a two-party system.

Suppose we have three well-defined political parties, each of which consistently attracts the following percentage of the voters under winner-take-all plurality rules: Business, 45 percent; Labor, 35 percent; Farmers, 20 percent. Assuming that the three parties remain intact and do not join into coalitions, it is obvious that the Business party will win every time, even though it does not have a majority of all votes. The Labor and Farmers parties thus face a dilemma: stay separate and win nothing, or sacrifice their individuality to win on the strength of their combined votes. The latter choice assumes that Laborites and Farmers are not so ideologically distant that they cannot cooperate, but U.S. history is filled with examples where the oddest of bedfellows have stuck together. Franklin Roosevelt's New Deal coalition of northern liberals, southern conservatives, urban ethnic Catholics, blacks, and Jews was one of the more fragile amalgamations imaginable, but it hung together for over thirty years on little more than a simple common desire to dominate and run government. Not until the late 1960s, when the forces that bound it together gave way to new issues that provoked sharp division (for example, civil rights, Vietnam), did the New Deal coalition fall apart.

The lesson is clear: The electoral system provides every incentive conceivable for smaller political factions to band together into larger and more potent voting blocs. When one bloc emerges, as it eventually will under winner-take-all rules, all remaining opponents must either join it or become part of another bloc to ensure some representation and forestall continual defeat. This dynamic of preelection coalition building almost always produces a two-party system in which the main parties are relatively large and internally diverse blocs of interests tied together largely by the desire to win.

Think about what U.S. politics might look like under an election system in which parties win a percentage of seats in the national legislature proportionate to their percentage of the total vote in a national election. Such a proportional-representation system would have the opposite effect on parties than does the current system because it actually would allow smaller and more ideological parties to thrive, to attain a share of governing power equal to their electoral success. Parties under a proportional-representation system have fewer incentives to abandon their distinctive identities and join with other parties before an election. They instead compete strenuously to win a percentage of the seats in the legislature and *then* work to construct a dominant legislative coalition if no single party wins a majority of seats. Coalition building in such electoral systems thus takes place *after* the election.

The ultimate problem with proportional representation is its tendency to produce *too much* electoral competition, to spawn too many small parties or factions. It is less likely under such circumstances that any single party will attain a large enough majority to govern by itself. This condition, in turn, can produce political instability because a government based on a coalition of parties tends to fall apart when even the smallest partner in the ruling coalition defects to the other side. When this happens, a new government must be formed, often after a new round of national elections.

It comes as no surprise that many Western European parliamentary systems, having suffered a high degree of political instability during the mid-twentieth century, abandoned pure proportional elections in favor of modified winner-take-all systems. In the process, of course, smaller political parties were forced to join with one another or, more frequently, with the larger parties, to ensure that some party members would get elected. The net impact in virtually every case has been to shift coalition building to the preelection phase, which eventually transformed relatively freewheeling multiparty systems into more stable two-party or two-bloc systems, just as in the United States.

The United States never had proportional representation, essentially because the founders feared the potential instability in government that might ensue with too many political factions. Although they could not remove the causes of faction without undermining the freedom of Americans to speak and assemble freely, the founders did create an election system designed to blunt the possible effects. By creating a system that forces coalitions to form before elections, the founders sacrificed true competition and meaningful representation of interests in favor of political stability and national cohesion. Imagine a United States with a pure proportional-representation system, in which liberals, conservatives, farmers, workers, antiabortionists, environmentalists, and business interests (to name but a few) all had separate political parties, and it is easy to see why the founders went in the other direction. In promoting stability and cohesion, of course, the founders consciously or unconsciously tamped down on

more open representation through the electoral arena.

TWEEDLEDUM AND TWEEDLEDEE

We are stuck with two dominant parties because our election system makes it so. This actually is good for the parties because it simplifies political debate and certainly makes voting easier for many citizens. But this system wherein the Democrats and the Republicans continuously jockey for position is pitifully narrow for true representation. Both parties must be large and broad enough to make winning possible, which forces them to move somewhat toward the great center of politics, where most voters allegedly are. Both thus must temper their ideological appeals—if such sizable aggregates of interests can be said to share a unified ideology—and rein in their various constituencies to appeal to as many voters as possible. Smaller parties, of course, can retain their ideological distinctiveness, but they cannot win.

The two parties thus often act like Tweedledee and Tweedledum during general elections, each trying hard not to move too far outside a decidedly narrow ideological spectrum. But this does not mean that Democrats and Republicans are equally open to all societal needs and views. To assume that interests such as labor or business shop around between the two major parties for the better deal is ridiculous. They usually have little choice because one party is bound to be totally hostile to their views. Labor unions, for example, tend to find a friendlier reception in the Democratic party, just as business groups tend to gravitate to the Republican. In this sense, both interests are going to their ideological homes; labor unions have never found life all that comfortable in the Republican party, and business groups tend to find among Democrats too many other interests not wholly friendly to commerce. Blacks and environmentalists typically perceive Republicans as hostile to their needs, and conservative Christians lately are repelled by Democrats as a matter of course. And so it goes down the line.

Still, the two major political parties are neither merely accumulations of nor captive to special interests, despite any rhetoric you hear in election years. It actually is pretty much the other way around when party leaders are savvy enough to realize it. Most organized interests are instead captives of a two-party system in which the choices between parties are extremely limited and where party needs supersede those of any constituent group. Party leaders enjoy tremendous leverage to force interest groups to swallow their particular agendas on behalf of party unity and victory because the groups usually have nowhere else to go. The Democrats in 1988 offered a particularly good example, with environmental, civil rights, housing, education, and liberal foreign policy activists all forced to accede to the demands of the party and its presidential nominee. The Republican party, though more homogeneous and narrower as a party, similarly imposed constraints on its various conservative groups. In both cases the party leaders, not the constituent interests, won out. After all, it is the two parties and their candidates, not the interest groups, that compete for victory, so the parties dictate how the game will be played. The groups, for their part, either join in loyally or defect, though they more often than not drop entirely out of the electoral sphere because the other party is no more accommodating to their views.

What is more, the party organizations and what they produce hardly represent a cross-section of society. If Stone castigates interest groups for being dominated by the more affluent and more educated, how can the parties escape the same criticism? The 1988 presidential nominating conventions of the major parties are but one case in point. Delegates to both conventions tended to be more educated, affluent, and distinctly ideological than most citizens. Delegates were far more likely to be white-collar professionals (teachers and lawyers, for example), business elites, or politicians than average working-class persons. Democratic delegates were far more liberal than the average voter; Republicans were far more conservative. The Democrats at least tried to ensure that their delegates represented a rough cross-section of the society in racial and gender terms—51 percent of the delegates to the 1988 convention were female; 22 percent were nonwhite—but delegates to the 1988 Republican convention were 74 percent male and 96 percent white.[1] Neither party could assert that it provided adequate representation of all voices.

Look also at the fruits that the electoral and party systems bear nationwide. Congress and state legislatures alike are dominated overwhelmingly by middle-aged white males, hardly representative of a society where more than half its citizens are female and about one-fifth are nonwhite. The U.S. Senate in 1988 had no blacks and but two women among its one hundred members, and the much larger U.S. House of Representatives was only marginally better.[2] Many sectors of this society may look to the electoral system and its winners to represent their needs and views, but pitifully few actually get included.

The parties thus control the electoral space. By reducing elections to simple choices between two big players, the electoral system effectively stamps down the "mischiefs of faction," but in the process distills the vibrant diversity of America into deadening blandness. It produces candidates who mouth the same middle-of-the-road platitudes, and gives us representatives far removed from the needs and experiences of too many citizens. Smaller groups or constituencies, especially those not part of the vaunted middle of the road, are particularly hurt by this dynamic, for their needs simply get lost amidst the major-party jockeying and the needs of party leaders to placate the mainstream of the electorate. Small wonder that whole sectors of the voting population are staying away from the polling places; they feel disenfranchised from an electoral system that produces mushy politics and ignores their more specific needs.

THE RISE OF INTEREST GROUPS

The political parties may be electoral juggernauts, but they are fundamentally weak in one critical respect: They do not govern. They only help to get their people into elected positions. In parliamentary systems, by contrast, the party that wins the majority of seats in the national legislature actually *becomes* the government, and the head of the majority party in parliament becomes the prime minister. There is no separation of powers, as in the United States, and the parties thus have every incentive to remain cohesive. It also comes as no surprise that interest groups in parliamentary systems are relatively dependent on the parties for access to government because governing power is placed in party hands. Where parties are strong, interest groups are weak; parties dominate both the electoral *and* the governing domains.

Where parties are made weak, as in the United States, interest groups are more numerous, stronger, and more independent because the parties do not dominate governing. Thanks to the founders, U.S. parties enjoy no constitutional role in setting up and running the show after the election is over but instead cede ground to governing institutions. The framers of the Constitution created a system whereby Congress and the president are elected separately, neither institution completely controls the other, and members of Congress owe their primary allegiance not to their parties but to their constituents. Members of Congress can go against their parties and still get reelected; the parties can do relatively little about it because constituents, not parties, vote. Members of Congress who go against their constituents in favor of their parties often discover this truth to their dismay.

Because U.S. parties do not govern, they really are overgrown weaklings that do not and cannot dominate the political space once the election is over. Because the parties cannot govern, it is irrational for any group of citizens to rely totally on the party system to push their particular issues. There is a good chance that neither party will even listen, much less adopt their causes, and there certainly is no guarantee that party platforms will mean anything after election day. Parties do not govern, so their platforms, and their promises, are structures of straw, likely to be blown away at the first change in the political winds.

Citizens over the past three decades have taken these lessons to heart and increasingly have decided that parties are irrelevant to their specific policy goals and local needs. Not only have Americans in droves abandoned the election system, they have taken matters into their own hands. Their participatory impulses have been transformed into organized interest groups, their efforts deflected away from electoral politics and directed increasingly at influencing those who occupy the seats of government power. The exponential growth of the interest group community is a perfectly rational response to the perceived hollowness of party politics.

Interest groups emerge essentially because like-minded citizens seek some organized means to express their common views and to press their common demands directly on those who make public policy. This makes perfect sense. Most of us would rather work and socialize with those who share our outlooks and interests. We feel less comfortable with persons whose views and demands oppose our own. We also realize that we cannot easily get access to or service from government officials—elected or otherwise—if we operate solely as individuals.

Save for the most local of agencies or offices, government today is a complex and depersonalized beast, and the lone citizen has little real chance for success. We of common interests and outlooks thus join together into some group, with varying degrees of formal organization, funding, and activity, to make our views and demands known in government. Wheat growers naturally organize to seek federal subsidies, and teachers assemble to promote educational issues. Citizens who care passionately about the environment, or about steel imports, or about animal research, eventually find one another and organize to maximize their numbers. Individually, citizens are but minuscule voices in the body politic, but together they can make great sounds.

And it matters remarkably little to those who band together for common purposes which party dominates Congress or which persons sit in particular congressional seats. Most interest group activity is decidedly separate from parties and elections because what matters most is whether or not the groups can gain access to decision makers and wield some influence over the crafting of their particular slice of national or local policy. Labor unions may gravitate more naturally to Democrats, but they can live with Republicans as long as their views are heard. They may not get so welcome a greeting, which obviously would motivate them to get more Democrats elected, but they do get attention. The same goes for any number and types of organized interests: party labels, and partisan attachments, lose much of their meaning once the election is over.

THE VOICE OF THE INTEREST GROUP IS HEARD IN OUR LAND

Why would any Republican in Congress listen to labor union requests or complaints from environmentalists in the first place? Why would a Democratic senator, who ideologically may favor consumers, listen sympathetically to the needs of business groups? The answer lies in the very structure of our system of government. It is a system characterized by fragmentation of governing authority, by locally elected representatives serving in a national legislature, by a separation of powers that cripples political parties but nourishes interest groups. The AFL-CIO, for example, is a powerful voice for labor because of its sheer size, but its influence in Congress depends less on its overall numbers than on *where* its constituent local unions are located. Members of Congress who have active labor unions in their districts or states are more likely, regardless of party, to at least listen to local labor initiatives. To turn a deaf ear is to alienate possible voters, a cardinal sin to any member of Congress seeking reelection. Members of Congress from rural areas obviously thus will curry favor with farm organizations, and those whose districts contain a high number of retirees will be more sensitive to issues concerning the elderly.

The localism embedded in congressional politics makes this dynamic possible because the first thing on the mind of any member of Congress is whether the group in question is a force among voters at home. If so, party or ideology does not matter. The member will listen, and will deliver, if that group can wield some influence among constituents. It comes as no surprise, for example, that groups opposing U.S. involvement in Vietnam fared much better when they organized by congressional district—and recruited middle-class parents of draft-age youths—than when students demonstrated at party conventions or tried to influence presidential elections. Even members of Congress supporting the war found themselves listening when concerned constituents came calling, and more than one member changed sides because of strong antiwar sentiment back home.

Citizens of course understand well this primary rule of congressional life and work diligently to mobilize at the grass roots, at the level where it most influences legislative behavior. And the grass roots are very fertile indeed. Americans over the past few decades have become more interested in practical politics and more aware of how government decisions affect everyday life. We are frustrated by the apparent inability or unwillingness of party organizations to address our needs, cynical about elections that seem only to produce candidates who care more about reelection than good public policy, and ever less ready to rely passively on elected representatives to protect our interests. We are, however, as a people more confident about our individual capacities to make a difference, and exhibit an ever greater desire to participate directly in influencing public policy.

And why not? The cost of organizing like-minded fellow citizens and promoting common concerns to those who make policy decisions certainly is a lot more reasonable than fighting largely fruitless electoral battles. The same decentralization of the U.S. system of government that frustrates party control in fact allows even a small group of citizens to have some influence over particular issues or programs. A determined band of activists—even though their numbers are few—can effectively stop the construction of a power plant by relying on the media and public opinion, by generating citizen pressure on government officials to intervene on their side. It makes less sense for them to rely on party organizations because there is little guarantee that the electoral route will even address their needs.

It thus is more strategically rational to organize fellow citizens and complain directly. If the federal bureaucracy seems deaf to your entreaties, seek out your member of Congress or go to court. Civil rights groups, environmental and consumer activists, antiabortion advocates, and numerous other interests have discovered that parties and elections are less useful than lawsuits, television coverage, or citizen mail to policymakers. Many groups also become active in party politics, primarily to help elect legislators sympathetic to their causes, but these strategies largely are secondary to direct action. There is no *need* in most cases to await elections to get what you want, and citizens across the land seem to have realized the lesson well.

Not only are interest groups more effective means for promoting diverse citizen causes, the interest group community itself certainly is a lot more open and diverse than the party system ever will be. From welfare recipients and gays to small businesses and religious groups, many sectors of society long shunted aside by the parties have discovered how easy it is to play the interest group game. The sheer explosion in the range and number of registered lobbyists, professional associations, and citizen groups evident in both Washington and the state capitals during the past twenty years attests this dynamic. So dramatic and so deep has been this participatory surge that today it is hard to imagine *any* segment of this society not represented somehow by at least one organized interest group. Try making the same claim for our political parties.

SUMMING UP

The tapestry that is the United States is far more colorful and vibrant than the two-party system and its restrictive elections can ever reflect accurately. What the parties represent instead is a dull monochrome, the blurry grayness of a narrow middle spectrum of political ideology and values. Any argument that the parties bind this nation and its people into a common good, that they somehow provide the tie that binds, is misleading at best and a complete lie at worst. What weaves diverse and energetic Americans into one nation are the institutions of government created by the Constitution, Congress in particular. And that is the way the founders intended, for they distrusted the potential tyranny of large majorities over those left on the outside. They did not want party government, nor do their descendants two hundred years later.

What is clear is that the thousands of interest groups more accurately and fairly represent the myriad needs and causes that motivate Americans in everyday life. It is in the conflict among these groups that truer democratic representation takes place. It is in Congress and the other institutions of government, at all levels of the political system, where these groups come together regularly to promote their views, seek compromises, and influence the directions of public policy. Interest groups are the rational answers of a people not content to act merely as passive voters but intent on practicing their daily roles as citizens. The nation as a whole is better served in the end.

If, as Stone argues, the health of democracy depends on competitive elections, then U.S. democracy is sickly. Our elections are competitive only insofar as voters get to choose between vanilla and French vanilla: a slight variation in flavor but not much of a selection. Few consumers would willingly patronize a store where the choices were so limited.

But, if democratic representation can be construed as resulting from the proliferation and everyday activities of thousands of smaller groups, each speaking for an equally important piece of the body politic, then we can be more certain that democratic politics is alive and flourishing. Democracy lives not in the machinations and contortions of two flabby behemoths grappling like electoral sumo wrestlers in their constricted ring but in the everyday tumult of the marketplace of thousands of groups and millions of citizens. It is a noisy, disorganized, fragmented, and fractious place, but its sounds are those of a free people seeking their democratic destinies. So be it.

NOTES

1. For data on the characteristics of delegates to the 1988 Democratic National Convention, see the *New York Times*, July 17, 1988, p. 1; for data on the delegates to the 1988 Republican National Convention, see the *Boston Globe*, August 15, 1988, p. 10.

2. Norman Ornstein et al., *Vital Statistics on Congress, 1987–1988.* (Washington, D.C.: American Enterprise Institute, 1988), pp. 35–36.

SUGGESTED READINGS

BERRY, JEFFREY. *The Interest Group Society.* 2d ed. Boston: Little, Brown, 1989. A short, very readable text on interest group politics in the United States. Berry discusses the various theories about interest group power, the explosion in the number and range of groups in the past three decades, the relations between groups and political parties, and the connections among groups, policymakers, and citizens.

LADD, EVERETT CARLL. *Where Have All the Voters Gone?* New York: Norton, 1982. A well-argued examination of the past several decades of parties and elections, in which declining voter turnout and the erosion of support for either of the political parties among voters manifest the weaknesses of the party system in the United States. Weak parties and unstable voting coalitions, Ladd argues, are unsuited for successful governance.

MANSBRIDGE, JANE. *Why We Lost the ERA.* Chicago: University of Chicago Press, 1986. An insightful examination of the grass roots organizations that emerged to fight for and against the adoption of the Equal Rights Amendment to the U.S. Constitution. This book is useful particularly for its discussion of how like-minded individuals unite to form organized interest groups, and the problems these groups face in mobilizing members and pursuing their goals.

The Parties and Electoral Democracy: Solving the Problem of Participation

Walter J. Stone

University of Colorado at Boulder

If I announce to my family that we are going to have a "good" dinner this evening, my children may think of hamburgers and french fries while my wife and I have more balanced fare in mind. In similar fashion, the concept of democratic government is susceptible to many different interpretations. Some define as democratic a political system that encourages the greatest possible participation by its citizens. Others emphasize economic equality as the defining characteristic of democracy. Still others link democracy to values such as equal opportunity, political competition, or free association and social diversity. A case can be made for any of these as defining characteristics of democracy. In this essay, I define *democracy* as a system of government that depends upon the consent of its citizens participating as equals in regular and competitive elections, and that enables its citizens to fix responsibility for the results of governmental actions. My thesis is that political parties are the institutions best suited to achieve this sort of democracy in contemporary American politics.

This definition of *democracy* emphasizes a division of labor between citizens who must consent to the government, and those in government who represent the interests of citizens who choose them. In a *representative* democracy of this sort, the government is not the people. The government is made up of only a few citizens who represent the people. Representative government works if the government is compelled to respond to the interests of the people. Elections force the government to attend to the people's interests because officeholders must satisfy those interests or be booted from office. In addition, elections further the democratic goal of political equality because citizens participate as equals (one person, one vote). This kind of equality is not realized anywhere else in the political process. Finally, when parties compete for control of government, elections are the means of registering popular consent and promoting political responsibility.

In contrast to my emphasis on equality and political responsibility, Professor Bosso's defense of interest groups rests on a conception of democracy that stresses social, economic, and political diversity. There is no doubt that American society is diverse, and that the variety of interests found in it gives rise to many groups clamoring for government to respond to their special interests. I agree with Bosso that these groups must be allowed to press their claims on government. However, to build one's ideal of democracy on such groups is to establish serious political inequalities at the center of government, to fragment national institutions beyond hope of coherence, and to frustrate genuine political responsibility to the larger public that democracy is supposed to serve.

To understand the case for parties and against groups, we must begin with the citizen in a large democracy. We must cut away the myths surrounding the role of the citizen and understand the problem of participation, a problem that burdens all forms of popular participation whether in elections contested by parties or in interest groups.

THE PROBLEM OF VOTING PARTICIPATION

The idea that elections enable citizens to participate as equals, registering their consent (or discontent) with the government, sounds good. The idea that governmental leaders are forced to be responsible to the people through the accountability brought about by regular, competitive elections also sounds good. But there is a problem. The problem, as democratic thinkers have known for a long time, is especially acute in large nations where millions of people are called upon to vote in national elections. In such systems, each individual voter's contribution to the outcome is a negligible drop in the bucket. To appreciate the implications of this problem, run the following mind experiment on the 1988 presidential election. Imagine all the speeches, the debates, the television advertising, the encouragements to vote, the hoopla, and then on election day, you vote. George Bush is the winner. Now rerun the 1988 presidential campaign once more. Imagine again all the speeches, the debates, the television advertising, the encouragements to vote, the hoopla. This time, however, on election day you stay home. Who wins? Bush wins. Indeed, you can run this experiment for any large election, such as for a U.S. Senate seat, a governor's chair, or even a U.S. House of Representatives seat. In every case, the mind experiment should achieve the same results: your individual participation as a voter does not determine the outcome of the election. If you were to stay at home, the election outcome would be exactly the same.

The candidates would not notice that you had stayed home, nor (alas) would they care. The winner of an election assumes the burdens of office while the loser licks his or her wounds, perhaps to return to fight another day. But whether or not you vote, dear reader, has no effect on the outcome.[1]

Whenever I make this argument to my students, I encounter resistance and even hostility. It flies in the face of assertions about U.S. democracy made every day (especially during election campaigns) that "your vote matters." Students also leap to the conclusion that I am arguing that because one person's vote does not determine the outcome of an election, I am also saying elections don't matter. So let's be clear: One person's vote is like a drop in the bucket. Its presence or absence in the whole will not be noticed or missed. But that does *not* mean the bucket is of no importance. The bucket of water can still be used to quench the fire even if one drop is removed. Of course, if *all* drops are removed, the bucket is empty and of no use. In the same way, elections are very important in determining who governs, even if each voter individually has no meaningful influence on the outcome. Take away one voter, and the election remains just as effective in determining the winner and establishing a government. Take away all the voters, and the election fails.

So elections can matter without each individual's vote determining the outcome. Thousands and millions of votes matter a great deal; one vote more or less does not. In the same way, blocs of votes (the union vote, the black or Hispanic vote, the women's vote) can also matter a great deal without any individual labor union member, black or Hispanic, or woman mattering in deciding the result.

Understanding this problem of participation is absolutely essential to understanding democracy in a large nation. The reason can be seen with another mind experiment. Take the example of a U.S. House election. Rerun in your mind the last U.S. House election in your home district. Did you vote? Did you have much information about the choice you made? In the average House district in 1986, when there was no presidential election, almost two-thirds of the eligible voters failed to vote. Of those who voted, the vast majority did so without much information about the candidates they were choosing.[2] Almost no one in the electorate could say what the candidates stood for, or what they had done when they were in office. So if you did not vote, or if you voted without much information about the choice you were making, you had plenty of company.

Now rerun the 1986 House election in your mind again and assume that you and you alone have the power to choose the next representative from your district. You must choose between the Democratic and the Republican nominees. Would you vote? Would you have more information about the choice you were making? You almost certainly would vote, *and* you would spend a great deal more time in getting information to make your choice.

The problem of voting participation is this: It is not reasonable to invest much time or effort in making a choice when the impact of that choice is very small or nonexistent. When the impact of the choice is great, the effort invested in making it is correspondingly much greater. Most reasonable people, to give another example, invest much more time and effort in the details of their private lives—their careers, their personal choices like raising a family, their private purchases—than they do in making public choices like voting. In their private choices, their effort is rewarded because the more they invest in their decisions, the better their life will be. But in voting, effort is not rewarded by a better outcome, because an individual vote doesn't influence the outcome. A citizen's vote has precisely the same effect (none) on the outcome whether he or she has spent a great deal of time and effort or none at all on deciding how to vote. Knowing this, most people don't commit much effort to their voting choice.

Does all of this mean that a democracy, based on popular elections designed to force leaders to be responsible to those who elect them, cannot work? Democracy is not ruled out by the problem of participation, but it certainly is made more difficult. For example, it is frequently charged that candidates take advantage of an indifferent citizenry by engaging in superficial appeals, promising more than they can deliver, and relying upon slick, media-based campaigns. There is truth in this picture of contemporary campaigns, but we must be careful not to blame the victim. Voters are not well informed about politics because they have too many other ways to spend their time and effort. Democracy must be made to work for people as they are, not as we might wish them to be in some idealized fantasy world where everyone reads the *Congressional Record* and spends all day long talking about politics.[3] What is needed is a way for citizens to make choices in politics that reflect their best interests without expecting them to invest heavily in the choice.

There are two schools of thought about how to escape the participation problem I have described. Both schools recognize that the problem creates a serious difficulty for democratic government. Both depend upon intermediaries between government and citizen to help connect the citizen to what is going on in government. Those who emphasize the importance of political parties in this intermediary role may be labeled *party theorists*. Bosso and others who look to interest groups to play this key role are *group theorists*. They deemphasize the importance of elections because groups are not especially comfortable in the highly public and visible electoral arena. They enter it when they must and then only reluctantly (such as by endorsing a candidate, or by forming political action committees [PACs] and contributing money to candidates).

POLITICAL PARTIES AS THE BASIS OF DEMOCRACY

Party theorists emphasize two values as critical to their conception of democracy: equality and responsibility. Political equality is achieved when every citizen has an equal say in what government does. This sort of equality is impossible to achieve in practice, but because elections are based on the principle of one citizen, one vote, they force those in government to attend to a broad constituency (that is, the one that elected them) and promote the ideal of equal political influence for all citizens. Political parties are organizations that seek to control government by winning elections. They nominate candidates they think will appeal to the electorate, they generate support for those candidates, and they try to promote policies when in government to help them win the next time. In contrast to Bosso's assertions, this is exactly what we want: political parties striving with all their might to win elections. We do *not* want parties committed primarily to narrow ideological stands, although both the major parties are in fact quite different in their ideological interests. When parties seek to win elections, they promote political responsibility in a way that helps solve the problem of participation. To see this, consider how responsibility works in the marketplace.

When a woman purchases a new automobile, it comes with a label. The label permits her to hold Ford Motor Company (or General Motors or Toyota) responsible for how the car runs. If the car does not perform up to her expectations, she tries a different brand when it comes time to buy another. If the Ford works well and she is satisfied, she buys another Ford. Automakers know that they are "responsible" in this sense, and therefore do everything they can to make a car that will measure up to consumer expectations. This works whether or not the consumer knows very much about how cars are made or the differences between Toyotas and Fords. All the consumer need know is how well her car worked to know whether she wants to buy the same brand again or change brands.

Voters are like the consumer and the parties are like the automakers. Voters, we have seen, ordinarily cannot be expected to have detailed information about where the candidates stand on issues of foreign policy, the balance of trade, crime fighting, economic prosperity, education, and so on. Expecting voters to have detailed information of this sort would be like expecting consumers to know how best to reduce gas mileage. Some have opinions on such matters, but most defer to the experts while retaining the right to judge the results. Just as consumers form an opinion about whether the fuel economy of their new Chevys is reasonable, so also voters can be ex-

pected to form an opinion about the state of the domestic economy. If the economy seems not to be working very well, voters can change "brands." To do so, they need know only that the economy is not doing well (information that is readily available) and which political party is in charge. The party label is on the ballot (along with the names of the candidates), so the decision facing the voter is immensely simplified if party responsibility can be fixed. If the voters judge that things are going well under the Republicans, they quite reasonably "buy" another four years from that brand. They need not worry about *why* things are going well. If, on the other hand, the economy is down, or if world peace is in jeopardy, they can vote to change parties, holding the Republicans responsible for failing to produce desirable outcomes. Voters who choose on the basis of party performance need not keep track of dozens of different candidates at the national, state, and local levels. They need not know who their representative in Congress is, or what he or she has done recently. They need know only how things seem to be going, and blame (or give credit to) the party in charge.

Politicians, like their counterparts who run automobile manufacturing concerns, are aware that they will be held responsible for how well things are going, so they try to produce desirable outcomes. Party theorists emphasize that it is ultimately *parties*, not individual candidates, who must assume this kind of responsibility. Political parties are organizations of men and women committed to the success of their "label" in much the same way that Ford Motor Company is a vast corporation made up of many people working to ensure its success. Just as no single person can build an automobile, no individual can produce policies that will promote peace and prosperity. That is especially true in U.S. politics, where power is shared among different (and often competing) individuals. The result in a fragmented system that divides power among national institutions (president, Congress, Supreme Court) and between the national and state levels is often a lack of direction to policy and an absence of political responsibility. When parties function as they should, Republicans in Congress have an incentive to work with Republicans in the White House and in the state governments to come up with policies that will work. The political fortunes of individual candidates and officeholders are inevitably linked together in the success of their parties when voters can fix responsibility for unpleasant results. Moreover, candidates will not promise more than they can deliver in election campaigns because to do so would only guarantee expectations that would outrun performance.

These happy consequences follow precisely because parties seek with all their might to win elections. In contrast to Bosso's implication, the interest parties have in winning is both desirable and necessary to the larger purposes of democracy. Just as manufacturing concerns like Ford Motor Company need to sell automobiles by satisfying customers who purchase cars, parties seek to attract votes by satisfying their market. The interests of voters are therefore joined with the interests of the party in control of government, and representative government is possible.

In the absence of party responsibility, what happens? When many are involved in making public policy, and the policy fails, it is easy to shift the blame. If unemployment is high, or the national debt pushes inflation upward, presidents blame their colleagues in Congress for not adopting all of their domestic pro-

grams, and members of Congress blame the president and one another. When unemployment and inflation are down, everyone steps forward to claim credit. In such circumstances, is it any wonder that voters are susceptible to slick media appeals, the image makers, and candidate promises to save the world?

PROBLEMS WITH PARTY THEORY

One of the biggest problems with the ideal of party responsibility described above is that it is a very imperfect description of how things actually work in U.S. elections. Some of the features of party theory work well, but some of the most important ones do not. It is true, Bosso's assertions notwithstanding, that the vast majority of voters identify with one or the other of the two parties. In doing so, they make their voting decision easier because they usually vote their party identification. It is also the case that every single representative and senator currently in Congress, the president and his cabinet, and members of the Supreme Court all have well-known partisan affiliations. Thus, it is not difficult to determine which party controls these institutions.

At the same time, there are some notable departures from what party theorists would prefer to see in American national politics. As occurred in 1988 when Republican Bush was elected president only to face a Democratic Congress, it is not at all uncommon to see the parties divide control of our major institutions. When this occurs, voters looking to fix responsibility on the "governing party" have obvious difficulties. The federal budget deficit is a case in point. In 1980 Ronald Reagan ran as a candidate committed to balancing the budget by 1984. He linked the deficit to the so-called "misery index," which combined the unemployment and inflation rates, and charged that the Carter administration (and the Democratic Congress) was inept. Reagan's electoral victory over Carter seemed to give him a mandate to carry out his program of balancing the budget. However, at the same time the Republicans were winning the White House and the Senate in 1980, the Democrats retained their control over the House of Representatives. As a result, Reagan could declare in the 1984 election that his failure to balance the budget was due to the recalcitrance of the Democrats in Congress. By the presidential election of 1988, with record deficits in the federal budget, the issue seemed attractive to Michael Dukakis and the Democrats. They blamed the deficits on Republican mismanagement in the White House, while Bush and the Republicans continued to fault the Democratic Congress: Voters, meanwhile, were left without a clear sense of just whom to blame.

Another major departure from party theory is that individual candidates have relatively few incentives to link their personal careers to the fortunes of their party. Most candidates in U.S. politics get nominated by their own efforts in soliciting money and other support. They contest a primary election that, if they win, gives them the party nomination without the necessary consent of the party leadership. As a result, candidates for office (even if they are already in office) can often escape political responsibility. This is especially true for members of Congress. Because a representative or senator is only one of 535 lawmakers, he or she can insulate himself or herself from unfavorable attitudes toward Congress by criticizing the institution.[4] He or she can also build a personal following that is based on creating a favor-able image, satisfying organized interests in the constituency, and delivering the "pork" to the home district.[5] When faced with a problem like the national deficit, members of Congress have few incentives to promote solutions like raising taxes or cutting programs.

Party theorists see these problems as strengthening, rather than undermining, their case. If fragmented governmental power and divided control of governmental institutions weaken political responsibility, something must be done to restore responsibility to governmental institutions. If individual candidates can insulate themselves from the failures of their institution, if they have incentives to promise the world or emphasize image over substance, these too are major departures from the ideal of responsibility, and something must be done. If citizens cannot easily fix blame or grant credit in their voting, something must be done to restore elections as the centerpiece of contemporary democracy.

The "something" that must be done is to strengthen party organizations. Parties must be strong enough to compete visibly in elections, they must have the resources to impose some degree of discipline over their membership, including candidates who run under their label, and they must be able to exert consistent programmatic influence over what officeholders in the party do in government. As things stand in the American system, individuals in Congress are responsive to the local interests in their districts and states that helped elect them. To be sure, the diversity that results is the basis for the famous checks and balances that define U.S. government, but it also provides a foothold for narrow, special interest groups that frustrate the ability of the parties to sustain a program. Individual officeholders can appeal to their local constituencies as individuals rather than as members of a party committed to a national program. The result is a failure of collective responsibility because office-holders can distance themselves from the unpleasant results of governmental actions. Indeed, parties do not have the resources to address difficult problems like the deficit head-on, and because no one's political career hangs in the balance, the deficit is allowed to continue growing. If responsibility for the deficit and its unhappy consequences could be pinned on the party in control, the parties would have the necessary incentive to make the hard choices needed to address it.

Strengthening the parties does not mean the diversity of the group system would be eliminated, but the *perception* that everyone can win by getting a piece of the action would be reduced. This is all to the good, and hardly amounts to the "disenfranchisement" alluded to by Bosso. In fact, many groups get access to government, but because of the decentralized and fragmented nature of power, losers in the political arena often do not know they are losing. The costs of monitoring what government does are too expensive for all but the well-heeled and highly organized to bear. When a party loses in the visible, public forum of an election, its members know what they have lost, and work all the harder to gain the upper hand next time around. The resulting conflict between the parties draws people—even those without political skills, without organized representation, and without great amounts of information—into the political fray. There will always be winners and losers in politics. In democratic systems, losers are fully aware of their losses and have the wherewithal to do something about it.

THE CASE AGAINST INTEREST GROUPS

Group theory offers a different solution to the problem of participation. Whereas it is true that citizens are not very active or interested in electoral politics, and it certainly is easy to show that levels of information about politics are extremely low, group theorists suggest we look outside the electoral process for the principal means of promoting representative democracy. People are connected to politics through their economic, social, and religious activities, which inevitably draw them into interest groups. Such groups, in turn, represent their members' political interests. Interest groups participate directly as lobbyists in Washington, or as part of associations that involve many groups with similar interests. Groups connect individual citizens to government by informing them of possible governmental actions that may affect their interests, by mobilizing action around issues of concern to the group, and by bearing many of the costs of monitoring what government does in a given policy area.

Group theory depends upon two fundamental propositions in order to make its case: (1) the interest group system includes the broad range of interests in society without significant bias, and (2) interest groups do a tolerably good job of representing the interests of their members. Both propositions are highly suspect in light of available theory and evidence.

First, the group system is not inclusive. That is, interest groups cannot adequately represent to government the full range of interests in society because there is a significant bias in the kinds of interests organized into groups. In his famous indictment of group theory, E. E. Schattschneider put it best:

The notion that the pressure system is automatically representative of the whole community is a myth fostered by the universalizing tendency of modern group theories. *Pressure politics is a selective process* ill designed to serve diffuse interests. The system is skewed, loaded, and unbalanced in favor of a fraction of a minority.[6]

There is ample evidence to back Schattschneider's claim. A recent study found that among groups with representatives in Washington, the vast majority are corporations, trade associations, and other institutions.[7] Kay Schlozman and John Tierney estimate that about 7 percent of the U.S. population in 1980 was employed in managerial and administrative occupations, while a whopping 71 percent of the organizations with Washington representation were corporations and trade, business, or professional associations.[8] Even among so-called membership organizations that rely upon voluntary members who are presumably committed to the group's goals, the bias in participation is strong. A study of the public-interest group Common Cause found that its members were much more highly educated and earned higher incomes than the general public.[9] Bosso correctly points out that delegates to national party conventions are not typical of the larger public in their education and income levels, in their occupations, and in their political attitudes. But he misses the point. Political parties, no matter how unrepresentative activist members are of the public, are formally responsible for their actions through elections.[10] Interest groups are accountable to no one; most often they are not even responsible to their own membership!

The larger reasons for a strong pro-business and upper-status bias in the interest group system are complex. Such interests have readily identifiable claims to press before government. Most important, they can afford to bear the significant costs associated with organizing and monitoring what the fragmented U.S. system of government is doing. Groups that are successful in their economic activity (such as a corporation or a university) pay for most of the costs of organizing out of that economic activity. They have lawyers and public relations experts on their payrolls, and much of their overtly political activity is a byproduct of their primary, economic activity. A political group that may seek to organize against an economic group (an environmental group concerned about toxic waste pollution by a chemicals plant, for example) must organize its efforts from the ground up. It faces the participation problem described above because its potential members may quite reasonably fail to join or pay dues or otherwise support the group's political agenda. Their involvement in the group's effort, after all, is a "drop in the bucket" that cannot possibly determine the success of the interest.[11] Corporations, universities, and other institutions do not face this problem because they directly compensate their "members" out of their economic activity; for example, they pay their employees a salary. The members are therefore directly remunerated for their efforts and need not worry about their contributions to the political goals of the group. As a result, many potential political groups do not form at all, or are significantly undermobilized. Bosso can point to the example of a "determined band of activists" committed to stopping the construction of a power plant. But far and away the most common scenario is one in which well-organized and wealthy corporate interests successfully pursue their interests with no or only token opposition. That's real political power, and only the political parties have the potential to bring to bear the even more significant power associated with the public interest.

The contention that groups represent their members' political interests is also suspect. Unlike political parties, most interest groups have little or no incentive to represent the political preferences of their members. It is true that most citizens are linked to government by virtue of their economic, social, and religious activities, which involve them, at least indirectly, in the interest group system. An employee of a corporation, a student at a university, and a member of a church all are "represented" in some fashion by their economic, educational, and religious affiliations. However, participation in groups of this type is not expressly political. As a result, the group's claims pressed before government need not be responsive to the *political* interests of the membership. A hypothetical example will illustrate the point.

Consider a student upset by his university's stand on a political issue, say, divestment of university funds invested in corporations doing business in South Africa. By becoming a student at the university and paying tuition, the student is supporting the university's activities, including its investment strategies. The student, if extremely interested in the issue, may make known his or her opposition to the university by writing letters to the student newspaper, staging protests, or meeting with administrators. Assume for the sake of argument that a majority of students agrees that the university should divest. Will the university respond by changing its investment strategies? Probably not, especially if administrators believe their investments are economically sound and if they themselves do not agree with the students' opinions. The reason is that few if any students will leave the university and stop paying tui-

tion if the university fails to divest. Students go to the university for an education. They seek a diploma and the accompanying knowledge and status. That's what motivates them to pay their tuition, not the political stance of the university. Thus, if the university fails to offer a quality education, shuts down a student's major, or otherwise fails to deliver on the bargain it has with tuition-paying students, it can expect to lose tuition dollars. But the university will not suffer these effects merely because its political actions differ from those of its membership.

The same can be said for many interest groups that are politically active. Labor unions, churches, and corporations all have implicit or explicit bargains with their members and employees that have little or nothing to do with politics. The group leaders may become active in the political arena, but there is little to ensure that their activity will reflect the interests of their group. In contrast, groups that are explicitly political— groups that, in other words, strike an expressly political bargain with their membership—are much more likely to represent the political interests of their members.[12] But group theorists do not depend on such groups as the basis for their version of democracy. The reason is simple: Most people are not members of groups that are expressly political in their purpose. Most people are involved in interest groups as a result of their economic, religious, educational, or social activities. Groups that strike an economic, religious, educational, or social bargain with their members can be expected to keep the bargain, but they cannot be expected to provide reliable political representation.

The argument for political parties as the basis for democracy rests on a simple insight: Political interests must be activated in order to get represented. Political parties are the institutions best suited to activate political interests in the public. Parties want to win elections so their members can control government. Well organized parties solicit popular support, alert citizens to the stake they have in political conflict, and mobilize them into the electoral arena. Parties do these things because they have powerful interests in doing them. In forming a government following electoral victory, a party makes it possible for citizens to pin responsibility for unfortunate results on those in charge. By first soliciting citizen support and then converting that support into a government, it creates the links between popular choice and governmental action necessary to forge democracy.

Interest groups fail for the reasons that parties can succeed. Interest groups most often do not depend upon the political interests of their members for their existence. They do not necessarily activate those interests, nor do they participate directly in governance. Interest groups become political when they lobby or otherwise press their claims before government, but there is no assurance they act on the interests of their memberships. Even if they do represent their memberships, they almost never can claim a broad popular mandate of the sort routinely available to the winning political party. As a result, groups seek narrow goals from government that are generated by their primary, nonpolitical, reasons for existence. There is nothing wrong with what interest groups do. Indeed, group activity is important to maintaining the diversity of society, and to the responsiveness of government. But interest groups cannot be the basis of democracy because the interest group system is biased, and because groups are an unreliable channel for political in-

terests. In the absence of strong parties, interest groups tend to fragment the political process and further undermine political responsibility. To be sure, as Bosso points out, interest groups can often win concessions in the courts, in Congress, and in the bureaucracy. They prey on a decentralized system that often lacks the political will to deny their special claims. Groups have an important role to play in democracy, but because of their limited and exclusive nature, the health of democratic institutions demands they play that role within a context set by strong political parties. It is the parties, not groups, that ensure democracy.

A MODEST PROPOSAL

The U.S. constitutional framework is more the natural habitat of interest groups than of strong national parties. Power is shared by institutions very differently constructed—as between House and Senate and among Congress, president, and Supreme Court. This arrangement of power fragments the policy process and provides many footholds for special interests to gain access.[13] James Madison's defense of the constitutional order was based in part on its ability to frustrate a majority faction (like the Democratic or Republican party) intent on monopolizing power. The institutional incentives that divide Democrats in the House from Democrats in the Senate, and Democrats in Congress from a Democrat in the White House, will many times overwhelm the common interests they have as members of the same political party. Therefore, the parties in our national politics always face an uphill fight.

Unlike some party theorists, I do not advocate junking the U.S. constitutional order because of its antiparty proclivities.[14] Nonetheless, we should have a national policy more favorable to the political parties. The goal should be to strengthen them as independent organizations capable of exerting greater control over what candidates and officeholders do in their name.

In part, our policy should not be quite so blatantly antiparty. Although it is true there are laws on the books that help the parties, there nonetheless is a strong antiparty strain in our culture that finds its way into public policy. For example, in an effort to democratize them, we have taken from the parties control over their most important resource: their ability to nominate candidates to run on the ticket. The primary election, which is the most common method for selecting party nominees, encourages popular participation in nomination contests. But it has a number of other effects as well, some of which are pernicious.[15] In particular, by removing the party organization from a formal role in nominations, primaries encourage candidates to build personal followings independent of the party whose nomination is in question. A Congress full of candidates so nominated is an institution composed of entrepreneurs playing to their individual "markets" (including organized interests) without much incentive to consider the collective implications of what they do.[16]

To offset this fragmenting tendency in electoral politics, I suggest we give the parties greater control over a key resource essential to electoral success: money. The strong version of my suggestion would be to forbid candidates for national office from spending any money on their campaigns that does not come from the parties. A weaker version would be to require all interest group PACs wishing to contribute money to do so through the parties. Some provisions to guarantee rough equality in moneys available to both major parties would have to be adopted. A variation of the current public financing of presidential nomination and general election campaigns could be extended to include the activities of all parties, minor as well as major.

The specifics of the proposal are less important than the goal. At one time the parties controlled a critical resource necessary for election: labor in the form of volunteer canvassers and other workers. But as campaigns have shifted from being labor intensive to capital intensive, the grip the parties had on the electoral process is slipping. A policy that would restore primary control over campaign funds to them would go a long way toward strengthening their influence, even in the house that Madison built.

In particular, the effect would be to give the parties some control over who runs for election and reelection. The parties could demand more attention from their candidates and officeholders, they could promote more unity on policy questions of central importance to their national fortunes, and greater electoral responsibility would result. A party truly committed to balancing the budget could invest its campaign funds most heavily in the races involving candidates dedicated to the party's goals. Divided government would still be a problem, but at least the congressional and presidential wings of a party would be more likely to work together.

The political parties are remarkably resourceful institutions. They have persisted and at times thrived in a constitutional framework hostile to their very existence. And today the parties are finding ways of raising their own money and doling it out to favored candidates.[17] Nonetheless, a greater recognition of the critically important role in democracy played by the parties will help us find ways of strengthening them and thereby more closely approximate the ideal of electoral democracy.

NOTES

1. See Anthony Downs, *An Economic Theory of Democracy* (New York: Harper & Row, 1957), especially chap. 14, "The Causes and Effects of Rational Abstention."

2. For an excellent analysis of voting in congressional elections, see Gary Jacobson, *The Politics of Congressional Elections* (Boston: Little, Brown, 1987).

3. E. E. Schattschneider, *The Semisovereign People* (Hinsdale, Ill.: Dryden Press, 1975), chap. 8.

4. See Richard F. Fenno, Jr., "If, as Ralph Nader Says, Congress Is the 'Broken Branch,' How Come We Love Our Congressmen So Much?" in *Congress in Change,* ed. Norman J. Ornstein (New York: Praeger, 1975); Glenn R. Parker and Roger H. Davidson, "Why Do Americans Love Their Congressmen So Much More than Their Congress?" *Legislative Studies Quarterly* 4 (1979): 53–62.

5. Bruce Cain, John Ferejohn, and Morris Fiorina, *The Personal Vote* (Cambridge: Harvard University Press, 1987).

6. Schattschneider, *The Semisovereign People,* p. 35.

7. Robert H. Salisbury, "Interest Representation: The Dominance of Institutions," *American Political Science Review* 78 (March 1984): 64–76.

8. Kay Lehman Schlozman and John T. Tierney, *Organized Interests and American Democracy* (New York: Harper & Row, 1986), p. 70.

9. Andrew S. McFarland, *Common Cause: Lobbying in the Public Interest* (Chatham, N.J.: Chatham House, 1984), pp. 48–49.

10. Presidents and members of Congress are much less representative of the public than convention delegates or, for that matter, interest group leaders and activists. But the fact that the U.S. Senate is full of millionaires educated at elite institutions is not especially important so long as senators are individually and collectively responsible to the people who elect them.

11. For a complete account of how the problem of participation applies to interest groups, see Mancur Olson, *The Logic of Collective Action* (New York: Schocken Books, 1968).

12. Such groups are sometimes said to rely on "purposive" incentives because members join them out of agreement with the purposes of the group. For a discussion of the implications of different incentives for participating in interest groups, see Robert H. Salisbury, "An Exchange Theory of Interest Groups," *Midwest Journal of Political Science* 13 (February 1969): 1–32.

13. The classic statement on this point is David Truman, *The Governmental Process* (New York: Knopf, 1951), p. 507.

14. For examples of party theorists committed to fundamental constitutional reform, see Charles Hardin, "The Crisis and Its Cure" and Lloyd N. Cutler, "To Form a Government," *Reforming American Government,* ed. Donald L. Robinson, chaps. 1, 2

(Boulder, Colo.: Westview Press, 1985).

15. See Nelson Polsby, *Consequences of Party Reform* (Oxford: Oxford University Press, 1983). On primaries, see James I. Lengle, *Representation and Presidential Primaries* (Westport, Conn.: Greenwood Press, 1981), and Larry M. Bartels, *Presidential Primaries and the Dynamics of Public Choice* (Princeton: Princeton University Press, 1988).

16. See David R. Mayhew, *Congress: The Electoral Connection* (New Haven: Yale University Press, 1974), and Morris P. Fiorina, *Congress: Keystone of the Washington Establishment* (New Haven: Yale University Press, 1977).

17. Gary Jacobson, "Parties and PACs in Congressional Elections," in *Congress Reconsidered*, 3d ed., ed. Lawrence C. Dodd and Bruce I. Oppenheimer (Washington, D.C.: Congressional Quarterly Press, 1985), pp. 131–58.

SUGGESTED READINGS

FIORINA, MORRIS P. "The Decline of Collective Responsibility in American Politics." *Daedalus* 109 (Summer 1980): 25–45. A lucid essay spelling out the importance of collective responsibility in U.S. politics, how parties provide it, and the recent sources of its decline.

SABATO, LARRY J. *The Party's Just Begun: Shaping Political Parties for America's Future.* Glenview, Ill.: Scott, Foresman, 1988. A practical account of the importance of parties to future development of U.S. democracy by a scholar well versed in the comparative advantages of groups and parties.

SCHATTSCHNEIDER, E. E. *The Semisovereign People.* Hinsdale, Ill.: Dryden Press, 1975. A scathing and influential indictment of group theory as an apology for U.S. democracy. Schattschneider was a leading party theorist whose writings provide an eloquent defense of party democracy.

V

THE MEDIA

Has Television Weakened Our Democratic Institutions?

Television is a ubiquitous fact of American government and politics. Attend an important congressional hearing, and the cameras are there—and the members play to them. Full-time advisers to the president (any president) spend their working days thinking about how television will cover major news events, or how to create "photo opportunities" and "sound bites" that will show the president to the best advantage. They do so with firm conviction that popular support, to be won through television, can be translated into support for the chief executive's policies. Increasingly, television even has come into the formerly

sacrosanct arena of the courthouse to report, live, on the drama of ongoing trials. No candidate for statewide office, let alone the presidency, has a chance unless he or she has a "media adviser" and a "media strategist" prepared to raise the money and prepare the commercials necessary for serious contention for such major electoral offices.

Neither Professors Hallum nor Shea would deny television's importance, and both would admit that television increasingly defines the public agenda, the major issues that decision makers must address. The question under consideration is whether or not the changes television has wrought in our politics have fundamentally weakened our democracy.

Hallum argues absolutely yes in "Television Undermines Democracy." She sees a people made passive and with an increasing sense of alienation and powerlessness that she traces to the growth of television politics. She argues that television provides only superficial coverage of most events, allows no time for reflection on their meaning, treats electoral politics like a horse race, costs too much money, and prevents officeholders from taking the time to prepare thoughtful and careful responses to major occurrences, such as foreign policy crises.

Shea does not say that television has not changed our politics, or even that all the changes are for the better in "Television Is the Messenger, Not the Problem." The essence of his argument is that, on balance, our institutions are no less democratic and, indeed, in some cases are better off because of television. Some of the changes Hallum sees (rising alienation, weaker parties) Shea concedes, but he places the blame elsewhere, pointing out that the events of the past thirty years themselves have had a profoundly negative impact on citizens' willingness to participate in the political process, and that such factors as the growth of civil service and the decline of patronage have also weakened our parties. In some areas, such as in the coverage of the war in Vietnam, Shea sees a profoundly positive influence of television, contending that the live coverage of the carnage of war may well make people less enthusiastic about using it as a means of settling international disputes.

Television will not disappear from our lives. The questions for you to consider are what has been, on the whole, the nature of its impact, and what, if anything, should be done to change the way it is used. In Great Britain the government has taken steps (that clearly would be unconstitutional here) to ban spokespersons for "terrorists" (that is, the Irish Republican Army and its allies) from access to not only television but all the media. We do not face such proposals, but there is no question that officials at all levels of government regularly seek to restrict the media's (and thus the public's) access to information both for security reasons and to avoid political embarrassment. How shall we judge the legitimacy of such efforts? Are there changes in our laws governing campaign financing that might ensure a better use of television? Should the broadcasting of election results before polls close be prevented by law?

Television is the latest technology to transform our politics radically. The full impact of the computer has, believe it or not, yet to be felt. Combined with direct mail, it offers the possibility of politicians more and more selectively targeting audiences so as to deliver a message with one emphasis to a given group of voters and quite different messages to others. Even the fax machine is becoming politically significant.

It has been noted many times that television or any other means of mass communication cannot tell us what to think, but it can and does tell us what to think about. What, if anything, is needed to safeguard the essence of our democracy in this, the age of the "information revolution"?

Television Undermines Democracy

Anne Motley Hallum
Stetson University

Twelve years ago political scientist Jarol B. Manheim asked, "Can Democracy Survive Television?"[1] His concern was that a growing number of Americans are relying upon television for their political information, yet the medium inherently requires a relatively low level of participation for viewers and generally provides simplistic, noninterpretive political content. Hence, a knowledge gap is developing between the majority of television viewers, who are losing their sense of involvement in politics, and the politically informed members of an elite, who are in a better position to manipulate the people. Manheim did not answer his rhetorical question, but he would undoubtedly agree with the title of this essay. The survival of democracy may not be at stake, but it will be argued here that television is, at a minimum, having a detrimental effect on basic democratic institutions. First, Manheim's concern about the central institution of an informed citizenry will be elaborated on. Next, television's impact on political campaigns will be outlined, followed by a look at some changes in national government operations brought about by television's pervasive presence.

Each of the network news programs has twelve to fifteen million viewers each

137

evening. The enormous size of this audience gaining exposure to political facts would appear to be a positive development for democracy, but certain characteristics of television news mitigate its supposed power to enlighten. For one thing, the audience may be large but it is also mostly passive. Many people watch the news only because it is too much trouble to turn it off while waiting for lighter fare. As they casually watch, viewers find that stories are usually unrelated to each other and are very brief. In fact, a transcript of an entire evening news program is equivalent to less than one page of a newspaper.[2]

Another point is that items are presented rapidly without the pauses that are essential for information to "sink in." One study of the recall of news immediately after a broadcast found that 20 percent of respondents were unable to recall even one item from the program.[3] Thus, people are not learning from television as much as they are simply gradually forming attitudes about their government. If viewers do not discuss politics or seek other interpretations that could alter these attitudes, they are especially vulnerable to television's impact. This impact is more likely to undermine the governmental system than to strengthen it because of television's preference for depicting conflict and scandal in government.

The critical stance toward government taken by reporters is not a partisan bias because it is levied on public officials across the board. This generalized negativism has far-reaching implications. Austin Ranney, for instance, contends that television has contributed to an overall impatience with government. People expect government to resolve problems quickly, as if reality were a television drama with a satisfying ending.[4] They are usually disappointed.

As early as 1952 one scholar worried that a result of the televised Kefauver hearings in Congress was a feeling of "social impotence" among the viewers. People were angry rather than apathetic at the committee findings about crime, but they did not engage in constructive action.[5] The term "social impotence" was later replaced by the concept of political inefficacy, or the general feeling that an individual has little effect on the political process. According to surveys, political inefficacy has been steadily increasing among the population since 1960. In addition, political cynicism has been on the rise in the United States since 1964, before Watergate but after the advent of television.[6] The combined effect of these two trends is a sense of political alienation for many citizens. It is difficult to prove that television is the cause of the alienation. The fast-paced complexity of current events and the modern lifestyle also contribute to feelings of helplessness. Nevertheless, political scientist Michael Robinson contends that television is the primary culprit. He lists six explanatory factors that also summarize our discussion thus far: (1) the television news audience is extremely large and usually passive; (2) the public perceives the networks to be highly credible; (3) most television news coverage is noninterpretive; (4) television news reports emphasize the negative; (5) network reporting emphasizes conflict; and (6) a frequent theme in network newscasts is antiinstitutional.[7]

In his defense of television Professor Shea contends that it is incorrect to blame the technology of television when it is really our shallow use of the technology that deserves criticism. He further reminds readers that news, by definition, will be negative, and he also notes that in-depth television news coverage is available on CNN, C-SPAN, and the PBS

MacNeil/Lehrer NewsHour. For example, Shea praises C-SPAN for allowing "avowed political junkies" like him to watch a live presentation of the 1988 Iowa caucuses. In response, I would point out that PBS and C-SPAN audiences are very small and are made up of elite members of society who also read newspapers and newsmagazines. They enjoy television political news but are not vulnerable to its impact because they use competing sources of information. As noted in the first paragraph, television is widening the knowledge gap between the informed elite and the majority of Americans who watch network television for their news and *think* they are informed. This is not a positive development for participatory democracy.

In addition, I argue that it is appropriate to blame the messenger, that is, the technology of television, because many of the weaknesses of television presentation are endemic to the technology itself. Television news is not just about interesting unusual events, as Shea asserts. It is about *selected* events that involve dramatic visual conflict with as little interpretation by "talking heads" as possible. In fact, Shea helps this case with his example of British television campaigns. In Britain each party discusses important issues in five-minute and ten-minute segments. The results are boring and the audience is small because television is *inherently* nonanalytical. When producers depart from the fast-moving visual format, only a dedicated few will watch. In the United States both the evening news and political campaigns are often reduced to thirty- and sixty-second spots in order to accommodate the television medium.

The visual conflict between good and evil during the 1960s civil rights movement suited television news criteria perfectly. Television was an invaluable asset to that movement, but television is *not* explaining the complexities behind the wars in Nicaragua or El Salvador, nor is it offering illumination of such concerns as the budget deficit or the trade imbalance. It is not the tool for such an educational effort; it only supplements print media by offering pictures.

Scholars often refer to television as a "passive" medium, which is another trait of the technology. Viewers do not have to be actively engaged in the newscast, whereas readers of the newspaper are actively concentrating on what they are reading. Television is not usually an interactive medium conducive to viewers' acquisition of information, but it does gradually shape general attitudes.

A final trait of the technology of television is the huge size of the audience. None of the most important newspapers in the nation has more than one to three million readers, but the three network news programs can reach over thirty-five million viewers each evening. This is what gives television its enormous power in our political system. News journalists can influence society because the technology allows their news choices and comments to reach large percentages of the population instantly. The impact of many new competing channels has not been fully assessed, but at present, the major networks are certainly holding their own in terms of the number of people they reach.

TELEVISION AND ELECTIONS

What about the impact of television on the democratic institution of elections? Here one finds several fundamental changes that have occurred since the advent of the television era.

To begin with, voter turnout in the United States is abysmally low for most elections and is declining. Reasons for the low turnout are varied, including too-frequent elections, complex voter registration procedures, and a growing pool of eligible voters that makes the decline in percentage of actual voters look more serious than it is. Nevertheless, citizen apathy is one factor contributing to low turnout. As discussed earlier, scholars are concerned about the effects of a medium that is too passive to mobilize viewers but does gradually foster attitudes of cynicism, suspicion, and political inefficacy. The sentiment "What's the point of voting? They're all crooks anyway" is heard all too frequently during the election season. Tracing the precise source of such an attitude is difficult, and Shea points out that many events occurred in the 1960s to disillusion citizens. Still, it is interesting that decline in turnout in presidential elections began in 1964 and continued until a slight upturn in 1984.[8] The election of 1964 was the first held after national television news had expanded from fifteen minutes to thirty. The Watergate scandal of 1972–1973 is sometimes cited as a turning point toward voter disillusionment and apathy, yet the drop in rate of electoral participation more closely parallels developments in television news.

Robinson pinpoints the lengthened national evening television news in the early 1960s as the beginning of "videopolitics."[9] Particularly during the primaries, videopolitics means "horse-race" coverage: who is ahead and who is behind rather than a stressing of campaign issues. Horse races are entertaining to watch, but they are spectator events. Thus, potential voters respond by staying at home to watch, forgetting that they are supposed to be the crucial participants.

Another aspect of the impact of television on presidential elections is less speculative: Television is a key factor in the determination of which candidates survive the primaries in the first place. The criteria for television's selection of viable candidates include such irrelevancies as impressive looks, use of emotional campaign symbols, scheduling that accommodates the evening news, and so on. Candidates will use virtually any tactic to gain favorable media attention, or else they will be forced out of the election even before the spring primaries. News journalists desire to narrow the field of candidates quickly in order to save the networks money in primary coverage. They exercise their inordinate power by labeling the front-runners early—not based on actual victories but based on how well candidates perform relative to media expectations. Before even 5 percent of primary delegates are actually chosen, television speculation about the candidates can build momentum for one or two and force out those less skilled at playing "videopolitics." The now classic example is Jimmy Carter's 1976 success after the media pronounced him the surprise "winner" of the Iowa caucuses; he had in fact won less of the Iowa vote than the uncommitted delegates.[10] Television commentary, it is obvious, can supplant voting results as the decisive factor in caucuses and primaries! Clearly, this is an example of television's distorting the electoral process, the defining democratic institution.

Meanwhile, political parties are struggling to maintain their central function of building electoral and government coalitions. The pivotal election of 1964 brought a significant shift in the number of voting decisions based on party cues toward voting based on issues and candidate personality. Thus, an early impact of rising television coverage of campaigns was the declining influence of parties. Candidates have realized that they can build their own organizations without benefit of party backing and, with enough money, can gain direct access to voters. However, the access to voters is not really direct. Instead of party structures as intermediaries, now media consultants, advertising experts, pollsters, and television reporters all shape the candidate's message to the public. Admittedly, television is not the only variable at work here, but it is a major factor forcing changes in our party politics. Without the parties as a screening mechanism, the electoral process is more crowded with unknown prospects and is less predictable. Furthermore, once candidates attain office without benefit of party, they display less party loyalty in policy-making. Television encourages individualism both before and after the election. It does not foster the kind of partisan teamwork essential for a productive government.

Political parties are now improving their fund-raising skills in order to return to a more central role in campaigns; however, the high cost of television commercials strains party resources and gives the advantage to wealthy candidates or incumbents who have name recognition. For any statewide or presidential election, fund-raising for television has become the name of the game. This is sometimes discouraging for qualified candidates who enjoy public service but not the exhausting and sometimes humiliating requirements of raising money. Today, 50 to 60 percent of resources in a typical statewide or national campaign go to broadcast advertising. In 1980 both Carter and Ronald Reagan allocated approximately $16 million, or 53 percent of their funds, for television commercials.[11]

In the U.S. Senate race in Florida, Senator Lawton Chiles chose not to seek reelection partly because he dreaded the rigors of fund-raising for the campaign. Popular former governor Reubin Askew briefly campaigned for Chiles's Senate seat before he dropped out of the race as well. Askew was favored in the election and his withdrawal shocked party professionals, yet he too cited the new unpleasant emphasis on raising money for television as his reason. Candidates in other states have made similar statements.

Shea suggests that we simply limit the amount candidates can spend on television and radio advertisements by law, yet this would be difficult to do absolutely without violating the First Amendment. In any case, it is time to ask whether or not the expense and volatility of television campaigning are driving away the most serious and thoughtful public servants. Television is certainly weakening democratic institutions if it is contributing to alienation among elected officials as well as the general public.

To be a viable candidate today requires not only a great deal of money but also a personality and appearance that come across well on the air. In 1980 presidential hopeful Senator Alan Cranston looked older than his years on television and was never taken seriously as a candidate. Walter Mondale confessed in 1984 that his major campaign failing was his inability to develop an effective television presence. Similarly, in 1988 Republican Alexander Haig had extraordinary governmental experience, but he came across on television as too hot to handle. I agree with Shea that television can make room for colorful politicians who are not attractive in the conventional sense. The concern is that being in some way "telegenic" has become a more important requirement for a successful candidate than being experienced or knowledgeable.

Shea makes the somewhat fatalistic argument that elections in the United States have never been of high quality, with or without television. Politicians have always indulged in cliches and inflated rhetoric. Early partisan newspapers were hardly responsible or objective in their campaign coverage. But again, I would counter that the concern about television technology is its capability of influencing millions of citizens instantly. The point is not that we have lost some mythical, intellectual campaign dialogue but that we are handing our electoral process over to a few television reporters and producers. At least in the past many diverse elements influenced the electorate: party machines, a variety of newspapers, opinion leaders, convention speeches, debates, and so on. Today a few television commentators and consultants can make or break a candidate. Should we not be concerned about the immense power of Tom Brokaw, Dan Rather, Peter Jennings, and other news "anchors" in a democracy? Should we not question the wisdom of allowing national conventions to be sets for a television program? Should we not worry that a few negative television commercials have more impact in a campaign than dozens of positive speeches by the candidate? The "downfall of democracy" is not imminent, but it does seem appropriate to examine critically the implications of current trends for representative democracy.

TELEVISION AND GOVERNMENT OPERATIONS

Television news coverage of government extends beyond the election season, as does its detrimental impact. Let us look at several recent changes in government operations, beginning with a look at Congress.

The defining traits of television news include timeliness, visual appeal, and themes of inherent conflict, either personal or organizational. For government officials to "make the evening news," they must meet these criteria for newsworthiness. Thus, for example, congressional hearings will be scheduled for the convenience of news producers. They will include celebrity witnesses and as much dramatic conflict as possible. A constant competition occurs on Capitol Hill in the battle to attract television cameras to committee hearings. Members of Congress want news coverage in order to advance their policy goals as well as their personal reelection goals; their motives are not entirely self-centered by any means. The point is that the requirements of television often shape the policy-making methods of government officials.

Prior to the 1960s, formal rules in Congress, party discipline, and informal courtesies all operated to help build policy coalitions. As Norman Ornstein points out, things have changed in the 1970s and 1980s:

> As media coverage expanded, the number of members of Congress who were brought to public attention mushroomed, and more and more of the publicized members came from the rank and file. . . . No longer did a member have to play by inside rules to receive inside rewards or avoid inside setbacks. One could "go public" and be rewarded by national attention; national attention in turn could provide ego gratification, social success in Washington, the opportunity to run for higher office, or, by highlighting an issue, policy success.[12]

Thus, when television and Congress discovered each other, it became more difficult for Congress to act decisively. Television reporters seek out individual personalities, not cohesive committees. Senators and representatives who are at the center of disputes and who tend to speak in catchy "sound bites" are especially newsworthy.

It is probably still true that the most respected members of Congress are not the publicity seekers. Yet even members who do not desire television coverage for themselves must adapt to the allure of the television cameras on the Hill for others. The real work of making policy involves tedious research and painstaking negotiation in committees. Too often, this work is neglected or distorted because of television grandstanding. Television may benefit certain members of Congress, but the workings of Congress as an institution are impeded by the presence of networks.

A second major effect of television on governance involves the executive branch as well as the legislative. Because political emergencies are now presented to an audience of around fifty million people almost as soon as they occur, government officials face enormous pressure to react quickly. Delayed, thoughtful response to foreign policy developments, for instance, is extremely difficult when such an enormous audience is impatiently waiting. Former White House counsel Lloyd Cutler gives several examples of this problem, such as the hasty *televised* reaction of Reagan to the 1983 downing of a South Korean airliner by the Soviet Union. Reagan accused the Soviet Union of deliberate murder of the innocent passengers. Later evidence confirmed that the Soviets had mistaken the airliner for a reconnaissance plane. Tensions were heightened during this period because of pressures to respond forcefully before the television audience.[13]

Cutler also notes that because of the brevity and visual nature of newscasts, the public receives an oversimplified and emotional reading of events. Television was relentless, for example, in covering the human interest side of the 1979 taking of U.S. hostages by Iran. Daily reports and interviews with family members pushed Americans to call for action as drastic as a declaration of war.[14] Fortunately, President Carter did not comply, but television coverage of the hostage crisis undoubtedly contributed to his subsequent defeat in the election.

Crises generally call for a cool head and patient diplomacy—tools that do not play well on the evening news. But television will not go away. Therefore, the challenge for public officials today is to learn the art of television presentation so that government, not the television camera, is shaping policy. To remain in control, government leaders must expend a great deal of effort in explaining their policy choices persuasively to the television audience. Shea and others have noted that the Reagan White House was expert in manipulating public opinion by means of television to support the president. The techniques used in manipulation involve exploiting the dependence of reporters on government officials for information about national and world events. If reporters do not describe events in terms favorable to the politicians, they can lose access to sources vital to their careers. Thus, by cooptation and occasional intimidation of journalists, government can shape and simplify news content.

Skillful management of news is particularly easy in the case of television because of the symbolic power of pictures. The president's media handlers, for instance, control the schedule and setting for presidential news. When the setting evokes patriotic emotions from the audience, any critical words by news commentators are overshadowed. When CBS White House correspondent Leslie Stahl presented a scathing piece on Reagan's blatant use of shallow imagery, she was called by the White House to thank her for the story. Why? Because the president had been featured in the item always smiling and surrounded by flags and red, white, and blue balloons. The White House handlers knew that these favorable trappings had far more impact on viewers than the critical substance of Stahl's words.[15] This experience was humbling for the journalist, and it also points to the role of television in molding public opinion without educating the electorate. Television places decision makers in a constant spotlight; they respond by using the medium in any way they can to garner support. Yet the potential for public deception on an inordinate scale is always present. The public's best bet, it seems, is to turn to diverse print media for information.

SUMMING UP

Television, operating in the private sector in pursuit of large audiences and profit, is an excellent entertainment medium.

That is its primary function. However, its influence reaches far beyond the private sector. Because it is a powerful medium, political candidates and government officials have adapted their style of campaigning and governing to the requirements of television. They produce dramatic commercials; they condense issues to oversimplified slogans; they accommodate the evening news with "media events"; they frequently "go public" with policies rather than working out policy compromises with colleagues. These adaptations are not simply benign. Overall, these trends are alienating the public, weakening the political party system, straining cooperative ties in government, and strengthening the power of television professionals. It is not enough to dismiss these problems with the argument that U.S. democracy has never worked perfectly. We should be concerned about television's impact, and we should educate ourselves to be critical consumers of its products.

NOTES

1. Jarol B. Manheim, "Can Democracy Survive Television?" in *Media Power in Politics*, ed. Doris A. Graber (Washington, D.C.: Congressional Quarterly Press, 1984), pp. 131–37.
2. Elihu Katz, Hannah Adoni, and Prina Parness, "Remembering the News: What the Picture Adds to Recall," *Journalism Quarterly* 54 (1977): 239.
3. Jacob Jacoby and Wayne D. Hoyer, "Viewer Miscomprehension of Televised Communications: Selected Findings," *Journal of Marketing* 46 (Fall 1982): 12–26.
4. Austin Ranney, *Channels of Power* (Washington, D.C.: American Enterprise Institute, 1983), p. 148.
5. G. D. Wiebe, "Responses to the Televised Kefauver Hearings: Some Social Psychological Implications," *Public Opinion Quarterly* 16 (Summer 1952): 172–200.
6. Seymour Martin Lipset and William Schneider, "The Decline of Confidence in American Institutions," *Political Science Quarterly* 98 (Fall 1983): 382–89.
7. Michael J. Robinson, "Public Affairs Television and the Growth of Political Malaise: The Case of 'The Selling of the Pentagon,' " *American Po-*

litical Science Review 70 (June 1976): 409–32.

8. Stephen J. Wayne, *The Road to the White House*, 3d ed. (New York: St. Martin's Press, 1988), p. 56.

9. Michael J. Robinson, "Television and American Politics: 1956–1976," *Public Interest* 48 (Summer 1977): 23.

10. Richard Joslyn, *Mass Media and Elections* (Reading, Mass.: Addison-Wesley, 1984), pp. 126–29.

11. Ibid., p. 83.

12. Norman J. Ornstein, "The Open Congress Meets the President," in *Both Ends of the Avenue*, ed. Anthony King (Washington, D.C.: American Enterprise Institute, 1983), p. 202.

13. Lloyd N. Cutler, "Foreign Policy on Deadline," *Foreign Policy* 56 (Fall 1984): 113–28.

14. Ibid.

15. Martin Schram, *The Great American Video Game* (New York: Morrow, 1987), pp. 24–26.

SUGGESTED READINGS

GRABER, DORIS A.   *Mass Media and American Politics*. 3d ed. Washington, D.C.: Congressional Quarterly Press, 1988. Graber's work is an excellent survey text on the mass media, including the press.

RANNEY, AUSTIN.   *Channels of Power: The Impact of Television on American Politics.* Washington, D.C.: American Enterprise Institute, 1983. Ranney's book is a strong warning about the harmful effects of television on government because the medium fosters cynicism and fragmentation.

ROBINSON, MICHAEL J.   "Television and American Politics: 1956–1976." *Public Interest* 48 (Summer 1977). Robinson's essay is a fascinating analysis of the subtle but powerful impact of television on political trends. He includes analysis of entertainment television.

Television Is the Messenger, Not the Problem

John C. Shea
West Chester University

That television has transformed American life, including our political life, should not be denied by any rational observer. Since the 1950s it has been the dominant influence in our popular culture. The "tube" is on for more than six hours daily in the average household, and students of the subject contend that more than 40 percent of the free time of the average American is spent watching television.[1] George Will, the conservative columnist whose political views make him controversial but whose love of baseball shows him to be a fundamentally sound human being, once observed that Americans probably would not have noticed if the Japanese had simply pushed aside such basic industries as steel and petrochemicals, but when they went after our automobiles and television sets, the primary artifacts of our civilization, we got angry.

What Professor Hallum and others would have us do, like the ancient Persians, is shoot the messenger (in this case, television) that brings the bad news of problems in our political system. Sometimes, however, the simple is the most important, so let us begin with a simple but major observation: Television is, fundamentally, just a technology. It is a very significant technology, and scientific-technological advances have many times in the past two centuries led to sweeping changes in the lives of human beings. Our whole society is a product of the industrial revolution that began in the late eighteenth century, and many have suggested we are in the process of a new information revolution that is at least as important. Some technologies, such as the development of vaccines for poliomyelitis, have had nothing but positive results for humankind. Others, such as the unlocking of the secrets of the atom, we would all undoubtedly be pleased to do without were it possible to do so. Of course, one of the realities of life is that it is not possible to wish such developments away; there are no "secrets" of nuclear physics or of television that can be undone by closing our eyes.

Most scientific-technological developments are more morally neutral than the discovery of vaccines or weapons of mass destruction. Railroads in the nineteenth century and the airplane in this one were both used to speed the movements of people and goods as well as the delivery of troops and bombs. The silicon chip and, yes, even television are inherently neutral and can be used for purposes that better our lot or to increase human misery.

Well, I am not going to argue with anyone who would make the case that a lot of miserable fare appears on television. It is not my burden, fortunately, to defend the artistic or aesthetic merits of "Crash TV" but, rather, to speak to the consequences for our democracy of television.

Hallum very capably lays out the standard case against television. Let me briefly summarize those arguments. (1) Television does not provide in-depth coverage of much of anything. The typical newscast is a series of brief stories, each unrelated to the foregoing and without any depth. (2) Television concentrates on (shades of the Moral Majority!) the bad news. Hallum tells us of television's preference for depicting conflict and scandal in government and that it may even encourage early retirement by government officials. (3) Television inspires a sense of alienation from government and the political process and, most important, television is responsible for the declining rate of participation in our electoral process. She argues that this dates from the mid-1960s, after the rise of television but before the events of Watergate. (4) Hallum discusses, as do most critics who make this case, television's ability to select the front runner in presidential campaigns, pointing to the famous 1976 example: Jimmy Carter, a virtual unknown, on the basis of television's declaring him the winner of the Iowa caucuses became the leading candidate for the Democratic nomination and eventually president. (5) Television has become the preferred method of campaigning; it is very expensive, and has led to the corruptive influence of money in our elections. Other points are made, but these seem to be the essential ones.

Let us deal with these charges serially. First, it is true that television network news typically deals with the news in an abbreviated, disjointed way, without providing the background and depth necessary to understanding. The same observation, however, might be made about most of the popular press, the newsreels that preceded television, and, indeed, the "penny press" of the turn of the century, which dealt in sensationalism and had little respect for the truth or accuracy. That surface reportage is a problem is undoubtedly true. That it is the fault of television is less clear. Hallum does not seem to value the "MacNeil/Lehrer NewsHour," available on PBS to most of the population. More important, she does not credit the influence of cable, now available to 50 percent of the people. Those who watch C-SPAN or the CNN service of Turner Broadcasting would not be making unfavorable comparisons with most daily newspapers in terms of depth of coverage. The truth, of course, is that the average newspaper reader does not read the *New York Times,* even in New York City, and the average television viewer does not watch "Washington Week in Review." This is a fact that is not the responsibility of the networks but, rather, one they exploit.

My response to Hallum's first charge is twofold. One, the news shows of Dan Rather, Peter Jennings, and Tom Brokaw do not suffer so much when the comparison is not with what we, as civic-minded scholars, might idealize as the best choice but with what real choices were made before television. Two, the evolution of television in the late years of the twentieth century promises greater variety to choose from, some of which will provide the in-depth coverage Hallum wants. In 1988 C-SPAN did not just show the results of the Iowa caucuses, it took those of us who are avowed political junkies to Iowa to watch a caucus live as it unfolded. Hallum says that it is not realistic to expect the average citizen to watch C-SPAN. But C-SPAN is symbolic of the growing world of cable and VCRs that each year diminishes the monopoly on information of the networks, a concern of Hallum's.

My answer to the charge that television concentrates on the bad news is that I certainly hope so. I am reminded of a news story in the mid-1960s when Dean Rusk and his entourage became stuck in a nonfunctioning elevator in the State Department building, an event all news sources reported. Rusk irritably commented that the networks did not report on the several elevators that ran normally

that day. Indeed, they did not. The very nature of news is that it deals with recent events, events of interest, and the unusual. Neither television nor newspapers carry stories on planes that land normally, on banks not robbed, on bureaucrats who do what they are supposed to do.

The argument that television brings about a sense of alienation among the populace and is responsible for the decline in voting is the most serious. Study after study has shown that Americans are increasingly unhappy with the performance of governmental officials. And that voting in presidential elections has dropped since 1960 almost steadily, except for a slight upward blip in 1984, and fell to less than half the electorate in 1988. The Lipset and Schneider study cited by Hallum makes that point very well, and accurately traces it to the mid-1960s.[2] She and they conclude that the decline is due to the rise of television because Watergate, the other likely culprit, did not occur until 1972–1974.

The only problem with this analysis linking diminished voter participation to growing television watching is that other significant events were occurring in the turbulent 1960s: the civil rights movement with the accompanying problems of urban riots, white backlash, and the assassination of Martin Luther King, Jr., the Vietnam War and college riots, challenges to the traditional roles of women, mounting crime, and alternative lifestyles—all of these threatened the social fabric. And as many commentators pointed out in 1988 on the twenty-fifth anniversary of the assassination of John F. Kennedy, we can see in retrospect that it was in that tragedy that America lost its youth, its sense that the nation could surmount any problem. Alienation in such an environment is not surprising.

Television, the bad-news messenger that Hallum and others would blame, in fact began its major role in U.S. politics not in the 1960s but at least as early as the 1952 campaign of Dwight Eisenhower. It was firmly established by the 1960 election, which had the highest turnout in modern history.

As for the contention that television's coverage of politics discourages well motivated (or otherwise-motivated) public servants from continuing in office, I can reply only that attrition in this regard must be hard to measure statistically. In fact, in 1988 98 percent of the members of the House of Representatives who sought reelection were successful, a percentage as high as any in our history.

Hallum's fourth and fifth arguments, that television has come to be the predominant instrument in politics and that modern campaigns are obscenely expensive, are entirely correct. They can be answered only in terms of the place of television in politics. It is to that we turn next.

TELEVISION AND DEMOCRATIC INSTITUTIONS

The precise charge that we are asked to respond to is that television has weakened our democratic institutions. To examine the charge systematically, we must first think briefly about the concept of democracy, which implies a lot more than simply free, competitive elections. Political democracy is, indeed, an important component of democracy but it is not the only one. Although Hitlerian Germany would not have permitted it, it is certainly reasonable to speculate that had there been a free election in Germany in, say, 1938, Hitler would have won overwhelmingly. In fact, he became chancellor of Germany in 1933 as the result of a democratic election, an election, by the way, that saw a higher percentage of Germans vote—88 percent—than in any other pre-World War II election. (That level of voter participation must please those who measure democracy in terms of turnout, but would they point with pride to the result as an example of what can be accomplished without television?)[3] Yet even if Hitler had won endorsement at the ballot box every six months, no credible philosopher of democracy would dignify his brutal regime with that term.

Democracy is more than majority rule; it also speaks to the important concept of individual freedom and dignity as represented by the twin ideals of civil liberties and civil rights. *Civil liberties* include the rights associated with free expression, freedom of conscience and lifestyle and protection from the unreasonable use of police power. *Civil rights* means that no group should be unreasonably discriminated against on the basis of ascribed characteristics, such as race, gender, and religion. What these concepts (as well as the majoritarian idea) have in common is the idea of equality: equality at the ballot box as well as in how we treat people as groups and respect them as individuals, each free to find his or her own way.

It is clear we have achieved a higher level of democratic equality with respect to both civil liberties and civil rights than was true at the dawn of the television era. Obviously, racism is still a major problem, but it is also true that African-Americans are clearly better off than they were, say, in 1948. And, despite recent retreats by the courts, civil liberties are just as secure as they were in that time. Certainly there is now room for greater diversity of lifestyles; there is more consciousness of the rights of the criminally accused; and freedom of expression is alive and well. It was in 1948, after all, that the New York City Board of Education sought to ban the *Nation* magazine from the city's public schools.

These developments have taken place as the result of many factors, among the most important of which were (1) the work of the Warren Court in the 1950s and 1960s; (2) the civil rights movement of those decades, especially the boycotts led by Martin Luther King, Jr.; and (3) the social revolution of the 1960s. Although these same factors also undoubtedly contributed to the conservative backlash that came to dominate our presidential politics after 1968, they widened greatly the scope of civil liberties and civil rights in this country. Did television play a role in all of this? There is no way of measuring its part precisely, but informed judgment would have to say yes, it did. The Supreme Court may not have been directly responsive to pressures, but there can be little doubt that those famous pictures of white police in Selma, Alabama, attacking peaceful black marchers with water hoses, cattle prods, and police dogs contributed mightily to public support for the momentous Civil Rights Act of 1964. Television is able to deliver all sorts of messages, and sometimes the messages result in positive changes in our society and make it more democratic.

To deal in such matters as civil liberties is to beg the question to some extent. Because when people speak of what television has done to weaken our democratic institutions, what is really meant are the institutions relating to political democracy. It is in terms of such concern that Hallum's strongest case is made.

My defense to this charge is multifaceted. I will argue that although in some ways the charge is true (some of our political institutions are probably weaker because of television), what is more important is that television has primarily changed rather than weakened

our democratic institutions. Sometimes the changes are, in fact, for the better because what existed before was not so admirable either. And finally, some of the changes—both desirable and not—that have come about in our democratic institutions have resulted, either wholly or in part, from factors other than television. These matters are all interrelated, so it will not be possible to deal with them in sequential fashion.

First, television is alleged to have weakened the political parties by rendering them almost irrelevant. People no longer need to depend on the parties to inform them about the candidates; instead, they can learn directly about them from television and other media. In the pretelevision days it was the party workers who brought literature to the door who were the main conduit for information about the people running for office.

There is some truth in this characterization, but it needs to be offset by other considerations. First, candidates for a host of local offices, often up to and including Congress, receive little or no television exposure. And the fact is that to most political workers, these offices are at least as important as the more prestigious offices, including the presidency, that hold television's attention. Yet, all candidates, including those for local offices (which are the life blood of politics), have seen a decline in the availability of party workers to push for their election. This ought to indicate to any clearheaded examiner of modern political reality that it is not television alone that has weakened the parties. The growth of the civil service at the expense of patronage appointments has also contributed. Public policy, too, has had a debilitating effect by making available through governmental programs the subsistence level assistance party bosses used to hand out in return for electoral support. And there has been a well documented wasting away of partisanship among the voters, which has had the same result.[4] Further, when people speak of the decline of parties in the age of television, what they often really mean is the relative decline of the Democratic party. As Michael J. Robinson of Georgetown University has pointed out, the national Republicans and many individual state and local parties have done quite well in adjusting to the new reality.[5]

Adapting to change has long been the order of the day in politics. William Jennings Bryan, three times the Democratic nominee for the presidency, was considered the leading political orator around the turn of the century. Among his speaking assets was his ability to bellow, to make himself heard in a crowded convention hall or across a field where a political rally might be held. There is little doubt that his style of campaigning, which had a good deal in common with the revivalist preaching at camp meetings, would not be well received today. Many would say that Bryan was long on wind but short on intelligence. However, there is little evidence that such a style should be paired with insufficient brainpower any more than is the laid-back style of today's made-for-television political personalities. Marshall McLuhan was the first to understand that television is, in his words, a "cool" medium; that is, it comes into our homes, where we are relaxed and not entirely focused on the little screen. Hence, it requires a personality that is not intense (hot) and that communicates conversationally.[6]

The effective politician adapts to the demands of the media of the day. Undoubtedly, this bars some who might be effective public servants and allows others to gain office who have few otherwise admirable attributes. Walter Mondale, for example, in his 1984 postelection news conference brushed aside the microphones and said he had never been comfortable with "those things." Some politicians succeed in spite of having a different style; Jesse Jackson is obviously a very "hot" but still effective television communicator. It is frequently alleged that Abraham Lincoln would not have done well in the age of television. That assumption is not necessarily true. Certainly Lincoln was not handsome by today's standards, yet television—and politics—has always made room for people who are not conventionally good-looking but who can communicate their intelligence and honesty; for example, U.S. Senator Sam Erwin of Watergate fame. It is rather difficult to judge across the years how Lincoln, a man of obviously deep compassion and intelligence, would "come across" in our living rooms today. Surely, the ability to master the major means of communication of the time should not be unexpected in an ambitious politician, nor taken as evidence of a person's suitability or unsuitability for high office. Lincoln might have "played well" on television or he might have been terrible; we have no way of knowing.

The most serious charge against television as a political instrument is that it trivializes serious public issues and reduces our consideration of them. The thirty-second commercial and one-minute news "bite" are the big guns in a kind of "bumper-sticker" combat. The charge is true, at least as politics has developed in the United States, but that is not necessarily entirely the fault of television. The values of our society must be factored in. In Britain there are no television commercials for candidates. Each major party is provided, free of charge, with blocks of time in five-minute and ten-minute segments. They use the time to talk about the issues and try to persuade the voters to support them. How does it work? In the words of Richard J. Ayre of the British Broadcasting Company (BBC), it "must be the most tedious television we produce, and the audience size reflects that. I think they have minimum impact on the way . . . the nation votes."[7]

Many people, including the candidates, believe that clever television advertisements, in and of themselves, often win elections. Certainly that has been charged about the 1988 campaign, in which, it is said, misleading Republican advertisements put the blame for the pollution of Boston Harbor on Michael Dukakis and—most tellingly in the invidious Willy Horton material—played to racist fears and fears of crime. These commercials were effective, and effective for two reasons in particular. The Dukakis campaign showed incredible ineptitude in responding. And although it may be argued that the Republicans do not, in fact, have any promising ideas on how to reduce crime, the Democrats have long failed to recognize that Americans, black and white, have a legitimate concern about lawlessness. Fundamentally, the Republicans won in 1988 for the same reason they won in 1984: The country was at peace; inflation was down and employment up from the end of the Carter administration. Peace and prosperity is a formula for victory that is hard to beat, no matter what commercials are on television. In fact, at the close of the Republican Convention and before the fall advertising blitz began, the Bush-Quayle ticket led in the polls by eight percentage points, just as it did on election day in November.

A telling study of the actual effect of television on the voters' behavior in campaigns is the Patterson and McClure study of the 1972 campaign, *The Unseeing Eye*. Although the study found that television news typically pays an inordinate amount of attention to the horse-race aspect of the campaign (that is, who is ahead) and the visuals and hoopla (balloons and photogenic settings), the voters still managed to arrive at fairly perceptive understandings of the issue differences between George McGovern and Richard Nixon. The real source of that understanding tended to be the commercials of the candidates themselves![8]

Studies of American voters most often show them increasingly more likely to indicate they make their electoral decisions on the basis of perceived issue divisions. Many people seem to think that is a desirable state of affairs.

It may well be that modern manipulators of popular opinion are able to go beyond commercials to use television to mold public opinion. Certainly, the Reagan White House, while Michael Deaver was in attendance, was expert in that regard. Indeed, it has been reasonably demonstrated that Deaver's people would often arrange "photo opportunities" of the president in settings that suggested concerns that ran directly contrary to the real priorities of the administration. If the president was being seen as uncaring about women's issues, why, just present some visuals of the president listening to women expressing concerns about those issues and let the pictures take the place of policy. The same thing could be done with Hispanics, education, whatever policy area was in question.[9]

Well, politicians have deceived the public before and undoubtedly will do so again, and in the age of television, that medium can be used to deceive. Lincoln's observation about the frequency with which one can fool people is probably still apropos. There are limits, however. After Reagan sent the Ayatollah of Iran a cake, a Bible, and guns for hostages and Nicaragua-bound cash, it was difficult for him to present himself as tough on the Iranians.

So the case for television as causing a decline in our democratic institutions seems rather weak at best. In fact, it gets even weaker. Politics in the age of television is discussed as if prior to the tube all campaigns were exercises in the Socratic method. Hardly. Here is Richard Rovere describing travels on Harry Truman's campaign train in 1948:

> Politics is a branch of show business, and life aboard a Presidential campaign train—a peculiar and somewhat wearing form of existence that I have been sampling on and off during the past couple of weeks— is like life in a fast moving road carnival.[10]

A few weeks later, four days after the election, the following appeared in the *New Yorker:*

> To the President-elect of the U.S. (and we don't know his name at the moment of writing this) we wish health, wisdom and courage for the next four years. And we take this opportunity to remind the President-elect (whose name we don't know) that he is already indebted to millions of his countrymen who sat dutifully at their radio sides through platitudes, banality, blarney and evasion in their attempt to render a fair decision. Only a term of unusual excellence in office can pay off this frightful and burdensome public debt.[11]

Where, oh where, is the evidence that earlier elections were conducted on the idealized high plane the absence of which is attributed to television? Nineteenth-century campaigns were largely mobilization contests in which the emphasis was on getting out the voters loyal to one candidate or the other. Discus-

sions of issues were conducted, if at all, by highly partisan and not particularly objective newspapers that often were more interested in commenting on the news than in reporting it, and very often providing details only in support of the political positions of the paper.[12] The Republican *New York Tribune* did not bother telling its readers in 1884 that Democrat Grover Cleveland had been elected president until two weeks after the election![13]

An example of highminded electioneering that is frequently mentioned is the famed Lincoln–Douglas debates, real debates in which the participants were able to develop their arguments in detail. Those debates, in fact, were held in 1858 in Illinois in the Senate contest between Stephen Douglas and Lincoln—and Lincoln lost. A few points need to be made. One, the Lincoln–Douglas debates were no more the standard for political discourse in the nineteenth century than they would have been in the twentieth. But if it is debates you want, turn to the televised appearances on the same stage of the presidential candidates in 1960, 1976, 1980, 1984, and 1988.

Of course, the last-named events were not real debates at all but joint press conferences, and the ones held in 1988 were constrained by ridiculous rules that prevented follow-up questions and allowed maximum evasion. But the fact is that they served to bring into focus the issue differences between the candidates, and the public gained some understanding of the relative abilities of the candidates to handle public pressure. There is also considerable evidence the debates informed the public and made a difference. No one could misunderstand the positions of Dukakis and Bush regarding such issues as abortion, cuts in the defense budget, and the relative likelihood of support by either of increased taxes. No one can doubt that Dukakis's legalistic reply to a bizarre question about whether he would favor the death penalty if his wife were raped and murdered showed more than simply the attitude of the man toward capital punishment. Similarly, the first Kennedy–Nixon debate established Kennedy as a serious candidate who could do more than hold his own with the far more experienced Nixon, and Carter was devastated by Reagan's asking watching voters, "Are you better off now than you were four years ago?" I am well aware that the effect of any given debate is often determined by the "spin" the media put on it in the days following the actual event, and that there are qualities far more important in determining who would be the better president than simply who can deliver the most facile answer. Still, it is hard to argue that this format is less productive as a means of informing the voters than what existed before television.

There is no question that modern campaigns cost too much. A great deal of the excess, as Hallum points out, has to do with television. But it has nothing to do with the technology of television and a lot to do with the campaign finance laws we enacted in the 1970s and the limits we place on ourselves. Although this is a subject for an entirely separate essay, briefly, we need (1) to limit Political Action Committees (PACs) to giving money solely to political parties and not to individual candidates, and (2) to limit stringently the total that can be spent on behalf of any candidate. Beyond those things we need to bite a larger bullet. Broadcast stations are creatures of our laws; they are given licenses, worth millions of dollars, to broadcast exclusively on limited frequencies. It would not be unreasonable to require, by law, that they provide a certain amount of free time to major candidates for public office, and then further to require that such

candidates, as a condition of receiving the free air time, could spend no money on television and radio advertising. Campaign costs are a problem created not by the nature of television but by restrictions we have placed on ourselves. We can correct the problem.

Finally, there are some things that television simply does better than any other media. Alistair Cooke, among others, has pointed out that it was television that brought the real meaning of Vietnam into our living rooms and helped to end the pointless carnage of that war. He suggests that television coverage of the Western Front in 1917 might have had the same effect on the slaughter during World War I.[14] Had that happened, it is safe to assume that the generals would have growled about the media, but it is hard to say whether Europe, and Germany in particular, would have drifted into the morass that produced Adolf Hitler.

Television can build up a person of questionable achievement, but it can also expose wrongdoing. Certainly, television in the days of Watergate carried a first-class civics lesson in the operation of key congressional committees under the able guidance of people such as Sam Erwin and Peter Rodino.

The endless presidential primary and caucus system has undermined our parties' ability to manage nominations at least as much as has television. It is a system that we Americans have jerry-built out of complex party rules and states competing for the limelight (and candidate promises). An excellent case can be made that it is only through television that the voters have any chance of being able to sort through the competing claims of the field of relatively unknown persons like, for example, those the Democrats fielded in 1976 and again in 1988.

Blaming television for whatever weaknesses exist in our democratic institutions is to look for a handy whipping boy. There are serious problems in our democracy and our society at the end of the twentieth century. In many ways the media reflect those problems. In some ways the media undoubtedly contribute to them. But television, on the whole, has not weakened the democratic nature of our institutions. On balance it has strengthened them. We are not justified in blaming the messenger for the bad news.

NOTES

1. John P. Robinson, "Toward a Post-Industrial Society," *Public Opinion* 2 (August/September 1979): 43.
2. Seymour Martin Lipset and William Schneider, "The Decline of Confidence in American Institutions," *Political Science Quarterly* 98 (Fall 1983): 379–402.
3. Chris Cook and John Paxton, *European Political Facts, 1918–1973* (New York: St. Martin's Press, 1975), p. 124.
4. Norman H. Nie, Sidney Verba, and John R. Petrocik, *The Changing American Voter* (Cambridge: Harvard University Press, 1976), pp. 46–71.
5. Michael J. Robinson, quoted in John D. Callaway, Judith A. Mayotte, and Elizabeth Altick-McCarthy, eds., *Campaigning on Cue* (Chicago: William Benton Fellowships Program, University of Chicago, 1988), pp. 53–54.
6. Marshall McLuhan, *Understanding Media* (New York: McGraw-Hill, 1964), pp. 36ff.
7. Richard J. Ayre, quoted in Callaway et al., *Campaigning on Cue*, pp. 127–28.
8. Thomas E. Patterson and Robert D. McClure, *The Unseeing Eye* (New York: G. P. Putnam's Sons, 1976).
9. Martin Schram, *The Great American Video Game* (New York: Morrow, 1987), pp. 30–31.
10. Richard Rovere, "Letter from a Campaign Train: En Route with Truman," *New Yorker*, October 9, 1948, p. 69.
11. "Talk of the Town," *New Yorker*, November 6, 1948, p. 23.
12. Bernard Roshco, "The Evolution of News Content in the American Press," in *Media Power in Politics*, ed. Doris A. Garber (Washington, D.C.: Congressional Quarterly Press, 1984), pp. 7–22.
13. Richard Jenson, "Armies, Admen and Crusades: Strategies to Win Elections," *Public Opinion* 3 (October/November 1980): 44–46.
14. Alistair Cooke, "Now Here Is the Nightly News" (June 7, 1970), in his *The Americans* (New York: Knopf, 1979), pp. 43–48.

SUGGESTED READINGS

BENJAMIN, GERALD, ED. *The Communications Revolution in Politics.* Vol. 3, no. 4 of *Academy of Political Science Proceedings.* New York, 1982. A thoughtful, scholarly, and still entertaining overview of the many areas in which innovations in communications have influenced politics, from elections to terrorism.

PARENTI, MICHAEL.   *Inventing Reality: The Politics of the Mass Media.* New York: St. Martin's Press, 1986. Be aware of Parenti's point of view; he is a Marxist and he makes the argument that it is capitalism and the desire for profits, along with a commitment to the maintenance of the system, that drive the media.

SCHRAM, MARTIN.   *The Great American Video Game.* New York: Morrow, 1987. Makes the case, about as strongly as it can be made, for politicians' ability to manipulate our opinions through television. The major thrust here is not campaigning, although there is some of that, but the tactics of the Reaganites and particularly of Michael Deaver, the former president's media genius, who believed it did not matter what was said on television but only what the pictures showed.

VI

CONGRESS

Can and Should There Be a Central Role for Congress in Setting American Foreign Policy?

Ask most Americans where responsibility for the conduct of foreign policy lies and they most likely will reply the president. That this has been true for most of the past fifty years, neither Professor Johnson nor Professor Oliver would deny. But this set of essays deals with whether this is desirable. The relevant questions turn on what role, if any, Congress should have in regard to foreign policy issues.

One relevant question deals with the constitutional responsibilities of Congress. Johnson makes a strong case in "Congress and Foreign Policy" that the founding fathers intended at least an equal role for Congress in national security policy. The president was to be the commander in chief of the armed forces, yes, and was empowered to deal with a direct attack on the United States by a foreign enemy. But policy making and control of funds for the military were clearly intended to be the prerogatives of Congress. Oliver counters in "The President Must Forge Foreign Policy" that in the recent past when the courts have been asked to rule on limitations Congress has sought to place on the primacy of the chief executive in the handling of foreign affairs, they have inevitably decided against the legislature.

157

Another relevant question fundamentally recognizes that our world is significantly different from the world of the founding fathers. Even a declaration of war by a European power in the eighteenth century would not have precluded Congress from taking time to consider how best to react, what armies to raise, what ships to fund. But by the twentieth century things were very different: The attack on Pearl Harbor a half-century ago demanded immediate action, and in this nuclear age a missile launch allows no time for deliberation. Is it possible in the modern world for a slow-to-act, often contentious Congress to help mold an effective foreign policy? Is Congress too responsive to narrow constituent interests? Too given to grandstanding? Can it be trusted not to leak sensitive national secrets? Many a president has hinted that it cannot. It is not hard for people who would respond in the negative to these questions to find examples of congressional incompetence, and even more instances when Congress was not consulted yet it promptly cheered popular results of decisive presidential action abroad. President Bush's decision to invade Panama comes to mind in connection with the latter point.

On the other hand, the record of foreign policy disasters undertaken by presidents is not a short one. The Iran–Contra affair involving White House officials running amuck with little regard for the law or overall policy considerations would not have happened had there been prior consultation with the legislative branch. Certainly in the national security arena, too, where Americans are frequently called on to spend not only their treasure but their blood, one might assume there would be greater national support for policies that might have tragic results if a more open political process helped to shape them.

Oliver closes his essay with a pessimistic assessment from Alexis de Tocqueville, the perceptive nineteenth-century student of our society, to the effect that democratic government does not seem as well equipped to conduct foreign relations as do other governments.

One might conclude that the ideal we are all searching for is that we, as a nation, might shape effective foreign policies, based on long-term national interests, and to insure in some way that such policies grow out of consent by the people's representatives. The broader question is whether or not that is possible today, or does the search for such an arrangement only create new hazards?

Congress and Foreign Policy: Remembering the Constitution

Loch K. Johnson
University of Georgia

The founders of our republic designed a government of separate institutions sharing power. With memories still fresh of their bondage under British tyranny, America's early leaders were "imbued with antipower values."[1] As they distributed power across three branches of government, they vowed to limit its abuse. "Ambition must be made to counteract ambition," declared James Madison (*Federalist Paper* 51).

With responsibilities and prerogatives spread across the executive, legislative, and judicial branches of government, the constitutional framers hoped to ensure that no one branch would grow so mighty as to dwarf the others or dictate to the people. "The greatest insight of our Founding Fathers was their recognition of the dangers of unlimited power exercised by a single man or institution," concluded a thoughtful U. S. senator recently, adding that "their greatest achievement was the safeguards against absolute power which they wrote into our Constitution."[2]

Although a separation of institutions with shared powers held an obvious attraction to a young republic still reeling from a war against the excesses of British monarchy, the new arrangements also contained the seeds of inefficiency. Foremost among them was the fundamental problem of coordinating dispersed units of government, each with formidable powers. How could these separate entities truly be made to share power and work together for the good of the nation? The answer remained in doubt, especially because the very Constitution that gave them their authority seemed— with its silences and ambiguities—to present, in Edward S. Corwin's memorable phrase, "an invitation to struggle."[3]

The men who drafted the Constitution were wise to concern themselves with the dangers of concentrated power; few students of history and politics would deny the truth of Lord Acton's famous aphorism "Power corrupts, and absolute power corrupts absolutely." Yet, in their headlong escape from tyranny had the founders embraced another serious threat to democracy: a paralysis resulting from a badly fragmented and disorganized government? If at one end of a power continuum stood the threat of absolute power, at the other stood anarchy.

The purpose of this essay is to examine the contemporary relevance for foreign policy of the original constitutional blueprint. At the heart of the argument is the question of governability. Do our public institutions permit the making of sound foreign policy decisions? Can collaborative government work as the founders intended, especially when dealing with the often tangled and dangerous problems of international affairs in a nuclear age? Have the precautions against the abuse of power, adopted over two centuries ago, led to a government that lacks sufficient centralized authority to react with dispatch and coherence to modern global threats? Or, are the concerns and prescriptions of the founders as valid today as they were at the nation's beginning?

In a search for answers to these vital questions, this essay focuses on the subject of power sharing between Congress and the executive branch, especially regarding the use of force—the war-making power—to achieve U. S. objectives abroad. The purpose is to explore the consequences for policy-making that flow from the decision of the founders to distribute power across institutions. The dominant theme that emerges from the argument may be succinctly previewed: Collaborative government—a partnership between the executive and legislative branches—not only can work in the modern era but, as the founders foresaw, provides an indispensable safeguard against the abuse of power.

THE CONSTITUTION AND THE WAR POWER

The Constitution lodges the war-making power predominantly in the legislative branch. In Article I, Section 8, the founders gave Congress the right to declare war; to raise and support armies; to provide and maintain a navy; to make rules for the governing and regulation of the armed forces; to provide for calling forth the militia to execute the laws, suppress insurrections, and repel invasions; to provide the organizing, arming, and disciplining of the militia; and to make all laws necessary and proper for executing the foregoing powers. In Article II, Section 2, the founders addressed the role of the executive during war and designated the president as commander in chief of the army and navy.

The constitutional framers were more concerned about the war-making power than any other, and with good reason. As colonists, they had viewed with alarm the ease by which King George III could commit Great Britain—and therefore the

American colonies—to war. They were determined in their new government to remove this momentous decision from the hands of a single individual. Even such a champion of executive power as Alexander Hamilton was wary of concentrated authority to make war. "The President is to be commander in chief of the army and navy of the United States," he wrote in *Federalist Paper* 69.

In this respect his authority would be nominally the same with that of the king of Great Britain, but in substance much inferior to it. It would amount to nothing more than the supreme command and direction of the military and naval forces, as first General and Admiral of the Confederacy, while that of the British king extends to the *declaring* of war and to the *raising* and *regulating* of fleets and armies—all which, by the Constitution under consideration, would appertain to the legislature.[4]

Thomas Jefferson, James Madison, and others similarly had no interest in turning over the weapons of war to the discretion of one person; better to keep this power harnessed within a popular assembly. "We have already given in example one effectual check to the Dog of war," wrote Jefferson to Madison in 1789, "by transferring the power of letting him loose from the Executive to the Legislative body, from those who are to spend to those who are to pay."[5]

A misinterpretation of Article II, Section 2, sometimes leads to the unwarranted conclusion that the president enjoys preeminent authority over the war power. Properly understood, this section gives to the president the right and obligation as commander in chief to make use of the armed forces to *repel* sudden attacks upon the United States when delay to consult with Congress would be foolhardy, even suicidal. As commander in chief, the president is responsible as well for leading the armed forces in ways specified by Congress. The president, however, is not to initiate hostilities. Senator and constitutional authority Sam Ervin, Jr. (D–North Carolina), once emphasized the difference with these words:

A distinction must be drawn between *defensive warfare* and offensive warfare. There is no doubt whatever that the President has the authority under the Constitution, and, indeed, the duty, to use the Armed Forces to repel sudden armed attacks on the Nation. But any use of the Armed Forces for any purpose not directly related to the defense of the United States against sudden armed aggression, and I emphasize the word "sudden," can be undertaken only upon congressional authorization.[6]

During the first hundred years of the nation's history, presidents largely honored this original understanding between the two branches. An important illustration is President Jefferson's handling of the Barbary pirates, who jeopardized U. S. shipping in the Mediterranean Sea. He dispatched a naval squadron to protect U. S. commerce in these waters; however, upon deciding that defensive action was insufficient, the president turned to Congress for permission to employ offensive measures against the pirates. He acknowledged that he himself was "unauthorized by the Constitution, without the sanction of Congress, to go beyond the line of defense," and requested permission to "place our force on an equal footing with that of its adversaries"—an offensive decision "confided by the Constitution to the legislature exclusively."[7] As a member of the House of Representatives, Abraham Lincoln observed in 1846 how "kings had always been involving and impoverishing their people in wars" and that the founders had properly "resolved to so frame the Constitution that *no one man* should hold the power of bringing this oppression upon us."[8]

Yet, the erosion of legislative control over the war power accelerated, slowly at first, and then in this century at an increasing rate. With congressional acquiescence, presidents during the late 1800s used military force abroad for limited, though sometimes clearly offensive, purposes, including the "hot pursuit" of criminals across international borders and operations against piracy and the slave trade. By the twentieth century, presidents would claim constitutional authority to direct military force against other sovereign nations. Although Presidents Theodore Roosevelt, William Howard Taft, and Woodrow Wilson never declared the right to launch full-scale war on behalf of the United States, they nonetheless did use the military to intervene repeatedly in the affairs of Mexico and other nations in Central America and the Caribbean. The precedents—and temptations—mounted for chief executives to exalt Article II, Section 2, of the Constitution over Article I, Section 8.

Then, early in the twentieth century, came the twin catastrophes of the Great Depression and World War II, both powerful catalysts for the further centralization of power in the White House. In this time of great peril for the nation, Americans were prepared to accept— they even demanded—aggressive leadership from the White House. In the worthy battle against the Axis powers, President Franklin D. Roosevelt exercised almost exclusive control over the war power. Strictly on his own authority and without meaningful consultation with Congress, Roosevelt in 1941—a time when the American people held strong isolationist sentiments—offered U.S.

forces for the protection of Greenland and Iceland against a Nazi invasion, assigned warships to accompany convoys loaded with supplies for war-racked Britain, and announced that U. S. naval ships would shoot on sight any German or Italian vessels of war discovered in the western Atlantic. The executive branch— by itself—had taken the United States into undeclared naval warfare in the Atlantic Ocean.

Few would dispute the merits of Roosevelt's cause, but by avoiding Congress he had established a dubious precedent for war-making that his successors could draw upon for purposes less clearly supported by the people. In 1950 President Harry Truman made the decision to commit American troops to a war in Korea without congressional authorization. Truman's only public explanation appeared in the *Department of State Bulletin*. "The President, as Commander in Chief of the Armed Forces of the United States, has full control over the use thereof," he opined, claiming an inherent constitutional right to make war based on a "traditional power of the President to use the Armed Forces of the United States without consulting Congress."[9]

Congress allowed this accretion of presidential power to pass with barely a murmur, though by 1951 the Senate leader, Robert Taft (R–Ohio), lamented that the president had "simply usurped authority, in violation of the laws and the Constitution, when he sent troops to Korea to carry out the resolution of the United Nations in an undeclared war."[10] Truman's secretary of state, Dean Acheson, found Taft's reference to constitutional questions quite improper: "We are in a position in the world today where the argument as to who has the power to do this, that, or the other thing, is not exactly what is called for from America in this very critical hour." Acheson declared magisterially that "not only has the President the authority to use the Armed Forces in carrying out the broad foreign policy of the United States and implementing treaties, but it is equally clear that this authority may not be interfered with by the Congress in the exercise of powers which it has under the Constitution."[11]

The Eisenhower administration took the argument a step further, requesting from Congress in 1955 a resolution that one leading senator called a "predated declaration of war" to defend the island of Formosa (Taiwan) against a Chinese attack.[12] According to historian Arthur M. Schlesinger, Jr., the Formosa Resolution failed to order a specific action or even to name an enemy: "Rather it committed Congress to the approval of hostilities without knowledge of the specific situation in which the hostilities would begin."[13]

The resolution passed, but Congress had at last become wary about its ebbing prerogatives. Two years later, in 1955, the Eisenhower administration sought passage of another resolution allowing the president to use military force, if necessary, in the Middle East against possible Soviet encroachments. Senator J. William Fulbright (D–Arkansas), chairman of the Foreign Relations Committee, complained that there had been:

> no real prior consultation with Congress, nor will there be any sharing of power. The whole manner of presentation of this resolution—leaks to the press, speeches to specially summoned Saturday joint sessions, and dramatic secret meetings of the Committee on Foreign Relations after dark one evening before the Congress was even organized, in an atmosphere of suspense and urgency—does not constitute consultation in the true sense. All this was designed to manage Congress, to coerce it into signing this blank check.[14]

Richard B. Russell (D–Georgia), widely regarded at the time as the most influential member of the Senate on military matters, concurred: "In my opinion, the Congress of the United States is being treated as a group of children, and very small children, and children with a very low IQ at that, in the manner that this resolution has been presented to us."[15] Senator Wayne Morse (D–Oregon) added:

> You have got a resolution here which, for the first time, suggests that the President of the United States can exercise discretion to proceed to protect the territorial integrity of some other country somewhere in the world attacked by some Communist country, because he thinks that eventually that may involve the security of the United States, and I think that is an absurd stretching of that alleged emergency power on the part of the President, and I think it would be a clear violation of the constitutional power of the president.[16]

The Senate agonized over the language of the resolution for many weeks, stumbling around in what Russell referred to as the "shadowland" that fell between the declaration-of-war and the commander-in-chief clauses of the Constitution. Finally, the senators decided to strike from the resolution the concept of legislative authorization; instead, the language would simply represent a statement of U. S. policy on the Middle East. On this basis the Middle East Resolution passed on March 12, 1957. The effect of the altered language was untoward. According to Schlesinger, Eisenhower became convinced "less of the need for serious consultation with Congress than of his inherent authority to employ armed forces at presidential will."[17] When the president sent U. S. troops to Lebanon later in the year, he neither invoked the Middle East Resolution nor requested authority from Congress but merely pointed to his authority as commander in chief.

The most fateful of the foreign policy resolutions passed by Congress was the Gulf of Tonkin Resolution, approved in August of 1964. Reacting to intelligence provided by the executive branch that suggested that U. S. naval vessels off the coast of Vietnam had come under enemy fire, legislators declared in the resolution: " . . . the Congress approves and supports the determination of the President, as Commander in Chief, to take all necessary measures to repel any armed attack against the forces of the United States and to prevent further aggression." Subsequently, Undersecretary of State Nicholas Katzenbach of the Johnson administration would point to the Gulf of Tonkin Resolution as the "functional equivalent" of a declaration of war by Congress—even though, according to a senior member of the Foreign Relations Committee who participated in the original debate, "Congress neither expected nor even considered at the time of the debate on the resolution that the President would later commit more than half a million American soldiers to a full-scale war in Vietnam."[18]

CONGRESS ON THE SIDELINES

Though the most visible and dramatic, control over the war power has been only one of many foreign policy options to experience a growth of presidential dominance. Others include the hidden use of the nation's intelligence agencies beyond the vision of legislative overseers, as well as reliance on secret executive agreements to bypass the constitutional treaty process.

In 1947 Congress passed the National Security Act, which established the modern intelligence community led by the Central Intelligence Agency (CIA). The purpose of the CIA and its sister agencies was to improve the gathering, analysis, and coordination of information (intelligence) in hopes of averting future surprise attacks like the one that devastated Pearl Harbor in 1941. Within months, however, executive officials turned to the CIA for quite a different mission: the secret conduct of operations (called covert actions) to influence other countries abroad and thwart Soviet expansion. The executive branch now had a new and virtually invisible arm to carry out its foreign policy—including the concealed use of force (known as paramilitary activity or "special operations").

The temptation for executive officials to resort to this approach, often as a means for bypassing congressional debate, has proven irresistible. A recent example is the Reagan administration's conduct of a secret war against the Sandinista regime in Nicaragua. As one of its leading officials told a congressional investigative committee in 1987, the administration "turned to covert action because they thought they could not get Congressional support for overt activities."[19] To avoid the restrictions Congress had placed on CIA covert actions in 1974 and 1980, the Reagan administration used the staff of the National Security Council (NSC) within the White House— a surrogate CIA—to carry out its secret operations. As a means of funding the operations, the NSC staff developed a network of private financiers: wealthy conservatives within this country and the leaders of selected foreign nations (South Africa among them).

According to the testimony of the key NSC staff aide involved in this subterfuge (Lieutenant Colonel Oliver L. North), the CIA leadership hoped eventually to establish an "off-the-shelf, self-sustaining, stand-alone" covert-action capability, free altogether of congressional interference.[20] To conceal this hidden power, North and other top officials simply lied to legislative overseers about its existence. The legerdemain made a mockery of the constitutional system of power sharing and checks and balances. Other administrations, too, have improperly used intelligence agencies. During the Kennedy years, the CIA attempted to carry out a variety of assassination plots against Fidel Castro, even hiring the Mafia to assist. Patrice Lumumba of the Congo (now Zaire) became another target for CIA assassins.

The executive branch has also used the intelligence agencies against legitimate dissenters within the United States—an internal police function expressly prohibited by the National Security Act. Government investigators discovered in 1975 that the CIA and a host of other secret agencies had spied on U. S. citizens, especially those who had protested the war in Vietnam. The Huston Plan, Operation CHAOS, Operation COINTELPRO, HQ-LINQUAL, and other codenames concealed an Orwellian assault against the privacy of Americans acting within their constitutional rights to dissent.[21] Congress might as well not have existed; the executive branch carried out its dark operations without debate or consultation, unfettered by the restraints of the law or the Constitution.

The erosion of the treaty power further illustrates the decline of democratic controls over foreign policy. In Article II, Section 2, the Constitution states that the president "shall have power, by and with the advice of the Senate to make treaties, provided two-thirds of the Senators present concur . . . " These words convey the idea of a partnership between the legislative and executive branches. As one prominent legal analyst of this treaty clause concludes, "The Founders made it unmistakably plain their intention to withhold from the President the power to enter into treaties all by himself. . . . "[22]

Yet, the historical record reveals that presidents and even middle-ranking officials in the executive branch have involved the United States in major foreign obligations without the requisite advice and consent of two-thirds of the Senate membership. Originally designed to be the solemn means by which the United States would enter into agreements with other nations, the treaty has been mostly abandoned by presidents in the modern era. Since 1946, less than 10 percent of the total number of international agreements have been approved through the treaty procedure; most have been based upon loosely worded statutes granting permission for negotiations (so-called statutory agreements), or, more troubling still, hidden transactions with other nations—sometimes sweeping in their import—carried out by the executive branch without meaningful consultation with Congress (executive agreements).[23]

As the war in Vietnam heated up in 1966 and threatened to spill over into Thailand, Secretary of State Dean Rusk warned that "no would-be aggressor should suppose that the absence of a defense treaty, congressional declaration, or U. S. military presence grants immunity to aggression." Rusk's motive was laudable enough, but members of Congress saw the declaration as a blow to their constitutional prerogatives. It "put Congress on notice," remarked a prominent senator, "that, with or without its consent, treaty or no treaty, the Executive will act as it sees fit against anyone whom it judges to be an aggressor. . . . It is indeed nothing less than a statement of intention on the part of the Executive to usurp the treaty power of the Senate."[24]

U. S. negotiations with Spain during the 1960s over military base rights provide another example of an attempt to bypass the Congress in foreign affairs. A series of secret understandings and communiqués between the executive branches of both governments created nothing less than a major security alliance. For the Senate Foreign Relations Committee, these secret negotiations represented an abandonment of constitutional procedure. "The making of such a commitment by means of an executive agreement, or a military memorandum," the committee reasoned, "has no valid place in our constitutional law, and constitutes a usurpation of the treaty power of the Senate." The committee referred to the Spanish bases agreement as a "quasi-commitment, unspecified as to exact import but, like buds in springtime, ready, under the right climatic conditions, to burst into full bloom."[25]

Looking more broadly at a wide range of international agreements entered into by the executive branch without legislative consultation, a committee member lamented: "It is really, under the existing situation, the President, and the President alone, who decides whether any agreement that is signed is going to be considered by this body at all. The President can dispense with Senate advice and consent merely by calling a treaty an executive agreement. I do not see that as a fair balance."[26]

Space in this volume does not permit an examination of additional attempts by the executive branch to exclude Congress in favor of foreign policy by administrative fiat: its efforts to monopolize information, its use of a "plumbers unit" during the Nixon years to stop leaks and harass White House enemies (and whose activities eventually produced the Watergate scandal), its use of "public diplomacy" to malign legislative critics and sway the U. S. public—often with misleading or false information (during the Reagan years this task was assigned to the CIA's leading propaganda expert, on leave to the NSC staff), and many other instances. Suffice it to say that the United States has drifted far away from the prudent system of power-sharing devised by the nation's founders.

CONGRESS REASSERTS ITSELF

Congress has become increasingly mindful of the dangers inherent in an "imperial presidency," a lesson the country learned anew through President Lyndon Johnson's misleading pronouncements on the Vietnam War, President Richard Nixon's complicity in the Watergate coverup, the revelations of CIA abuse, and the Iran–Contra scandal of the Reagan administration (in which arms were sold illegally to Iran and the profits diverted, again illegally, to the anti-Sandinista Contra guerrillas in Nicaragua). As a result, legislators have taken important steps to restore their eroded powers.

In 1973 Congress passed the War Powers Resolution, requiring the executive branch to report to Congress within forty-eight hours after introducing U. S. forces into an area of "hostilities." The president must withdraw the troops within ninety days unless Congress votes to approve their continued presence—an attempt to curb a future drift into war, like the escalation of fighting in Vietnam without open debate and approval by the plenary legislative membership. With the

1980 Intelligence Oversight Act, Congress required the executive branch to report in advance to the House and Senate intelligence committees (or, in times of acute emergency, to eight top legislative leaders) on any important intelligence operation. As for international agreements, all significant negotiations must now be reported to the House and Senate foreign affairs committees so that Congress will be aware of any agreement making outside the normal treaty procedure. Additional laws have been passed to institute democratic controls on other policy fronts.

The effects of these laws have been uneven. Presidents have usually chosen to ignore the reporting requirements of the War Powers Resolution, and legislators have been passive in their demands for reports. The Intelligence Oversight Act has had more success, but during the Iran–Contra operations the intelligence reporting requirements were ignored, as were (among other laws) the Boland amendments barring military aid to the Contras. And the law requiring reports on international agreements (the Case-Zablocki amendment of 1972) has been complied with only in a spotty fashion; sometimes the reports from the executive branch are over a year late.

Executive officials have resented this congressional resurgence. Many would prefer life without Congress and its nettlesome habit of debate and even saying no. This "micromanagement" from Capitol Hill can be, in their view, a nuisance at best. Their preference for "presidential unilateralism is usually couched in terms of constitutional prerogative or national security imperative," note two foreign policy specialists. "But the underlying reason has a more telling label: power politics. Presidents deliberately exclude Congress because they do not want Congress involved and because

members will ask too many questions and might actually oppose presidential decisions."[27]

This anti-Congress attitude is damaging to the country. In times of utmost national emergency, of course, no one expects the president to consult with the legislative branch; he or she must react quickly for the safety of the nation, as Lincoln did during the Civil War. Nor does anyone expect the executive branch to share delicate secrets widely on Capitol Hill, such as the names of U. S. spies overseas or the intricacies of operational plans and weapons systems. These secrets rightly belong in the secure safes of the appropriate agencies. But short of these exceptions, a return to the constitutional principles advocated by the founders would benefit the nation significantly. The founders wisely understood, as the late Senator Ervin often put it, that "one of the great advantages of the separation of powers is that it is difficult to corrupt all three branches at the same time."[28]

Reliance on the executive branch alone to conduct American foreign policy is simply too risky. Should one elected official in the White House decide whether you will go to war? One-person decision making is a prescription for poor policy. Good policy, by definition in a democracy, rests upon public debate and widespread citizen support, not upon secret communiqués, private funding, and sweeping national commitments made by a single individual—or, worse still, aides acting on what they think the president might approve, as evidently happened in the Iran–Contra operations.

Congress comprises elected officials from across the wide land. They remain in close communication with voters back home and, as a consequence, represent a sensitive barometer of public sentiment. Legislators can be an invaluable source of support for a president. They can legitimize an administration's policies and serve as an excellent sounding board with much collective wisdom and experience in foreign affairs. The opportunity to draw upon the combined experience and judgment of elected representatives in both branches of government is a great strength of American democracy.

As a former undersecretary of state notes, this kind of partnership or "compact" between the branches calls "for restraint on the part of the Congress—for Congress to recognize and accept the responsibility of the Executive to conduct and manage foreign policy on a daily basis." The executive branch, in turn, must be prepared to provide Congress "full information and consultation," and "broad policy should be jointly designed." For its part, Congress should only rarely, in extreme circumstances, attempt "to dictate or overturn Executive decisions and actions. . . . "[29] Advance consultation with members of Congress (or with a small group of their leaders in times of emergency) and congressional approval for major policy initiatives— here is the key to successful, bipartisan external relations rooted firmly in the soil of public support. They are the sine qua non for an effective, sustainable foreign policy.

Seeking consultation and approval from Congress may slow down the policy process somewhat (though legislators, too, can react quickly in times of emergency), but students of democracy must remember that higher values than efficiency are at stake in a free society. "The doctrine of the separation of powers was adopted by the Convention of 1787, not to promote efficiency," stressed Supreme Court Justice Louis Brandeis, but to limit the exercise of arbitrary power.

NOTES

1. James Sterling Young, *The Washington Community: 1800–1828* (New York: Columbia University Press, 1966), p. 81.
2. Frank Church, "Of Presidents and Caesars: The Decline of Constitutional Government in the Conduct of American Foreign Policy," *Idaho Law Review* 6 (Fall 1969): 14.
3. *The President: Office and Powers, 1787–1957*, rev. ed. (New York: New York University Press, 1957), p. 171.
4. *The Federalist* (New York: Modern Library, 1937), p. 448.
5. Julian P. Boyd, ed., *The Papers of Thomas Jefferson*, vol. 15 (Princeton: Princeton University Press, 1955), p. 397.
6. Senate Committee on Foreign Relations, *U. S. Commitments to Foreign Powers: Hearings*, 1967, p. 194; emphasis added.
7. James D. Richardson, ed., *Compilation of Messages and Papers of the Presidents*, vol. 1, Congress, Joint Committee on Printing (New York: Bureau of National Literature, 1897), p. 314.
8. Letter to William H. Herndon (February 15, 1848), in *The Collected Works of Abraham Lincoln* (New Brunswick: Rutgers University Press, 1953), 1: 451–52, cited in Senate Committee on Foreign Relations, *National Commitments*, April 16, 1969, *Report No. 91–129*, pp. 12–13 (the committee's emphasis).
9. *Department of State Bulletin* 23 (July 31, 1950): 173–77.
10. *Congressional Record*, January 24, 1955, p. 601.
11. Testimony, in Senate Committees on Foreign Relations and Armed Services, *Assignment of Ground Forces of the United States to Duty in the Eu-*

ropean Area: Hearings, February 28, 1951, p. 306.

12. Cited by Senator Robert Byrd (D– West Virginia), *Congressional Record,* April 28, 1986, p. S4963.

13. Arthur M. Schlesinger, Jr., *The Imperial Presidency* (Boston: Houghton Mifflin, 1974), pp. 159–60.

14. Byrd, *Congressional Record,* April 28, 1986, p. S4964.

15. Senate Committee on Foreign Relations, *Executive Sessions of the Senate Foreign Relations Committee Together with Joint Sessions with the Senate Armed Services Committee (Historical Series),* vol. 9, *1957* (Washington, D. C.: Government Printing Office, 1979), p. 267.

16. Ibid., p. 310.

17. Schlesinger, *The Imperial Presidency,* p. 162.

18. Church, "Of Presidents and Caesars," p. 10.

19. Testimony, May 11, 1987, Robert McFarlane, former national security adviser, in Senate Select Committee on Secret Military Assistance to Iran and the Nicaraguan Opposition and House Select Committee to Investigate Covert Arms Transactions with Iran, *Hearings.*

20. Testimony, July 9, 1987, ibid.

21. On these operations, see Loch K. Johnson, *A Season of Inquiry: Congress and Intelligence* (Chicago: Dorsey Press, 1988).

22. Raoul Berger, "The Presidential Monopoly of Foreign Relations," *Michigan Law Review* 71 (1972): 39.

23. See Loch K. Johnson, *The Making of International Agreements: Congress against the Executive* (New York: New York University Press, 1984).

24. Church, "Of Presidents and Caesars," p. 4.

25. Senate Committee on Foreign Relations, *U. S. Commitments to Foreign Powers,* pp. 28–29; emphasis added.

26. Senator Dick Clark (D–Iowa), *Congressional Record,* June 28, 1978, p. S10010.

27. Morton H. Halperin and Gary M. Stern, "Lawful Wars," *Foreign Policy* 72 (Fall 1988): 174–75.

28. Senator Ervin, conversation with the author, University of North Carolina, Chapel Hill, May 16, 1970.

29. Warren Christopher, "Ceasefire between the Branches: A Compact in Foreign Affairs," *Foreign Affairs* 60 (Summer 1982): 999.

SUGGESTED READINGS

FRANCK, THOMAS M., AND EDWARD WEISBAND. *Foreign Policy by Congress.* New York: Oxford University Press, 1979. An analysis of efforts by Congress to restore its foreign policy prerogatives.

JOHNSON, LOCH K. *America's Secret Power: The CIA in a Democratic Society.* New York: Oxford University Press, 1989. An examination of the use (and misuse) of the Central Intelligence Agency, and of the attempts to bring intelligence operations within a framework of democratic controls.

SCHLESINGER, ARTHUR M., JR. *The Imperial Presidency.* Boston: Houghton Mifflin, 1973. An influential chronicle of the rise in executive dominance over foreign (and domestic) policy.

The President Must Forge Foreign Policy

James K. Oliver
University of Delaware

With the exception of a brief period in the mid and late 1970s, Congress has occupied a peripheral position in the formulation of U.S. foreign policy since World War II. Furthermore, however salutary its penetration to the center of the policy making process may have been in hastening the end of the Vietnam War and curbing other overextensions of U.S. power, the means fashioned by Congress at the time have proved of limited utility and appropriateness in sustaining the expanded congressional role. Furthermore, their continued application has too often been merely disruptive, contributory to policy making stalemate, and, therefore,

ultimately made Congress vulnerable to charges of incompetence and irresponsibility.

The constitutional design provides Congress and the president with different capabilities that are appropriate to different kinds of foreign policy activity. World and domestic politics have evolved and combined to create a policy making environment in which the potency of the presidential mix of policy making capabilities has increased while the congressional mix has become more difficult to apply. In addition, the character of the contemporary Congress as an institution, that is, the political incentives and limitations working on the membership of the House and Senate, has not proved advantageous. The combination of these changes in the policy making environment and Congress as an institution leads to what former Senator John Tower has referred to as the "clear-cut issue of the efficacy of Congressional involvement in foreign policy."[1]

Thus, the kind of institution Congress has become and the character of the world in which it must operate, as much as claims of constitutional intent and legally defined powers, have been decisive in determining the role Congress can and should play in the making of foreign policy. There are important limits on congressional power—limits recently reaffirmed in a series of important judicial decisions—but they are only a part of the reason that Congress cannot play a positive and central role in the setting of foreign policy. This essay will trace the evolution and interaction of the executive–legislative relationship and the world role of the United States as a means for identifying the sources of Congress's problematic foreign policy making potential.

THE MAKING OF FOREIGN POLICY IN REVIEW

Two hundred years ago the United States was positioned both figuratively and literally on the edge of the international system. Its involvement with the world, after the intensive diplomatic activity to terminate the Revolutionary War, was ideally to have been confined to commercial relations conducted largely by private individuals. In the classic formulation of George Washington's farewell address, the United States was to minimize its diplomatic contacts and avoid altogether the kinds of foreign entanglements that would necessitate the "efficient" activity of a strong president. [2] Foreign involvement of the extensive and intensive sort undertaken by the great powers of the late eighteenth and early nineteenth centuries was deemed imprudent for the new and weak United States. Thus, the divided constitutional grant of power and a limited foreign policy were sufficient to ensure a central role for Congress. To the extent that the United States became involved in international relations, the normal mode of engagement was to be by means of treaties, advice and consent to which was a clear Senate prerogative and necessary under the Constitution for any such agreement to become binding as law. The diplomatic agents responsible for the conduct of such diplomacy were subject to approval by the Senate. And insofar as war was initiated through formal declarations and conducted at what would now be thought a glacial pace, control of involvement in war was very much within the grasp of Congress. Finally, mobilizing resources for the conduct of diplomacy, whether by normal or military means, was very much a legislative act in that the control of ways and means was solely within the congressional ambit.

The president's prerogatives clearly included those of the chief diplomat, and he could, of course, administer wars as commander in chief. But even this limited grant of explicit authority was a sufficient basis, when combined with the events of the late eighteenth and early nineteenth centuries, to lead to an expansion of the president's role in foreign policy. The protection of American commercial activity, the opportunities for continental expansion by means of activist diplomacy, and most important, defining and protecting the interests of the United States vis-à-vis the global strategic maneuvering of Britain, France, Spain, and Russia all contributed to the de facto inflation of the foreign-policy presidency. Nevertheless, a central role for Congress was not precluded—though it was certainly complicated—by these events. Indeed, a hundred years later, Congress would demonstrate that it retained the capacity to check and decisively curtail the attempt of Woodrow Wilson to institutionalize a position of global leadership for the United States in what Wilson insisted was a transformed international system. For more than twenty years after the defeat of American involvement in Wilson's League of Nations, Congress was the policy making focus of a foreign policy that echoed Washington's axioms even as the American economic and military security became more globally interdependent.

Ironically, however, it was the success of Congress in asserting its centrality, even primacy, in the making of foreign policy in the interwar period that undercut its legitimacy as a central player after World War II. American isolationism was seen as a contributing factor in the collapse of world order in the 1930s. Furthermore, Congress was understood to be the institutional embodiment and agent of that isolationism. This image of an obstructionist and myopic Congress was compounded by the less than enthusiastic early reaction given by a Republican-controlled Congress to President Harry Truman's postwar program of containment by means of the Marshall Plan. In the post-World War II era of U.S. global involvement and activism, Congress was viewed, therefore, as an institution to be feared and co-opted but, ultimately, insulated from the presidential center of policy making. For the executive branch "cold warriors" of the late 1940s, this was one of the central lessons to be learned from the Wilsonian experience.

No less important for the diminution of the congressional policy making role was that the leadership of Congress came to accept the executive's analysis of congressional limits. Until the mid-1950s there was at least a debate as Truman struggled to build support in Congress for containment built on massive economic assistance and reconstruction programs in Europe and the non-Western world, culminating in a military alliance with the West Europeans, the North Atlantic Treaty Organization. Throughout this process, the congressional leadership was courted and consulted as a necessary condition for the construction of a consensus for the new U.S. world role. But the onset of the cold war was marked by escalating tensions with the Soviet Union, its emergence as a nuclear power and its consolidation of control over East Europe, and the ascendancy of communism in China. Finally, in June of 1950, North Korea attacked South Korea and the administration acted unilaterally to insert U.S. troops into an undeclared war in Korea. This step was followed in late 1950 with a presidential decision to increase U.S. ground forces in West Germany without consultation of Congress. A ferocious "Great Debate" ensued in the Senate over Truman's claim to inherent powers as commander in chief to use troops in combat in Korea and increase forces in Europe without congressional approval. In the end, Congress was unable or unwilling to check the president. When, finally, Senator Joseph McCarthy launched his viciously partisan attack on Truman, the Democrats, and ultimately even Republican supporters of containment, including the Eisenhower administration, the appearance of an impotent Congress was compounded by the evident irresponsibility of one of its members.

The "lesson" of Wilson's bitter defeat

was seemingly confirmed. Though Mc-Carthy was eventually checked, the leadership of Congress seemed chastened. Two cold war presidents—one a liberal Democrat, the other a conservative Republican—had both insisted that the world had changed dramatically. Nuclear weapons, Soviet aggressiveness, and the global nature of the threat all meant that a foreign policy and global activism that the founding fathers would have regarded as imprudent and dangerous for republican institutions were now deemed necessary and realistic. Crises, including the threat and use of force, nuclear weapons, secrecy, and covert operations, were all to be normal modes of strategic engagement and diplomacy. Under these circumstances, "bipartisanship" had to become the watchword of policy formulation. And although the notion originally meant the suppression of partisan conflict between the parties on foreign policy, it came, operationally, to mean more. Insofar as Congress was controlled by the Democrats and the White House by the Republicans throughout most of the 1950s, bipartisanship worked to suppress institutional conflict and the ceding of foreign policy leadership and primacy to the president. When in the 1960s the Democrats regained control of the presidency, the subordination of a Democratically controlled Congress was confirmed.

Senator J. William Fulbright summarized the conditions that led to the displacement of Congress from the center of policy making:

> The circumstance has been crisis, an entire era of crisis in which urgent decisions have been required again and again, decisions of a kind that the Congress is ill-equipped to make with what had been thought to be the requisite speed. The President has the means at his disposal for

prompt action: the Congress does not. When the security of the country is endangered, or thought to be endangered, there is a powerful premium for prompt action, and that means executive action.[3]

Senator Fulbright, who would during the Vietnam years lead the attack on the "imperial presidency" and thereby energize the "Vietnam revolution" in executive–legislative relations, could be found saying on the eve of John Kennedy's presidency:

> So it is the President that must take the lead, and we would help him. We would accede to his requests. If he puts it the other way around, it is going to fail, and I think he makes a mistake in not taking a stronger stand in this field. . . .
>
> I'm talking about political management . . . of the Congress. Our strong Presidents always have, if they are successful in this field, to counteract the parochial interests of our Congress.[4]

His position was by no means an eccentric one at the time.

It is not surprising, therefore, that throughout the 1950s and well into the 1960s, Congress by overwhelming margins granted to a succession of presidents of both parties a series of resolutions encompassing enormous latitude to manage the great crises of the cold war: Formosa, the Middle East, the Cuban missile crisis, and finally, the Tonkin Gulf Resolution. Moreover, these same presidents were extended virtually complete freedom in managing the military budget and covert operations. Congress possessed little information concerning diplomacy, economic and military assistance programs, arms sales, covert and overt operations, or budgetary planning or expenditures other than that provided by the executive. The operational definitions of the diplomatic and commander in chief's functions—areas long agreed as within the province of the executive—had already expanded dramatically in response to the demands of the cold war and global containment. Now, even the legislative and programmatic powers of Congress atrophied or were appropriated by the president. The president had accumulated—largely with congressional assent—powers that, in President Truman's words, "would have made Caesar, Genghis Khan or Napoleon bite his nails in envy."[5]

The exercise of those powers proved, however, catastrophic as first John Kennedy, then Lyndon Johnson, and finally Richard Nixon sought to implement global containment in the Vietnamese arena. As evidence of the failure of policy mounted, the credibility and legitimacy of the imperial presidency were undermined and ultimately collapsed. As the Nixon administration was consumed by Watergate, Congress filled the vacuum and advanced a series of measures designed to constrain the president by increasing Congress's ability to intervene in the making and conduct of foreign and defense policy. Thus the War Powers Act of 1973, the Congressional Budget and Impoundment Control Act of 1974, and amendments to the Arms Export Control Act and the Foreign Assistance Act were all designed either to preempt presidential foreign policy initiatives in certain areas or to guarantee that Congress would be able to veto presidential initiatives once taken if it objected to their premises or effects. During the mid-1970s, Congress used its newly claimed powers to force detailed revisions of several major arms sales agreements in the Middle East, to embargo arms to Turkey when that country invaded Cyprus in 1974, and to severely restrict the ability of the Ford administration to intervene in

the Angolan civil war in 1975 and 1976. Finally, through a series of hearings and amendments to the Foreign Assistance Act, Congress exposed many of the intelligence establishment's cold war failures and expanded congressional involvement in the monitoring and approval of covert operations.

Taken together, these acts constituted a virtual revolution in executive–legislative relations. Talk of the codetermination of foreign policy and "congressional government" was commonplace. At a minimum, it was assumed that Congress had reclaimed much that had been lost to the president during the cold war of the 1940s, 1950s, and 1960s.

Yet, a decade later, President Ronald Reagan ordered the invasion of a sovereign country, Grenada, and replaced its government without consulting Congress. He subsequently provided tens of millions of dollars of military assistance to the Contras operating from Honduras and Costa Rica against Nicaragua, notwithstanding a law prohibiting such aid. Earlier, U.S. troops were sent to Lebanon—where some 241 of them were killed—without Reagan's agreeing that congressional approval was necessary (but welcoming it when it was offered). He ordered the bombing, without prior consultation of Congress, of another sovereign state, Libya, in an attempt to kill its leader, Muammar Qaddafi, and to punish the Libyan government for supporting terrorist attacks on American military personnel in West Germany. The president secretly sold arms to Iran, a country identified by him as the chief source of terrorism in the world, and attempted to use the profits from the sale to support the Contras. Finally, with no congressional consultation, Reagan sent the U.S. Navy to escort American-flagged and ultimately neutral shipping through the Persian Gulf in the presence of major hostilities between Iran and Iraq, hostilities that in time involved major damage to and death aboard U.S. warships and attacks by the navy on Iranian military forces.

In its totality, this exercise of presidential initiative was certainly as great and consequential as that undertaken by Presidents Johnson and Nixon during the Vietnam years. Whatever the presumed constraining force of the legislation emanating from the revolution in executive–legislative relations in the 1970s, the presidency of the 1980s remained institutionally potent and quite capable of seizing the foreign policy initiative from Congress and pursuing a policy course often at odds with a majority of the legislature.

The sources of this abrupt reversal of fortune for an ascendant Congress and a presidency deemed in decline only months before the arrival of Reagan in office are numerous. Clearly, Reagan's popularity and his capacity to use the media to communicate his optimism and commitment to bringing America "back" from the "decline" of the late 1960s and 1970s are key factors in explaining the resurgence of the presidency. But there has been more involved than personality and skillful manipulation of the inherent advantages of the presidency as the central mediator of most Americans' view and understanding of the world. In the first place, newly claimed congressional prerogatives were brought into question by the courts. No less important, the limits of Congress as a foreign policy making institution became increasingly apparent by the end of the 1970s even as the revolution in executive–legislative relations seemed at its peak.

Even before Reagan became president, the courts in a series of decisions during the Carter years reaffirmed the primacy of the president in the foreign policy field.[6] Members of the House of Representatives challenged the constitutional authority of President Jimmy Carter to transfer the Panama Canal to the government of Panama under the Panama Canal treaties ratified by the Senate. When relations with the People's Republic of China were normalized in 1978, previously ratified treaties with Taiwan were terminated, evoking a legal challenge by Senator Barry Goldwater to the president's authority to terminate the treaties without the concurrence of the Senate. Earlier, in 1977, a similar question had been raised concerning the Carter administration's return of the symbolically important "Holy Crown of St. Stephen" to the Hungarian government without senatorial consent. Later, in 1979, the president's authority unilaterally to suspend, during the course of negotiations over the return of American hostages held by Iran, legal provisions concerning claims against the Iranian government was challenged in the courts. In proceedings during 1979–1981 the power of the president to withhold a passport for national security reasons was challenged. In every one of these cases the federal courts or, ultimately, the Supreme Court upheld the president's power and prerogatives in the foreign policy area.

Finally, in the landmark case *Immigration and Naturalization Service v. Chadha,*[7] the Supreme Court struck at the very heart of the congressional "Vietnam revolution" against presidential primacy in foreign affairs. Specifically, the Court declared unconstitutional the provisions for legislative vetoes of presidential actions that were central to the War Powers Act and numerous other pieces of foreign policy legislation passed during and immediately after the Vietnam War. Congress had asserted that simply by passing concurrent or one-house resolutions not subject to presidential veto it could, for example, stop the executive from using U.S. armed forces in hostilities or circumstances where hostilities were imminent (War Powers Act).[8]

The lower federal courts and the Supreme Court in these cases maintained a position consistent with previous decisions refining the constitutional foreign policy powers. First, the courts are extremely reluctant to become involved in foreign policy questions. But second, when they do become involved, they almost invariably uphold the primacy of the president as *the* central actor in the formulation and conduct of foreign and defense policy. In the famous case of *U. S. v. Curtiss-Wright Export Corporation et al.* (299 U.S. 304), the Court held that with respect to negotiations, the president "alone has the power to speak or listen as a representative of the nation" and thereby established a principle of presidential primacy that over the next fifty years has been refined and extended to cover virtually every aspect of foreign affairs except those that touch on First Amendment freedoms[9] or the role of the judiciary itself.[10] Thus, even as the superior political skills of Reagan were supplanting congressional claims of a central role in the foreign policy process, the courts were undercutting Congress's legal and constitutional bases for such a role.

It should also be recalled that Congress's move to the center of policy making in the 1970s occurred by default. The collapse of the presidential center under the burden of massive policy failure and the breakdown of policy consensus within the foreign policy making elite opened the door to congressional activism. But only after public opinion turned against the Vietnam War and after Nixon's self-inflicted wound did the executive–

legislative "revolution" occur. Moreover, it is important to understand the nature of the instruments that Congress devised to assert its claim to policy making centrality.

Each of the major legislative acts was either reactive, negative, or both. The War Powers Act, arms export control, foreign assistance, and intelligence oversight all centered on procedures that were triggered by a presidential proposal or action. The Senate's investigation of covert intelligence activities, the changes forced in arms sales agreements, the Turkish arms embargo, the prohibition of intervention in the Angolan civil war—all were reactive and negative. In all cases Congress had waited for presidential action and then intervened to force a change or modification of a presidentially initiated foreign policy departure. Seldom if ever does Congress appear during this period to be advancing new policy initiatives.

In large measure this reactive behavior is because of the nature of Congress's policy making powers. Congressional leverage on the policy process is most evident with respect to investigation, publicity, and programmatic policy making.[11] This means that whereas Congress is well positioned to exercise a restraining power on policy or even to veto policy, it is not able to respond with great agility to the day-to-day vagaries of specific bilateral relations, developments in a particular country, or crises. The tools developed during the congressional "Vietnam revolution" were in fact blunt instruments more effective as threats than as means for systematic participation in policy making or the conduct of diplomacy. Congress can question and check, but it cannot easily initiate and follow up on policy at an operational level.

In part this is the result of Congress's powers being essentially programmatic.

It is also due, however, to the political constraints operating on and in the Congress. Two are most important: the constraints imposed by the electoral calendar, and the representational character of Congress. Insofar as all of the House members and one-third of the senators must face the electorate every two years, the planning horizon of the congressional politician is usually about two years out. No matter how "safe" the seat of a senator or representative, the influence of the electoral calendar is pervasive on the *institution* and imposes on the members of Congress an essentially short-term perspective on international events and reactions to them. This short-term perspective is compounded by a preoccupation with the particular that also results from the political and "representational" function of Congress. Insofar as the Congress responds to pressures from constituents and interest groups, institutional attention is fragmented as members focus on the increasingly well-organized and -financed pressures of the moment.

Finally, within Congress itself, the "Vietnam revolution" led to a dramatic democratization of the institution. A major part of the reform thrust of the 1970s was the transformation of the power structure of Congress even as the executive–legislative relationship was being changed. Internally, this meant a significant reduction of the traditional centers of control. The seniority system that for decades had guaranteed that centralized control of the substance and flow of legislation would be concentrated in the hands of the House and Senate leadership and key committee chairs was modified. And the number of committees and subcommittees proliferated, especially in the Senate, as newer and more insistent members entered Congress demanding a greater say in its operation. These in-

dividuals were in turn less dependent upon the parties for their election and reelection as organized political action committees and television became more important. The capacity to mobilize money and ensure one's personal visibility in Congress became more important to political success than party or institutional loyalty or attention to the details and nuance of issues.

The upshot has been an overall decline in institutional coherence and capacity to focus in a systematic fashion on issues and policy. Insofar as episodic intervention in the conduct of policy proves profitable politically, it will be undertaken; for example, revelations about the outrageous costs of hammers and toilet seats sold to the Defense Department. But how thorough or sustained is the probing of the policies, assumptions, and strategic thinking underlying the defense budget? The latter would indeed be the mark of Congress's playing a central role in the setting of foreign and national security policy. The willingness and capacity of Congress to play such a role, *however desirable it may be*, are, sadly, not self-evident.

SUMMING UP

In the final analysis, Congress became through the revolution of the 1970s more "democratic" and "representational" but not necessarily more "competent."[12] Former Senator Adlai Stevenson III, one of the leaders of the congressional reform effort of the 1970s, has recently summarized the skepticism of many who would perhaps prefer a central congressional role in the making of foreign policy but doubt its likelihood:

> There are, it seems to me, inherent limits to any reasonable expectations

of the Congress. It is representative. Congress represents the interests of people and organizations which are diverse and often in conflict. It mirrors. It amplifies the discordance which seems to be natural to our country. Its 535 individuals, unleashed by the reforms of the seventies, preoccupy the Secretary of State and the executive branch at large with hearings *ad infinitum* before a myriad of committees and subcommittees, all with overlapping jurisdictions and conflicting interests to represent. This is not a process which you can reasonably expect to produce policy, sound or unsound, except by way of supporting policies of the president.[13]

Absent such support, the congressional process becomes a thing unto itself, preoccupied with its own perfection and the political survival of its members. Predictably, therefore, when presidentially initiated and conducted foreign policy is successful, most members of Congress will cheer and applaud whatever the legal basis of the action; for

example, the bombing of Libya and the Grenada and Panama invasions. If, however, policy fails, congressional booing and hissing will be the accompaniment to a newfound congressional concern for redefining and asserting the congressional role at the center of the foreign policy making process. There is little in the postwar history of these efforts, however, to support the expectation that Congress can sustain these episodic intrusions into the center of the policy process with the necessary measure of sensitivity to international complexity, clarity as to American goals and objectives, or command of the necessary policy means. Sadly, a similar argument might be mounted against the contemporary presidency. But this is not a sufficient argument to lift the indictment lodged against Congress. Rather, it compels us to contemplate anew de Tocqueville's anxious lament: "As for myself, I do not hesitate to say that it is especially in the conduct of their foreign relations that democracies appear to me decidedly inferior to other governments."[14]

NOTES

1. John G. Tower, "Congress versus the President: The Formulation and Implementation of American Foreign Policy," *Foreign Affairs* 60 (Winter 1981/1982): 232.

2. See Felix Gilbert, *To the Farewell Address* (New York: Harper & Row, 1961).

3. Statement of Senator J. William Fulbright in Senate Subcommittee on Separation of Powers of the Judiciary Committee, *Separation of Powers*, 90th Cong., 1st sess., 1967, p. 42.

4. "Meet the Press," June 7, 1959, quoted in James Robinson, *Congress*

and Foreign Policy-Making, rev. ed. (Homewood, Ill.: Dorsey Press, 1967), pp. 185–86.

5. Cited by Clinton Rossiter in *The American Presidency*, 2d ed. (New York: Harcourt Brace Jovanovich, 1960), p. 30.

6. For a review of these years and decisions, see Warren Christopher, "Ceasefire between the Branches: A Compact in Foreign Affairs," *Foreign Affairs* 60 (Summer 1982): 989–1005.

7. No. 80–1832 (June 23, 1983).

8. For a review of the impact of the *Chadha* decision, see House Com-

mittee on Foreign Affairs, *The U.S. Supreme Court Decision Concerning the Legislative Veto Hearings*, 98th Cong., 1st sess., 1983. Especially useful is the essay by the Congressional Research Service's Raymond J. Celada, "Effect of the Legislative Veto Decisions on the Two-House Disapproval Mechanism to Terminate U.S. Involvement in Hostilities Pursuant to Unilateral Presidential Action," at pp. 296–326.

9. See *New York Times Co. v. Nixon* 403 U.S. 713 (1971), the "Pentagon papers" case.

10. *U.S. v. Nixon*, 481 U.S. 683 (1974).

11. See I. M. Destler, "The Constitution and Foreign Affairs," in *A Reader in American Foreign Policy*, ed. James McCormick (Itasca, Ill.: F. E. Peacock, 1986).

12. See the exchange between former Senator Adlai Stevenson III and Professor Benjamin Page in Benjamin I. Page, "Representation as Well as Competence: Congress and President in U.S. Foreign Policy," Working Paper Series prepared for presentation at the Constitutional Bicentennial Conference, Nelson A. Rockefeller Center, Dartmouth College, Hanover, N. H., February 17, 1987, pp. 30–37.

13. Ibid., p. 32.

14. Alexis de Tocqueville, *Democracy in America* (New York: Vintage Books, 1945), 1: 243.

SUGGESTED READINGS

CHRISTOPHER, WARREN. "Ceasefire between the Branches: A Compact in Foreign Affairs." *Foreign Affairs* 60 (Summer 1982). An argument for a balanced approach to foreign policy-making, but one in which presidential initiative is seen as central.

HENKIN, LOUIS. "Foreign Affairs and the Constitution." *Foreign Affairs* 66 (Winter 1987/1988). An overview of executive and legislative foreign policy powers and their development that lends some support to advocates of congressional primacy.

TOWER, JOHN G. "Congress versus the President." *Foreign Affairs* 60 (Winter 1981/1982). A strong attack on the competency of Congress in foreign policy-making that asserts the central role of presidential leadership.

VII

THE PRESIDENCY

Is America Best Served by a Powerful Presidency?

The casual reader might think Professors Milne and Robertson are simply rehashing the issues addressed by Professors Johnson and Oliver, but the focus here is both broader and narrower than in the two previous essays. Broader in that Milne and Robertson are free to consider a wider range of issues, including domestic as well as foreign policy concerns. But narrower, and more pointed, because the emphasis is more explicitly on the workings of the executive branch.

Milne makes the case in "The Power Presidency" that given the challenges of the modern world, we have no choice but to rely on a strong presidency in order to address our national problems. Congress, he believes, is simply ill-prepared to deal with not only foreign policy problems but major domestic issues, such as civil rights, in a meaningful comprehensive way. He concedes that some presidents have been less effective in using their office to accomplish their goals, but when problems are effectively addressed, it is through the presidency. The Supreme Court also has been forced to act on issues that Congress has ignored, but it ultimately must depend on presidential enforcement of its decisions (as well as on presidential appointment of its personnel). Further, because of its nature, the Court moves only reluctantly into many areas of political dispute. Only the presidency can command the attention of the media, avoid the parochial interests of the members of Congress, and speak effectively to a myriad of national problems.

That recent presidents have exercised enormous power Robertson does not dispute. That the presidency has become the most powerful of the three branches of our national government is also taken by him as a matter of fact. But Robertson is not so sanguine about the results as is Milne. Indeed, in "The Covert Presidency" he sees development of a "covert government" in the White House, in which the president has built around him a government-within-the-government that is used to circumvent not only Congress but the regular executive departments of the government. Facts are manipulated and powers interpreted in such a way as to build, behind the security of the White House walls, a government that would seem to challenge the very existence of representative government.

The charges made by Milne about the venality and ineffectiveness of the modern Congress (justifying the need for a strong chief executive) and those raised by Robertson concerning the growth of the covert presidency as an unhealthy commentary on the democratic nature of our government are serious concerns. They have to do with problems that exist today, but each essayist obviously would project his own view into the future and expect existing trends to worsen. Both arguments raise anew the constitutional question of separation of powers that has permeated the concerns of other authors in this volume (Blessing, Saffell, Johnson, and Oliver).

In many ways the issue for the reader is what measure of efficiency does the modern world, and the problems it presents, demand from our governmental system and at what price? Do ideas for reinvigorating the plan of separation of powers and checks and balances come to mind? What other measures might be taken to assure that our system can work without sacrificing the goal of a responsive, representative system?

The Power Presidency

James S. Milne

West Chester University

The American political system . . . has worked best as a presidential system. Only strong presidents have been able to overcome the tendencies toward inertia in a structure so cunningly composed of checks and balances.[1]

The president, Congress, and the Supreme Court are constitutionally equal, each branch having the power to check potential abuses by the other two. Such is the typical argument of American constitutional theorists. In reality, the United States of the twenty-first century is positioned within a complex, international environment of an interdependent worldwide economy driven by multinational corporations. National politics is intertwined in this web of international activity. In such a context, the executive, judicial, and legislative branches of the federal system simply do not function as coequal constitutional partners. When the president of the moment is not perceived as "strong," the system does not produce decisions effectively and efficiently. What is needed is a powerful president, one who can impose his or her will if necessary![2]

Throughout the country's history presidents have utilized great power (some argue unconstitutionally so) to marshal whatever national forces were necessary to cope with perceived threats to national supremacy or international security. The examples necessarily include George Washington and the "Whisky Rebellion," Thomas Jefferson and the "Barbary pirates" and the Louisiana Purchase, Abraham Lincoln and the Civil War, William McKinley and the Spanish-American War, Franklin Roosevelt and World War II, and the numerous nondeclared, "cold" and "hot" wars dictated by presidential decision making since 1945.

Professor David Robertson's point of view in his essay "The Covert Presidency" suggests the assertion of power by "strong" presidents is somehow unnatural and, therefore, "wrong." His argument strikes this writer as another in a spate of unrealistic criticisms of the American presidency in the context of the modern world. While emphasizing how dreadful the assertion of power is by contemporary presidents, Robertson necessarily is implying that the system should operate in a vacuum. It is interesting, however, tht he never spells out his visionary world; he never explains to us how the political system will identify objectives, initiate actions, and operationalize policy in the absence of strong presidential leadership. The belief here is that Robertson does not because he cannot!

Robertson's charges about the abuse of presidential power are not only unrealistic but also incorrect. The reality of the national emergency powers invoked by presidents historically is that such were and remain extraconstitutional. Presidents succeeded in using these powers precisely because Congress either didn't want to act—or couldn't. With few exceptions, the other branch, the Supreme Court, also has always laid low in the face of domestic upheaval or international security questions.[3]

Throughout his essay Robertson not only acknowledges the central part presidents play in domestic and international policy making but also portrays the increasing role modern presidents have played as initiators and agenda setters. He discusses the "enormous pressures for enhanced presidential power" in international affairs and states as well that "the president has been expected to exercise leadership as the chief domestic policy initiator and executive of the national government." Robertson acknowledges, "A yawning gap separates these enormous responsibilities and limited presidential powers [the executive possesses] to live up to them." He proceeds to lace his essay with examples of limitations on presidential power, stemming from actions of other branches and those of the bureaucracy, the media, and the international environment. Robertson laments the presidential assertion of the very powers he delineates. It appears not to occur to him that these very presidential powers emerged and are deemed appropriate by the American public precisely because their effective use is essential for national survival.

In fairness to Robertson, his assertion that the president is too powerful is rooted in the American culture. Tyranny was feared by the founding fathers, and the fear of tyranny has been imbued in every generation since. The irony is that the American people do want a strong government. Indeed, they do not want the key components of democracy undermined, but they do want a government capable of effective action. Such action requires creativity, initiative, and rhetoric, to be sure. Realistically, however, if effective programs and policies are to emerge, strategic plans must be developed, budgets built, negotiations completed, diplomatic agreements reached, and operations implemented. Only under the leadership of a strong president can these practical outcomes be achieved.

The Supreme Court is constitutionally structured to be incapable of achieving any of these outcomes. Certainly, it has the ability, if it has the will, to call the nation's attention to critical constitutional issues. The myriad of civil rights decisions in the 1960s amply demonstrates this. Nonetheless, even the most strident supporter of these Supreme Court initiatives acknowledges that "success" was achieved only with the concomitant strong support of Presidents John Kennedy and Lyndon Johnson.

Congress, in turn, speaks with 535 voices. Robertson's point about the severe weakening of the political parties is correct, but what he fails to sense is that the present state of the parties actually destroys any realistic hope that Congress can act cohesively in the nation's best interest. Because of the disintegration of the already relatively weak parties, combined with the image making of the television era, Congress is now composed of 535 political parties, one for each member. Representatives label themselves Democrats or Republicans as part of their campaign strategies. However, they have built their own political entourages and used them, first, to gain office and, second, to retain their positions. The high percentage of incumbents reelected is staggering. Such a pattern can be achieved only if the members cater to the narrow interests that have contributed to their enormous war chests and self-promotional campaigns. Such catering not only constitutes "marginal bribery" but also negates any possibility of cohesive congressional action for the national good.

Typically, Congress has complained about what it perceived to be presidential usurpations of power but yielded nonetheless. In fact, legislation passed by Congress, especially the Budgeting and Accounting Act of 1971 and the Full Employment Act of 1946, in effect "mandated presidents to be the general managers of the economy. . . . the president, not Congress [is] recognized as the initiator of anti-employment and anti-inflation policies."[4]

Prior to World War II there was an ebb and flow to perceived national emergencies. After each subsided, Congress and the Court would engage in a flurry of activity designed, in retrospect, to reinstate the intended constitutional equilibrium among the three branches. Since 1945, however, the United States has been in a constant state of national emergency. "Hot" and "cold" wars, driven by the "containment" foreign policy adopted by all post-World War II presidents since Harry Truman, have dictated the national security concerns of most Americans. "The power of the presidency lies largely in the public's perception of his leadership capabilities. The electorate may be willing to accept an austere budget but not a weak-appearing commander-in-chief."[5]

This public expectation of a strong commander in chief reflects that presidential power, as an issue, centers on foreign affairs. Quite commonly, presidential scholars depict two presidential models, one concerned with domestic policies and the other with foreign policies.[6] These models typically show that presidents have much greater leeway, and thus success, in directing defense and foreign policies than in directing domestic ones.

Conversely, the president's domestic hands are tied by the myriad of interest groups represented, however indirectly, by the equally diverse personal political "parties" congressmen and senators have built to retain their seats. The consequence of this is that Congress, as presently constituted, has become a drag-weight on effective policy making. Despite the democratic myth, Congress has failed to address adequately most of the major issues of modern U.S. history. For example, the great economic issues made apparent by the Great Depression and the whole range of civil rights policies that make the pre-1964 American culture seem like ancient history today became the country's new norms as a consequence of leadership external to Congress. In fact, Congress not only did not move on these issues on its own initiative but also continually blocked rational and dispassionate discussion until forced to do otherwise by public pressure generated by presidential leadership.

In the economic arena, President Franklin Roosevelt was the prime mover, stimulating congressional action while overcoming Supreme Court "vetoes." Eventually, the Court retreated and Congress became enlightened enough to pass the Full Employment Act of 1946 during the presidency of Harry Truman. The civil rights policies so well known today would not have become more congruent with historical American values without presidential leadership. Even before the Supreme Court decided and Presidents Kennedy and Johnson enforced major desegregation decisions in the 1960s, Truman had desegregated the armed forces and federal civil service by executive order. Undoubtedly, his actions contributed mightily to focusing the American mind-set on the issue of equal treatment of its citizens.

In many ways Truman set the national agenda that the United States has been addressing since World War II. That conflict had changed the face of the national culture—forever. Sectionalism was eroded. Masses of citizens became mobile either because of their military involvement or because of wartime employment needs and opportunities. Concomitantly, the television era was emerging

and radio was in full bloom, creating a national awareness never before possible.

It was in this post-World War II era, while simultaneously grappling with the reconstruction of Europe and Asia and "containing" communism, that Truman established a truly national agenda for domestic policy. He articulated three primary areas for the national government to address: civil rights, the economy, and health care.[7] These issues, established as national obligations by strong presidential action, still need continual attention in the 1990s. Such attention can come only with strong presidential leadership. It was obvious that the United States addressed economic and taxation policy questions during the Reagan years because Ronald Reagan focused on these quite strongly. Conversely, the Reagan administration exhibited almost a disdain for civil rights and had what many perceived to be a callous attitude toward health care for the poor and disadvantaged. Consequently, positive domestic policies on these latter two areas were never developed.

In recent years the intensity of the East–West conflict has abated somewhat because of both the complexities of international economic competition and the appearance of a myriad of new security questions triggered by international terrorism, domestic economic sluggishness, the world population explosion, intractable world poverty, and the emergence of militant factions demanding theocratic states (Shiite Muslims), national territories (Palestinians), or control over their own domestic destiny (South African blacks).

Thus, the causes of the constant state of national emergency have changed, but the need for a strong national leader in the face of new challenges has increased. The new problems are complex and, because of the technology of the modern world, ever changing and diversifying. Congress simply is ill-equipped to address expeditiously concerns driven by the domestic environment, let alone the international one.

> The Chief Executive . . . must be the vital center of our whole scheme of government. The nature of the office demands that the president place himself in the very thick of the fight . . . that he be prepared to exercise the fullest powers of his office—all that are specified and some that are not.[8]

By the 1980s reality confirmed the perception cited above and had "expanded and recast the Presidency around three 'subpresidencies'—foreign affairs, aggregate economics and domestic policy, and quality of life issues." In fact, the presidential staff and cabinet are now organized around these three substantive areas.[9]

Robertson correctly states that "the expansion of the mass media, especially television, has made the president a national celebrity." However, he misses two critical points about this national celebrity and leadership. Precisely because of the era of television, the president alone among national decision makers can lead the public, generating the support to operationalize policies. Study after study has shown that today at least 80 percent of Americans get most of their news from television. The focus of national political news is the presidency. Thus, presidents will be the center of national attention regardless of personal attitudes about the effects of the electronic media.

National political power flows from the White House. Period! Either the president can be used to direct the nation's attention to serious problems it must address—housing, transportation, industrial renaissance, pollution, disease control, and so on—or the president can play ostrich. If the chief executive plays ostrich, the public will as well. Why can't Congress play the leadership role? Running the country is not like writing a romantic novel. Congress has already established that it does not have the intestinal fortitude to carry the flag on controversial issues.

Recent presidencies and presidential campaigns have demonstrated the effect of the modern media on leadership quite clearly. Jimmy Carter and Michael Dukakis were generally perceived by most Americans to be superior intellects compared to Ronald Reagan and George Bush. In fact, the general impression of Reagan was that he was unable, either because of personality or because of ability, to grasp complex matters. Yet, Reagan was a leader. Except for a couple of stumbles, his popularity remained remarkably high throughout his presidency. Critics passed this popularity off as a consequence of his communication skills honed by an acting career. Be that as it may, the "Great Communicator" was still leading the country, making people feel positive about the nation and its policies to the very end of his presidency.

Carter, on the other hand, was never able to articulate a positive national agenda. Yes, he was very capable intellectually. He understood the intricacies of complex issues down to the minutest detail. Yet the full significance of his great international achievements, such as the Camp David agreement between Egypt and Israel, was never fully understood by his own people. Instead, he became bogged down in the Iranian hostage situation, letting events overwhelm his presidency. Rather than defining these events in the proper perspective of international politics, he became obsessed with them.

This obsession, in turn, became the obsession of the country, probably leading Carter to defeat in the presidential election of 1980. The important point is that Carter was still leading, albeit in a direction he neither understood nor wanted. In the modern media era, the nation's attention will be focused on the president of the moment regardless. This phenomenon must be understood. Only the president can keep the nation upbeat and productive. Conversely, presidents who fail to understand the electronic age will lead the nation into malaise and despair.

The presidential election campaign of 1988 provides another example of the effect of the modern media on the presidential process. Bush, a woeful public speaker, handily beat Dukakis, a person of acknowledged intellect and humanitarian concern. Why? Quite simply, Dukakis didn't understand the modern media and public expectations any better than Carter had.

Is an understanding of the electronic age and sophisticated use of the media bad? Realistically, it doesn't make any difference. This is what Robertson does not seem to understand. The United States is in the era of media image making. The phenomenon cannot be reversed. Presidents have to understand that and use the available tools to the nation's advantage. Indeed, it is the obligation of a modern president to be a strong leader through effective use of the media.

Will such tactics lead to the abuse of power and the destruction of democracy? No, far from it. Ironically, Robertson himself explains to us the protections the media provide when he says, "Presidents sacrifice their privacy, living in a fishbowl of public attention." Moreover, "presidential mistakes and misstatements are amplified immediately." Precisely, Rob-

ertson, precisely. The president must present a positive national program clearly articulated to the American public or he or she will sacrifice any possibility of a successful administration. The same public that will support a strong president with a good, well-managed set of policies will also lower the boom on a presidential nerd. This is the best protection a democracy can have in the modern era, and is far better than depending on a Congress that has sold its soul to special interests.

Congress is a quagmire. Perpetuation of the lifestyles of its members seems to be its major driving force today. Congress is unable or unwilling to legislate, let alone lead, on any matter on which the members' constituencies are divided. Members' actions or, more likely, inactions are more directly related to advice from their pet pollsters than to any logically developed process that factors in the national "good." When a crisis erupts, congressional members usually don't have time to test the wind to determine which direction they should "blow." Consequently, Congress has passed, at critical times in the nation's history, "several hundred statutes giving the President virtual 'emergency powers' to seize property, oversee production, assign military forces, control communication and travel abroad, etc."[10]

This is a sorry scenario, indeed, unless one perceives the national "good" to be dependent upon the reelection of the incumbent legislators, as most of these "public servants" themselves seem to do. Reading the overnight polls is a must at breakfast. Any aspect that could affect an incumbent's reelection is addressed by the staff, and strategies are concocted to position the legislator in the most favorable light vis-à-vis the polling information.

Thus, Congress is inherently incapable of national leadership. As weak as its role has been historically, its present capacity to give direction to the system has worsened. The system is fragmented, "set off by the 'gold rush' among special interest groups." The "glue" of the old political party structure has come unstuck with the advent of television and the new breed of politician. The sheer volume of extragovernmental activity is staggering. "The whole non-governmental sector now outnumbers federal employees in Washington."[11]

Although the modern president is also caught up in this "power game," unlike Congress, the executive is inherently capable of strong leadership. "The President is the only person who can speak with a clear voice to the American people and set a standard of ethics and morality, excellence and greatness."[12]

The judicial branch, headed by the Supreme Court, also has a role to play in United States politics, but it is a domestic one. Ironically, in modern times, it has had to step into the role of settler of domestic differences (civil rights, abortion, capital punishment, and so on) that are the appropriate purview of Congress. Because of Congress's ceasing to function effectively for the reasons outlined previously, it has had to use its judicial powers in a quasi-legislative way. Where it has succeeded has been in moving the domestic environment closer to the rhetoric of the American political culture and constitutional intent.

An important footnote to the apparent domestic power of the post-World War II Supreme Court is that its power was really dependent upon presidential support and enforcement. Presidents Eisenhower, Kennedy, and Johnson's use of the powers of the office to enforce the Supreme Court's momentous social and political decisions of the 1950s and 1960s changed the face of American society.

In retrospect, common American social, political, and economic norms of two decades ago now seem to have been incomprehensible, medieval practices, not everyday standards in the United States. They could have and, perhaps, should have been remedied by Congress but were not. The Supreme Court nudged the system. Presidential power effected the changes.

Internationally, neither Congress nor the Supreme Court has ever had a pattern of sustained involvement, except to ratify presidential acts. Much can be argued about presidential "wars" and unconstitutional "executive agreements." The fact is, however, that wars, declared or not, cannot be fought without corollary congressional ratification of the presidential decisions. Wars cost money; Congress provides the money. Wars require personnel; Congress creates the legislation to supply the warriors.

The country's inherent need for strong presidential leadership in international relations was acknowledged from the first days of the republic. In the *Federalist Papers*, Alexander Hamilton stressed that only the executive office met the necessary criteria to engage in foreign relations with "unity, secrecy, and dispatch."[13] In the modern era these foreign policy assets inherent in the presidential office are even more critical, arguably even vital to the survival of the nation itself. Congress is not equipped by either concept or will to act with the decisiveness and dispatch required by the rapidly moving international events of the contemporary world. In such a context, U.S. presidents cannot be the compliant, nonassertive executives portrayed as optimal by Robertson.

If Alexander Hamilton saw the critical role of the presidency in foreign affairs two hundred years ago, before the office was even institutionalized, how much more essential would he conceive it to be in the modern context? To this writer, the perceptive Hamilton would see Robertson's views as quaint. Romantic, perhaps, but views that would ill equip the United States to operate in the modern world. The country's foreign policy initiatives cannot be judged against some ideal notions of a utopian international community. Old-style diplomacy simply doesn't fit a world of international terrorism. Modern wars are not fought with Napoleonic military tactics. It is often contended that generals train troops in the strategy and tactics of the previous war. By analogy, Robertson is arguing for a presidential diplomatic role even more antiquated. That is, he would constrain the president, placing him or her in a historic, romantic conceptualization of the presidential role.

As Hamilton's statements support, a "separated institutional" implementation of U.S. foreign policy was never the intent of the founding fathers. They saw quite clearly how the international community operated even then. Today summits are common. World leaders are in constant, direct communication with their counterparts, addressing such issues as terrorism, nuclear proliferation, conventional arms reduction, humanitarian disaster relief, multinational trade, and a myriad of international economic concerns. The president of the moment is engaged in negotiating these questions with world leaders who, for the most part, can "deliver" their countries. That is, whether the other leaders be prime ministers of democratic states or autocratic heads of closed societies, they are in a position to commit their national resources to whatever agreements are made.

Historically, U.S. presidents have not had the assurance in international negotiations that agreements made with foreign heads of state would, in fact, be supported at home. These embarrassments range from those suffered by Woodrow Wilson at Versailles to the Senate's refusal to approve the more recent Strategic Arms Limitation Treaty (SALT II) during the Carter years. The speed of modern communication, coupled with the rapidly changing international situation, means that international presidential negotiation on behalf of the country is only going to increase, in both number and importance.

It is not being suggested here that presidents be given dictatorial power in international relations. It must, however, be fully understood that they must have considerable leeway and support in diplomatic negotiations. Only in the most extreme circumstances should the country's commitment not be forthcoming after a president reaches agreements with the national leaders of other countries. To do otherwise will increasingly handicap a president in reaching international resolutions favorable to the United States.

Without strong leadership from its chief executive, the United States will find itself increasingly isolated internationally as the world moves toward the year 2000. Its views will be given short shrift or even be bypassed by leaders of other nations as these leaders grapple with the world's agenda. With the weak president envisioned by Robertson, the United States will find itself at the mercy of world events by the early years of the twenty-first century. Such a scenario would be an ironic turn of the wheel compared to the dominant international role the country and its president enjoyed in the decades immediately succeeding World War II. The modern world must be understood. The United States needs strong leadership. Given the realities of the 1990s, the only institutionalized office capable of providing effective direction to the nation's policies is the presidency. The American people must understand and support that role. There is no other alternative!

Indeed, Robertson's weak executive will more likely lead to negative consequences than the strong executive proposed here. Promoting the wimpish executive desired by Robertson will result in world events overwhelming the nation. U.S. policies will not be established by priorities set by the American people. Instead, international actions will take place independently of the president and, therefore, the people. The country will be thrown into a whirlpool it can't control. For the national good, presidents must assert themselves internationally and Congress and the Supreme Court must support such presidential initiatives.

Historically, Congress has demonstrated its understanding of the necessity of this presidential role by, generally, supporting international use of presidential power. For its part, the Supreme Court also has had a historic pattern of nonintervention. Realistically, it has no other choice. Without presidential support to enforce its decisions, the Court is moribund. It can only demonstrate its ineffectiveness. To avoid a public display of its weakness vis-à-vis the president on international issues, the Court opts to do nothing.[14] For example, as recently as the Vietnam War, the Court had several opportunities to accept cases designed to "test" the constitutionality of this "undeclared war." It declined the challenges, knowing it could do nothing in the face of contrary presidential power.

Thus, of the theoretically coequal branches of U.S. national government, only the presidency has demonstrated

sustained effectiveness in both the domestic and international arenas since 1945. Congress has virtually ceased to function constitutionally. It is a public relations club for incumbents, designed to perpetuate each member's lifestyle. Instead of serving the republic for two or three terms from a sense of the public good, most members now strive for career survival. Such is not conducive to the exercise of power in the face of the complex issues of today.

In turn, the Supreme Court was never designed to be a prime initiator; it is structured to react to what is brought to it. It may reach a tad if faced with what it perceives to be gross injustices in the contemporary culture, but other forces also must be at play, "testing" the culture against its values, for the Supreme Court to enter the policy arena. Moreover, as was emphasized previously, the Court cannot effect its decisions without presidential support.

> To be reminded that it was not meant to be—that the Framers envisioned a vastly more modest chief executive—is only to recall that, had the blueprint been incapable of expanding beyond the Framers' designs, the nation could not have persisted through two centuries of turmoil. We are . . . a society led by two equal branches, with one permanently "more equal" than the others; as the Supreme Court and Congress are preeminent in constitutional theory so the presidency is preeminent in constitutional fact.[15]

The evolution of a powerful presidency as portrayed here was the natural consequence of the real needs facing this once underdeveloped nation as it grew, became economically interdependent, and emerged as the dominant force in international politics after World War II. As noted, presidential strength always exceeded that of Congress and the Supreme Court in times of domestic and international crises. It is not surprising, then, that these two branches became confused and uncertain whenever faced with new and different national or international emergencies.

In the early days of the twentieth century and before he had become president, Woodrow Wilson had analyzed the president to be "the only national voice in affairs. . . . No other single force can withstand him; no combination of forces will easily overpower him. . . . He is the representative of no constituency but of the whole country."[16] What is suggested here is that Congress and the Supreme Court never were really powerful in the face of crises simply because neither is really equipped constitutionally to address such issues expeditiously. Only the president is. Hence, since the United States faces nothing but a series of crises in the modern world, the president must be powerful. He or she must assume leadership in the constitutional powers vacuum created by the realities of the modern world and domestic politics.

"Italian politics is often held up to ridicule as comically unstable. . . . But how much different in practice is [the United States] . . .? The real decision-making power gets passed around here to those strong enough to grab it."[17] The argument here clearly establishes that the United States has direction only when the president is "strong enough to grab [power]." Only the president has the potential to use political capital to overcome the influence of special interests on Congress.[18]

It is true that not all presidents have used the potential powers of the office effectively. Furthermore, in the abstract, an "imperial" presidency is anathema to most Americans. In practice, however, the people want and the country needs a strong president to solve its complex problems. Americans look to their president to satisfy at least three sets of needs: reassurance, progress and action, and a sense of legitimacy.[19] Instead of weakening the president, "what is needed are measures to give presidents more power to pull together governing alliances in Congress, to increase the cohesive force of political parties, to reduce prospects of partisan-government and to promote more collaboration across party lines."[20] With this power, presidents must lead. Great achievements usually have been accomplished by people with a degree of "irrational self-confidence." "Men and women of vitality have always been prepared to bet their futures, even their lives, on ventures of unknown outcomes. If they had all looked before they leaped, we would still be crouched in caves sketching animal pictures."[21]

Americans might not now be living in caves, but they are facing as uncertain a future as their earliest ancestors. Without strong leadership, the country is bound to flounder. Only a perceptive "power president" can lead it through the labyrinth of international intrigue and domestic gamesmanship by vested interests so that future generations can continue to enjoy the equilibrium of the American Dream!

NOTES

1. Arthur M. Schlesinger, Jr., *The Politics of Hope* (Boston: Houghton Mifflin, 1962), p. 9.

2. See Richard E. Neustadt, *Presidential Power* (New York: Wiley, 1960), and Richard E. Neustadt, *Presidential Pow-*

er: The Politics of Leadership (New York: Wiley, 1980).

3. See Robert McCloskey, *The American Supreme Court* (Chicago: University of Chicago Press, 1960).

4. Thomas E. Cronin, *The State of the Presidency*, 2d ed. (Boston: Little, Brown, 1980), p. 91.

5. Dom Bonafede, "Bad News from Abroad," *National Journal*, February 27, 1979, p. 318.

6. See Aaron Wildavsky, "The Two Presidencies," in *The Presidency* (Boston: Little, Brown, 1969).

7. See Robert Sickels, *Presidential Transactions* (Englewood Cliffs, N.J.: Prentice-Hall, 1974).

8. Arthur M. Schlesinger, Jr., *A Thousand Days* (Boston: Houghton Mifflin, 1965), p. 120.

9. Cronin, *The State of the Presidency*, pp. 145–54.

10. J. Malcolm Smith and Cornelius P. Cotter, *Powers of the President during Crisis* (Washington, D.C.: Public Affairs Press, 1960), and Harold C. Relyea, "Declaring and Terminating a State of Emergency," *Presidential Studies Quarterly*, Fall 1976, pp. 36–40.

11. See Hedrick Smith, *The Power Game* (New York: Random House, 1988), pp. 20–30.

12. Jimmy Carter, quoted in *National Journal*, August 7, 1976, p. 993.

13. Alexander Hamilton, Federalist Paper 7047, in *The Federalist Papers* (New York: New American Library, 1961), p. 424.

14. See McCloskey, *The American Supreme Court*.

15. Larry Tribe, *American Constitutional Law* (Westbury, N.Y.: Foundation Press, 1978), p. 157.

16. Woodrow Wilson, *Constitutional Government in the United States* (New York: Columbia University Press, 1908), pp. 67–73.

17. Michael Burns, *Washington Post*, December 15, 1985, P-Ci.

18. Mitchell Bard, "Interest Groups, the President and Foreign Policy," *Presidential Studies Quarterly*, Summer 1988, pp. 583–600.

19. James D. Barber, "The Presidency: What Americans Want," in *Perspectives on the Presidency*, ed. Stanley Bach and George T. Sulzner (Lexington, Mass.: Heath, 1974), pp. 144–51.

20. Smith, *The Power Game*, p. 715. See pp. 715–18 for Smith's suggestions for achieving greater presidential power.

21. John Gardner, *Morale* (New York: Norton, 1978), p. 152.

SUGGESTED READINGS

CRABB, CECIL, AND PAT M. HOLT. *Invitation to Struggle: Congress, the President and Foreign Policy.* Washington, D.C.: Congressional Quarterly Press, 1984. Delineates inevitable conflicts between Congress and the president over control of foreign policy initiatives and decisions. These are seen as inherent in the concept of the U.S. Constitution and its subsequent reinforcement of "shared" governmental powers.

PFIFFNER, JAMES P. *The Strategic Presidency: Hitting the Ground Running.* Chicago: Dorsey Press, 1988. Emphasis on the need for presidents to enter the White House with an in-place "strategic plan" consistent with business-oriented chief-executive-officer planning responsibilities. For example, Pfiffner stresses that it is critical for incoming presidents to establish policy control over the bureaucracy expeditiously or important administration initiatives will not be effected as conceptualized.

SICKELS, ROBERT. *Presidential Transactions*. Englewood Cliffs, N.J.: Prentice-Hall, 1974. Argues Harry Truman was the first modern president. Shows how the United States was changed so significantly and permanently by World War II that its historic sectionalism was eroded. These changes plus modern communications permitted, even necessitated, Truman's setting a national agenda for his presidency and for succeeding ones as well.

The Covert Presidency

David Brian Robertson
University of Missouri–St. Louis

In his essay "The Power Presidency" Professor James Milne persuasively explains why Americans have come to expect a strong president. They want a leader who will articulate a compelling vision of the country's future, energize Congress and the bureaucracy, confront forcefully any threats from abroad, and negotiate shrewdly with foreign heads of state. Citizens want the president to maximize economic prosperity, to humanize social programs, and to ensure that government policy is efficient, effective, and fair.

Milne believes that constitutional checks and balances excessively hamper the president's power to achieve national goals. He expresses the popular view that presidential power should be strengthened further because the president is the only national figure who can bring any measure of unity to national policy making. But Milne's view mistakenly assumes that the president is a hapless Gulliver who is frustrated by the small-minded, self-interested, and cowardly officials in Congress, the courts, and the bureaucracy with whom he must share power. In fact, presidents have always exercised a wide range of formal and informal powers, and these powers steadily have grown in this century. This expansion of power has been largely *co-*

vert: presidential power has grown through the inconspicuous manipulation of personnel and budget rules, of information, and of the policy agenda rather than conspicuous legal or constitutional changes. Gradually, presidents have stretched their powers by making loyalty to the president the primary criterion for appointment to office, by centralizing budget powers in the White House, and by controlling information through manipulation, secrecy, and deception. Especially disturbing is the tendency to exaggerate threats to national security in order to enhance presidential independence and popularity. Congress and the federal courts have foreclosed some tactics (such as the presidential refusal to spend funds approved by Congress), but these setbacks have only spurred the development of alternative—and hardier—techniques of presidential control.

The covert techniques evidently tempt presidents to abuse their power. Despite occasional backlash against an individual president unleashed by such abuses as Watergate and the Iran–Contra affair, the covert techniques of modern presidential power are growing ever more effective and threatening to democratic government.

The strong covert institution that is now evolving in the White House is the inevitable dark side of the idealized textbook version of the heroic presidency. It would be a grave mistake to enhance this covert presidency with additional legal powers. Milne and other proponents of increased presidential power depend on a half-truth: any expansion of presidential power would enable the president to do more good. In fact, the emerging covert presidency permits the abuse of presidential power on an unprecedented scale. Additional presidential power would increase the risks of presiden-

tial wrongdoing even more. We cannot depend on Congress and the courts to correct such abuses. The emerging covert presidency poorly serves the best interests of the United States because it threatens government accountability and thus American democracy itself.

My argument should be kept separate from three other potential objections to a strong presidency. First, it does not assert that the formal powers of the president are unchecked; presidents must still share legislative and appointment power with Congress, and civil service requirements still limit presidential control over the bureaucracy. Nor does my argument oppose the election of presidents with strong personalities and the will, positive attitude, and leadership abilities necessary to harness effectively the circumscribed powers of the modern presidency without devolving into despair or paranoia. Finally, it is not an argument against a government strong and effective enough to protect individual security and implement equitable policies.

PRESIDENTIAL POWERS AND RESPONSIBILITIES: A DIFFICULT BALANCE

Enormous pressures for enhanced presidential powers long have been hard to resist. Ever since the New Deal of the 1930s the president has been expected to exercise leadership as the chief domestic policy initiator and executive of the national government. His responsibilities include management of a far-flung bureaucracy and the annual presentation of proposals for new policy initiatives. His leadership extends to economic growth, employment, inflation, investment, and other key components of prosperity. He claims credit and attracts blame for economic problems despite the limited ability of any government to shape the complex factors that affect economic performance. As the nation's commander in chief and chief diplomat, the president is responsible for the nation's military and the nation's foreign relations.

The expansion of the mass media, especially television, has made the president a national celebrity whose activities flash across television screens more frequently than those of the most famous entertainers. Since Theodore Roosevelt began to use the presidency as a "bully pulpit" to sway public opinion, presidents have used the mass media with increasing sophistication. By influencing public opinion, presidents can directly (and, because of public opinion polls, demonstrably) improve the favorable perception of their proposals. But in exchange for national celebrity, presidents sacrifice their privacy, living in a fishbowl of public attention. Presidential mistakes and misstatements are amplified immediately.

A yawning gap separates these enormous responsibilities and limited presidential powers to live up to them. Although executing federal law is the most fundamental presidential responsibility, the president's executive power is severely circumscribed. No one could easily manage dozens of federal agencies and three million civilian employees, of course, but civil service protections further complicate management by restricting the president's appointment power to about 1 percent of the federal work force. In at least some agencies, therefore, a president is likely to find himself confronted by tenured bureaucrats hostile to his agenda.

Congress is the main obstacle to presidential control because the president must share most powers with the legislature. Presidential proposals to reorganize the bureaucracy often founder in Congress. Congress usually amends or rejects presidential budget and legislative proposals. The longer presidents are in office, the less successful they are in persuading Congress to enact their recommendations. The president's informal role as leader of his political party does little to compensate for the limits to his formal powers because voters' attachment to the parties' and the strength of parties, organizations have withered in recent decades.

THE HEROIC PRESIDENCY, PROS AND CONS

Advocates of greater presidential power usually emphasize presidential weakness, as does Milne. Concern about a presidency overmatched by more powerful institutions is rooted deeply in American thought. The authors whose defenses of the Constitution appear in *The Federalist Papers* argued that "in republican government, the legislative authority necessarily predominates."[1] In the nineteenth century Woodrow Wilson identified Congress as the "predominant and controlling force" in the federal government.[2] Still, admiration for a strong presidency has increased with each positive experience laid to the incumbent of the White House: Theodore Roosevelt's aggressive stand against corporate irresponsibility, Woodrow Wilson's progressive reforms, Franklin Roosevelt's New Deal and wartime leadership, John Kennedy's New Frontier, and the astonishing success of Lyndon Johnson in breaking long-standing stalemates in civil rights, health, education, and welfare policies in 1964 and 1965.

By the mid-1960s many experts (such as Arthur Schlesinger, Jr., whom Milne quotes) portrayed the president in heroic terms and suggested that presidents use every means at their disposal to enhance the power of their office. A strong presidency was in the nation's best interest in this view because the office elevated the incumbent and motivated him to exert leadership toward positive goals, such as international security, economic planning, and social justice.[3] Strong presidents were portrayed as struggling to exercise power within the confines of antiquated institutions. In perhaps the most widely cited analysis of presidential power, Richard Neustadt emphasized the weakness of the office and defined presidential power chiefly as the power of persuasion. Even the perceived abuses of power in the Johnson and Nixon administrations "were in a sense illusory," Neustadt asserted in a 1980 edition of his book, "for these are also the symbols of their self-destruction."[4]

But even former proponents began to question the heroic presidency in the late 1960s and early 1970s. The Vietnam War and the Watergate scandal prompted former presidential assistants Schlesinger and George Reedy to publish books warning of the enormous opportunities for the abuse of power inherent in inflated presidential expectations.[5] In the mid-1970s Congress seemed to descend on the presidency with the wrath of usurped politicians. It enacted the War Powers Act to force the president to share war-making power and the Budget Control and Impoundment Act to circumscribe presidential budget power, and it began to attach provisions to many bills designed to give Congress the power to veto executive actions.

By the 1980s the conventional wisdom suggested that power had swung too far in the direction of Congress. Both scholars and political leaders expressed grave fears that the United States was becoming ungovernable. Even Reedy remarked in a new edition of his book that

he had underestimated the resiliency of the American political system and that "we . . . have buil[t] counterbalancing forces that are bringing us back to reality."[6]

THE GROWTH OF THE PRESIDENCY

Although opinions about the strong presidency vary as circumstances change, the presidency has steadily and almost invisibly gained power. Presidencies inherit the lessons about power that their predecessors learned. There is now a recognizable pattern that can be labeled a covert presidency: the pursuit of enhanced presidential power through indirect techniques of political control over personnel, budgets, and information; the manipulation of the media; and the temptation to use national security to control the political agenda. Superficial variations in presidential personality and partisanship mask the steady growth of presidential power through the refinement of these tactics.

Presidents have responded to the limitations of their power over federal personnel by creating a counterbureaucracy of loyalists in the Executive Office of the President. Presidents have learned to use this counterbureaucracy with increasing effectiveness to assure greater White House control of policy formation and execution.

Before World War II the president had but a handful of personal aides. In response to the growth of the federal bureaucracy, the presidency has become an enduring institution employing hundreds of people. By 1970 the White House staff had grown to about five hundred. After each initially pruned the White House staff, Presidents Jimmy Carter and Ronald Reagan permitted the staff to grow back to that size by the end of their terms. The White House staff is a part of the larger Executive Office of the

President, which in 1988 employed more than seventeen hundred people and had a budget of $140 million. This extended presidential staff includes agencies originally intended to advise the president on his many roles. The Office of Management and Budget has evolved from its predecessor, the Bureau of the Budget, and explicitly aims to increase presidential control of federal spending and policy management. The Council of Economic Advisors and the National Security Council were intended to help the president coordinate economic, diplomatic, and military policy.[7]

The growth of the presidential staff is no accident. Compared to established bureaucracies, such as the State, Defense, and Treasury departments, this "presidential bureaucracy" is much less inhibited by strict personnel regulations. Once they are confirmed by the Senate, these presidential appointees can provide a shadow bureaucracy that owes its allegiance solely to the incumbent of the White House. Indeed, many scholars applauded the larger presidential staff for its potential to bring more coherence to the executive branch. This staff has the will and increasingly the capacity to centralize control over the federal establishment for the president's benefit. Over time the staff has invented more skillful techniques for reducing the discretion of civil servants.

In each recent presidency political control has gravitated away from cabinet-level departments (such as Health and Human Services, and Defense) to the Executive Office of the President. Both Richard Nixon and Carter originally appointed many independent-minded cabinet secretaries to manage federal departments. It was precisely these independent-minded people who were the most willing to challenge presidential errors and abuses. The White House staff wrested control from the cabinet within

three years after the start of both the Nixon and Carter presidential terms.

In the Nixon White House, Chief of Staff H. R. Haldeman, Domestic Policy Advisor John Ehrlichman, and other staffers so dominated access to the president and decision making that they earned the title "Palace Guard." After 1972 these staffers partially implemented a sophisticated plan further to centralize political control over the day-to-day operations of departments by using loyalty to Nixon as the criterion for appointment to cabinet and especially to subcabinet positions (such as assistant secretaries).

Carter also started with independent-minded cabinet officers who were allowed to name their own subcabinet officials. He also promised not to appoint a chief of staff because Haldeman's office had become so closely identified with Watergate. However, the administration was in a crisis by 1979. Several of the most independent-minded cabinet officials were pressured to resign or were fired. More complaisant officials were named to replace them. Carter revived the White House Chief of Staff position, naming his longtime associate Hamilton Jordan to the post.

For Reagan's advisers, these experiences drove home the importance of political loyalty. President-elect Reagan's transition staff paid careful attention to appointing devoted Reagan conservatives to key cabinet and subcabinet positions. These included James Watt, a secretary of the interior committed to reversing federal restriction of private use of public resources; Ann Gorsuch (later Burford), director of the Environmental Protection Agency, bent on reducing business regulations; and William Bradford Reynolds, committed to reducing federal enforcement of civil rights laws.

At the same time that loyalists were placed in control of many key agencies, management grew increasingly political and centralized. One of the most direct efforts to control the civil service bureaucracy followed the appointment of Donald Devine as the director of the Office of Personnel Management (OPM), the agency responsible for managing the civil service system. Devine believed his job to be explicitly political in the sense that "there must be response to what the elected officials of the government want." By "elected officials," clearly he meant the president. Under Devine the OPM used "reductions in force" to cut the number of career civil servants and to downgrade other positions. At the same time more federal personnel were hired without the protection of civil service, some as political appointees (under Schedule C rules). Devine defended this practice by noting that it marked no break with the past. During the Carter administration the number of Schedule C appointees had increased from fewer than 1,000 to 1,566 (there were 1,615 Schedule C appointees in 1983). Temporary employees provided another way to ensure more loyalty in the federal work force because the jobs of temporary workers are harder to protect from political influence. In 1983 Devine granted agencies "broad new authority" to hire temporaries, who already numbered more than 111,000.[8]

Far from remaining titular but helpless heads of the executive branch, presidents have developed an increasingly effective set of techniques for effecting their policy priorities through the manipulation of personnel. The techniques are not idiosyncratic to individual presidents, nor are they exclusive to one political party; they are logical steps in the evolution of a presidency with powers better suited to the role expected of it. At least two recent books treat the Reagan efforts as steps toward a mature model of presidential control. James Pfiffner, for example, concluded that "a new administration can best insure that its policies will be carried out effectively if it establishes policy control over the bureaucracy as quickly as possible."[9]

However appealing a powerful presidency can be, these presidential gains expose a darker side of the covert presidency. Along with increasing administrative control has come an increasingly sophisticated use of these tools in the battle for executive branch supremacy over other branches of government.

PULLING POLITICAL PURSE STRINGS

Along with the control of personnel, the control of money is essential to political power. In formulating the federal budget, Congress constitutionally shares power with the president. Over time Congress has relinquished the formulation of the budget, but it has retained its power to check the exercise of discretion in presidential spending. For example, when the first unified budget was formulated in 1921, Congress authorized creation of the executive Bureau of the Budget (now the Office of Management and Budget) but also created the General Accounting Office to monitor federal spending. When Nixon tried to use an old technique (impoundment, or the refusal to spend money appropriated by Congress) to change spending priorities, both court decisions and a new law ended the practice.

In the midst of the highly visible budget struggles between Congress and the president, the Office of Management and Budget has quietly grown into a far more potent and explicitly political force. In 1973 the Nixon administration used the OMB as its principal agent for controlling the bureaucracy through spending and personnel controls. Political appointees constituted a growing number of the OMB staff. By the mid-1970s Congress accused the agency of exaggerating expenditures and understating revenues in order to enhance President Gerald Ford's image before the 1976 election. Carter further politicized the agency by appointing Georgia banker Bert Lance, a personal friend, as OMB director. During the Ford and Carter years the agency made political interests of the president increasingly central to the budget process.[10]

All these trends accelerated in the 1980s, guided by David Stockman, director of the OMB from 1981 to 1985. The politically astute Stockman was the first OMB director with experience as a member of Congress. He turned a relatively obscure provision in the Congressional Budget and Impoundment Control Act of 1974 (reconciliation, which originally was intended to increase congressional leaders' control over the budget) into a tool for exercising executive leverage in the congressional budget process. In defending budget requests before congressional committees, the OMB increasingly superseded agencies. Under Executive Order 12291 the OMB received the power to review proposed regulations for their cost effectiveness, giving it virtually a veto power over a wide variety of executive branch activities. After 1981 the OMB's budget projections routinely were viewed as a set of numbers manipulated for political goals.

Indisputably the OMB's budget power relative to congressional committees and civil servants has reached unprecedented levels. Once budgeting was a "bottom up" process in which career civil servants typically developed budget requests (often with the tacit consent of the congressional committee with jurisdiction over the agency). The Budget Bureau aggregated these requests, marginally cut them, and sent the package to Congress. More recently budgeting has become a "top down" process, with the OMB imposing the president's priorities on agencies and acting as his advocate in Congress. By the end of the 1980s OMB was viewed as "more efficient, more political, more controversial and more central to White House policy making than ever."[11]

THE MANIPULATED MEDIA

Despite the evolution of techniques for enhancing presidential control of personnel and budgeting, the civil service and Congress constitute formidable obstacles to direct presidential control in these areas. By manipulating public opinion, presidents can undermine the will of these institutions to obstruct presidential goals. It is not surprising that each recent presidency has contributed to the steadily growing elegance with which presidents manage the public's perception of themselves and their opponents.

Presidents grasped the potential of direct communication with the electorate early in the century. Theodore Roosevelt began the custom of presidential press conferences. On average his cousin Franklin met with the press nearly seven times a month. But press conferences are difficult for presidents to control. Reporters may pose embarrassing questions, or elicit ill-informed or mistaken responses. No wonder, then, that the press conference has slowly disappeared. Truman held an average of fewer than four press conferences a month. Eisenhower, Kennedy, and Johnson held about two a month; Ford and Carter fewer than one and a half a month; and Nixon and Reagan averaged a press conference only every other month.[12]

Presidents have learned to present themselves and control their message more effectively. The glamor of the Kennedy White House offered the first hint that television would focus public attention on the president. Richard Nixon learned that deliberate "packaging" could enhance both presidential electability and power. In the Carter administration a pollster (Patrick Caddell) and a media expert (Gerald Rafshoon) exercised unprecedented influence in the day-to-day operations of the White House.

During the Reagan administration the media became central to the very task of governing. Advisers carefully designed the presentation of the president to deflect criticism and to maximize his popularity and influence (and, in 1984, his votes). One technique was the "line of the day," by which the White House manipulated information to ensure that network news shows would present the president's view of major issues. Against the backdrop of classrooms in several states Reagan forcefully reasserted his views on teacher certification, school desegregation, and a strict curriculum during the 1984 campaign, thus defusing Walter Mondale's criticism of the Reagan administration's education budget. The White House also emphasized reassuring visual images of the president. To deflect concerns about his age, the White House persuaded *Parade* magazine to feature a cover story of the president lifting weights.

Presidents have increasingly demonstrated the will and ability to manage public opinion in order to achieve a climate of opinion supportive of their goals. For example, in the Reagan administration

[Michael Deaver's] image-game tactics leaned heavily on polling, used the way soap and cosmetic companies work mass marketing. . . . [Richard] Wirthlin's firm, Decision Making Information, Inc., would "pretest" public attitudes before Reagan went barnstorming on issues. . . . Wirthlin's firm . . . can do national polls on hot issues within twenty-four hours. Frequently this speed put the Reagan operation far ahead of Congress, the television networks, of Democratic rivals in figuring out the best political line with the public.[13]

In turn, the polls permit presidents to calibrate their popularity and translate that popularity into political influence. The Constitution's framers intentionally designed a government whose branches would be difficult to align in support of a particular initiative. The manipulation of information, images, and popular attitudes permits the president to short-circuit the system by creating precisely the outpouring of sentiment that the Constitution's framers feared most. Such a wave of public opinion in turn can bring about the alignment of these fragmented institutions in support of the president's agenda. This is precisely what happened in 1981 when the Reagan administration won stunning victories for its budget and tax cuts. The administration was unable to sustain its influence over public opinion at that level, but Reagan left office with the highest public approval rating of any departing president since the 1940s.

Certainly the growing executive power to monopolize and restrict policy information suggests one set of techniques for maintaining the presidential initiative. All presidents have complained about embarrassing leaks of information and all have taken steps to restrict those leaks. The Reagan administration tried to go further than most. It altered the Freedom of Information Act to limit more strictly access to government documents, and in 1983 it sought to force 200,000 government officials to make a lifetime commitment to keep information secret.

THE USES AND ABUSES OF PRESIDENTIAL POWER

Presidents usually invoke national security to justify their efforts to control information. Presidents can legitimately claim that a generous interpretation of presidential power is essential for fulfilling the presidential role as diplomatic and military leader. Indeed, presidential actions that would be viewed as abuses in domestic policy are tolerated, even encouraged, in military and foreign affairs. Here, the abuse of power is especially tempting, for "[a]ny president acting as commander-in-chief and chief diplomat will be more powerful than when acting as chief executive, legislative leader, or opinion/party leader."[14]

Particularly in a crisis, as when U.S. troops are under fire, Congress and the nation rally behind the president and defer to his leadership. But even in more routine foreign and military policy Congress has had to delegate extensive control over personnel, money, and information to the White House. Few members of Congress, much less the public, have any idea of the national budget for intelligence activities, though estimates are as high as $20 billion. Virtually all government documents dealing with potentially embarrassing information about foreign or military policy are classified under a system evolving since the 1940s.[15]

As in the case of the Office of Management and Budget, the National Security Council (NSC) has become partisan and more central to policy making in each succeeding presidential administration. Presidents Kennedy and Johnson elevated the NSC role by relying heavily upon the advice of such national security advisers as McGeorge Bundy and Walt Rostow. Henry Kissinger, the dominant foreign policy expert in the Nixon administration, built the largest staff in NSC history, and it often wrested policy control from the State and Defense departments. Although Carter expressed an intention to return to cabinet responsibility, he came to rely increasingly on his national security adviser, Zbigniew Brzezinski. Disputes among the NSC, the State Department, and the Defense Department contributed to the perception of disarray in the making of foreign policy in the Carter years. Secretary of State Alexander Haig attempted to reinvigorate cabinet influence in the early years of the Reagan administration, but soon he was eased out of his post and such NSC advisers as William Clark, Robert McFarlane, and John Poindexter became more prominent in many foreign decisions than Haig's successor, George Schultz.[16]

Nowhere is the potential for abuse of presidential power clearer than in foreign affairs, where presidential discretion is so great. Deception in military and foreign policy making is a constant across administrations. The Pentagon papers, first published by newspapers in 1971, revealed that the Eisenhower, Kennedy, and Johnson administrations had misinformed the press and the public about the nature of the conflicts in Vietnam and the purposes of intervention. Without congressional approval, President Nixon ordered the secret bombing of Cambodia. Although the War Powers Act aimed to prevent such unilateral actions in the future, Reagan's administration secretly mined harbors in Nicaragua in 1984. The president's ability to manage information about these actions is suggested by the administration's ban on newspaper coverage of the invasion of Grenada in 1983.

The most disturbing trend in the evolution of the covert presidency is the creation of secret, *ad hoc* agencies to execute presidential policy goals. Irate and embarrassed by such leaks as the "Pentagon papers," Nixon approved the creation of a "plumbers" unit. Justified on national security grounds, the plumbers burgled the offices of the psychiatrist of Daniel Ellsberg, who had leaked the papers to leading newspapers. The 1972 presidential election campaign erased the line between national security and the president's political interests. Eventually, the plumbers attempted to tap the telephones of the Democratic National Committee in the Watergate office complex in Washington and they were arrested in the process. Although much confusion surrounded the Watergate scandal as the conspiracy unfolded, in retrospect its consequences are clear. The president used his national security powers to keep himself in office—actions hardly distinguishable in principle from those of authoritarian regimes abroad.[17]

The Iran–Contra scandal that surfaced in 1986 proves that the abuse of the president's national security power is endemic to the modern presidency. The National Security Council staff, notably Lieutenant Colonel Oliver North, established a secret foreign policy network termed "the Enterprise" that bargained with numerous foreign governments, sold arms to Iran, and channeled profits to the Nicaraguan Contras despite a congressional ban on U.S. government assistance to the Contras. A full accounting of this shadowy organization's budget is difficult, but between June 1984 and 1986 it apparently received $10 million from private contributors and $34 million from foreign countries, including $3.8 million from the sale of arms to Iran.

With this money "the Enterprise" purchased airplanes, built an airstrip, bought weapons in Europe, and delivered them to the Contras. Deceiving outsiders was critical. As North told Contra leader Adolfo Calero, "We need to make sure that this new financing does not become known. The Congress must believe that there continues to be an urgent need for funding."[18]

The plumbers unit and "the Enterprise" were very different organizations, but both are predictable responses to circumstances in which all presidents find themselves. Although Congress and the courts might act to prevent a recurrence of the specific abuses involved in a particular scandal, the circumstances that prompt these abuses have not changed, nor has the inventiveness of presidential staff. The combination of expectations, constraints, and informal opportunities channels presidents toward exercising power by emphasizing national security and bypassing established institutions.

One might argue that however dangerous is presidential power in foreign affairs, the potential abuse of power is more limited in domestic policy. Presidential scholars commonly distinguish between the domestic presidency and the foreign policy presidency, implying that the discretion the president enjoys in foreign affairs is not and will not be matched in domestic policy. Presidential power over the civil service and the budget may have advanced incrementally over the past generation, but these small steps are insignificant in light of the Constitution and customary limits to presidential power in domestic affairs.

Yet the "two presidencies" are much more interdependent than this distinction implies. First, his role as commander in chief gives the president a status unequaled by other domestic policymakers and enhances his influence on a wide range of issues beyond military affairs; a visit to the White House engenders no little awe and support, no matter what the issue at hand. Second, foreign crises and events enhance presidential standing in public opinion polls, which in turn can be utilized for a variety of domestic political goals. In 1964 the dubious Gulf of Tonkin incident not only prompted Congress virtually to surrender war-making power to the president but also boosted President Johnson's reelection prospects that year. The temptation to manufacture foreign policy problems in order to enhance a president's standing in public opinion polls is hard to resist. Third, the policy consequences of military and foreign policy decisions increasingly spill over into domestic politics as the American economy becomes more integrated into international markets.

If there are growing incentives for presidents to expand the meaning of "national security" to domestic problems, so are there opportunities. In 1988 both presidential candidates endorsed the definition of drugs as a national security problem and the use of the U.S. military to combat drugs. As more policy problems are linked to national security, both presidential power and the risks of the abuse of that power will expand.

SUMMING UP

The evolution of the covert presidency has not alarmed most observers of American politics because they view many of these developments as peculiar to each president (and thus not a pattern), because they believe that these abuses are separable from the strong presidency, and because they view the abuse of presidential power as self-correcting. But

none of these viewpoints can be supported.

The presidential struggle for control has been a constant in the post-New Deal presidency, not a variable. Presidential staff has steadily increased, and the staff's power over personnel, money, and information has steadily grown. This expansion is bipartisan. Former members of President Carter's White House expressed admiration for the way that the Reagan administration handled the media, for example.

These developments are inseparable from the heroic presidency. It is impossible to increase the power to do good without also increasing the opportunity to abuse power. Control means control over money, people, and information, whatever the purpose. And even when the ends are thought good, does diminished accountability justify them? It is comforting to view the Tonkin Gulf incident, Watergate, and Iran–Contra as exceptions to presidential conduct that cannot recur because the system corrects itself through congressional backlash and responsible court decisions. But one should reassess this contention in the cold light of history. Presidents are by trial and error discovering ways to enhance their power at the cost of democracy. As they explore and exploit the fault lines of the political system, presidents find new ways to exercise control. Because Americans maintain such high expectations, presidents will continue to turn up untried control modes and their successes will mount.

Although Congress has reacted to specific presidential abuses, it is unreasonable to suppose that the abuse of presidential power corrects itself. The means and the motive make the covert presidency too tempting. The Budget Control and Impoundment Act of 1974, the War Powers Act of 1973, and even the informal consultations between the White House and the intelligence committees during the Reagan administration addressed individual abuses. They did not alter the trajectory of presidential power.

A strong presidency, as it is being defined incrementally in the United States, is not in the best interests of democracy. Whatever the flaws in contemporary political arrangements, the covert presidency holds out the prospect of a future government that will be far less accountable, accessible, and responsive to American citizens.

NOTES

Note: Thanks to Calvin Mouw and Dennis Judd for comments that improved this argument.

1. James Madison, Federalist Paper 51, in *The Federalist Papers,* ed. Clinton Rossiter (New York: Mentor Books, 1961).
2. Woodrow Wilson, *Congressional Government* (New York: Meridian Books, 1956), p. 31.
3. James MacGregor Burns, *Presidential Government: The Crucible of Leadership* (Boston: Houghton Mifflin, 1966).
4. Richard E. Neustadt, *Presidential Power: The Politics of Leadership from FDR to Carter* (New York: Wiley, 1980), pp. xi–xii.
5. Arthur M. Schlesinger, Jr., *The Imperial Presidency* (Boston: Houghton Mifflin, 1973); George E. Reedy, *The Twilight of the Presidency: From Johnson to Reagan,* rev. ed. (New York: Mentor Books, 1987).
6. Reedy, *The Twilight of the Presidency,* p. 179.
7. John P. Burke, "The Institutional Presidency," in *The Presidency and the Political System,* ed. Michael Nelson, 2d ed. (Washington, D.C.: Congressional Quarterly Press, 1988), pp. 357–59.
8. Robert Pear, "Temporary Hiring by U.S. Is Pushed under New Policy," *New York Times,* January 2, 1984, p. 1.
9. James P. Pfiffner, *The Strategic Presidency: Hitting the Ground Running* (Chicago: Dorsey Press, 1988), p. 161. See also Richard P. Nathan, *The Administrative Presidency* (New York: Wiley, 1983).
10. Lance T. LeLoup, *Budgetary Politics,* 4th ed. (Brunswick, Ohio: King's Court, 1988), pp. 107–10.
11. Lawrence J. Haas, "What OMB Hath Wrought," *National Journal,* September 3, 1988, pp. 2187–91.
12. Hedrick Smith, *The Power Game: How Washington Really Works* (New York: Random House, 1988), p. 432.
13. Ibid., p. 417.
14. Raymond Tatalovich and Byron W. Daynes, *Presidential Power in the United States* (Pacific Grove, Calif.: Brooks/Cole, 1983), p. 447.
15. LeLoup, *Budgetary Politics,* p. 235; Schlesinger, *The Imperial Presidency,* pp. 331–76.
16. Karl F. Inderfurth and Loch K. Johnson, "Transformation—Editors' Introduction," in *Decisions of the Highest Order: Perspectives on the National Security Council,* ed. Inderfurth and Johnson (Pacific Grove, Calif.: Brooks/Cole, 1988), pp. 89–103.
17. Theodore H. White, *Breach of Faith:*

The Fall of Richard Nixon (New York: Dell, 1978), pp. 190–96.

18. *Report of the Congressional Committees*

Investigating the Iran–Contra Affair, abridged ed. (New York: Random House, 1988), pp. 11–34, 59.

SUGGESTED READINGS

REEDY, GEORGE E.   *The Twilight of the Presidency: From Johnson to Reagan*. Rev. ed. New York: Mentor Books, 1987. One of the earliest books to warn about the potential abuse of the heroic presidency, written by a special assistant to President Johnson.

SCHLESINGER, ARTHUR M., JR.   *The Imperial Presidency*. Boston: Houghton Mifflin, 1973. The most lucid portrait of the temptations of presidential excess, written by a noted historian and aide to President Kennedy who changed his mind about the heroic presidency after witnessing its abuses.

WHITE, THEODORE H.   *Breach of Faith: The Fall of Richard Nixon*. New York: Dell, 1978. A prominent journalist's account of the Watergate scandal that details the Nixon administration's abuse of presidential power.

VIII

THE SUPREME COURT

Is the American Supreme Court Consistent with Democracy?

What is meant by *democracy?* Undoubtedly for most people, democracy means, above all else, majority rule, that at given (and regular) intervals the people choose their leaders. It further means that what those leaders do in office, the laws Congress passes for example, and the policies the president follows, are generally based on majority support. But doesn't democracy also include respect for the rights of minorities? The right of those who follow unusual religious beliefs to do so in peace? The right of those who espouse unpopular political ideas to express those views? What happens when rights collide? When the majority

wishes to pass laws that abridge the right of minorities to hold to their own practices and beliefs? What if the majority wants to require schoolchildren to be vaccinated against contagious diseases and Christian Science parents dissent?

In our system, the great protector of minority rights has often been the Supreme Court. More than once, the Court has used its power of judicial review to strike down barriers to human freedom. The Court first claimed that power, which is nowhere mentioned in the Constitution, in the 1803 case of *Marbury v. Madison*, when it declared an act of Congress, the Judiciary Act of 1789, to be in conflict with the Constitution and therefore null and void. Subsequently, the Court extended judicial review to apply to actions of the president and other executive officers, as well as to acts of the states.

The Court's awesome power means that a majority of nine justices, appointed in effect for life, are the final arbiters of what is and is not permitted under the Constitution. It means they can strike down, and indeed have struck down, laws and actions that have widespread popular support.

Our authors agree that sometimes the power of the Court has been used in ways that expand our freedoms and, at other times, in ways that have cruelly reduced them. On balance most seem to accept the proposition that it is the Supreme Court that is the boldest of our major institutions in acting to enlarge and safeguard the benefits of liberty. Surely, neither the executive nor the legislative branch was prepared to move, as did the Court in *Brown v. Topeka Board of Education*, to end the legal basis of segregated public facilities. (But in fact, the Court was tearing down the racist edifice it itself had ratified in 1896 in *Plessy v. Ferguson*.) Certainly neither Congress nor most presidents would have provided us with as broad a definition of the First Amendment guarantees of free expression and freedom of assembly as has the Supreme Court.

Perhaps we can agree these are desirable goals. But are they consistent with democracy? Professor Urey argues in "The Supreme Court and Judicial Review" that democracy means more than simple majority rule, that in the American context it places equal values on the protection of minority rights. Professors Heck and Arledge would agree in "Judicial Review Is Not Majority Rule" that we have other important political values, including federalism and separation of powers, but by their nature these are not democratic values. This is, indeed, an argument over semantics, the meaning of words. But because *democracy* is a very powerful word in the world, it is not a hair-splitting argument of no importance. It forces us to confront what significance we attach to majoritarianism as opposed to those institutions and processes that serve to protect our freedoms. Many have observed the irony that it is often the Supreme Court, the least democratically chosen of our three branches, that, precisely because it does not answer to the voters, is best able to ignore popular (and majority) passions to protect the rights of various minorities.

Learning about American government means learning about a variety of principles that underlie our political system. These include constitutionalism, separation of powers, federalism, and the presidential system. What happens when these principles collide, and to what extent are all of them united under the umbrella concept of democracy?

The Supreme Court and Judicial Review: In Defense of Democracy

Gene R. Urey
Susquehanna University

Chief Justice John Marshall once said of a case before the Supreme Court that the issue raised was "of great importance, but not of much difficulty."[1] Similarly, the issue of the compatibility of judicial review with democracy is of great importance to our appreciation of the constitutional system of the United States, but not of great difficulty if judicial review, democracy, and our constitutional philosophy are properly understood.

In defending the compatibility of the Supreme Court's exercise of judicial review with a democratic system, four basic arguments will be developed. The first is that the concept of democracy must be viewed in its particularly American context. The second is that judicial review is simply an aspect of the basic constitutional system of limited government created by separation of powers, checks and balances, and federalism. The third argument is that throughout much of the twentieth century, the Court has used judicial review to protect, defend, and expand democratic government. Finally, it will be argued that the Supreme Court itself is subject to both internal and external constraints that prevent judicial review from being used to subvert democracy.

THE CONSTITUTION
AND DEMOCRACY

The starting point in any discussion of judicial review and democracy must be to elaborate on the concept of democracy. *Democracy* is a slippery word. There are nearly as many different definitions as there are definers. The United States and France call themselves democracies; so do Albania and Cuba. Surely, these nations, so very different, cannot all be democracies if the word is to have any substantive meaning. But rather than finding a common definition to cover the myriad varieties of democracy, the discussion will be better served if confined to the meaning of *democracy* in the American context.

Perhaps in his Gettysburg address Abraham Lincoln best summarized the essence of American democracy with his famous words "government of the people, by the people, for the people." Measured by that standard, even the opponents of judicial review concede that the United States is a democracy, but a closer examination is necessary.

Obviously, some writers propose to define *democracy* simply in terms of majority rule—that government "of the people, by the people" must mean that government is to do simply what "fifty percent plus one" of the people of the country demand, regardless of the consequences for individuals, minorities, and the general welfare. Lincoln and the framers of our Constitution were too intelligent, sophisticated, and politically experienced to believe that majority rule alone produced democratic government. Majority rule had to be weighed against other democratic values: the protection of minority rights and the protection of the political, legal, and economic liberties of all the citizens of the nation. The fundamental constitutional principles of separation of powers, checks and balances, and federalism were not designed simply to prevent governmental abuses of power. They were intended to put limits on the power of a majority to do harm to minorities.

Government "of the people," or popular consent, lies at the heart of the establishment of the United States Constitution. Those who worked through the hot Philadelphia summer of 1787 recognized as a fundamental political principle that ultimate political authority rested with the people who had the right to consent or withhold consent to be governed. Government was not to be imposed on the people. The consent essential to legitimize political authority could even be withdrawn, as it was by the Declaration of Independence of 1776. But the act of consent, represented in the Constitution by its first three words, "We the people," by the requirement of popular ratification, and by the extraordinary majorities required in the ratification and amending processes, does not establish majority rule. "Of the people" is not the same as "by the people," in which a popular majority has its voice.

Although the framers were committed to the principle of consent, government "by the people," one responsive to the people's demands, posed a greater challenge. The delegates were not blind to what they saw as the weaknesses of human nature. As James Madison put it, "If men were angels, no government would be necessary";[2] human experience demonstrated that men are not angels. Although people at times act altruistically and rationally, they are just as likely to act on the basis of passion, emotion, or greed and to act irrationally. These all too human characteristics must be restrained in any free government, especially when people inevitably form groups to pursue their own selfish ends. The effects of these groups, or "factions" as Madison called them, had to be controlled, whether they were minorities or—even more dangerous to liberty and the common good—a majority.

A central problem, then, in drafting the Constitution was how to have a government "by the people" but one that impeded, if it did not prevent, the formation of a majority faction acting on the basis of its own narrow, selfish interests and threatening the liberty of minorities within the American community. In other words, unrestrained majority rule was no democracy but the rule of the mob. A government simply "by the people" was not necessarily a government "for the people," at least not one for *all* "of the people."

Other values were of equal importance to that of majority rule: the protection of the rights and interests of minorities, of individual liberties, both political and economic, of basic political and legal equality for those deemed citizens (a limited category in 1787), and ultimately the promotion of the common well-being of all of the people, not just the few, or even the many at the expense of the few. A majority could rule but not at the expense of other democratic values.

The document that emerged from the Constitutional Convention contained several devices to effectuate these values. The system was to be a representative democracy, not a direct democracy. The people were expected to choose as their representatives those of greater experience, talent, and, perhaps, even civic virtue, hence filtering out some baser, popular instincts.

The House of Representatives was where the voice of the majority was to be heard, muffled somewhat by a representative system but still subject to popular demands and passions. The fear and, indeed, expectation of the House's being swayed by demands of the mob required a restraining influence—the Senate—selected not directly by the people but by state legislatures for terms of six years. Let the House respond to the mob; the Senate was insulated from popular passion. It was here, even within the legislative branch, that the effects of even majority factions could be controlled.

The bicameralism of Congress was not the only means of restraining majority rule. As Madison explained it, the very nature of a large, heterogeneous nation with a wide variety of regional, economic, religious, and political interests would erect barriers to the easy formation of national majorities. In a sense, although factions were dangerous, there was safety in large numbers of factions. The larger the number and the greater the diversity of interests, the lesser the likelihood that any one faction would become dominant. Factions would be forced to form coalitions with other factions in order to broaden their political support, to find something approaching a consensus. Only a widely shared view of the common good would move Congress to act. Legislation would not be voluminous, but the legislation produced was likely to be wise legislation— legislation "for the people."

The constitutional structure of Congress coupled with the diversity of interests in the nation would place limits on majority power in the interest of protecting the political and economic liberties of minorities. A simple, parochial majority was unlikely to have dominant power in Congress, but even that was not a sufficient guarantee against the tyranny of simple majority rule. Something else was needed.

For most of the delegates to the convention, a fundamental principle of constitutional government was that all political power should not be placed in the hands of a single institution any more than in the hands of a single individual. Governmental power had to be separated into its component parts: legislative, executive, and judicial. If Congress had the power to make the law, it would be a guarantee of tyranny for Congress to also execute and interpret the law.

Article II of the Constitution grants to the president the executive power with at least implied discretion as to how the laws are to be "faithfully executed," as well as the power to veto congressional action. The president, independent of the legislative will, and being chosen by the people for a rather long, four-year term, is by constitutional design largely insulated and removed from popular passions and is a check on the power of Congress and unrestrained majority rule.

These fundamental constitutional elements lead to the inescapable conclusion that our democracy was not intended to promote decision making by simple majority rule. The document created in 1787 established what may be called a "constitutional democracy," in which the power of the majority is tempered by the need to protect minority rights. Leaving aside the descriptor *democracy* that some other nations apply to themselves, we can rightfully say that ours is a constitutional democracy with restraints on the power of majorities to do as they will. Unless we are willing to undertake a fundamental reassessment of human nature and to engage in basic constitutional change, constitutional democracy is a fact of American political life that cannot be ignored. It is designed to be a government of, by, and for *all* of the people, not just a majority of the people. Definitions of *democracy* that ignore minority rights are irrelevant to the American experience.

The concept of constitutional government speaks directly to the role of the Supreme Court in our system. The Constitution not only places limits on popular majorities but also places limits on the power of government itself. The Constitution, in its most basic form, determines what actions government may take and what actions are forbidden. The Constitution through separation of powers, checks and balances, and federalism created a limited government. Governmental action was necessary, but unlimited government could threaten basic rights and liberties.

Although the broad purposes of the Constitution are specified in the Preamble, the national government may not do anything it chooses under the guise of promoting the "General Welfare" or insuring "Domestic Tranquility." Government may use only those powers granted to it by the Constitution or reasonably implied from those grants of power. Other governmental activities are assigned by our federal system to the states. The people consented to a government exercising only those powers contained in the Constitution. Unless the Constitution is amended by the people acting in their sovereign capacity, even they cannot legitimize action exceeding constitutional powers.

Federalism, as a basic principle, goes beyond simply limiting the power of the national government. It, too, like the separation of powers and checks and balances, limits majority power. Any group seeking to use the national government must have political strength in more than a narrow region of the country if it is to have any hope of controlling national policy decisions. Regardless of whether the Court interprets the scope of federal and state power broadly or narrowly, this fact of constitutional life remains.

Unfortunately, a constitution is only

words, and words are ambiguous and not self-interpreting. What institution is to interpret the ambiguities, to make the limits meaningful? The people? The states? Congress? The president? The Supreme Court? The Constitution provides no clear answer. The records of the convention are themselves ambiguous. Scholars are unsure of the intention of the framers. The Federalist Papers generally avoid the subject. Yet, for nearly two hundred years, it has been the Supreme Court that has been the ultimate interpreter of the meaning of our constitutional system and our constitutional democracy through the power of judicial review.

Judicial review, broadly viewed, is the power of the courts to declare acts of Congress, the president, administrative agencies, and state governments null and void because those acts conflict with the Constitution. Or to put it more starkly, it is the power of the Supreme Court, often by a five-to-four margin, to override the decisions of 435 members of the House, 100 senators, and a president. That power may seem to be completely incompatible with government "by the people" in any form. How can that power, exercised by nine justices, appointed by the president and confirmed by the Senate, and holding office for life, if well behaved, possibly be consistent with democracy, constitutional or otherwise?

The answer lies in the nature of the Constitution. As Chief Justice John Marshall argued in *Marbury v. Madison* in 1803, the Constitution represents the ultimate will of the people in determining the fundamental rules by which they will be governed. The act of consent through ratifying the Constitution means agreeing to be bound by the rules of the Constitution. It is the most basic democratic act of the people. As such, the Constitution represents a law higher than the

day-to-day acts of governmental institutions. What happens, though, when an act of Congress violates those rules by going beyond the powers delegated to it in Article I, or when it violates a specific prohibition on such action?

Marshall's response was that it was the duty of the Court to interpret the law. When an act of Congress, ordinary law, came before the Court, and it conflicted with the Constitution, the supreme law, it was the duty of the Court to "determine which of these conflicting rules governs the case." Marshall went on, "If, then, the courts are to regard the constitution, and the constitution is superior to any ordinary act of the legislature, the constitution, and not such ordinary act, must govern the case to which they both apply."

Marshall asserted that it is the responsibility of the courts in interpreting the law to protect the most basic political act of the people: the establishment of, and consent to, the fundamental rules of the political game. The Court must protect government "of the people." Nor is that argument novel; Marshall largely borrowed Alexander Hamilton's position in Federalist Paper 78. Also, the Court, seven years before the *Marbury* decision, implied that it had the power of judicial review, while upholding an act of Congress in that case.[3] Judicial review is justified as the most effective means of protecting the most basic democratic act of the people from self-interested majorities or minorities that have temporarily gained political power. As to the question of majority rule, the Court is only an additional check, a safeguard, when other constitutional protections from majority tyranny have failed. As such, it is an essential element in our constitutional democracy.

Despite declarations to the contrary

throughout our history, and most recently from the Reagan administration, the Court has not abused the power of judicial review. It has been used sparingly. From its first use in 1803, it was not used again against a congressional act until *Dred Scott v. Sandford* in 1856. Today, fewer than 150 federal acts have been voided.[4]

Although many more state than federal actions have been struck down by the Court, that form of judicial review has not generally been subject to the same degree of criticism as Court nullification of national acts. The supremacy clause of Article VI establishes a firm foundation for the position that state actions that conflict with the Constitution, federal laws, or treaties are not to be enforced by the courts.

The importance of the Court's role as a protector of constitutional democracy has increased dramatically in recent years. The Constitution of the 1990s is in several respects very different from the Constitution of 1787. The likelihood of mass democracy, or mob rule, as Madison saw it, is much greater today than two hundred years ago. No longer is the electorate limited to white, male property owners or taxpayers. The Fourteenth, Fifteenth, Nineteenth, and Twenty-sixth amendments, along with federal enforcement legislation, have expanded the electorate to include virtually all citizens over the age of eighteen years. The Seventeenth Amendment, providing for the direct election of United States senators, has weakened the Senate as a restraint on the majoritarian House of Representatives. The development of political parties has increased popular influence on the president, and has changed the Electoral College role to largely one of a rubber stamp of the popular vote, even if potentially a faulty rubber stamp.

THE SUPREME COURT AND DEMOCRACY

The impact of these changes on both formal and informal constitutional structure is to increase the potential for majoritarian government in violation of the framers' intentions. Unless human nature has dramatically improved in two hundred years, a proposition for which there is little evidence, the potential for repressive, intolerant, self-interested legislation has increased. The most effective remaining institutional restraint to protect the interests of individuals and minorities who are not part of the temporary majority is the Supreme Court. In fact, a dominant role of the Supreme Court over the past fifty years has been not only to protect the political and legal rights of minorities but, through that protection, to move us to a position where the majority is a "real majority," one that includes all citizens regardless of race, sex, residence, ethnicity, or wealth.

This function of judicial review was first suggested by Justice Harlan F. Stone in a footnote in the *Carolene Products* case in 1938.[5] There he suggested that the appropriate role for the Court might be to examine closely legislation touching on the Bill of Rights and legislation that imposes burdens upon "discrete and insular minorities." His concern was to protect access for all citizens to the political process, to ensure, as far as the Court could, that the process of forming a political majority was open to all. If a majority was to rule, it was to be an inclusive, not an exclusive, majority. This was a concern similar to that expressed by Justices Oliver Wendell Holmes and Louis D. Brandeis nearly twenty years earlier in a series of First Amendment cases,[6] when they argued that the Constitution and our political values required a free marketplace of ideas. No one, not even a powerful majority, had a monopoly on truth. Constitutional democracy requires a political process open to all, with free access to information.

That the Court has acted to promote these values is evident from several recent and highly controversial cases. The decision in *Brown v. Board of Education* in 1954, declaring racial segregation in public education unconstitutional, was a first step in opening educational opportunities, and the political and legal processes as well, to all Americans regardless of race. The Court acted after the failure of our "democratic" institutions to end the shame of segregation and racism.

It was the Supreme Court that took crucial steps toward ending political, legal, social, and economic gender-based discrimination,[7] falling most heavily against women who had long been victims of discrimination, even if not a "discrete and insular minority." The Court also struck down racial gerrymandering, poll taxes, lengthy residency requirements for voting, and numerous other impediments to access to the democratic process.[8]

The Court's decisions in a series of reapportionment cases, beginning with *Baker v. Carr* in 1962, had a profound impact by opening the political process to city dwellers, who, because of the "crazy quilt"[9] pattern of drawing both congressional and state legislative district lines, had seen their voting power diluted at the hands of rural minorities. The reapportionment decisions, perhaps more than any others, demonstrate that judicial review can be and has been used by the Supreme Court to effectuate majority rule by opening the democratic process to those excluded by an entrenched minority.

The Court's decisions on the First Amendment issues of speech, press, and religion have also expanded our commitment to democratic values. For example, the decision in 1971 permitting publication of the "Pentagon papers"[10] allowed more informed public debate on the vital issue of our involvement in Vietnam. Several decisions making it more difficult for public officials to win libel actions against newspapers and other critics expanded information available to the public.[11] Nor have these decisions been limited to the public at large. The right of public school students to free, nondisruptive speech has been protected, and school boards have been prevented from arbitrarily removing books from library shelves.[12]

The school prayer decisions of the Court,[13] subject to so much criticism by the political and religious Right, also have promoted the values of constitutional democracy by restricting the power of a local majority or minority to impose their religious values on members of the community who do not share those values.

The criminal justice decisions of the Court, such as *Miranda v. Arizona*, although widely criticized, have a firm foundation in democratic values. Protection of the individual from arbitrary, unreasonable governmental action and protection of legal rights, regardless of the ability to "buy" justice, lie at the heart of government "for the people," not just the wealthy, powerful, or favored.

Finally, the extension of these limits on governmental action to the states through the process of incorporation, begun in 1925,[14] has gone a long way toward guaranteeing that state and local governments will be democratic. Incorporation, which simply means that the Bill of Rights will be applied to the states just as to the federal government through the due process clause of the

Fourteenth Amendment, was heavily criticized by the Reagan administration, particularly through Attorney General Edwin Meese. Despite his criticism, however, the effect of the incorporation doctrine has been to protect and expand constitutional democracy. The national rights of free speech and press, the right to be free from governmentally imposed religion and free from governmental oppression in the criminal justice system—essential liberties—are no less important for citizens vis-à-vis state and local governments, federalism notwithstanding.

THE SUPREME COURT AND JUDICIAL REVIEW

Does judicial review, even when used to protect, promote, and expand democracy, mean that we are ultimately ruled by a judicial "aristocracy"? Are we dependent for our rights as citizens on the continued goodwill of at least five Supreme Court justices? Clearly, the answer is *No!*

Just as the powers of a popular majority, of Congress, and of the president are subject to checks in our constitutional system, so is the power of the Supreme Court. In fact, Alexander Hamilton, while arguing in Federalist Paper 78 in support of the power of judicial review, called the courts "the least dangerous branch," restricted both externally by the constitutional system and internally by self-imposed rules that recognize the Court's lack of independent political power.

The first external check on the Court's power is found in the nature of the judicial function itself. Article III of the Constitution requires that the judicial power extend only to "cases or controversies." Although a complex subject, the requirement that there be a case or controversy means, in part, that a person alleging an injury must bring a claim to the courts. Courts do not actively roam through legislation looking for constitutional violations. They are passive institutions: only when someone brings a claim before them may they make a decision.

The vast bulk of the Court's business consists of appellate cases. It is here that Congress may impose an important check on the Court's power, for the appellate jurisdiction of the Court is subject to change by Congress. If Congress is unhappy about the Court's reapportionment decisions, for example, it could attempt to remove reapportionment cases from the Court's appellate jurisdiction. The effect would be to leave those decisions in the hands of the lower federal courts or the highest state courts where, supposedly, the decisions would be more "favorable" to the dominant congressional interests.

The other major check that Congress has on the Court is the constitutional power to change the size of its membership. The Constitution does not specify the number of justices; the current number of nine, in effect for over one hundred years, is fixed by law. Congress can reduce the number to prevent the filling of vacancies or enlarge the number to permit new appointments in an attempt to overwhelm an unpopular majority. It was the enlargement option that was proposed by President Franklin Roosevelt during his battle with the Court in the 1930s. Although his "court-packing" proposal was rejected by Congress, some observers have suggested that the proposal played a part in creating a court majority more favorable to the New Deal legislative program, and hence contributed to the judicial revolution of 1937.[15]

Courts also face the problem of having no power to enforce their decisions and orders. For this they are dependent on the executive branch, which may not be sympathetic to the judiciary's position. President Andrew Jackson allegedly once said, "John Marshall has made his decision, now let him enforce it."[16] More recently, in 1958, the Supreme Court faced the issue of what to do about the refusal of the state of Arkansas to implement a federal court order desegregating the schools of Little Rock. The Court's decision in *Cooper v. Aaron* may be viewed as an attempt to pressure President Dwight Eisenhower into bringing the full force of federal power to enforce the court order.

The Court's approach in *Cooper v. Aaron* illustrates both its strength and its weakness. The unanimous opinion, uniquely signed individually by each justice, not only upheld the desegregation order but also stated firmly that Supreme Court decisions on constitutional issues were constitutional law, not just interpretations binding upon only the parties in the case. This broad claim, viewed as overly broad by some critics, was an appeal to the tradition of compliance with Court decisions, but it was only an appeal. The president still could have refused to act, leaving the Court's ringing pronouncement an empty promise

Still another external influence on judicial review is found in the selection process. Presidential nomination decisions from the earliest days have been motivated by the desire to select for the Court appointees who will promote and protect the president's political, social, and economic agenda. Although presidents are not always able to predict accurately the future behavior of their appointees, one or two appointments may be enough to create a balance on the Court favorable to a president's program. Beginning in 1937, President Roosevelt's appointments influenced the Court's di-

rection for over thirty years. President Ronald Reagan may also have had a similar effect on the Court. Only President Jimmy Carter of recent presidents did not have the good fortune of filling a vacancy on the Court during his term.

The Senate role in the confirmation process also needs to be noted. Clearly, presidents do not have a free hand in appointment, as President Reagan discovered with his nomination of Robert Bork to the Supreme Court. The Senate may decide that a nominee is too far removed from the judicial mainstream and popular opinion to be confirmed, thus preventing the formation of a majority on the Court that is antithetical to public hopes and aspirations.

A more direct external constraint on the Court is the amendment process. Constitutional interpretations may be reversed by amending the Constitution. Admittedly, amendment is a complex and difficult process, but it is one that reflects the importance and extraordinary nature of constitutional rules. The Equal Rights Amendment and the efforts to pass school prayer and antiabortion amendments say less about the lack of effectiveness of the amendment as a check on the Court than they say about the divisions within the American public. It is not just a small majority but something approaching consensus regarding wrongful interpretation that makes amendment possible.

The effects of these external constraints on the Court are buttressed by internal institutional constraints as well. Despite the certainty with which opinions are written, Court decisions are not chiseled in stone tablets. The rule of *stare decisis* (holding to principles previously decided) does not bind the Court in deciding constitutional issues. The Court can reverse, and in many cases has reversed, its decisions on constitutional issues. The makeup of the Court changes, and justices change their minds.[17]

The Court has also recognized the weakness of its political position by developing internal rules that may preclude decision in some cases. The political question doctrine is one such device. The Court will refuse to decide issues for which the Constitution has vested decision-making authority in another branch of government. The standing doctrine, which requires that a party bringing an action demonstrate concrete personal injury, is also a means by which the Court may choose not to decide a constitutional issue. It was a combination of the political question doctrine and standing rules through which the lower federal courts avoided a number of challenges to the constitutionality of the United States involvement in the Vietnam War,[18] thus permitting the democratic process to work, as painful as that proved to be.

Even if standing and political question problems are avoided, the Court has virtually complete discretion in choosing the cases it will take on. Of the five thousand or so cases the Court is asked to decide each term, less than 5 percent receive full hearing and decision. Many important issues, important at least to the litigants, remain unresolved by the nation's highest court. Only those cases that the Court itself deems the most important are given its attention.

Critics of the Court's role argue that the picture of a Supreme Court dedicated to protecting democratic values and subject to external and internal checks on its power is a distorted vision of reality, and to a limited extent they are correct. Throughout the history of the Court, decisions have been made that have been the antithesis of constitutional democracy. The *Dred Scott* case was an unmitigated disaster.[19] The decision was reversed only by the Civil War and passage of the Fourteenth Amendment. Forty years later, the Court approved Jim Crow laws in *Plessey v. Ferguson,* and thereby guaranteed the continued existence of a segregated nation for the next sixty years.

For approximately the first one-third of this century, the Supreme Court frequently struck down federal and state legislation designed to ease the worst conditions spawned by the industrialization and commercialization of the nation. Minimum wage laws, maximum hour laws, child labor laws, and consumer protection laws usually faced an insurmountable barrier in the Court.[20] Matters came to a head in the 1930s during the Great Depression when several key provisions of President Roosevelt's New Deal legislative program were struck down by a conservative Court. Those decisions, based as they were on an unpopular and outdated economic philosophy of laissez-faire, created a crisis of public confidence in the Court, which was giving greater weight to economic liberty than to the voice of the majority. Constitutional democracy and judicial review were on a collision course, and only because of an amazing change of direction by the Court was the collision avoided.[21]

Other instances can be cited in which the Supreme Court seemed unconcerned with supporting democratic values. The decision upholding the internment of Japanese-American citizens during World War II has only recently partially been rectified.[22] Court decisions during the 1950s did little to limit McCarthyism, our national preoccupation with Communist infiltration.[23] More recently, the decision permitting states to punish consensual homosexual acts[24] is seen by many as a denial of the rights of a minority; as being inconsistent with the rights of privacy established by the Court in

Griswold v. Connecticut and *Roe v. Wade;* and, more basically, as being inconsistent with individual freedom, dignity, and equality.

No, the Court has not always been the champion of the values of constitutional democracy, nor have our other, more "democratic" institutions, but on balance the record of the past half-century clearly demonstrates the Court's commitment to constitutional democracy. Judicial review has frequently been used to expand, not limit, democratic government despite opposition from Congress, presidents, states, and popular majorities.

A key factor in this development is the change in the dominant judicial philosophy of the Court following the crisis of the 1930s from judicial activism to judicial restraint in dealing with economic issues. The Court withdrew from issues of economic regulation and turned to a position similar to that of Justice Holmes who argued in dissent in *Lochner* in 1905 that the Constitution did not protect any particular economic philosophy. That change meant that the government was free to respond to the majority's economic demands; the political process, not the courts, would determine economic policy.

The corollary to this position was that the Court would closely examine governmental actions, both national and state, that impinged on the democratic process, as Justice Stone had suggested in the *Carolene Products* case in 1938. The Court was saying, in effect, that democratic values of liberty and open access for all were of greater importance to constitutional democracy than protection of property rights. Human rights would be actively and vigorously protected; economic rights would receive only a cursory review. It is this activist use of judicial review that has aided in the trans-

formation of an arguably undemocratic device into a vital instrument of constitutional democracy, balancing majority rule, minority rights, and fundamental liberties for all.

Those who criticize the activist approach to judicial review frequently do so not on the basis of democratic principles but because they disagree with the substance of the Court's decisions. The exercise of judicial restraint that permits repressive legislation to stand does not serve democracy.

The most important constraint on the Court remains unexplored: the ultimate check by the people of the United States. Court decisions clearly and consistently out of touch with the values of the people are doomed, as illustrated by the result of the confrontation between President Franklin Roosevelt and the Court in the 1930s. Judicial review restrains but does not destroy majority rule. The Court's ultimate power is not the force of its legal opinions and certainly not its superior moral judgment. Its real power is to convince the American people that it is conscientiously attempting to preserve the Constitution and constitutional democracy. Decisions that lack public support and persuasive rationales, that do not rest on widely held values, are bound to be only footnotes in our constitutional history. The Court cannot for long stand firm in the face of a popular majority bound to have its way. Perhaps, in fact, too often the Court has succumbed to unenlightened public pressure.

The Constitution is not, as Justice Charles E. Hughes once said, "what the judges say it is."[25] The Constitution is an amalgam of its own words, of what Congress and the president do, of how the Court interprets it, and most important, of what the people want the Constitution to be. As Madison knew so well, a constitution can be only as good as the people permit it to be. The Court can suggest, sometimes restrain, and occasionally lead, but, as it should be in a constitutional democracy, the people will finally decide. Even with judicial review, and in large part because of judicial review, this nation remains a balanced constitutional democracy, as Madison had hoped.

NOTES

1. *Barron v. the Mayor and City Council of Baltimore,* 32 U.S. 243 (1933).
2. This quotation and the discussion that follows are based on Federalist Papers 10, 47, and 51.
3. *Hylton v. United States,* 3 U.S. 171 (1796).
4. Henry R. Glick, *Courts, Politics and Justice,* 2d ed. (New York: McGraw-Hill, 1988), p. 341.
5. *United States v. Carolene Products Co.,* 304 U.S. 144 (1938).
6. See, for example, the concurring opinion of Justice Brandeis in *Whitney v. California,* 274 U.S. 357 (1927).
7. See Craig R. Ducat and Harold W. Chase, *Constitutional Interpretation,* 4th ed. (St. Paul: West, 1988), pp. 806–18.
8. See, for example, *Gomillion v. Lightfoot,* 364 U.S. 339 (1960); *Harper v. Virginia Board of Elections,* 383 U.S. 663 (1966); *Dunn v. Blumstein,* 405 U.S. 330 (1972).
9. See the concurring opinion of Justice Tom C. Clark in *Reynolds v. Sims,* 377 U.S. 533 (1964).
10. *New York Times Co. v. United States,* 403 U.S. 713 (1971).
11. Beginning with *New York Times Co. v. Sullivan,* 376 U.S. 254 (1964).
12. See *Tinker v. Des Moines Independent Community School District,* 393 U.S. 503 (1969), and *Board of Education v. Pico,* 457 U.S. 583 (1982).
13. In particular, *Abington School District v. Schempp,* 374 U.S. 203 (1963).
14. *Gitlow v. New York,* 268 U.S. 652 (1925).
15. Ducat and Chase, *Constitutional Interpretation,* pp. 405–7.
16. Quoted in Alfred H. Kelly and Winfred A. Harbison, *The American Constitution,* 4th ed. (New York: W. W. Norton & Co., 1970), p. 303.
17. The Court reversed its position on the compulsory flag salute in only three years. See *Minersville School District v. Gobitis,* 310 U.S. 586 (1940), and *West Virginia State Board of Education v. Barnette,* 319 U.S. 624 (1943).
18. See, for example, *Holtzman v. Schlesinger,* 484 F. 2d. 1307 2nd Circuit (1983), cited in Ducat and Chase, *Constitutional Interpretation,* pp. 130–32. For a thorough discussion of these issues, see *Baker v. Carr,* 369 U.S. 186 (1962).
19. Here the Court held that the Constitution did not permit blacks to be citizens of the United States.
20. A classic example is *Lochner v. New York,* 198 U.S. 45 (1905).
21. See, in particular, *Schechter Poultry Corp. v. United States,* 295 U.S., 495 (1938).
22. *Korematsu v. United States,* 323 U.S. 214 (1944).
23. *Dennis v. United States,* 341 U.S. 494 (1951).
24. *Bowers v. Hardwick,* 106 Sup. Ct. 2841 (1986).
25. Ducat and Chase, *Constitutional Interpretation,* p. 3.

SUGGESTED READINGS

MARBURY V. MADISON,   5 U.S. 137 (1803), in the original, or found in any constitutional law casebook; for example, Craig R. Ducat and Harold W. Chase, *Constitutional Interpretation*, 4th ed. (St. Paul: West, 1988), pp. 16–27. A "must read" for anyone wishing to understand the foundation of judicial review, the political restraints on the Supreme Court, and John Marshall's inventive arguments.

MARSHALL, THOMAS R. *Public Opinion and the Supreme Court* (Winchester, Mass.: Unwin Hyman, 1989). A study of the relationship between Supreme Court decisions and public opinion that concludes that the Court is no less majoritarian than other governmental institutions.

THUROW, SARAH BAUMGARTNER, ED. *E Pluribus Unum: Constitutional Principles and the Institution of Government*, vol. 2 (Lanham, Md.: University Press of America, 1988), pp. 149–219. Contains a set of five lively essays on the appropriate place of judicial review in democracy, includ·ing two essays that are highly critical of judicial review.

Judicial Review Is Not Majority Rule

Edward V. Heck
San Diego State University

Paula C. Arledge
Northeast Louisiana University

"Can the Supreme Court, a politically non-responsible body, block the will of the majority in the name of minorities and still be considered a democratic institution?" In those words Supreme Court scholar Alpheus T. Mason formulated a crucial question in an ongoing debate about the nature of the Supreme Court and its role in the American political system. Despite the importance of the Court's role of protecting majority rights, the authors of this essay take the position that the answer to Mason's question is no.

Ultimately, this debate turns on the nature of democratic government. To de-termine whether the Supreme Court's position in the political system is con-sistent with democracy, it is necessary first to understand the meaning of the key term *democracy*. This task is by no means as simple as it might first appear, because there are literally hundreds of definitions of *democracy*. In its simplest and most basic sense, *democracy* means "rule by the people." In the modern world, democracy is more likely to take the form of indirect rule by the people through elected representatives that di-rect popular rule. Even so, there is wide-spread disagreement about the pro-cedures necessary to ensure that "the people" actually do exercise political power. In a comparative study of nations generally recognized as stable democracies, political scientist Arend Lijphart identifies two basic models of democracy derived from differing definitions of the term: the *majoritarian* model and the *consensus* model.[2]

The authors of this essay take the position that a definition of *democracy* in terms of the majoritarian model is most appropriate if we wish to address the question of whether the United States Supreme Court is a democratic institution. Crucial to any such definition of *democracy* is recognition of the principle that in a democracy ultimate control over government must rest in the hands of the majority. In a provocative analysis of judicial review and the Supreme Court, Jesse Choper observes that "majority rule has been considered the keystone of a democratic political system in both theory and practice."[3] In this view the key to democracy is the power of a majority of citizens to choose (and remove) their representatives and political leaders through elections. Henry Mayo has defined a democratic political system as "one in which public policies are made, on a majority basis, by representatives subject to effective popular control at periodic elections which are conducted on the principle of political equality and under conditions of political freedom."[4]

In general, nations in which members of the national legislature are selected by the voters in meaningful elections and the voters may have a decisive voice in the choice of the head of government (president or prime minister) are classified as democracies under this definition. Australia, France, Canada, Costa Rica, and the parliamentary democracies of Western Europe are among the nations in which voters exercise control over government through elections. Similarly, it seems fair to conclude that the United States meets this definition of a democracy. Primary responsibility for the making of public policy at the national level is in the hands of a president and Congress chosen in elections in which virtually all citizens are free to register and vote, and also to discuss and debate the issues, the qualifications of candidates, and the past performance of officeholders. Similarly, the making of public policy at the state and local levels is largely in the hands of elected governors, mayors, legislatures, and city councils.

Despite adherence to basic democratic principles, the actual functioning of political institutions in the United States and in other democratic nations may embrace practices that are not fully consistent with the principle of majority rule. A British prime minister, for example, may win office if his or her party controls a majority of seats in the House of Commons even if an overall majority of voters did not vote for candidates of the prime minister's political party. In the United States the functioning of the electoral college might in rare instances mean that a president could be elected with fewer popular votes than the opposition's candidate. The basic argument of this chapter is that the United States Supreme Court is another example of a political institution that is inconsistent with the democratic principle of majority rule.

The U.S. Constitution provides that members of the Supreme Court are chosen by the president, with the approval of the majority of the Senate, and serve "during good behavior," in practice until death or retirement. Unlike presidents, governors, mayors, and members of Congress and state legislatures, Supreme Court justices are not elected and may not be removed from office either by the voters or by the president. Yet, the Supreme Court plays a significant role in government and in the making of public policy in the United States.

The power of the Supreme Court in the American political system rests on its power of judicial review. Judicial review may be defined as the power of a court—in a case properly before it—to determine the constitutionality of acts of other branches of government. If the Supreme Court determines that an act of Congress or a state legislature, or for that matter an action of the president or the procedure employed by a local police department, is inconsistent with the Constitution, the Court may overturn such an act. In theory, judicial review rests on the proposition that the courts have a special responsibility for interpreting and enforcing the Constitution. In the famous case of *Marbury v. Madison* (1803) Chief Justice John Marshall justified the power of the Court to declare an act of Congress unconstitutional by asserting that "it is emphatically the province and duty of the judicial department to say what the law [including the Constitution] is."[5] In practice, the power of judicial review allows the Supreme Court to overrule decisions of democratically elected political leaders, including the president and Congress at the national level, as well as governors, state legislatures, and local officials at state and local levels. When the justices "exercise the power of judicial review to declare unconstitutional legislative, executive, or administrative action—federal, state, or local—they reject the product of the popular will by denying policies formulated by the majority's elected representatives or their appointees."[6] As historian Henry Steele Commager once wrote,

> The philosophical basis of judicial review is undemocratic. The assumption behind judicial review is that the people either do not understand the Constitution or will not respect it and that the courts do understand the Constitution and will respect it.[7]

The position that the power of the Supreme Court to overrule decisions of elected officials on constitutional grounds is inconsistent with democratic principles plays a significant part in an ongoing debate among students of the Supreme Court and the justices themselves about *how* the Supreme Court should use its power of judicial review. In simple terms this debate matches proponents of judicial restraint (or deference to the legislative and executive branches) against judicial activists. Justices committed to restraint are characterized by "their reluctance to exercise the judicial power to invalidate legislation," a reluctance based on their recognition of the "intrinsically undemocratic nature of the Supreme Court."[8] Justice Felix Frankfurter, widely recognized as one of the foremost advocates of judicial restraint, once declared that for the Court to uphold an act of Congress "is to respect the actions of the two branches of our Government directly responsive to the will of the people and empowered under the Constitution to determine the wisdom of legislation." As a result, Frankfurter continued, "the awesome power of this Court to invalidate such legislation . . . must be exercised with the utmost restraint."[9] Other judges and scholars have sought to minimize the political power exercised by a nondemocratic judiciary by arguing that the justices must determine the meaning of the Constitution solely in light of its literal language or in a way that is consistent with the original "intent of the framers."

Despite the connection between judicial restraint and democracy, there is general agreement that most Supreme Court justices have been judicial activists, at least in recent years. Many elements of judicial activism have been identified, including willingness to overturn precedent, limited concern with the "intent of the framers" of the Constitution, and specificity in prescribing policy to be followed by other branches of government.[10] The essence of judicial activism, though, is use of the power of judicial review to negate "the will of legislative majorities."[11] Whereas the proponent of judicial restraint hesitates to use the power of judicial review to overturn the acts of another branch of government, the activist is more aggressive in the use of judicial power. Activist justices may be "outraged at injustices and are quite willing to declare statutes or actions of government officials unconstitutional," particularly when the goal is the protection of civil liberties and civil rights.[12]

Although aggressive use of the power of judicial review may be inconsistent with democracy, it does not follow that judicial restraint is the only proper posture for the Supreme Court, nor that judicial activism is inconsistent with the American constitutional system as a whole. Majoritarian democracy is by no means the sole principle of the Constitution. Rather, democracy is only *one* of a number of distinct values embraced by it. Among the other fundamental principles of the Constitution are federalism, separation of powers, checks and balances, and limited government (the principle that provides for protecting the rights and liberties of individuals).[13] In the words of Henry Abraham:

> Our system of government was designed . . . as a system characterized by representative democracy, popular sovereignty, majoritarianism, duly limited by observance of minority rights, a federal structure, a written Constitution capable of growth or contraction, and separation of powers.[14]

Even if the democratic principle of majority rule is the most important of these constitutional principles—a position that would certainly have been rejected by those who drafted the original Constitution and the Bill of Rights—these competing principles cannot be ignored. It is the argument of the authors that the Supreme Court acts in a way that is inconsistent with the democratic principle of majority rule when it uses the power of judicial review to strike down the acts of elected officials. Yet, vigorous exercise of this undemocratic power is essential to the protection of other fundamental constitutional values. Many examples can be cited of Supreme Court decisions that overturned the acts of other branches of government in order to promote the fundamental constitutional principles of federalism, checks and balances, and limited government.

Federalism The constitutional principle of federalism "calls for political authority to be distributed between a central government and the governments of the states."[15] Although the national Constitution, laws, and treaties take precedence over the constitutions and laws of the individual states in cases of conflict, the original seven articles of the Constitution clearly envision a significant and partially independent role for the states in the governmental system. This principle of federalism was given more concrete form in the Tenth Amendment's provision that powers not granted to the national government are reserved to the states.

Historically, the Supreme Court's role in enforcing the constitutional principle of federalism has involved both enforcement of the supremacy of the national government and protection of the independent role of the states. The Court was particularly aggressive in protecting state independence between 1890 and 1936, often striking down acts of Congress as inconsistent with the reserved powers of the states. Since 1937 the Court has generally accepted expansion of the power of the national government, but recent decisions reveal that some justices still consider it the responsibility of the Court to use the power of judicial review to guarantee the "separate and independent existence" of the states. In 1976 a majority of the Court went so far as to strike down a federal law extending the national minimum wage and maximum hours laws to employees of state and local governments.[16] Although this decision was reversed nine years later, four dissenting justices made clear their continuing commitment to the Supreme Court's role of "protecting the States from federal overreaching."[17]

Judicial enforcement of the principle of federalism is not the major component of judicial activism in an era of national power, but the Court still retains ultimate power to overrule any act of the people's representatives that the justices deem inconsistent with this principle.

Checks and balances Even more significant than federalism in a political system marked by the growth of executive power is judicial enforcement of the constitutional principles of separation of powers and checks and balances. "Separation of powers is the assignment of the lawmaking, law-enforcing, and law-interpreting functions to separate and independent legislative, executive, and judicial branches of government," and "the constitutional system of checks and balances is a means of giving each branch of government some scrutiny of and control over the other branches."[18] Although these principles are distinct and to some

extent inconsistent, the U.S. Constitution provides for a system in which the two principles interact "to ensure that one branch will not dominate the government."[19]

Perhaps the best example of judicial enforcement of these principles was the Court's decision in a 1952 case that President Harry Truman's attempt to seize the nation's steel mills without the approval of Congress (in order to prevent a threatened strike that would disrupt military production) violated the principle of separation of powers.[20] Similarly, the Supreme Court's decision in the Watergate tapes case[21] may be seen as a classic example of the use of judicial power to enforce the principle of checks and balances. By ruling that President Richard Nixon must hand over recordings of White House meetings for use in a criminal prosecution, the Court acted to prevent abuse of presidential power and assured that the president would have to resign or face impeachment and removal from office for his role in efforts to cover up high level involvement in the Watergate scandal. More recently the Court has invoked the separation of powers principle to strike down acts of Congress providing for a "legislative veto" of acts of administrative agencies and delegating to an official responsible to Congress the authority to reduce the federal deficit by mandating across-the-board reductions in federal spending.[22] On the other hand, the Court has upheld an act of Congress giving lower court judges limited power to appoint special prosecutors to investigate and prosecute executive branch officials accused of abuse of power despite the Reagan administration's assertion that the law unconstitutionally restricted executive power.[23]

Limited government By far the most important function of an activist judiciary is aggressive use of the power of judicial review to strike down acts of other branches of government that interfere with the rights and liberties of individuals. Constitutional provisions that protect individual rights by limiting the power of government may be found in the Bill of Rights (the first ten amendments to the Constitution) and the Fourteenth Amendment. Various provisions of the Bill of Rights guarantee the freedoms of speech, press, and religion (First Amendment), protect individuals against "unreasonable searches and seizures" (Fourth Amendment), specify procedural guarantees for those accused of crimes (Fifth and Sixth amendments), and prohibit the imposition of "cruel and unusual punishments" (Eighth Amendment). The Fourteenth Amendment protects individual rights by prohibiting the *states* from taking actions that deny "due process" or "equal protection of the laws." Although the Bill of Rights was originally designed to prevent the abuse of power by the national government, the Supreme Court has ruled that the provisions of the Bill of Rights that are deemed "fundamental" limit the states as well.

In introducing his proposal for addition of a bill of rights to the Constitution, James Madison declared:

> If they [provisions of the proposed bill of rights] are incorporated into the constitution, independent tribunals of justice will consider themselves in a peculiar manner the guardians of those rights; they will be an impenetrable bulwark against every assumption of power in the legislative or executive; they will be naturally led to resist every encroachment upon rights expressly stipulated for in the constitution by the declaration of rights.[24]

Although the Supreme Court was slow in accepting the role of enforcing the Bill of Rights contemplated by Madison, it is in the performance of this function that the modern Supreme Court is most likely to engage in judicial activism. The Court has enforced provisions of the Bill of Rights by striking down a few dozen federal laws and hundreds of state and local laws that the justices believed invaded rights protected by constitutional guarantees of individual liberty. In addition, the Court has frequently ruled that certain police practices, such as warrantless searches or interrogations without warnings of constitutional rights, violate the Fourth or Fifth Amendment.[25]

Particularly noteworthy are Supreme Court decisions striking down the acts of state legislatures that the justices found to be in violation of the Fourteenth Amendment's vaguely worded guarantees in such famous cases as *Brown v. Board of Education* and *Roe v. Wade*. In the *Brown* case, the Supreme Court interpreted the equal protection clause as prohibiting state legislatures from requiring racial segregation in public schools.[26] In *Roe v. Wade*, the Court ruled that a right of privacy, which included a woman's right to choose whether to terminate a pregnancy, was part of the "liberty" protected against state interference by the due process clause of the Fourteenth Amendment.[27] In neither case were the justices able to rely on unambiguous constitutional language to support their decisions. Rather, they performed what Justice Robert H. Jackson once described as the task of "translating the majestic generalities" of constitutional provisions that limit government in order to protect individual rights "into concrete restraints on officials dealing with the problems of the twentieth century."[28] In both cases— as well as in hundreds of other cases striking down governmental acts that the justices regarded as inconsistent with the

Constitution—the justices acted in conformity with Madison's vision of the courts as guardians of constitutional rights. As unelected judges overruling the acts of elected representatives of the people, they acted inconsistently with the democratic principle of majority rule. Rejecting the notion of judicial restraint, they used their power of judicial review aggressively to enforce another fundamental constitutional principle: the idea of limited government.

JUDICIAL REVIEW:
A BALANCING PROCESS

Professor Urey, author of the companion essay in this book, is among the supporters of judicial review who argue that the Supreme Court's power to strike down the acts of elected officials in the executive and legislative branches is not inconsistent with democratic principles. At least two aspects of this argument should be acknowledged here. Many distinguished scholars have reasoned that the Supreme Court is rarely out of touch with the views of elected officials in the executive and legislative branches, and that the Court can be brought into line with the wishes of the populace through the president's power to appoint justices. Others have noted that the Court has on occasion promoted democracy by striking down laws that interfered with voting or fair representation. The authors of this essay have no quarrel with these propositions. In the long run, the Court does tend to follow the election returns. The election of George Bush to the presidency assured that future Court appointees would be more conservative than those who would have been selected if a Democrat such as Michael Dukakis had been

the choice of the voters. Moreover, there is no doubt that some of the Court's most noted activist decisions have promoted meaningful exercise of the right to vote.[29]

Yet, even if the *results* of judicial review are ultimately consistent with the will of the people, it does not follow that the *process* of judicial review is democratic. Ultimately, conclusions about democracy and the Supreme Court turn on definitions. In the words of political scientist Charles Hyneman, "Whether our highest tribunal is a democratic or a nondemocratic institution depends on the meaning which is given to democracy, and what meaning that word ought to carry is hotly debated in the literature."[30] Definitions of *democracy* in terms of its "particularly American context" run the danger of circular reasoning. If "democracy" is equated with the "American system of constitutional government," a discussion of judicial review may lead to little more than the obvious conclusion that the American constitutional system is consistent with the American constitutional system. Our definition of *democracy* in terms of majority rule provides a standard by which to judge the performance of American institutions. The authors of this essay agree with Henry Abraham's assertion that "regardless of periodic efforts to 'democratize' the Court, its nature is intrinsically *undemocratic*—which is precisely what the Founding Fathers intended it to be."[31] Its ultimate function is not merely to give its stamp of approval to acts of elected officials, as proponents of judicial restraint tend to argue. Rather, its responsibility is to balance the Constitution's commitment to the democratic principle of majority rule with its commitment to such competing fundamental principles as federalism, checks and balances, and individual rights. It is this function—a function essential to the overall system of checks and balances itself—that the Court performs when it strikes down acts of elected officials that the justices deem inconsistent with the Constitution.

NOTES

1. Alpheus T. Mason, "Judicial Activism: Old and New, "*Virginia Law Review* 55 (April 1969): 398.
2. Arend Lijphart, *Democracies: Patterns of Majoritarian and Consensus Government in Twenty-One Countries* (New Haven: Yale University Press, 1984).
3. Jesse H. Choper, *Judicial Review and the National Political Process* (Chicago: University of Chicago Press, 1980), p. 4.
4. Henry B. Mayo, *An Introduction to Democratic Theory* (New York: Oxford University Press, 1960), p. 70.
5. 1 Cr. 137, 177 (1803).
6. Choper, *Judicial Review and the National Political Process*, p. 6
7. Henry Steele Commager, *Majority Rule and Minority Rights* (1943; reprint, Gloucester, Mass.: Peter Smith, 1958), pp. 79–80.
8. Philip B. Kurland, *Mr. Justice Frankfurter and the Constitution* (Chicago: University of Chicago Press, 1971), p. 5.
9. *Trop v. Dulles*, 356 U.S. 86, 128 (1958) (Justice Frankfurter dissenting).
10. Bradley C. Canon, "A Framework for the Analysis of Judicial Activism," in *Supreme Court Activism and Restraint*, ed. Stephen C. Halpern and Charles M. Lamb (Lexington, Mass.: Lexington Books, 1982), pp. 386–87.
11. Gregory A. Caldeira and Donald J. McCrone, "Of Time and Judicial Activism: A Study of the U.S. Supreme Court, 1800–1973," in *Supreme Court Activism and Restraint*, ed. Halpern and Lamb, p. 110.
12. Marcia Lynn Whicker, Ruth Ann Strickland, and Raymond A. Moore, *The Constitution under Pressure: A Time for Change* (New York: Praeger, 1987), p. 79.
13. Gary Wasserman, *The Basics of American Politics* (Glenview, Ill.: Scott, Foresman/Little, Brown, 1988), pp. 26–32.
14. Henry J. Abraham, "Line-Drawing between Judicial Activism and Restraint: A Centrist Approach and Analysis" in *Supreme Court Activism and Restraint*, ed. Halpern and Lamb, p. 202.
15. Wasserman, *The Basics of American Politics*, p. 29.
16. *National League of Cities v. Usery*, 426 U.S. 833 (1976).
17. *Garcia v. San Antonio Metropolitan Transit Authority*, 469 U.S. 528, 567 (1985) (Justice Powell dissenting).
18. Kenneth Janda, Jeffrey M. Berry, and Jerry Goldman, *The Challenge of Democracy* (Boston: Houghton Mifflin, 1987), p. 84.
19. Ibid, p. 85.
20. *Youngstown Sheet and Tube Co. v. Sawyer*, 343 U.S. 579 (1952).
21. *U. S. v. Nixon*, 418 U.S. 683 (1974).
22. *Immigration and Naturalization Service v. Chadha*, 462 U.S. 919 (1983); *Bowsher v. Synar*, 106 S. Ct. 3181 (1986).
23. *Morrison v. Olson*, 108 S. Ct. 2597 (1988).

24. Alpheus T. Mason and Gordon Baker, *Free Government in the Making* (New York: Oxford University Press, 1985), p. 293.
25. For example, *Katz v. U.S.*, 389 U. S. 347 (1967); *Miranda v. Arizona*, 384 U.S. 436 (1966).
26. 347 U.S. 483.
27. 410 U.S. 113 (1973).
28. *West Virginia State Board of Education v. Barnette*, 319 U.S. 624, 640 (1943).
29. *Reynolds v. Sims*, 377 U.S. 533 (1964).
30. Charles S. Hyneman, *The Supreme Court on Trial* (New York: Atherton Press, 1963), p. 241.
31. Abraham, "Line-Drawing between Judicial Activism and Restraint," p. 210.

SUGGESTED READINGS

HALPERN, STEPHEN C., AND CHARLES M. LAMB. *Supreme Court Activism and Restraint.* Lexington, Mass.: Lexington Books, 1982. Provocative discussion of activism and restraint from a variety of perspectives in fifteen essays.

CHOPER, JESSE H. *Judicial Review and the National Political Process.* Chicago: University of Chicago Press, 1980. A carefully formulated argument that the Court should use the power of judicial review to protect individual rights, leaving problems of federalism and checks and balances to the more democratic branches of government.

MASON, ALPHEUS T. *The Supreme Court: Palladium of Freedom.* Ann Arbor: University of Michigan Press, 1963. Supreme Court decisions discussed in light of the desire of the framers of the Constitution to create a system of "free government."

IX

CIVIL RIGHTS
Is Affirmative Action Just?

It is time to recall two points made in the introduction. First, our authors are serving as advocates; they are acting as lawyers do, making the strongest case for each side that it is possible to make. Second, this book is intended to promote arguments, to cause you to think, to examine your own ideas and assumptions about what is and is not true and just.

It is quite likely that one side or the other in this set of essays is going to make you angry, perhaps produce stronger feelings than you have had about any of the earlier essays. This is because the subject under consideration, affirmative action, is in fact one of the most contentious policies of modern American society and politics.

The advocates of affirmative action, in this case represented by Professors Lenz and Stetson in "Affirmative Action: Constitutional and Just," see it as "benign discrimination" meant to help right centuries of wrongs against such groups as blacks and women. They would not pretend that in a perfect world such policies would be necessary; in such a place there would be no history of slavery nor of the subjugation of women. But we do have a history of slavery, racial segregation, and legal discrimination against women (as well as other groups). The idea of affirmative action is simply to help members of those groups achieve something of their "rightful share" of employment and educational opportunities, but to do it in such a way that no member of the majority is automatically excluded because of race or gender.

Professor Allen speaks for many when he argues passionately, in "Affirmative Action: The Ideology of Race," that affirmative action is simply reverse discrimination. He contends that the past cannot be undone, and the remedy is to proceed on the basis of equal opportunity, which always should have been our standard: to judge each person on his or her merits. To do otherwise, he suggests, is to reduce us to nothing but members of racial or gender groups and to ignore our merits, or lack of them, as individuals. Indeed, he believes that affirmative action hurts the talented members of "favored" minorities by tainting them with the brush of affirmative action: the suggestion that except for governmental preference they would not be where they are. Moreover, he believes the Supreme

Court deliberately and clearly ignored the precise intent of the Civil Rights Act of 1964 and took on itself the responsibility of making social policy that could not win majority approval. This, he argues, promotes racial-politics antagonisms that the advocates of affirmative action declare they want to remove.

The arguments made here are blunt and not couched in the careful language of politicians seeking not to offend. But these are the arguments that are in fact made by supporters and opponents of affirmative action. As with the following set of essays, the concern here is with "rights," and the concern often is in terms of rights that define what we consider to be unique about our system of government.

There is no question that affirmative action gives, and is designed to give, special opportunities to selected groups. The question is whether this is justified in terms of our democratic philosophy and history, and whether such programs undermine other values that we place on an equal or higher level.

Affirmative Action: Constitutional and Just

Timothy O. Lenz and Dorothy McBride Stetson

Florida Atlantic University

Americans fondly describe the United States as a melting pot where people from different ethnic, social, and racial backgrounds live and work together, sharing the fruits of their labor. This heartwarming image is false. Professor Allen's rhetoric about individual rights and unlimited equal opportunity ignores the fact that individuals born male into families of European descent are often privileged. It is true that the most blatantly discriminatory laws have been changed: slavery is illegal and women can enter voting booths, courts, and universities. But racism and sexism persist because of deeply rooted attitudes, established relationships, and social structures. People still find themselves restricted to low-paid jobs and deprived of the benefits of education because of their race or sex.

Political experience and social history demonstrate that it is not enough to pass laws that declare that everyone is equal. In 1868 the Fourteenth Amendment guaranteed equal protection of the laws and expanded the commitment to equality, but it left significant barriers to the participation of all as full citizens. The Fourteenth Amendment did not prevent states from enacting poll taxes and literacy tests to keep some citizens from voting. Local school boards passed regulations prohibiting married women from being teachers despite the Fourteenth Amendment. Only after decades of struggle and protest has the Fourteenth Amendment been interpreted by the courts to ban such discrimination. Thus, more than one hundred years after the Constitution was amended to require equal treatment, blacks and Hispanics remain clustered at the bottom of the economic and educational ladder. Women won the right to vote in 1920, but women are still clustered in a "pink-collar ghetto" earning only two-thirds of what men earn. These circumstances are not the result of choice, genetic inferiority, or chance; members of these groups are shortchanged due to social structures and beliefs that reinforce racism and sexism. Achieving equal opportunity requires more than legal declarations for equality and against discrimination. It requires a social commitment to abolishing racism and sexism. This is what affirmative action is all about.

Allen considers affirmative action to be a dangerous concept that undermines the republic and threatens the very foundations of Western civilization. An examination of actual affirmative action programs demonstrates why Allen's rhetoric has little to do with the way the policy works.

As a public policy concept, affirmative action originates in the labor politics of the 1930s. For decades employers had used brutal means to prevent workers from organizing labor unions. The National Labor Relations Act of 1935 outlawed these intimidating practices, but Congress realized that workers might be afraid to exercise their new rights after so many decades of hostility. So the act required employers to take *affirmative action* to inform employees that the employers'

past actions were now illegal. This recognized the need to go beyond nondiscrimination to achieve equality.

The concept of affirmative action was first applied to civil rights after World War II, when, despite government regulations prohibiting companies that received federal contracts from discriminating against blacks, most jobs went to white workers. In 1961 President John F. Kennedy issued a new executive order that required contractors to go further by taking affirmative action to improve the representation of minorities. Later, President Lyndon B. Johnson expanded the order to include women. The growing commitment to an integrated work force resulted in Title VII of the 1964 Civil Rights Act, which prohibits private employers from discriminating on the basis of race, sex, national origin, or religion. One section of the law authorizes courts to order "such affirmative action as may be appropriate" in cases where an employer has been found guilty of discrimination.

Thus, affirmative action was not imposed on the American people by an imperial judiciary or created out of thin air by social engineers or "new mandarins" as Allen asserts. It is certainly not intended to punish anyone. It is the product of widespread movements for equality that engaged hundreds of thousands of Americans in labor, civil rights, and women's rights movements. These movements reflect the desire to extend the ideals of the founding fathers to all people, not just white men of property.

Affirmative action is a policy option used by all levels of government, federal, state, and local, to overcome the effects of past discrimination. Not all affirmative action programs are mandated by government. There are also many voluntary programs in labor-management contracts and university admissions policies. An examination of these programs illustrates how affirmative action works.

Manufacturing, particularly the metals industry, has traditionally provided some of the highest paid craft jobs in the country. For years labor unions and companies refused to give blacks an opportunity to perform these jobs. Consequently, ten years after Title VII outlawed race discrimination in employment, there remained great disparities between the percentage of blacks in craft jobs and the percentage in the local labor force. At Kaiser Steel Company, where blacks were 39 percent of the local labor force but only 1.83 percent of the craft workers, civil rights groups pressured management to negotiate with the union a temporary program to recruit and train black workers. The voluntary affirmative action plan, which reserved 50 percent of its positions for minority workers, was upheld by the Supreme Court (*U.S. Steelworkers v. Weber*, 443 U.S. 193 [1979]).

The Court has also upheld voluntary programs as they apply to women. A case in point involved a county road construction agency that offered some of the highest paid jobs in Santa Clara, California. The Santa Clara Transportation Agency had no women among its 238 skilled craft employees until Diane Joyce was promoted to road dispatcher in 1980. In choosing her from among a group of comparably qualified applicants, the agency director took the county's affirmative action plan into account, along with Joyce's background, expertise, and interview test scores. On the interview, another applicant, Paul Johnson, earned a score of 75 points; Joyce scored 73. On this basis, Johnson asserted he was the better qualified candidate and sued. The Supreme Court ultimately upheld the affirmative action program, emphasizing

that the promotion criteria were subjective and the interview was biased; one of the interviewers had once referred to Joyce as a "rebel-rousing, skirt-wearing person" (*Johnson v. Transportation Agency, Santa Clara County*, 55 U.S.L.W. 4379 [1987]).

Affirmative action is especially important in educational institutions because job opportunity depends on access to training, the chance to acquire qualifications for professions and well-paying jobs. Although educators have long believed in the value of a diverse student body, some consider affirmative action incompatible with the commitment to academic excellence and individual merit. In 1970 the Medical School of the University of California at Davis developed an admission plan to increase the percentage of ethnic minorities. Allan Bakke, a white male denied admission to UC/Davis, challenged the constitutionality of the plan, asserting reverse discrimination. An unusually divided Supreme Court declared that admissions programs based solely on race are unconstitutional, but the justices allowed admissions officers to develop special programs that take race or ethnicity into consideration when admitting students (*Board of Regents v. Bakke*, 428 U.S. 265, [1978]).

Although the Supreme Court has accepted many voluntary programs in principle, affirmative action remains one of the most controversial issues in contemporary social and legal policy. It raises important and complex questions about law, philosophy, and public policy. Fundamentally, they can be expressed in fairly simple terms: Is it constitutional to consider an individual's race, gender, age, or ethnicity when making decisions regarding employment or education? To be just, must all such decisions be race and gender neutral or may group characteristics be taken into consideration? Affirmative action is constitutional, it can be just, and thus it constitutes good social policy.

The Supreme Court has established criteria for determining the constitutionality of using race or sex in employment and educational decisions. People may not be denied jobs or places in a school or university solely because of their race or sex. These characteristics may be only one factor among many relevant factors considered. All black applicants are not favored over whites. The decisions must be made in the context of coherent and temporary plans for integration. Employers are not legally authorized to promote unqualified minorities over more qualified candidates. Universities are not allowed to deny admission based on race alone. Thus, affirmative action means neither an institutionalization of mediocrity nor rigid quotas.

It is sometimes difficult to distinguish between quotas and goals because they share an underlying principle: preferential treatment of a minority. The difference is in the relative weight attached to status as a minority. With quotas, decisions are made solely on the basis of race or sex. With goals, race and sex are among many relevant characteristics taken into consideration.

Some critics of affirmative action maintain that it does not make any difference whether an individual's gender or race is the exclusive factor, the primary factor, or merely one of many factors. Such critics advocate neutrality and object to any programs or policies that evaluate individuals on the basis of group characteristics rather than individual merit. Former Assistant Attorney General William Bradford Reynolds provided a succinct and fairly typical summary of this criticism of affirmative action programs: ". . . discrimination on account of race is simply wrong. To me a quota or a goal or a timetable or any other numerical device that assigns a preference to one person and disadvantages another because of race is discrimination itself and is wrong, because it is not dealing in either case with the victims of discrimination."[1] According to this view, race or sex may be taken into consideration only to compensate an individual who has been the victim of discrimination based on race or sex. This "identifiable-victim" standard for remedial affirmative action requires proof that an individual actually suffered discrimination. It is not enough that past discrimination against a particular group occurred: for a remedy to be just, it must benefit only the person who was a victim of discrimination. Without this restriction, so the argument goes, affirmative action is little more than a form of reverse discrimination that perpetuates race- or gender-conscious decisions.

The argument that all discrimination is wrong is simplistic. In fact, one common usage of the word *discrimination* means to exercise good judgment or to recognize legitimate distinctions between individuals. This is the basis for the legal distinction between benign and invidious discrimination. Benign discrimination refers to "helpful" discrimination, such as job programs, designed to benefit a minority without penalizing or depriving the majority. Invidious discrimination refers to acts intended to harm an individual who is a member of a minority group. In the past, invidious quotas in professional schools were used as ceilings on the number of students from a targeted group. In contrast, affirmative action goals simply place a floor beneath which minority representation should not fall. These goals are a benign form of discrimination, and they do not deprive members of the majority of any opportunity that they had before the program went into effect. There was no certainty Paul Johnson would have been promoted to road dispatcher in Santa Clara, California, if the director had not promoted the female candidate. Johnson was just one of the several men who were qualified. Similarly, Allan Bakke would probably not have been admitted to the medical school before the minority plan was adopted. His "place" was not given to a minority student. Admitting minorities did not take away his place because he had no place to begin with. True, a white male with his qualifications would very likely have been admitted twenty years earlier when medical schools routinely kept out the competition from women with strict quotas. After 1972 and Title IX, when males had to compete on an equal basis with females, some found they didn't make the grade.

Affirmative action is still criticized for violating individual rights, one of the fundamental principles of the American legal and political tradition. There are inherent tensions between affirmative action programs, which promote group interests, and the rights of individuals. It is possible, nevertheless, to reconcile group rights and individual rights. Individualism is not the sole principle sustaining the U.S. Constitution. The polity and its laws are based on a balance between public good and private choice, and between social justice and personal freedom. The political system is not as antagonistic toward groups as is commonly assumed. Allen is mistaken when he makes group-based politics seem alien to American culture. In fact, modern theories of American democracy recognize that groups play a vital role in representing the interests of individuals. Affirmative action is not contrary to the theory or practice of American politics.

There is also reason to be skeptical of the argument that affirmative action rewards mediocrity not merit, violates principles of equality, and interferes with the marketplace allocation of values. The white male's newfound faith in equality, excellence, and marketplace efficiency, and his criticism of affirmative action as a departure from these standards of individual merit belie the fact that affirmative action did not introduce "discrimination" on the basis of group characteristics any more than court-ordered school busing introduced the policy of transporting students to school based on considerations of race. In the good old days when the good old boys took care of their own, political patronage was a time-honored prerogative that ignored merit in favor of connections and loyalty. Blacks and whites were required to take buses to maintain segregated schools. There was never a "golden age" of individual rights that is now threatened by affirmative action. The opposite is true: affirmative action will help undermine long-standing racist and sexist biases.

The assertion that affirmative action interferes with marketplace efficiency in rewarding individual merit is based on the assumption that the market is naturally just. But in fact, markets are social institutions wherein decisions reflect values and preferences. They are not objective or neutral or natural. Seemingly objective job and education qualifications mask biases. Evidence shows that quantitative measures, such as I.Q. and aptitude tests, are frequently biased against racial and ethnic minorities. Even a seemingly simple measure like "years of job experience" is deceptive. "Years of experience" rarely includes highly skilled work in volunteer organizations and thus may undervalue women's qualifications. Further, ranking applicants always involves some subjective judgment, and the more responsible the position, the more likely subjective evaluations will be important.

The language of the Constitution does not prohibit race- or gender-based classifications. The Fourteenth Amendment prohibits a state from denying to any person within its jurisdiction the equal protection of the laws, but equality does not mean treating everyone the same. Governments make valid classifications among people, even based on accidents of birth. For example, the very young are different from the very old, and laws can treat them differently. The Court's problem is to determine which classifications are acceptable and which are arbitrary. When the Supreme Court reviews affirmative action programs in order to determine whether they are constitutional, it decides whether the positive discrimination is reasonably related to an important government objective. Despite some divided opinions, the courts are clear on one point: affirmative action is constitutional.

The Supreme Court's efforts to reconcile laws that classify people with the Fourteenth Amendment's mandate to treat them equally have produced some rather complicated schemes involving suspect criteria, fundamental rights, and levels of judicial scrutiny. These concepts are based on the commonsense recognition that some rights are more important than others. Some legal classifications are suspect and others are not. The courts will closely scrutinize laws that affect fundamental rights based on suspect classifications, such as race. They will be less vigilant about reasonable classifications, such as age. In each case the test is whether the law treating people differently because of race, gender, or age serves a valid, important governmental interest. This is consistent with the dictionary definition of *discrimination* as the exercise of good judgment in recognizing valid differences. Equality is an important component of justice, but neither the Constitution nor common sense requires that everyone be treated the same.

In deciding if affirmative action is just as a form of social policy it is important to recognize the purpose of the policy, study the complexities of the problem it is to address, and weigh it against available alternatives. The debates on this subject sometimes confuse integration and equality with complete rejection of all differences. It has become a cliché to criticize affirmative action by appealing to the ideal of a color-blind society. It is ironic that this ideal, once the rallying cry of the civil rights movement, has been adopted by the opposition. Allen goes so far as to label some struggles against discrimination and for improvement of women's status and minority opportunity as racist and neotribalist, provoking fear among white males that a quest for equality is really a drive for superiority and revenge. (Men get so emotional at times!)

Color blindness has become a slogan because "colorvision" is troubling. Americans have a difficult history of race consciousness, so, in order to be nondiscriminatory, we think we have to treat skin color like eye color and say it is irrelevant. But race and gender are characteristics that cannot be ignored; they are essential aspects of a person's identity and relationships with others. Race and gender consciousness are facts of American life. They are neither created nor increased by affirmative action. In fact, affirmative action forces the often painful recognition of underlying bias, and encourages social reconciliation.

Affirmative action is difficult precisely because it makes us think about how people should be treated by the government, educational institutions, and private employers. The real question for social policy is not whether affirmative action is just in principle, but whether it is just in practice. A major concern is the identification of the individuals for preferential treatment. A just program targets a truly "discrete and insular" minority. This phrase includes criteria for identifying a minority for the purposes of affirmative action and preferential treatment. The word *discrete* refers to identifiable, distinctive, and immutable characteristics, such as race and gender. It excludes mutable attributes, such as political party affiliation or economic status. The word *insular* describes the group's status as separate—apart from society's established power centers—with a history of disadvantage. Thus, insularity is not a permanent condition because an outgroup can be integrated and gain power.

Try to apply the "discrete and insular" test to these difficult cases:

1. Are Louisiana Cajuns a minority that qualifies for the benefits of federal civil rights legislation?
2. Do Asian Americans deserve special consideration?
3. Are there circumstances under which white males should be eligible for preferential treatment?

Some of the misunderstanding of affirmative action is rooted in our concept of equality. Guaranteeing equal protection of the laws does not require treating everyone the same. Such a view reflects a fundamental misunderstanding of the meaning of equal treatment. Differences among people can be taken into account. Age, for instance, is a voting qualification. Citizenship may be a requirement for public employment. Statutes that give preference to veterans (who tend to be overwhelmingly male due to sex quotas in the armed forces) for federal and state civil service jobs have strong public support. It is thus conceivable that race and gender differences may be relevant for some areas of public policy. The fact that there are few circumstances under which race and gender are relevant does not mean they are never appropriate. The real problem in formulating just public policy is to determine which discrimination is appropriate—that is, treating people differently because of characteristics appropriate to the goal of policy—and which is discrimination based on inappropriate factors.

A particularly important yet difficult concern in evaluating a policy is whether it treats individuals as they deserve. Veterans get preference because of their service to the nation even though others are denied jobs as a result. Public resentment of affirmative action, the perception that it is unfair, is partly due to the feeling that some individuals are being asked to sacrifice for social justice and others are the beneficiaries of preferential treatment. Is it fair to hire a black woman instead of an equally qualified white male, under an affirmative action program, even though neither personally benefited from or was victimized by past discrimination? Is it just that upper-middle-class Hispanic men go to Harvard when bright working-class Anglo males are rejected? These difficult questions make it all the more important that affirmative action plans ensure that race and gender are never the sole basis for allocating opportunities.

In weighing the merits of affirmative

action policy, it is important to consider alternative means to achieve goals of equality of opportunity and social integration. One alternative might be to limit preferential treatment to situations where an individual has proven that he or she was the victim of intentional discrimination. Achieving social integration case by case would be as burdensome as achieving school integration one student at a time. It would require each person to file and win a lawsuit, and the remedy would apply only to the two parties in the case. Furthermore, proving intentional discrimination means producing evidence about the state of mind of the employer or admissions director or promotion and tenure committee when a decision was made. It is almost impossible to meet this burden of proof. Some Supreme Court justices have even recommended abandoning trying to make a distinction between intentions and effects because it is so difficult to determine why someone acted. They argue that affirmative action is justified whenever there is evidence of results of discrimination, for instance, where admissions policies create a law school student body that is all white or 90 percent male.

Affirmative action can be a useful means to achieve desirable social ends. It is not an end in itself, so it must be evaluated in terms of its effectiveness at reaching integration. Existing programs must be sufficiently flexible to adapt as circumstances warrant. Policies must be crafted to avoid invidious discrimination against individuals. But public officials should not be deprived of this useful instrument to promote an important governmental objective: greater equality in the marketplace and in academic institutions.

This objective might be furthered by changing the emphasis of affirmative action from race- and gender-conscious programs to another, more familiar kind of affirmative action: programs designed to benefit those who are economically disadvantaged. Governments have traditionally assisted the poor. Programs such as Head Start use public funds to provide special care and education to very young children, but only from poor families. The idea is to give these disadvantaged youngsters help in developing necessary orientations and skills so they can compete equally with more advantaged children when they all start out in first grade. Such programs to help children have widespread support. But Americans have been reluctant to sponsor a vigorous effort to bring poor adults out of poverty. If economic status replaced race or gender as the primary basis for affirmative action, realistic governmental efforts to achieve greater equality would have to be even more activist, more "affirmative." Not only are antipoverty programs politically difficult but they won't work to achieve integration.

Although there is a correlation between race and income, and the feminization of poverty is increasing in the United States, focusing only on the economically disadvantaged will not remove race and sex barriers or achieve equality of opportunity. Special treatment for blacks and women is warranted apart from economic status because they face prejudice that poor, white males do not. The history of race discrimination compounds the problems of economic disadvantage and justifies race-conscious programs. Effects of the separation of women into traditionally dependent roles linger regardless of their family income.

This argument that race-, ethnic-, and gender-conscious social policy serves general values of equality of opportunity may be further supported by looking at the specific values it achieves in certain professions. The case of medicine is illustrative. Getting into medical school has become extremely competitive as the prestige and income of doctors rise. Medical schools have raised the entrance requirements, both GPA and MEDCAT scores, narrowing the pool of applicants and reducing the likelihood the pool will include blacks and Hispanics. This has aggravated the ability of the medical profession to provide necessary service to lower income areas where ethnic and racial minorities cluster. Because there may be an association between ethnic heritage and willingness to work with a people, affirmative action programs to bring minorities to the profession of medicine are likely to have direct effects on improving health care.

Affirmative action programs in academic institutions illustrate why it is a mistake to assume that equal opportunity is achieved when discrimination ends. The lingering effects of discrimination make the familiar footrace analogy inappropriate. According to this analogy, the pursuit of success is like a footrace, with participants competing to go as far as they can. The American commitment to equality extends only to making sure that everyone has an equal start. From that point on, they must rely on their own abilities. Americans are comfortable with the footrace analogy because it embodies the image of competitive individualism. Consequently, affirmative action is sometimes criticized for giving unfair advantage—literally a head start—to minorities. But it is unrealistic to give individuals positions at the starting line and then expect them to compete on equal footing if they are burdened and unprepared. An equal opportunity to compete requires a sustained commitment to training. In academic institutions, it requires assistance in overcoming the hardships that continue to limit performance. Affirmative action is not an

attempt to handicap competition so that everyone crosses the finish line at the same time, thereby undermining excellence. It simply targets some competitors for assistance in developing their abilities.

Modern governments have developed a wide array of programs that are designed to assist individuals and groups. Allen suggests that it is inappropriate to use law for social purposes. This is absurd. Government exists to create social policies; this profoundly conservative idea is consistent with the intentions of the framers of the Constitution. They also intended the courts to protect minority rights guaranteed in the Constitution, which is a *minoritarian* document. Allen's real target is not excessive government regulation but the greater commitment to equality that has spread throughout government and society since the beginning of the modern civil rights movement.

There are good reasons to be concerned that the expansion of governmental power into areas previously considered private might restrict freedom. But government regulations can also increase the range of choice of many by limiting a few. Civil rights legislation has restricted employment practices in both the public and private sectors. Job discrimination is now illegal. By these laws, the government can guarantee individual rights that have been threatened by unfettered discrimination. The first stages in the effort to achieve greater equality focused on political and legal equality in areas such as the right to vote. Current efforts focus on even more difficult problems, including the social and economic barriers to opportunity. Affirmative action is now an established part of employment practices and admissions standards. It is accepted and it is effective.

The problem of reconciling our commitment to equality with our commitment to individual liberty is one of the perennial issues in American politics. It is not an engineering problem, such as putting a man on the moon, where the policy ends once the goal has been reached. It is a complex interaction of values, social practice, and government action. Affirmative action involves continuing pursuit of greater equality in both the public and the private sectors. Carefully developed affirmative action programs are an integral part of a society that values individual and social justice.

NOTE

1. *Affirmative Action and the Constitution* (Washington, D.C.: American Enterprise Institute, 1987), p. 17.

SUGGESTED READINGS

COHEN, MARSHALL, THOMAS HAGEL, AND THOMAS SCANLON, EDS. *Equality and Preferential Treatment.* Princeton: Princeton University Press, 1977. This collection of philosophical writings examines the meaning of equality. It includes an explanation of how public policies that treat people differently can be justified.

HEINS, MARJORIE. *Cutting the Mustard: Affirmative Action and the Nature of Excellence.* Boston: Faber & Faber, 1987. This book provides a thorough, detailed response to the argument that affirmative action undermines the American commitment to excellence.

STRAUSS, DAVID A. "The Myth of Colorblindness." In *The Supreme Court Review, 1986,* edited by Philip Kurland, Gerhard Casper, and Dennis J. Hutchinson, pp. 99–134. Chicago: University of Chicago Press, 1987. Strauss provides an insightful analysis of a very familiar legal doctrine. He shows how the colorblindness standard has been oversimplified by critics of affirmative action.

Affirmative Action: The Ideology of Race

Wayne Allen
Louisiana State University

False assumptions make for bad public policy, especially in a republic. In the United States the principles of republican government form the essential and final objectives of policy formation. Indeed, these principles were the method for the declassification of groups for their final incremental incorporation into American life, but as individuals. Everything from the Missouri Compromise and the Emancipation Proclamation, to the Thirteenth and Fourteenth amendments, up to the *Brown* decision, is a tribute to these principles. It was also these principles that served as the moral assumptions of the early civil rights movement.

These moral assumptions of the early civil rights movement have been turned upside down today. Current "civil rights" thinking and its supporting policy of affirmative action (AA) are a dangerous outgrowth of perverse assumptions that are hostile to republican government. In fact, these new assumptions are not the answer to current race problems; they are the source of the problems. They degrade the principle of American law into a guardian of ethnic and racial privilege. The principle of individual right, which incorporates the person into citizenship and thereby guarantees him membership in the community, has been perverted into privileges for classes of people: blacks, browns, women, and homosexuals.

Because of the increasingly violent assertion of these new privileges and the concomitant effort to overturn American republicanism, we are now expected to reconcile propositions that are logically contradictory. As with George Orwell's "doublethink," we are supposed to believe simultaneously in the commitment to hire based on race and equal opportunity to be hired without regard to race. As we will see, this logical absurdity, present in race-specific programs, quotas, and ethnic, racial, and gender representation, is formed from dangerous assumptions about genetic and collective responsibility. These assumptions oppose 2,500 years of Western philosophical and legal development.

The new mandarins of race consciousness, masking their economic and political motives under the veil of "civil rights," have succeeded only in undermining Western legal values by introducing the volatile forces of neotribal warfare. We will see how this new tribalism corrupts community and humanity through the disintegrative forces of group combat.

THE WORKINGS OF MINORITARIANISM

The rise of race consciousness in the United States, or the belief that race must be made the basis of policy, began in the 1960s, not the 1950s, when the civil rights movement began. It took the romantic form of an attack on the "establishment." The establishment was a vague symbol for white Anglo–Saxon Protestants (WASPs) and what they represented. American community in the 1960s was a composite of racial and religious groups largely influenced by WASP aspirations, ethics, and power. The establishment was emblematic not only of WASP virtues but also of the capitalist economy, which reflects and is nourished by these virtues. The virtues include hard work, self-discipline, self-reliance, duty, devotion to family, reverence for God, and respect for law that promotes the delicate relationship between the individual and community. But the spokesmen for cultural and moral relativism, with their passion to overturn the establishment, sought not to add to this mosaic of American cultural life but to supplant it.

The American New Left recognized the futility of trying to break up the WASP economic and moral order by exploiting class antagonisms, so it turned to the amazingly old idea of using race as an instrument for uprooting the "system" by shaping the masses of minorities into a new order. Henceforth, race would be the dominant feature in politics, and the single distinguishing factor in reallocating social benefits. Today this is called social justice.

The new mandarins of education, themselves raised in the moral void of cultural relativism, thus began to do exactly what our founding fathers warned against: cultivate factions not for the sake of dispersing power but for the sake of seizing it. The American "melting pot" soon became a cauldron of toiling trouble precisely because race was introduced as an instrument to acquire political power.

The Timothy Lenz–Dorothy Stetson rejection of the melting pot image is done in ignorance of history, statistics, and the art of cooking. The first black U.S. senator was elected after the Civil War, not in the 1960s. Mexicans fought with Texans in the battle for the Alamo (1836). American Indians have been honored in our history from Hiawatha, to Pontiac, to

Pocatello. Second, their rejection ignores the historical and social reality that each group seeking shelter in the United States has subordinated itself in order to be "melted" into the pot. Every good cook knows that if an added spice maintains its complete integrity (taste) the cook has overspiced. A cook does not add salt to a stew in order to taste salt. To separate the components or ingredients of this "pot" is to factionalize American community for the sake of group integrity. Thus, affirmative action does not reveal the failure of the "melting pot" image, it destroys it entirely.

Of course, this destruction is having the expected results. With no common bond between groups, solidarity has given way to interracial combat. Without a vision of the public good, because everyone is now defined in terms of race, various groups have begun to compete for the always scarce resources of society. This is particularly evident in the black–brown tensions in Miami, New York, and Los Angeles. And there is the ongoing blacks–Jews struggle in Chicago, as well as the incessant gender struggles in universities.

Rather than seek sources of commonality, the very essence of political association, for political reasons the minoritarians began to deform the very meaning of civil rights. Civil rights is no longer a movement; it is an ideology. This is painfully evident in the shift of civil rights objectives.

The Emancipation Proclamation of 1863 and the Thirteenth Amendment of 1865 liberated blacks from bondage by severing the relationship between owner and owned. But the act of liberation and the foundation of freedom are different activities, often leading to vastly different results. Liberation is a concrete, tangible act of separation from the past, but it leaves the future open to doubt.

There is an abyss between the "no more" and the "not yet." Individuals are without association. Just as the Declaration of Independence signaled our break with England, the formation of a republic was by no means a natural result of that separation. Equally, once they were liberated, the foundation of freedom for the former slaves was in doubt. The process of association, an agreement between the freed and the free, would take time to form.

Political freedom, as history continues to show, is never the automatic consequence of liberation. Freedom is a political act that requires the founding and guarantee of certain rights for which the liberation was sought. Thus the Fourteenth Amendment (1868) could not by itself secure politically what could be undone socially. "Jim Crow" laws and other forms of social discrimination effectively undermined the political gains asserted by constitutional law. As one would expect, law cannot do what only the community can: integrate individuals.

But slowly the National Association for the Advancement of Colored People (NAACP) took legal action to challenge segregationist social practices. Lawsuits formed the front line of political offense for the protection of individual rights formerly denied through social custom. In most cases, it was the Fourteenth Amendment that was the vehicle for this political transformation.

However, by the late 1960s there was a shift from an emphasis on legal right to social ends: ends that have precious little to do with political rights or integration. The Supreme Court began to abandon law in favor of "social needs," and the justices assumed the role of psychologists, rendering decisions based on group income and psychological wants. Their concern was not merely to avoid separation of the races but to take positive, affirmative action to "promote" racial mingling. Presumably, the law could command people to like one another.

The now-famous *Brown* case (1954) demanded integration of public facilities. It overturned the 1896 case of *Plessy v. Ferguson*, and with it the doctrine of "separate but equal."[1] The *Plessy* case was overturned under the principle of a "color-blind" Constitution. Thus, color consciousness in law or policy was declared a thing of the past. But the minoritarians soon made race, then ethnicity, then "sexual preference" the very basis for constitutional protection. The emergence of the "color-blind" principle was actually in the best tradition of American republicanism: to recognize not only the distinctness of individuals but their uniformity under law. The law unites *only* when it does not discriminate. The Constitution loses its binding nature, its authority, the minute it is pressed into the service of a group. First this group, then that one; principle finally yields to the passions of the masses. Thus, *Brown* did not stand outside law but reaffirmed these principles in the face of social bias. But now we are told that what was wrong under *Plessy* is right today. Principles thus give way to vengeance.

Although the 1964 Civil Rights Act followed *Brown* by ten years, it went further than the Constitution permits by treating race relations through clumsy government policy rather than by neutralizing them through law. Behind the act lay some never-mentioned indebtedness that whites incurred for the economic backwardness of blacks. Hence, the worst of its supporting provisions, affirmative action—despite the bad history provided by Lenz and Stetson—was a politicized policy established by Lyndon Johnson through Executive Order 11,246 in 1965. This is when "goals and timetables" and "representation" of race were made a matter of policy. This is also the point at which race was firmly incorporated into American politics.

The original argument for affirmative action was theoretical and, at first blush, did not generate great hostility: in any activity of hiring, admission, or award, "all things being equal," the advantage should go to a minority. Of course, rarely, if ever, are "all things equal" in the world of human affairs. The intention was to offset any prior advantage of whites. By itself, this policy probably would not have generated open and widespread anger.

But soon the ideologists of race, who were seeking to acquire power rather than share it, degraded even this modestly harmful policy into the vulgar demand for quotas. Ethnic, racial, gender, and homosexual representation became the most important criteria for hiring and admission policies around the country. Defying the assertion of Lenz and Stetson that it is a "simple public policy," the Democratic party in 1984 went so far as to set aside a seat on its platform committee for a homosexual. Simple, indeed! Universities and businesses have been put into a position of having to justify why they do not hire a minority person. Turning an old legal axiom upside down, an employer is guilty of discrimination until proven innocent.

Being the special places of employment that they are, universities have gotten partially around this problem through a form of intellectual featherbedding. By creating departments or programs (moves that deplete financial resources) that specialize in such parochial concerns as black or women's studies, the general level of incompetence resulting from quotas is minimized. Universities can hire minorities that study themselves. But with increasing budget constraints, many academic departments are forced to hire someone who specializes in minority studies but who teaches out of a major department. Thus, a history department will be forced to use its budget to hire someone for black studies when it really needs a historian. Of course, the inability of these programs to justify themselves intellectually or in terms of enrollment is obvious in the demand by minoritarians that "minority studies" be made a general education requirement. Because the number of white males who teach such limited subjects is small, this effectively allows a university to meet its quota without appearing to have been legally coerced.

Yet, coercion is still a major instrument in minoritarian politics. Responding to the many "racial incidents" on campuses around the country, mostly carried out by minority students, universities are plainly abolishing any distinction between affirmative action and quotas. Some schools are going so far as to hold department heads accountable for not pursuing AA vigorously enough. The president of Ohio State University said in 1987 that he "is prepared to levy sanctions against units of the institution that fail to meet their goals in recruiting minority students and hiring women and minorities." Of course, this only encourages "racial incidents" by minorities—the politics of extortion. Lenz and Stetson seem to justify such programs under the general heading of patronage. Doing so, they confuse legal arguments with social practices. They point out that in the "good ol' days" the "good ol' boys" helped one another. But this was not under cover of law. It was a social practice that aided one's *friends* based on loyalty or debt, not race. In its place we have the "ol' girl" network under the affirmative action title of "Women's Studies." Only today it is mandated by law.

Now the system of rewards for one's kind is reduced to race or gender. In the past whiteness never assured anyone a seat in a medical school, or a job; one had to meet certain minimal standards. Friendship or debt may have helped an individual in particular situations, but patronage never extended to anyone based on anatomical plumbing. Universities are faced with particularly troublesome incidents with the new legal patronage.

The problem arises (quite often these days) during promotional hearings when the affected minority has failed to meet the research standard set for white males. Racism or sexism is heard behind the halls of ivy. Most often the department caves in to such charges, fearing a court hassle under the general heading of "discrimination." Apparently "equality" doesn't mean playing by the same rules. But the minoritarians have scrambled around this problem by creating journals that specialize in black, Chicano, or women's studies. These journals offer a "research" outlet to the minorities who cannot get their work accepted in mainstream academic journals. Of course, the atmosphere of intimidation is so thick no one would dare suggest these narrow journals are inadequate for promotional consideration. *Ms.* magazine is now defined as "scholarly" by some departments.

By the mid-1970s affirmative action was recognized as a failure even by many of its proponents. It was too obviously an insult to genuine equality; social causes must be found for minority failure. In order to shift social policy (and money) toward the "subordinate culture," minoritarians next seized on the idea of incorporating it into the best of American principles: equality. To save the new theory of racial preference, it was coupled to the more palatable notion of equal opportunity. Together they form one of the more absurd self-contradictory policies in American politics. We began to see job announcements, "scholarship" offers, and the like concluding with the acronym AA/EO.

In essence, equal opportunity "asserts that each man should have equal rights and opportunities to develop his own talents and virtues and that there should be equal rewards for equal performance." This definition is offered by John Schaar, a well-known American liberal scholar, who also points out that "no policy is better designed to fortify the dominant institutions, values, and ends of the American social order . . . for it offers *everyone* a fair and equal chance to find a place within that order."[2]

This is the original definition of *equal opportunity*, and it is probably acceptable to most Americans. It represents the traditional value of individualism, a principal tenet behind the U.S. legal and moral order. It is basic to the Puritan ethic because *each* man is to be judged by *his* works. But it is precisely this principle that is under attack. In fact, the 1967 article by Schaar in which this definition appears was the first liberal attack on the doctrine of equal, individual, opportunity as it was originally understood.

Schaar merely used this customary definition of *equal opportunity* as a point of departure for a wholesale assault on individualism and the American belief in personal achievement. In its place we are offered quotas and set-asides for categories of people whose "equality" is measured by group results. According to the new formula, equality is measured not by achievement but by income tax returns. These returns must reflect the success of various groups based on skin or sexual type: blacks, browns, homosexuals. The new "equality" is in fact a leveling mechanism determined by outcomes, results.

It thus robs the individual of his worth (his dignity) because his achievements are calculated into the average of the group he represents.

Here Lenz and Stetson suggest a distinction between goals and quotas typical of the new ideologists. But it is a distinction without a difference because it confuses (which is their intention) ends with means. Any "marketplace," whether business or educational, is a place of scarce resources and reduces *all* sought-for advantages to a sum-zero relation. The job or scholarship a black gets because he is black is the advantage a white does not get because of his whiteness. Further, if the goal of affirmative action is integration into the marketplace (as opposed to a harmony between the races) based on "proportional representation" of minorities in society, then this *necessarily* transforms goals into quotas at the beginning of the process.

Because blacks constitute 12 percent of the population, and because the goal is economic parity with whites, then clearly this means assuring at least 12 percent of the blacks "success" by admitting them to college, guaranteeing them passable grades, and granting them a job ahead of whites when they emerge from the college experience. This means special, privileged treatment in college because education is seen (sadly enough) as the beginning of the economic marketplace. Besides the logical gymnastics employed by Lenz and Stetson to promote confusion between goals and quotas, they ignore the painful truth that human beings often resist the goals we set for them. Who is to blame for the underrepresentation of blacks in physics? This explains the mounting pressure on faculty to pass minorities in college courses they otherwise would fail—the outcome is more important than the opportunity.

When one attaches this new formulation of results to affirmative action programs that have goals or timetables, both a fair beginning (based on individual worth) and a fair ending (determined by effort or talent) are perverted. The open market (freedom to compete), ambition, hard work, dedication, and, of course, excellence are brushed aside for the sake of equal distribution of resources based on group affiliation. Thus, "equal" access to success is restricted in favor of race or sex classification. What started as equal opportunity for the individual—the best of American tradition—is now transformed into a guarantee of results for the group.

The present effort to guarantee outcomes for groups is well documented and carefully rebutted by Thomas Sowell as he describes the degeneration of the early civil rights movement. Instead of treating rights as something bestowed, Sowell reminds us that civil rights were something earned, from the Magna Carta (1215) to the American Revolution. With a mine of data, Sowell points out that using statistical results for a determination of discrimination not only is deceitful but is a perversion of the early civil rights vision. In *Civil Rights: Rhetoric or Reality?* Sowell tells us that American Chinese make 10 percent more money on the average than do whites.[3] Who is the minority here? This is certainly no way for a black Ph.D. in economics to get the attention of the media. But the counterfactual evidence Sowell presents to rebut minoritarian ideology puts him at odds with the media-made darlings of the new movement.

Sowell is at his best while explaining the degeneration of the early movement into the new ideology. This ideology, he points out, followed "logically from the civil rights vision" only because the early vision was clouded with distortions of civil rights history.[4] Formerly, a civil right meant a claim of freedom the *individual* has *against* government; a civil liberty was a claim of freedom the *individual* had against other individuals. In other words, rights designate freedom from government; liberties designate freedoms within government. Prior to the 1960s this *was* the essence of liberal constitutionalism. However, the general policy of AA/EO, and the hidden assumptions on which it is based, changed the very meaning of legal status and the politically important principle of citizenship. As an ideological weapon, rather than a principle of law, the idea of right now attaches to classes of people defined in terms of race or gender.

The growing problem of interracial tension that arises from this ideology derives from the new belief that right attaches to groups. Race or gender has become the very basis of social and legal identity. This contradicts the early civil rights vision. Indeed, the oft-quoted portion of M. L. King, Jr.'s "I have a dream" speech expresses the hope that everyone will be judged *not* by color of skin but by content of character. His dream now becomes an ideological nightmare. Compare this with a recent statement of Jesse Jackson's: "The most important thing about black people is that they are black." Of course, the new ideology of right reaches dangerous proportions when made the basis of public policy.

Recently, the city of Corpus Christi, Texas, began a new (elitist) program to reflect its growing concern with educational excellence. In order to assure "equal opportunity" in access to the program, one standard on the admission test (92) is required of whites (male and female), while another standard (75) is required for blacks and Hispanics. Thus, administrators see "equality" between 92 and 75. This is also equality to Lenz and

Stetson. Yet, this is a program for the better students, even though it reduces excellence to the lowest common denominator: 75. Of course, no one dares ask what happens to the white who scores 91. Public education has always been confronted by intellectual "averages" as the basis for teaching, but now it is masked as "excellence."

The new right's ideology also does away with the Western legal and moral principle of responsibility. Because "right" now attaches to race or gender, failure by an individual can be affixed to the group he represents. But group condemnation is forbidden. This prompts the search for the real villain. The failed individual or his apologists soon locate the source for this failure in some vagary termed the "system," or "establishment," or worse, the white-male-dominated culture. The lack of statistical equality between the races (which Sowell easily accounts for) is seen to prove "racism" and relieve the individual of a failure that in fact is his own. Thus, there is an ideologically built-in excuse for the failure of any minority member.

Of course, the real danger in this is that the failed individual is now seen to encompass his group. The black who fails represents black failure. Accordingly, employers are *very* apprehensive about terminating a black employee. The likely charge of "racism" thus assures a certain amount of tolerated incompetence and negligence by any large employer.

All of this is the result of the fact that the individual is now seen as a member of a group. Yet, the whole historical development of right through the growing influence of constitutionalism *was* focused on the effort to declassify persons for the purpose of legislation and protection.

This is exactly why Lenz and Stetson abandon their own moral theory of "just deserts" by rationalizing AA in terms of results. Just deserts requires an equivalent moral consequence for one's own actions, a reward or punishment appropriate to individual conduct. But results theory degrades individual achievement into a group average. This is like the logic of the relativist. Such a theory makes no distinction between a Mafia hit man and a dentist because they both make the same amount of money, the result. Therefore, it is not what one does or how one gets there that matters; it is what one is, defined by one's group.

Because most Americans are acutely aware of race problems, without being racists, they deliberately avert implications of "racism," and consider it an insult. But in their desire to avoid this slur they set aside principles to avoid verbal intimidation. Academic standards are lowered for minorities, special "scholarships" are established, extra funding is offered to black fraternities, black studies is offered more money than its enrollment justifies, and so on. Yet, when Jesse Jackson refers to New York as "Hymie Town," or Louis Farrakhan (a black Muslim) calls Judaism a "gutter religion," or the black fanatic Steve Cokely accuses Jews of inoculating black children with AIDS, they do not even warrant the charge of insensitivity.

Reminiscent of Big Brother's "hate week," anything short of support for affirmative action now prompts the charge of "insensitivity," a crime as used by minoritarians that implies unconscious or repressed racist feelings that are visible only to the anointed. Even lukewarm support for any or all minority grievances means insensitivity or a lack of compassion.

Especially on college campuses, each

of the increasing demands by minorities (now including homosexuals) serves a segregationist end that is their purpose. They are usually couched in the language of "cultural diversity," "multicultural education," or liberation from the "hegemonic culture." Such isolationist and self-serving platitudes, when unmasked for what they are, reveal the fact that difference invites comparison. Thus, "multicultural education" is a forum for white-male bashing, dramatized in Marxist rhetoric as a struggle between oppressor and oppressed. Under the early civil rights movement "separate but equal" was outlawed. Today it is demanded. The only possible outcome this can have is a polarization of academic life. Formerly a unifying experience where enlightenment leads to liberation of the soul, education has been degraded into the politics of race. Where blacks once grieved over exclusion from a liberal education, today they demand it.

TORTUOUS REASONING, TORTURED RESULTS

Of course, the radicalized civil rights movement would have been blunted by the democratic process had it not been for the Supreme Court, which, under the cover of "minority rights," was able to give legal protection to the new ideology. In his 1985 address to the American Bar Association, Justice William Brennan reveals disdain, even contempt, for the majority. He speaks of the need to use "coercive force . . . to countermand the will of a contemporary majority." He further attacks the "majority process" and seeks "to rectify claims of minority rights."[5] Instead of seeing democracy as a process that works only if there is a majority, Brennan attaches some virtue to being a minority. He thus turns democracy upside down, making it an oligarchy from the bottom up.

According to Brennan, being in the majority automatically puts one in the wrong. In his new formula, the idea of right attaches to those certified by him as a minority through the very policies his legal decisions have shaped. Instead of the inglorious, awkward process of counting noses (as required in democracies) to determine public intentions, Brennan prefers to substitute his perceptions for those of a majority in the democratic process. It is this very arrogance of the Court that prompted Thomas Jefferson to warn against making judges "the ultimate arbiters of all Constitutional questions." It is, he said, "a very dangerous doctrine indeed."

The initial civil rights movement started with good and honorable intentions, and was thus able to attract a broad spectrum of support. But it soon degenerated into an ideological movement latent with insidious notions of genetic guilt and collective responsibility, the bane of Western civilization. The decomposition of traditional philosophical principles unmasks the hidden economic and political motives behind recent Supreme Court decisions intended to subjugate and punish white male Americans. This is painfully obvious in the person and opinions of Thurgood Marshall, a longtime justice and black activist during the early rights movement.

A crude revenge and thinly veiled race hatred are the dual motors driving the legal decisions of Marshall. This is evident in his opinion in the now famous *Regents v. Bakke* case, in which sixteen places in the Medical School at the University of California, Davis, were set aside for entering minority students.[6] Marshall agreed with the majority of the

Court precisely because "it permits a university to consider race of an applicant in making admission decisions."

The very racial policies once condemned by blacks Marshall now reverses, and goes one step further. In *Plessy v. Ferguson* (1896) the Court allowed only for segregation of the races based on the doctrine "separate but equal." Yet separation, while requiring a distinction for the purpose of separation, is not exclusion. A quota system designating persons to be included based on race is exclusionary by definition. It denies categorically, and by law, that any white male could fill one of the protected seats. It goes further than *Plessy* by replacing separation with exclusion. Bakke could not go to a separate facility.

Lenz and Stetson are correct to say Bakke never had a seat in the medical school. But they clearly misunderstand equal opportunity. Bakke had a better record (grades and test scores) than *all* the students admitted under affirmative action. He was *denied access* to compete for those sixteen seats; his abilities and record were dismissed for reasons of race. This is no more than prior discrimination, that is, racism. Additionally, their distinction between "benign and insidious" discrimination is a valid one. Indeed, if it is so valid why doesn't it apply to whites? "Insidious" is a moral term. Why should only certain groups be protected against it based on race? The fact that moral language now applies only to certain designated groups reveals the ideological nature of the current race movement.

Of course, the pressure to fill quotas can hardly be comforting to some unsuspecting patient whose surgeon was admitted to medical school to satisfy a new social policy. This makes the Lenz and Stetson argument dangerous on another count. A recent study on professional training "reveals that of *blacks admitted* to medical school, the average score on the Medical College Admission Test (MCAT) is *well below the average* of *whites* who are *rejected*."[7] And Lenz and Stetson say there is still merit in affirmative action. Then again, a physician can always bury his mistakes.

At this point Justice Marshall turns the old axiom "Two wrongs don't make a right" upside down. He uses history punitively, to rationalize the very practice he had earlier condemned. "Now when a state acts to remedy the effects of that legacy of discrimination," he says in *Bakke*, "I cannot believe this same Constitution stands as a barrier." His reasoning here is not only badly flawed but reveals a vengeance unequaled in American jurisprudence.

One of the painful truths about history is that it is irremedial, incorrectable. It is impossible to remedy or correct the acts, events, or crimes that form the fabric of human history. That which *was*, will *never* be again. It thus defies remedy. But vengeance, at least in its most noble form, seeks redress against an aggressor, the perpetrator of a wrong. It does not do what cannot be done: seek to make right that which has passed. Instead, vengeance can only establish a consequence of equivalent moral worth for a particular act. This is the underlying premise of retribution.

A perpetrator is an initiator, one who *causes* that which otherwise would not be done. Vengeance then seeks a harmony, a balance, between the act committed and its consequence. This has been the principle behind Western criminal justice for centuries. But Marshall's "remedy" is punitive without a perpetrator. It is directed against those who are innocent. He thus transforms guilt into a function of race relations and thereby removes it from the pale of human conduct.

Marshall's "class based remedy," as he puts it, for past wrongs reveals one of the oldest rejected theories of Western legal thought: genetic guilt. It is guilt by association, only with a more dangerous twist. According to this "class based remedy," current and future generations of whites are to be the instrument of "remedy" for historic discrimination by *some* whites against *some* blacks. The "sins of the fathers" are to be visited upon unknown but racially identifiable white children. Anonymous whites are now being punished for acts when their only connection to those acts is by way of skin color. Marshall and his fellow ideologists thus attach wrongdoing to race: the very premise of Hitler's persecution of the Jews.

Genetic guilt obliterates individual conduct and accountability, and attaches wrongdoing to blood or race relation. Western jurisprudence has aways located guilt in acts, or those who knowingly contribute to them. Indeed, we even go so far as to ascertain motives and intentions, not just deeds. Intention and action, not race relation or heritage, have formed the traditional foundation of responsibility, hence punishment.

Marshall's reasoning and the insidious assumptions behind it convert every anonymous white male into an heir of every slave owner. He attaches guilt and punishment to those who have committed no wrong themselves but who are related historically to a particular group by way of blood relation. As he puts it, "It is because of this legacy of unequal treatment that we must permit the institutions of this society to give consideration to race in making decisions about who will hold the positions of *influence, affluence,* and *prestige* in America."[8]

Of course, the attributes of social power mentioned by Marshall (influence and the like) defy the public pronouncements of "equal opportunity" the minoritarians assert are the principle behind their politics. Also, Marshall's opinion in *Bakke* makes no reference to law or the Constitution as the basis for his decision. Behind the veil of rights respectability lurks another group seeking power for itself.

To be sure, influence and affluence can be guaranteed by administrative fiats using the coercive power of the state to impose quotas. But how shall Marshall and the new mandarins guarantee prestige, which is an individual quality based on earned achievements rather than administrative racial preference? When was the last time you heard someone boast of getting a job through affirmative action? The real losers in all of this are the truly gifted minorities who have their dignity stolen from them by the group whose quota they help meet.

Prestige, like character (as the Reverend King understood), is an individual trait. It is particular. If not unique, it is singular. Race is not; it is general, and conjures the formation for stereotyping that denies character and the earned achievements that lead to prestige. Under systems of racial quotas the individual is subsumed in the group; his achievements are robbed from him and degraded into "role models" for the group he represents. Any self-respecting person would have to doubt "success" conferred by a system that requires proportional representation based on race or gender.

It is obvious now that Marshall is demanding reparations as the result of a *legacy* not bequeathed to whites by their predecessors but imposed by present-day power seekers. The present generation of whites (and how many more?) is expected to repay present-day blacks for damages done to their ancestors. This is "social justice"? It is in fact an abuse of the law used to subordinate whites and redistribute wealth to large *groups* of people under the guise of "remedy." On close inspection, Marshall's "remedy" is nothing but color-conscious hostility seeking reparations based on a dangerous abstraction, race.

This reparations mentality is particularly evident in James Foreman's *Black Manifesto,* and was proffered by him to churches and synagogues whose members believe in genetic guilt. Foreman says that it is "only a beginning of the reparations due us as a people who have been exploited and degraded, brutalized, killed and persecuted." He sees race as the single criterion for holding and wielding political power, proclaiming, "We must assume leadership, total control . . . inside of the United States of everything that exists. The time has passed when we are second in command and the white boy stands on top." To bring this reversal of power positions about, Foreman recommends the use of "whatever means necessary, including the use of force and the power of the gun to bring down the colonizers." More recently, State Senator Bill Owen of Massachusetts has been demanding monetary reparations for "African Americans." Thus, power hunger today is no longer a class but a race phenomenon.

By identifying race and gender as essential aspects of a person's identity, Lenz and Stetson reduce humanity to racial types for political and legal judgment, hence racism. This is clearly what the Reverend King wished to avoid, and it simultaneously calls for whites, especially males, to assert themselves in a counterracial defense.

This guilt-oriented reparations ideology, whose real motive is the acquisition of political power, is not confined to the mandarins of race. The feminists are more openly vicious and self-serving. This is clear in Valerie Solanis's *SCUM Manifesto.* The Society for Cutting Up Males has no other purpose than to blame men for the problems of women in particular and the world in general.[9] The feminists, too, have a logical absurdity they want us to accept. They assert that men have historically oppressed women. Yet they also assert women are equal to men. This simply cannot follow. A struggle between equals can end in a stalemate, or it can end in death, but it can never end in oppression. Oppression and equality are mutually exclusive; where you have one you simply cannot have the other. Thus, the rise in intersexual combat is not observed by minoritarian ideology, it is the purpose of it.

If we consider Marshall's "legacy" theory seriously, it fails on the very ground on which he seeks to found it. The argument goes something like this: Whites brought blacks to America to be forced into slavery. The absence of consent, rather than the slavery itself (after all, Benjamin Franklin was an indentured servant to his own brother), forms the basis of guilt. Therefore, the whites, as barterers in human flesh, are condemned collectively, genetically, and indefinitely into the future. Yet, it was the Arabs and the blacks themselves who were the largest slave traders. The Spanish and Portuguese, of course, now vaguely defined as Hispanic and a protected class, populated much of South and Central America with black slaves who did the drudgery work considered beneath the colonizers.

While many American students are being taught only one end of the slave trade in order to push this racial guilt nonsense, the front end of the enterprise is ignored entirely. The white man did not seize slaves; he bought them. The slaves were, in the jargon of today, prisoners of warring tribes. If we follow Aristotle's ethics on such matters, both ends of this barter are equally condemnable because buyer and seller need each other to make the crime beneficial to each. Then aren't blacks as guilty as whites for slavery, because without each other the crime would not have taken place? There is enough guilt to go around here. But at least, this "legacy" theory by blacks must be self-condemnatory.

The purpose in understanding history is to bring to light facts and meanings of events so we might better know who we are as a people. This understanding should not be sought to ferret out racial enemies who might be prosecuted through government policies, for the purpose of demanding reparations from those who are remote from the historical scene of the crime. The "constitutionality of race-conscious remedial measures," as Marshall has it, targets the coercive power of the state at those who are innocent. This can succeed only in heightening interracial tensions.

Every society has its negative, asocial forces, whether grounded in race, caste, or religion. To identify all whites in the United States with the worst practices of *some* of them is no more valid than to praise American whites because one of them invented the light bulb. Generalizing guilt is the first step in race-thinking.

Collective guilt renounces action in favor of association. It removes accountability from the individual as arbiter over his own conduct, and attaches it to a generalization. Indeed, Hitler's Nuremberg Laws, the legal first step in the destruction of the Jews, identified the Jews, then Jewishness, as responsible for Germany's defeat in World War I. From this beginning Jews were condemned for all of the problems of Germany. Guilt is thus focused on someone not for what they have done but for who they are. Now instead of Jews it is whites, and instead of Jewishness it is maleness.

But Marshall goes one step further by substituting "remedy" for reparations, and by locating guilt in a "legacy" of which no one living is a part. He and his minoritarian power brokers, masking themselves as civil rights advocates, ignore or defame the very Constitution that has allowed a forum for their new theory of racial incrimination. In fact, the destruction of genuine, individual equal opportunity reinstates the White Man's Burden with a new twist: collective guilt determined by blood relation now shapes the screening process for everything from "scholarships" to job access. This affronts the early civil rights leaders primarily because of their rigid reliance on a strict interpretation of the Constitution for protection not as groups but as individuals. The 1960s rights leaders could seek reform under the Constitution by imploring application of its stated principles. The Fourteenth Amendment specifies that "no person shall be deprived. . . ." There is no reference to race or gender.

Taking the Constitution seriously thus rejects a color-conscious interpretation of any sort, for reasons of good or ill. Rejecting race and gender entirely on a strict interpretation of the Constitution precludes the necessity of the Court's acting as a determiner of anthropological and biological traits that are suitable for protection—or prosecution. This is merely the traditional recognition that individuals are the carriers of law, not groups. Groups, by definition, have to be defined in terms of a peculiarity, a trait, that sets them apart from others. To recognize group traits for the purpose of legal or policy action is to build the battlefield for intergroup combat.

Lenz and Stetson mistakenly believe

that "modern" theories of democracy condone groups as the basis for legal protection, if not moral preference. This suggests considerable ignorance of democratic theory and republican principles. That groups are the bane and sorrow of republican government was recognized by the "father" of the Constitution. James Madison points out in *Federalist 10* that group politics would be the ruin of the nation. Theodore Lowi, a widely respected expert on American politics, has identified the death of liberalism with interest-group combat.[10] If the normal adversarial relationship between economic and political groups is translated into racial terms, conflict will intensify because race is much more personal and inescapable.

Formerly seeking protection under natural and political rights, those considered inalienable by our founding fathers, blacks could demand what was theirs by law, even if it had been withheld by social custom. In fact, the broad spectrum of support the early rights leaders received was derived from a commonly accepted source, the Constitution. Would that same support be present today with our knowledge of affirmative action, quotas, and forced busing? But guided by the relativism of the new mandarins, truth—and its constitutional symbolization, inalienable rights—is set aside for the sake of group vanity. The black power movement, for instance, emerged from the early rights movement and took the typical Marxist position that the Constitution is nothing more than a document intended to serve the interests of the white, capitalist class. But the worst failure of black nationalists, now embodied in Louis Farrakhan, was to demand identity as blacks rather than human beings seeking rights. Racial rather than legal identity allows for the demand of reparations based on racial distinctions.

This all had the effect of degrading law as a guardian of rights into a protector of racial privilege. Not universal rights for all men as individuals but color type is now the basis for protection under a Constitution whose sole purpose is to see color with a vengeance. Individuals, any men, with prescribable rights untainted by notions of peculiarity, have had to yield to racial, ethnic, and gender discrimination. This is no doubt what prompted Thurgood Marshall's comment to a white friend: "You guys have been practicing discrimination for years. Now it is our turn."[11]

THE RETURN OF TRIBALISM

The new ideology of race, whose premise is genetic guilt and whose argument rests on the statistical failure of preferred groups, sees this failure in a conspiracy of the white race. One now hears the language of paranoia: "Equal opportunity is not enough," "Opposition to AA is racism," "majority tyranny," "dominant culture jingoism," "Birth control for blacks is genocide," and so forth. These linguistic clichés form the foundation of a conspiratorial mentality. As reported in *The Chronicle of Higher Education* in March 1986, Clark University was ordered by a federal judge to rehire a woman dismissed on academic grounds ten years earlier. The judge described her department (sociology) as "generally permeated with sexual discrimination." Yet, absolutely no evidence of such discrimination was offered or even mentioned during the tenure review process.

Affirmative action has been so sanctified that opposition to it now appears to be a mask for some hidden racial motive. Thus have public policy and law become the source, rather than the mediator, of interracial tensions. Rather than the law's serving to constrain the factions of race, by deciding cases based on individual grievances, it now assumes race and gender to be the fundamental bases for determining right. Law thus gives way to the disintegrative feelings of racial consciousness. We no longer see ourselves as individuals but as blood and gender types.

The former integrating forces of state, nation, and law have succumbed to the corrosive and primitive thinking of tribalism, a blood characteristic. This neotribalism is based on an appeal to qualities that are supposed to be inherent in the individual, the very mystical characteristics of blood and spirit. This neotribalism is more inverted than the idea of state or law as principles for determining individual conduct. It relies on pseudomystical elements in one's own soul that are generalized in a blood type, the tribe. Everything is then reducible and finally explained in terms of racial characteristics. This inevitably leads to a confrontation between one's own and all outsiders. The new racism, then, has its source in the breakdown of law as an arbiter over individual citizens.

Today this intertribal combat has been given constitutional protection by a high court that has warped our democratic tradition and now leads the country in policy formation. In *United Jewish Organizations v. Carey* (1977) the Supreme Court upheld reapportionment plans enhancing the electoral power of blacks and Puerto Ricans in New York that adversely affected the Hasidic Jewish community. Here Justice Marshall's "remedy" was directed against those he himself identified as innocent. Again, in 1977 the Court upheld in *Califano v. Webster* that sexual discrimination against men generally is acceptable because its purpose is "the permissible one of redressing our society's long standing disparate treatment of women."

Marshall himself notes that in neither case had there been any "constitutional violations" of an individual's rights. In other words, no law had been broken. The sole purpose of the decision was to shape a policy that would avenge "some type of past discrimination." Again, his target is anonymous whites and males. His "policies" are not only without a perpetrator, they are without a victim. In language that defies legal precedent, he argues that such decisions are valid "without the need for a finding that those who benefited were actually victims of that discrimination." He clearly uses the Supreme Court as an instrument not for determining legal principle but for shaping public policy that guarantees group combat based on earlier blood relationships. Tribalism is thus embedded in constitutional interpretation.

Today's call for tribal unity found in such expressions as "soul brother," "Chicano," "sisterhood," and "gay power" only serves to mobilize whites in a counterracial defense. Whites are forced to be aware of their whiteness. This intensifies race consciousness, hence those ugly things that go with it, and transforms the state into a political prize that can be won only in intertribal warfare. The mere fact of birth, one's genetic origin, becomes the source of factional strife. For instance, what Lenz and Stetson did not tell you about the *Weber* case was that it overturned the seniority principle of "last hired, first fired" and introduced racial preference into a union priority. The state, formerly a guardian of law and protector of individual rights, has been put into the position of having to mediate blood feuds.

Besides the corruption of cultural and political unity, affirmative action denies the very idea of equality and humanity that civil rights were intended to serve because everything now is reducible to racial distinctions. It ignores the fact that men are unequal as a consequence of their natural origin, their different organization, and their fate in history. They are equal only in rights, which must be seen in terms of human purpose. This purpose can be understood only in light of the Jewish–Christian tradition of a common origin beyond human history, therefore beyond human interference. This history is divine and serves as the philosophical foundation for political equality that ascribes purpose to each individual act. It thus explains man's presence on earth. However, nineteenth-century positivism and progressivism, now masquerading as cultural and moral relativism, perverted this purpose of human equality when they set out to prove what cannot be proven, namely, that men are equal by nature and different only by history and circumstances.

Under the new civil rights ideology men are not equalized by rights but by the present effort to shift circumstances and alter education based on racial identity. Yet tribalism, the effort to make blood the criterion for privilege, obliterates the very notion of humanity by explaining history in terms of race, a natural not a divine origin. Race, clearly a distinguishing feature, cannot suggest either a common origin or purpose for humanity because, by definition, it points to differences, the very antithesis of humanity. Hence, no human dignity is possible if the individual, now a member of a race or tribe, owes personal value only to the fact of having happened to have been born black, brown, white, or female. In the absence of human purpose, whose origin is God and whose destiny is the divine, we as individuals are reduced to tribal warriors.

NOTES

1. *Plessy v. Ferguson*, 163 U.S. 537, 16 S.Ct., 1138, 41 L. Ed. 256 (1896). This case established the doctrine of "separate but equal" facilities for blacks. The *Brown* case overturned *Plessy*. *Brown v. Board of Education*, 347 U.S. 483, 74 S.Ct. 686, 98 L. Ed. 873 (1954). This case established the principle of a "color-blind" Constitution, which, as we will see, has been ignored entirely.

2. John Schaar, "Equal Opportunity, and Beyond," in *Equality: Nomos IX*, ed. J. R. Pennock and John Chapman (New York: Atherton Press, 1967), pp. 228–49. John Stanley points up the influence of Schaar's article on the academic profession in "Equality of Opportunity as Philosophy and Ideology," *Political Theory* 5 (February 1977): 61–73.

3. *Civil Rights: Rhetoric or Reality?* (New York: Morrow, 1984). Sowell is frequently referred to as an "Oreo cookie" (black on the outside and white on the inside), an appellation attached by his black critics. His white critics condescend to say he is disloyal to his people. See his first chapter on the false statistics used to support minoritarian politics.

4. See Sowell, *Civil Rights*, chap. 2, for a marvelous brief but historically correct summary of this movement.

5. "The Constitution of the United States: Contemporary Ratification." Reprinted in Alpheus Mason and D. G. Stephenson, Jr., *American Constitutional Law*, 8th ed. (New York: Prentice-Hall, 1987), pp. 607–15.

6. *University of California Regents v. Bakke*, 438 U.S. 265, 387 (1978). The

Davis campus medical school refused admission to Bakke, whose academic credentials were clearly superior to those of all sixteen students admitted under its quota system.

7. Charles Murray, "The Coming of Custodial Democracy," *Commentary*, September 1988.

8. My italics. The outcomes Marshall describes (influence and so on) only reveal his concern to redistribute power, not to uphold an ethical standard.

9. Solanis's attempted murder of Andy Warhol is well known, but the general mentality that led to it is portrayed well by Marcia Cohen in *The Sisterhood* (New York: Simon & Schuster, 1988).

10. *The End of Liberalism*, 2d ed. (New York: Norton, 1979).

11. Cited by Walter Williams, a black scholar and essayist, in his book, *All It Takes Is Guts: A Minority View* (Washington, D.C.: Regnery Books, 1987), p. 6.

SUGGESTED READINGS

GLAZER, NATHAN. *Affirmative Discrimination*. New York: Basic Books, 1975. One of the first thorough criticisms of affirmative action.

SHORT, THOMAS. "A New Racism on Campus." *Commentary*, August 1988. A careful description of the politics of race on college campuses.

SOWELL, THOMAS. *Civil Rights: Rhetoric or Reality?* New York: Morrow, 1984. A fine synthesis of statistical data and theoretical construction that describes the historical and legal degeneration of the civil rights movement into a new ideology.

X

CIVIL LIBERTIES

"Does the Emphasis on Individual Rights in America Endanger the Freedom and Well-Being of Ordinary Citizens?"

A few years ago the government of the USSR, in response to the arrest of one of its own for spying in this country, arbitrarily arrested and imprisoned Nicholas Daniloff, *U.S. News and World Report's* correspondent in Moscow on trumped-up espionage charges. The reaction from the United States was overwhelming, and the pressures applied to secure his release involved threats by the United States to major areas of relations between the two countries. The Soviets soon realized we were very serious and a deal was struck. A Western European diplomat observed at the time that he thought the "fuss" was out of all proportion to the importance of one journalist—and entirely characteristic of the United States.

The observer was certainly correct on the second point. Americans do value the freedom of the individual. We, as Huck Finn's father declared in the musical *Big River*, "don't want government's hand in the pocket of our britches. . . ." Nor for that matter, do we want it on our shoulder showing us, no matter how wonderful its intentions, the road we should travel in life. We want to think and say what we want, to worship or not worship as we choose, to live our lives as best we can, thank you, entirely according to our own lights.

There is no question that this freedom has its price. The ordinary citizen is undoubtedly safer walking on Beijing's streets than New York's. The people most apt to perform the acts of random violence encountered on city subways are more likely, we all know, to be off the streets in Beijing—and safely tucked away—than they are in New York. But that means most of us have to use a good deal of judgment about where and when we venture in our cities. Our freedom of travel, in that sense, is more restricted than in a police state.

Access to pornography may or may not be necessary to guarantee freedom of political speech, and it may or may not incite acts of crime, but there is no question that its presence debases our lives and is forced on many people who are made extremely uncomfortable by it. And, which is the greater right: the right of airline pilots, like the rest of us, to be free of random drug testing or the right of airline passengers to be relatively secure in the belief that the people to whom they entrust their lives are substance free? These are the sort of questions that Professors Scott and Riley address in this set of essays in a robust, free spirited, no-holds-barred sort of confrontation. The relative merits of each position you have to decide for yourself, but it is important that you develop a position.

The balance between rights is always relative. If I want to be free to throw rocks in the air (as a matter of observance of my religion), you as my neighbor want to be free of the threat posed by my rocks when they come down to earth. Although institutions such as the Supreme Court may set limits on what the majority can do to followers of offbeat religions ("Just lock those rock throwers up; they belong to nothing but a cult"), it is also ultimately true that the Supreme Court, in the long term, is responsive to public opinion. For that reason, as well as many others, it is essential that all educated citizens seek to understand where, logically for them, restrictions on freedom are necessary to ensure the greater liberty of all, and where they are arbitrary and excessive.

The proper balance between "freedom" and "responsibilities," then, is in many ways the subject of this pair of essays. It is also true here (as in other cases) that our writers are making very strong cases on behalf of their respective sides. They do so in the hope of provoking very strong, but thoughtful, responses on the part of you, the reader.

Restricting the Rights of Law-Abiding Citizens

Jo Ann M. Scott

Ohio Northern University

Does the emphasis on individual rights in the United States endanger the freedom and well-being of ordinary citizens? At the outset, we are confronted with two questions: First, how could the emphasis on individual rights endanger freedom (and incidentally, what are those rights)? Second, who are ordinary citizens? Let's take the second question first.

Do we mean by "ordinary" citizens members of neo-Nazi organizations (such as the Skinheads or other hate groups), individuals who profit from the sale of pornography or other obscene publications, atheists or individuals who subscribe to extreme religious beliefs, those who prey on society by committing crimes, or people who voluntarily and knowingly use drugs and thereby potentially cause harm or even death to unknown others? Clearly, if these are the ordinary citizens, then the answer must be an unqualified *no*. The emphasis on individual rights has not endangered their freedom or well-being. This, of course, assumes that their freedom and well-being are tied in some significant way to selling pornography, consuming drugs, or committing crimes. But are they truly "ordinary" citizens? I contend that they are not, although I admit that at specific times thay may appear to be ordinary. Rather than the "unusual" or perhaps "exceptional" citizen, the "ordinary" citizen in the United States is law-abiding, free from drug use or addiction, not a purveyor of pornography (although ordinary citizens may, from time to time, knowingly or unknowingly, be consumers of pornographic material), and God-fearing and religious. In short, ordinary citizens are virtually the same today in terms of values, judgments, and expectations as the ordinary citizens of the late 1700s and the early 1800s, when the Constitution and Bill of Rights were ratified. And the ordinary citizens of today are being harmed (that is, their freedom and well-being are endangered) by the continued emphasis on individual rights for the "unusual" citizen.

You may ask, how could the emphasis on individual rights ever endanger the freedom and well-being of individuals? You may even say weren't the Constitution and Bill of Rights written and ratified to protect individual rights? The answer to this question is, of course, yes. The Constitution and Bill of Rights were adopted to protect individual rights, but one must always remember that individual rights are not absolute. The rights of religious freedom and speech may be restricted if it is determined that the exercise of these rights is injurious to society generally or some individuals specifically. But religious expression and free speech are not the only individual rights that may be injurious to society or specific citizens. The so-called criminal defendant rights (particularly the application of the Fourth Amendment's protection against unreasonable search and seizure through the exclusionary rule), and the right to privacy as it relates to mandatory drug testing, sexual behavior, and the procurement of abortions may be, and oftentimes are, injurious to both society and specific individuals. Each of these issues will be discussed in the following essay.

Is pornography constitutionally protected speech? If so, do democratic principles require that ordinary citizens endure and accept pornographic material merely because some profit from it and others apparently enjoy viewing it? Does pornography endanger the freedom and well-being of ordinary citizens, and who are those ordinary citizens?

The First Amendment guarantees that Congress shall make no law restricting the freedom of speech, but does that include all expression, including material that is pornographic in nature? Clearly and absolutely, the answer is *no*. Although freedom of speech is guaranteed, it is not unlimited. Government can and does place reasonable restrictions on the exercise of free speech (and other expression). For example, it is unlawful to yell "fire" in a crowded theater, unless, of course, there is a fire, because it represents a potential harm to others. Likewise, individuals are prohibited from using their freedom of speech to incite others to riot or rebel against the government. And laws prohibit manufacturers from exercising free speech to fraudulently mislead the public or falsely advertise their goods. Yet, purveyors of pornographic material insist that the First Amendment guarantees of free speech protect their right to produce, sell, and distribute their material.

The framers of the Bill of Rights intended to protect speech that is not injurious to the "health of the self-evidently proper kind of polity—a republic."[1] In short, political speech, because it strengthens fundamental values and community development, is protected; however, pornography does not strengthen fundamental values nor does it contribute to the development of the community.

Quite the contrary is true. The distribution of pornography ultimately leads to the weakening of fundamental values and often undermines community development. Even though political speech is considered a preferred freedom and therefore is granted a greater degree of latitude than mere speech, it too is not absolute. The high court, in numerous cases, has held that if political speech presents a "clear and present danger," it may be regulated or prohibited altogether. Surely, the government has the right to protect its own existence even from the remote chance that the people will rise up and follow a demagogue of the stature of a Hitler, Huey Long, or Father Coughlin. If the government can regulate a preferred freedom, then it follows logically that the same government has the right, and perhaps even the duty, to protect its citizens against pornography. Perhaps former Chief Justice Warren Burger said it best when he declared, "To equate the free and robust exchange of ideas and political debate with the commercial exploitation of obscene material . . . demeans the First Amendment and its high purposes in the historic struggle for freedom."[2]

Pornography does endanger the freedom and well-being of ordinary citizens. In fact, four identifiable groups in society are clearly harmed by the production and distribution of pornography: women, children, adolescents, and the family.

The freedom and well-being of women are endangered by pornography. The very purpose of pornography is to show women in a sexually submissive and dehumanizing manner, and thus it degrades, brutalizes, discriminates against, and victimizes women. Pornography depicts women enjoying, almost reverently, the exploitation and sometimes brutalization of their bodies solely for the pleasure of men. The result, of course, is that pornography leads to an increased incidence of violence against women simply because many men who view pornographic material believe that some, or even all, women secretly desire to be treated in this manner. As Riley correctly points out in the following essay, "More than one grisly crime has been committed by an individual 'addicted to pornography.'" Perhaps one of the most celebrated examples of this was mass-murderer Ted Bundy. Just hours before he was executed, Bundy admitted that he was driven, at least in part, by the pervasive display of sex and violence on television and in theaters.

Children are also endangered by pornography. All too often we read or hear of instances where children have been forced into performing sexual acts with adults. Although it is rarely suggested that these children enjoy this activity or subjugation, it is nevertheless true that the children, clearly the victims of crime, are emotionally scarred by the experience. Moreover, these children would not have been victimized if some individuals were not making a substantial profit by their exploitation. As is true with women, children are seen as mere sexual objects, intended solely to satisfy adults' desires.

Adolescents are the third group who are endangered by pornography. It is unreasonable to argue, or even think, that young adults are not exposed to or don't receive the messages set forth by pornographic material. How likely is it that adolescents will be able to resist viewing pornographic material, especially if it is displayed in a corner of the local supermarket? Or what is the likelihood that adolescents will be able to differentiate among "true love," irresponsible sex, violent sex, aberrational sex, and sex that is a statement of love and commitment? Surely, the traditional values of family, morality, responsibility, and commitment are compromised or even disregarded by pornography. The message transmitted to adolescents is clear: Sex is nothing more than a physical and biological need. People are not distinguishable from animals, and people, including adolescents, therefore ought to satisfy that need whenever and with whomever they choose.[3] What are the consequences of pornography on adolescents? It leads to teenage pregnancies, abortions, premature marriages, venereal disease, and AIDS.[4] Clearly, prohibiting pornography will not eliminate all of these undesirable consequences; however, it will significantly reduce their likelihood or occurrence.

The fourth, and final group endangered by pornography is the family. America is traditionally a Christian society and the family is an integral component of that tradition.[5] Families are endangered by pornography precisely because it encourages attitudes that challenge their sanctity and continuance. Pornography implies that extramarital sex is not only permissible but desirable. As a result, the very cornerstone of American society, the stability of families, is threatened.

If pornography does endanger the freedom and well-being of individuals, and I submit that it does, what can and ought to be done? Clearly, the intent of the framers was not to protect all speech. Moreover, the Supreme Court, in a series of cases, has held that pornography is not constitutionally protected speech.[6] As such, material that lacks serious literary, artistic, political, or scientific value should be subject to reasonable restrictions enforced by local communities. It is frequently argued that complete elimination of pornography can never occur in a free and democratic society. Although

this may be true, that rationale should not be the basis for refusing to enact and enforce stronger pornography laws.

Riley contends that a government that can regulate, and perhaps outlaw, obscenity can also determine that "the real obscenity lies not in sex and violence but in social, economic, and political opinions different from those held by the people who run that government." The implication, of course, is that those social, economic, and political opinions will ultimately be outlawed and democracy will be lost to all Americans. The position is one of an alarmist and is as remote as Riley's argument regarding the possibility of Americans following a demagogue. Certainly, examples can be found where Congress enacted statutes that restricted political, social, and economic opinions. The important point, however, was not that these laws were enacted but rather that they were held in check by both the executive and judicial branches. Moreover, Riley argues that pornography is the price we must pay for democracy. The true measure of democracy is not whether individuals have an unbridled right to say and do anything they choose. Rather, the true measure of democracy is whether individuals use freedom of speech in a responsible manner.

The second issue that faces us is religious freedom, specifically, the First Amendment's no establishment clause. Unlike the free speech problem, and its application to pornography, the no establishment clause seems, at first glance, to be direct and explicit. Government is not supposed to establish a religion. As a result, one would think that ordinary citizens may freely exercise their religious beliefs, including prayer and Bible reading in schools, without governmental intrusion. But is this the case? Absolutely not! Government continues to intrude into this area of fundamental rights and continues to prohibit prayer and Bible reading in public schools.

Let's stand back and look at the First Amendment's provision for a moment. Does the amendment require that government, all government, maintain a hands-off policy toward religion? If not, what did the framers intend when they adopted this clause and, further, what was the purpose of the no establishment clause?

A literal reading of the First Amendment indicates that all government was not to be restricted in the area of religion. The amendment specifically states that Congress shall "make no law respecting an establishment of religion, or prohibiting the free exercise thereof." A reasonable interpretation of this provision, therefore, is that only Congress (and one may read that as the national government) was to be prohibited from intruding into this sphere. To support this argument further, one need only glance at the history of the United States, both prior to and immediately following the Revolution and adoption of the Constitution. The Declaration of Independence, written by Thomas Jefferson, mentions God at least four times. Additionally, the thirteen original state constitutions not only acknowledged the existence of God but also God's preeminence. At the beginning of the Revolution, nine of the thirteen original colonies had established, state-supported churches, and incidentally, four of those churches were still functioning when the Constitution was adopted.[7] This evidence suggests that rather than preventing all government intrusion, the framers intended only to restrict the actions of the national government.

If the framers did not intend to restrict all government activity in the area of religion, what is the purpose of the First Amendment's provision? Simply put, the constitutional purpose is twofold. First, the amendment intended to prohibit a national religion. This purpose is easily met by restricting (or prohibiting altogether) interference by the national government in religious matters. Second, states are allowed control over the issue of religion. Remember, the United States is a federal system, and the Tenth Amendment reserves to the states, or the people, all powers not specifically delegated to the national government or prohibited to the states. There is nothing in the Constitution that prevents states from acting with respect to religion.

Not only does the Constitution, as intended by the framers, permit state activity, so does American tradition. That "wall of separation" between church and state, so forcefully argued by opponents to school prayer, is of both recent vintage (although admittedly used by Jefferson for consumption only in Virginia) and thin construction. For the first 175 years of U.S. history children were allowed to pray or read the Bible in school. The Supreme Court, in 1952, held: "We are a religious people whose institutions presuppose a supreme being."[8] Although the Court decided that school prayer and Bible reading violate the "wall of separation," the same Court has never held that other religious practices at the national level, such as chaplains in the military, "In God We Trust" on our coins, and opening sessions of the Congress and the Supreme Court with a prayer, constitute a similar violation.[9] If the "wall of separation" exists, all of the above practices would have to be prohibited.

Are ordinary citizens' freedom and well-being endangered by recent court decisions? Clearly, they are. Individuals, primarily school-age children (the very citizens whom the Constitution was intended to protect), are being harmed. Riley contends that evidence does not exist that suggests that children would function any differently if they started their day with a prayer. Yet, the following quotation demonstrates that children are taught that God is not relevant, that religion is a lie, and that the state, rather than being neutral toward religion, is hostile to diety-based religion but not secular religion. It also suggests that many students would function differently if the free exercise of religion were permitted in our schools.

> We have been taught that the Constitution guarantees us freedom of speech. But we feel that here we have been discriminated against, because we can picket, we can demonstrate, we can curse, we can take God's name in vain, but we cannot voluntarily get together and talk about God on any part of our campus, inside or out of the school.
> We just feel frustrated because we don't feel like we are being treated equally.[10]

The argument most frequently advanced by opponents to school prayer, including Riley, is that the Court never said students could not pray. All the Court said was that there could not be organized prayer; nor, of course, could there be silent meditation if it was preceded by a suggestion to pray. Silent prayer has, of course, always been permissible in the Soviet Union. If our constitutional standard is reduced to silent prayer, then individual rights will be lost for all citizens. The only viable solution is a return to the intent of the framers: let states determine for themselves if prayer and Bible reading are permissible within their schools or other public places, such as the courthouse steps in Pawtucket, Rhode Island.

Assuming for a moment that a "wall of separation" does exist between church and state, an assumption I contend is unwarranted and historically unjustifiable, that wall extends only to direct state action with the church and similarly direct church action with the state. Surely, Baptists who dispense theology with soup and Catholics who organize to lobby against abortion would be permitted to continue. Neither activity receives state funding, nor is the church attempting to run the state. In both instances, it is private citizens, regardless of their religious affiliation, who are exercising their constitutional rights and not the church.

Although ordinary citizens are endangered by pornography and the prohibition on the free exercise of religion, their freedom and well-being are far more endangered by the Court's required application of the exclusionary rule. The rule mandates that all evidence, regardless of its probative value, be suppressed if the police failed to obtain either a consent for the search or a warrant prior to conducting the search.

As is the case of school prayer and Bible reading, neither the Constitution nor American tradition prohibits the practice of introducing probative evidence, however secured, during a criminal trial. It wasn't until the Court decided *Mapp v. Ohio* in 1961 that the exclusionary rule was made applicable to the states. Prior to *Mapp*, the rule was applicable only in federal cases, where the Supreme Court had supervisory powers; state criminal defendants had to rely upon civil remedies to redress any alleged wrongdoing. The difficulty with civil remedies developed only because states granted police officers immunity from prosecution. That immunity must be discarded and police officers must be held accountable for their actions.

Why did the Supreme Court impose the rule on state proceedings? In part because the Court felt that other remedies (for example, civil action against the police) were faulty, and in part because the integrity of the judicial system demanded nothing less than that the "criminal go free because the constable blundered."[11]

Riley contends that the exclusionary rule is there not only as a protection for individuals but also as a deterrent for unlawful police conduct. Has the rule effectively deterred police from conducting unreasonable searches? The answer is simply *no*. The exclusionary rule applies only if an arrest is made and only if formal charges are brought against the accused. The rule does not approve the conducting of unreasonable searches of innocent persons by police officers. It expects that police officers, often at a moment's notice, will be able to analyze all of the relevant judicial positions on search and seizure and then act accordingly. This expectation is both illogical and absurd. Moreover, the application of the exclusionary rule is directed against the wrong agent within the criminal justice system. Police are not brought before the bench and held to answer for their conduct. Rather, prosecutors are prohibited from charging and prosecuting the accused. If the physical evidence supports the charge that the accused committed the crime, then prosecutors should be allowed to enter the evidence at trial. It is important to note that physical evidence, unlike coerced confessions, is an independent indicator of the guilt of the accused.

A second difficulty with the exclusionary rule is that it imposes a single, inflexible, and drastic sanction without regard to the circumstances and facts of a particular case.[12] The rule does not differentiate between an honest mistake on the part of the officer and outrageous conduct by the officer. The result is always the same: The guilty party must be released and the state is prohibited from securing a conviction. There is a qualitative difference between these alleged wrongdoings, yet the rule does not provide for different remedies. Moreover, the framers did not intend to have the Fourth Amendment used as a vehicle to escape prosecution and punishment for wrongdoing.

A third difficulty with the exclusionary rule is that it deprives juries of probative evidence. Surely, coerced confessions should be suppressed primarily because they are not voluntarily and willingly made. The same cannot be said, however, for tangible evidence secured as a result of a search. That tangible evidence is reliable, regardless of how it was secured, simply because it is independent of the accused. Denying the jury this evidence diminishes the likelihood that the jury will be able to fulfill its primary function: the determination of guilt or innocence based on the evidence and facts of a given case. Instead, the jury is required to render a decision based on only a portion of the evidence.

A fourth, and final, difficulty with the exclusionary rule relates to the concept that a not-guilty verdict, however obtained, is a statement that the defendant is not guilty of a particular crime. Theoretically, and perhaps ideally, this concept may be true, but in a pragmatic sense it is incorrect. Defendants who are factually guilty (that is, they committed the offense for which they have been charged) are able to escape punishment because they cannot be declared legally guilty. The only reason this declaration is not forthcoming is due to the fact that evidence of the defendant's guilt must be withheld from the jury or the court.

It is frequently argued that the judicial system's integrity suffers when arbitrary justice is applied or when corrupt or overly zealous police officers engage in a search. But does the application of the exclusionary rule actually maintain, or even enhance, the integrity of the judicial system? Shortly after the Court announced the *Mapp* decision, researchers began studying the issue of police compliance. Interestingly, the evidence suggested that a "new epidemic" had developed. Some Americans suddenly became afflicted with a new disease called "dropsy"; immediately upon their passing police officers, contraband and other questionable material fell from their pockets, jackets, or wherever. Additionally, officers would testify either that the evidence was in plain sight (and therefore not subject to the *Mapp* holding) or that they, indeed, had obtained consent for the search. Surely, neither of the above instances enhances the integrity of the judicial system. Although on its face this example appears to suggest that officers should be controlled, and thus that the exclusionary rule is necessary, the example actually demonstrates the absurdity of the exclusionary rule. What we, as a society, are doing is making "criminals" of law enforcement officers. Surely, officers who egregiously disregard the law ought to be punished, but society must not handcuff all officers and thus prevent them from appropriately carrying out their responsibilities.

More important, however, is the integrity of the judicial process enhanced (or maintained) when guilty people are freed because of a technicality? The courts were created to administer justice. Justice is not served, nor are the victims or society, when guilty people are allowed to escape punishment because of a rule established by the courts. The only reason criminal defendants desire to have the evidence suppressed is that it

does establish their guilt. Rather than enhancing the integrity of the judicial system, the exclusionary rule fosters disrespect and distrust for the system. Criminal defendants do not respect and trust the process because they know if they are fortunate enough, an attorney will be able to hide their guilt. Ordinary citizens do not respect or trust the system because, all too frequently, they see guilty people returning to the streets to prey upon them once again.

The Fourth Amendment is an integral and important part of the Constitution, for it does protect the liberty and fundamental rights of citizens. Yet, that very important component of the Constitution has been turned upside down so that it protects the "exceptional" citizen to the detriment of ordinary citizens. As such, the rule should be modified to cover only the most egregious form of police misconduct. The good-faith exception, which states that evidence may be used during the trial if an honest mistake or subsequent invalidation of a warrant is made, should be expanded. In the final analysis, the message should be clear: The guilty will *not* be freed because the constable blundered.

Just as each of the individual rights discussed above is not absolute and unlimited, neither is the right to privacy. The Constitution does not secure the right to privacy for individuals; rather, the right was shaped through judicial enactments. Regardless of how the right was secured, it is important to remember that it is neither absolute nor unlimited.

One of the obligations (or duties) of government is to protect the health, welfare, morality, and safety of ordinary citizens. In an effort to fulfill this duty, the government may enact reasonable restrictions on the right to privacy. One example of this restriction is drug testing. Governmental policy, at least as it is currently enforced, is that all ordinary citizens are *not* subject to mandatory testing. The policy, simply stated, is that only citizens in sensitive positions, where national security could be threatened or where demonstrable harm to significant numbers of people could occur, will be tested. It is foolhardy to believe or argue that ordinary citizens would not be harmed if our national security is compromised. Likewise, the argument is not that airline pilots are "exceptional" citizens and therefore subject to more governmental regulation. Rather, the argument is that an airline pilot puts the ordinary citizen in an extraordinary position. Airline pilots, as well as air traffic controllers, railroad engineers, and bus drivers, are responsible for hundreds of lives on a daily basis. It is reasonable, therefore, to expect these ordinary citizens to be drug free and to reduce the likelihood of an accident or loss of life. If we lived in a perfect society where people routinely considered, and acted upon, the welfare of others, then drug testing would not be necessary. Unfortunately, as recent evidence indicates, that is not the case. As a result, the government must fulfill its obligation to protect the safety and welfare of people by requiring drug testing on certain ordinary citizens.

Riley is correct in arguing that legalized abortion has worked to increase the security and well-being of one segment of society, women who choose, for whatever reason, to terminate their pregnancies. At the same time, however, legalized abortion has worked to decrease, or more precisely eliminate, the security and well-being of another segment of society, namely, unborn children. These citizens are never given the opportunity to be born, to grow, to enjoy the protections of the Constitution, or to contribute to the advancement of our society.

The argument or concern should not be whether women ought to be allowed to continue or terminate a pregnancy. Rather, the concern should focus on education and a return to traditional American values. Women of all ages should be educated on how to prevent unwanted pregnancies, and young people must be taught that sex is an expression of love and commitment and not merely a physical need to be fulfilled. The answer cannot, and must not, be the unlimited right to secure an abortion in order to avoid a pregnancy.

As was true with the issue of abortion, the overriding concern with homosexuality is not, as Riley suggests, that a decision to expand housing and employment rights of gays threatens most Americans. Certainly, most reasonable people would conclude that these decisions do not threaten most Americans. Nor, for that matter, are homosexual adults any more likely to seduce young children than are heterosexual adults. Nevertheless, there is a vitally important concern that plagues all Americans and that is the current AIDS epidemic. Although it is unreasonable to argue that AIDS is God's way of punishing an errant society, we must recognize that the two largest groups afflicted with the deadly disease are homosexuals and intravenous drug users. Surely, government, through its police powers, has not only the right but also the duty to protect the health, welfare, and safety of citizens even when those citizens do not seek that protection. The issue of the right to privacy must be balanced against the rights of society to be free from the very real threat of a deadly disease. When these two rights collide, as they surely do with AIDS, then it is reasonable to conclude that the individual right to engage freely in potentially dangerous sexual activity must be regulated or prohibited altogether.

How can individual rights endanger the freedom and well-being of ordinary citizens? The answer is all too simple. All we need to do is emphasize the rights of "exceptional" citizens. Ordinary citizens— women, children, adolescents, and families—are endangered when purveyors of pornography are given license and constitutional protection to peddle their wares. Likewise, ordinary citizens are endangered when the national government puts federalism and state wishes aside and mandates that God be removed from the classroom and other public places, except, of course, those public places where members of the national government have a direct and prevailing interest. Ordinary citizens are also endangered when criminals can twist constitutional protections to hide their guilt and avoid conviction and punishment. The well-being and perhaps even the lives of ordinary citizens are jeopardized each time an airline pilot, bus driver, railroad engineer, or air traffic controller reports for duty after using drugs. Finally, the security and well-being of one segment of society, the unborn, are threatened when women are given an unlimited right to secure abortions.

Certainly, individual rights must be protected against excessive and unlawful government intrusion. To do otherwise would mean that no one has any rights. But, in the end, the rights of individuals, whether ordinary or exceptional, must be balanced with the needs and rights of society as a whole. Democracy does not mean that each individual has the right to act as he or she pleases at all times. Democracy means that each individual, while exercising his or her rights, must be mindful not to tread on the rights of others. Whenever individuals fail to do this, government has an obligation and a duty to act in the best interests of all.

NOTES

1. George Will, "Nazis: Outside the Constitution," in *Points of View*, ed. Robert E. Di Clerico and Allan S. Hammock (Reading, Mass.: Addison-Wesley, 1982), p. 293.
2. Reo Christenson, "It's Time to Excise the Pornographic Cancer," in *Points of View*, ed. Robert E. Di Clerico and Allan S. Hammock (Reading, Mass.: (Addison-Wesley, 1982), p. 302.
3. Ibid., p. 303.
4. Ibid., p. 304.
5. This is not to suggest, however, that non-Christian societies are supporters or advocates of pornography or that they are any less family oriented.
6. *Miller v. California*, 413 U.S. 15 (1973); *Jenkins v. Georgia*, 418 U.S. 153 (1974).
7. Senator Jeremiah Denton, "In Defense of School Prayer," in *Points of View*, ed. Robert E. Di Clerico and Allan S. Hammock (New York: Random House, 1986), p. 290.
8. *Zorach v. Clauson*, 343 U.S. 306 (1952).
9. *Engel v. Vitale*, 370 U.S. 421 (1962); *Abington School District v. Schempp*, 374 U.S. 203 (1963).
10. Denton, "In Defense of School Prayer," p. 293.
11. *People v. Defore*, 242 N.Y. 13 (1926).
12. Charles G. Douglas III, "The Exclusionary Rule Should Be Abolished," in *Opposing Viewpoints: Criminal Justice*, ed. Robert J. Kaczorowski, vol. 1 (St. Paul: Greenhaven Press, 1983), p. 119.

SUGGESTED READINGS

CHRISTENSON, REO. "It's Time to Excise the Pornographic Cancer." *Christianity Today*, January 2, 1981, pp. 20–23. In this essay, Christenson asserts that pornography is not constitutionally protected and should therefore not be entitled to the same consideration as political or other speech. He also presents in detail the groups that are harmed by pornography and calls for legislation to prohibit pornography.

DOUGLAS, CHARLES G. "Time to Overrule the Exclusionary Rule." *Human Events*, October 9, 1982. Douglas first presents a historical background for the exclusionary rule and then sets out to demonstrate that the rule is both unnecessary and dangerous to the American legal system and to the American public. Douglas states that the exclusionary rule hampers law enforcement officials, the jury, other participants in the judicial system, and finally, American citizens.

EPSTEIN, CYNTHIA FUCHS. "The Problem of Pornography." *Dissent* 25 (Spring, 1978): 202–4. Epstein explores many of the problems associated with pornography, including the effects it has on the sensitivities of men, the degradation it brings to women, and the violence that oftentimes is associated with it. She concludes with a plea that as civilized and intelligent people, we should be as upset with pornography as we are with the dangerous effects of nuclear warfare.

Individual Rights Are Good for Ordinary People, Too

Dennis D. Riley

University of Wisconsin, Stevens Point

Does the emphasis on individual rights in the United States endanger the freedom and well-being of ordinary citizens? My first reaction to the question was, *what* emphasis on individual rights? From the middle 1950s on into the 1970s, the U.S. Supreme Court—aided in no small measure by Congress and even by a couple of presidents—advanced the cause of individual rights further than it had come in the first 150 years of our existence as a nation. But Earl Warren stepped down as chief justice of the United States more than twenty years ago, and except for that frustrating interlude called the Carter presidency, the White House hasn't shown much leadership in the area of individual rights in that same two-decade period. And in any case, Carter's individual rights emphasis was aimed more outside the country than inside it. The nation isn't willing to accept the equal rights amendment, and the Supreme Court is now led by a man who once held that Suffolk County, New York, could regulate the length of the hair worn by its law enforcement officers because the county had a compelling interest in "mak[ing] police officers readily recognizable to the members of the public."[1] Emphasis on individual rights, huh?

But that's not really an answer. Besides, we may not emphasize individual rights in the way I believe they ought to be emphasized, but when compared with the rest of the world, even when compared with the world's democracies, we do pay a good deal of respect to individual rights. So, I'll accept the premise and give you an answer. That answer is *no*. This essay will try to tell you why.

The place to start is by asking yourself, which rights have we emphasized? Four spring readily to mind. The first two are found in the First Amendment to the U.S. Constitution, namely, freedom of expression and freedom of religion. Next, the fourth, fifth, and sixth amendments offer a number of important protections to individuals accused of crimes. Finally, there is the vague but extremely important right to privacy. Let's take them in that order.

As you compare this essay with the one written by Professor Scott, you will quickly see that there is one question over which she and I find ourselves in complete disagreement. Before I go any further, I'd like to address that question. I think it is essential to do so, not simply because it separates Scott and me so thoroughly but because it is the one question that hangs over all discussions of individual rights—indeed, that hangs over all discussions of the Constitution itself. Would James Madison recognize the version of the Bill of Rights I am about to defend, and maybe more to the point, does it matter whether or not he would?

That was really two questions, of course, and I'm convinced that the answers are *no*, and emphatically *no*. Trying to discern the appropriate contemporary meaning of a constitutional provision— particularly one as important as the First Amendment clause prohibiting the establishment of religion, or the Fourth Amendment prohibition against unrea-

sonable searches and seizures—by reference to the "intent of the framers" is impossible. It's also silly.

In the first place, who exactly are the framers? There were fifty-five people in Philadelphia, and many of them even stuck it out to the end. But they didn't draft the Bill of Rights. That came later. So, should we look to the first Congress, the one that drafted and passed those amendments? Or how about the people who insisted that the Bill of Rights was the price for ratification of the original document? Or maybe the state conventions that ratified the amendments themselves? Or, why don't we make it the people who elected the men who attended those conventions? Wasn't the creation of a government based on the consent of the governed the real "intent of the framers"?

Then there is the question of figuring out what that intent might be. If we conclude that only Madison and Hamilton— with a few bones tossed to John Jay— should count, we can look at the Federalist Papers, but they hardly provide a very clear guide as to whether or not we ought to exclude illegally obtained evidence from criminal trials (Fourth Amendment), and they are similarly silent on the question of whether or not mandatory drug testing constitutes self-incrimination (Fifth Amendment). The problem only gets worse if we widen the circle of people we agree deserve to be considered framers. The debates of the first Congress aren't much help, nor are the records of the various state ratifying conventions, such as they are. We could look to the custom and practice of the late eighteenth century, but we wouldn't look there for guidance on much of anything else. Why should government be an exception?

In short, if we want to know what the First Amendment means in the 1990s, we are pretty much on our own. Madison rarely agreed with Hamilton, and Jefferson seldom saw eye to eye with Adams. Washington occasionally tired of all of them. But they did leave us one important guide. They wanted to create a government based on two great principles. Government belongs to the people, and the people have rights that government ought never to abuse. It is our job to figure out how those two great principles apply to the questions we face, just as it was their job to apply them to the questions they faced. Let's be glad they left those two principles and be on with it.

Now to the substance of it. How could free speech endanger ordinary citizens? There is the outside chance, of course, that a demagogue with the talent and ambition of an Adolf Hitler could use his right to speak freely to build a mass movement that would take over the country and wipe out the right of free speech for everyone else. No one can say with complete confidence that Americans would never follow a Hitler-like character, but the possibility seems remote. Unlike Germany, we made it through the perilous 1930s without doing so, and despite the temporary stardom of figures as frightening as Louisiana Governor Huey Long and Michigan's racist preacher Father Charles E. Coughlin, even in that desperate time we never really came close to selling out our democratic heritage.

But it isn't the fear of another Hitler that worries most ordinary Americans when they think of the threat posed by free speech. It is rock music. It is *Penthouse* and *Playboy*. It is X-rated movies, sometimes available on videotape in a corner of the local supermarket. And worse. In short, it is "pornography," and it worries people from the Christian right to the feminist left. It very obviously worries Scott. Should we be worried, too?

More than one grisly crime has been committed by an individual "addicted to pornography," and newspapers and television have been quick to point that out. There have even been laboratory experiments in which individuals viewing extremely violent films were willing to administer greater and greater electric shocks to other human beings. Still, most grisly crimes were committed by people who have no more interest in pornography than do the rest of us, and, more to the point, most of the people "addicted to pornography" commit no worse crime than feeding their habit.

And there's one more thing, one more very important thing. Scott tells us that it is only "political" speech that ought to be protected. Perhaps, but keep this in mind. A government that can define—and outlaw—obscenity can conclude that the real obscenity lies not in sex and violence but in social, economic, and political opinions different from those held by the people who run that government. That's what Jefferson and friends feared most when they insisted on the First Amendment and its guarantee of free speech. Pornography is the price we have to pay for that guarantee. It's a real price, sometimes a high price, but in the end there is no choice but to pay it.

Religious freedom poses an even trickier question. Government—and despite Scott's argument to the contrary, we have long since concluded that the Bill of Rights can have meaning only if it applies against the states as well as the national government, and that a religion imposed on a group of citizens is just as offensive if the imposer is Wisconsin as it is if the imposer is the national government—isn't supposed to establish religion, and it isn't supposed to prohibit the free exercise thereof. That's a difficult tightrope. The establishment clause doesn't just say to government, don't favor one religion over another. It says, don't favor religion over nonreligion. How can government protect nonreligion without endangering the free exercise of religion?

Under most circumstances, and probably for most people, there is no real problem. Religious people can go to their "church" on Sunday morning—or on Saturday night, Friday night, or just about any other time—and practice their particular religion unhindered, and nonreligious people can play tennis, read the newspaper, go to a movie, or sleep, and no one will care much one way or the other. But there are times and places that are different. Religious people want to practice their religion(s) in school, on the courthouse steps, or in shopping malls and airports. Nonreligious people—or sometimes just people of different religions—don't want them to. Now the government has a choice to make, and it isn't an easy one.

Often as not it is the Supreme Court that ends up making the decision, and despite a lot of rhetoric to the contrary, it hasn't always come down on the side of nonreligion. The citizens of Pawtucket, Rhode Island, were told they could keep a manger scene on the courthouse steps—provided they had other universal symbols of Christmas, like Santa Claus and his reindeer there as well— and tax money is used to bus students to parochial schools.[2] Still, religious people have lost a number of such contests, including the one that seems to arouse their ire the most, the battle over prayer in the public schools.[3] Interestingly enough, even our secular religion—in the form of the pledge of allegiance to the flag—lost in a contest with a religious religion when the Supreme Court ruled that a mandatory flag salute to begin the school day violated the First Amendment rights of the Jehovah's Witnesses.[4]

Now, what does all of this have to do with the freedom and security of ordinary Americans? Not all that much, I suspect, but that's the point.

Ordinary American kids may not get to start the day at school by mumbling the pledge of allegiance, but that hardly affects their day dramatically. They don't get to start it with a prayer service, either, though it is important to understand that the Supreme Court did not say they couldn't start it with a prayer. No one can stop silent prayer, and the Court had no intention of doing so. What it said to the schools was, in essence. "Don't organize a prayer service. Don't have a prayer said out loud. Don't let the teacher lead a prayer. Don't have the school board write a prayer. But if the children want to pray on their own, in their own way, that's fine." To suggest, as Scott implies, that this would put religious freedom in the United States on a par with the historical position of religious freedom in the Soviet Union is simply silly. Anyway, there is no evidence that these kids would function much differently in school if their day did start with a prayer service.

The fact that American schoolchildren can't start the school day with a prayer service certainly annoys many of their parents, and even some of the children themselves. In a sense, it probably even restricts their freedom. But it protects the freedom of lots of other students and parents—and probably more than a few teachers and principals—and in this, as in so many other cases, both sets of people cannot be "free," at least not as they define freedom. Something (someone) had to give, and in this case it was the religious—and most particularly Christian—people, and they didn't really have to give up all that much.

Nor do most of us give up all that much when we have to get up from the television to answer the door when the Mormons come calling, or when we have to try to dodge the "Moonies" when changing planes in Washington or Chicago. Not that those aren't annoying things. But once more, it is either freedom *for* the Mormons and the "Moonies," or freedom *from* them. Only one set of us can be free—if freedom really does mean able to have our own way without interference or compromise—and nice as it might seem not to have to miss an inning of the game being polite to the Mormons or no longer to have to feel that vaguely uncomfortable feeling one gets when approached by the "Moonies," can we really justify buying that "peace" at the expense of the right of those groups to try to get us to "see the light"? Remember, a government that could tell the Mormons they can't ring doorbells asking to talk about God, could tell Catholics they can't organize to try to outlaw abortion, and Baptists they can't dispense theology along with the soup in their downtown missions. That's a price none of us should feel comfortable paying.

For most ordinary Americans, the most perplexing of individual rights are those guaranteed to individuals accused of crimes. On an abstract level the connection between democracy and freedom of speech and between democracy and religious belief seems much clearer than the connection between democracy and the rights of criminal defendants. Maybe more to the point, it is far easier for an ordinary American to envision the circumstances in which he or she might wish to exercise freedom of speech or of religion than to believe that he or she will ever need the protections of the Fourth, Fifth, and Sixth amendments.

There is no reason to engage in a full-scale discussion of the rights of criminal defendants, but I think it would be a good idea to give you a quick sketch of the key ingredients in these three important constitutional amendments. Then we can consider why they upset people so much, and the point of all of this, why there is no real need to be upset.

The Fourth Amendment prohibits unreasonable searches and seizures. Determined to protect our privacy—and worried about the possibility that corrupt (or just overly zealous) police might plant evidence—we have told law enforcement officials that they cannot search a home, office, or person and take with them things they believe constitute evidence of a crime unless that searching and taking are deemed to be reasonable. It is reasonable to search—and to take evidence—if the owner of the property to be searched agrees it is reasonable. Beyond such informed consent, searches and seizures are also reasonable if the police have obtained a valid search warrant, that is, a warrant signed by a judge who has been convinced that there is a sufficient reason to believe a crime has been committed and that evidence of that crime is in a particular place. In fact, the police have to give the judge a pretty clear idea of just what sort of evidence it is they are looking for. There are other categories of reasonable searches—each carved out by the courts in response to some particular situation—but most of the time police looking for evidence of a crime will need a valid warrant or the informed consent of the property owner.

The Fifth Amendment, in addition to its guarantee of due process of law, states that no person "shall be compelled in any criminal case to be a witness against himself." There is no piece of evidence quite as convincing to a jury as a signed confession, and the purpose of this so-called self-incrimination provision is to guarantee that any confession an individual might give is truly voluntary. It doesn't take too much imagination to figure out why we want to make certain that law enforcement officials aren't out there obtaining involuntary confessions.

Finally, the Sixth Amendment guarantees an individual's right to "have the Assistance of Counsel for his defence." A courtroom can be a frightening and confusing place. Its language is arcane, and its procedures esoteric. But most of all, our whole system of justice is based on the assumption of an adversarial proceeding. Each side is represented by an attorney dedicated to the cause of victory for that side. Justice emerges from the clash. To be without counsel is to be unarmed, and the Constitution forbids sending an unarmed defendant against the fully armed state.

These amendments frighten people because they raise the specter of dangerous criminals remaining on the streets because some lawyer that we paid for—the public defender—"got them off," or because the police couldn't get a search warrant, or worst of all, because their convictions were overturned on a "technicality."

Such things do happen. *Hill Street Blues* once did a marvelous show illustrating the problem and its frustrations. The detectives investigating a murder in a gay bar got an anonymous tip that could lead them to the murder weapon and almost certainly to the killer himself. But it is not possible to obtain a warrant based on an anonymous tip, so with an ironic twist that bordered on the tongue in cheek, they hit on the idea of having one of their favorite street characters break into the apartment in which they were sure the gun could be found. The detectives just happened to catch him in the act but in the confusion forgot to read him his rights before he confessed to the breaking and entering. One good technicality deserves another. It didn't work. The chief of detectives saw through it, and so did the public defender and the gun was never used as evidence.

I realize that a television script, even one from a show as well done as *Hill Street Blues*, doesn't constitute evidence of anything. But that show wasn't written in a vacuum. It was done after considerable research, and it represents what can happen, does happen, and maybe most important of all, what an awful lot of people are afraid happens all too often.

Guilty people do end up going unpunished, and there is no denying that sometimes the reason they go unpunished can be found in a judge's application of the Fourth, Fifth, or Sixth Amendment in an individual case. But there are two reasons that we shouldn't be extremely worried about it.

First, it doesn't happen all that often. For all the talk about the exclusionary rule—the Supreme Court ruling that declares that illegally obtained evidence cannot be used to convict someone—there is no systematic evidence indicating that more than a handful of prosecutions per year are lost because crucial evidence was thrown out by the judge. The same is true of illegally obtained confessions, and although public defenders do help a few real criminals go unpunished, privately hired attorneys do an even better job of that, and, in any case, the whole idea of an adversarial system of justice presumes that a not-guilty verdict—however obtained—is just that: a statement that the individual is not guilty of that particular crime.

Second, these applications of the Fourth, Fifth, and Sixth Amendments—particularly the use of the exclusionary rule to throw evidence out of court—are there not only as protections for us but also as deterrents for the police. If the police violate one of those provisions, they blow a case. It is hard to imagine anything much more upsetting to someone whose job it is to enforce the law than to know that his or her conduct made it impossible to see that the law actually was enforced. Guilty people going free has to stick in the craw of any law enforcement official. To know that he or she made the mistake that set that guilty person free has to make it that much worse. Indeed, it is more than a little ironic that some of the people most convinced that swift, sure, and severe punishment serves as a deterrent to street criminals and shoplifters are quite unable to see the need for some sort of deterrent against the actions of incompetent, corrupt, or overly zealous police. If we need the protections of the Fourth, Fifth, and Sixth amendments, then we need some way to make sure that the police respect them. The exclusionary rule, with its promise of a case lost on a "technicality," is that way.

Once more there is that final question, the really important one. What would American society be like for most of us without these rights? Police who could search where they pleased and obtain confessions as they saw fit, and courtrooms with only one lawyer, the prosecutor. Remind you of anyplace in particular? I don't mean to ignore the very real—if rare—threat to specific individuals that comes from the criminal who should have been convicted and wasn't. But maybe that threat can be better dealt with by forcing police to play by our strict set of rules than by loosening those rules. More to the point, real as that threat is, it doesn't compare to the threat posed by a society in which individuals are no longer protected from unreasonable searches and seizures, forced confessions, and unarmed confrontations with skilled and determined prosecutors.

Finally, there is the right to privacy. The right to privacy isn't specifically mentioned anywhere in the Bill of Rights, but the very existence of the Constitution itself is an expression of our commitment to limited government, and it is hard to see how limited government can have real meaning unless there are areas of an individual's life that are off-limits to that government.

Once again, at first glance it seems that ordinary Americans would be enthusiastic supporters of a right to privacy. Nearly everyone wants to be left alone. But ordinary people don't always want everyone else left alone, and therein lies the rub, for the right to privacy has been used to justify liberalized abortion regulations and expanded rights for homosexuals. Likewise, it has been used as an argument against mandatory drug testing. If we decide to continue to emphasize the right to privacy, do ordinary Americans have much of anything to fear?

Whatever one feels about the morality of abortion, liberalized abortion laws have worked to increase not to decrease the security and well-being of one segment of ordinary Americans, namely, women who decided, for whatever reasons, that their own pregnancies had to be terminated. Strict abortion laws never prevented wealthy women from securing abortions, nor did they force those women into the hands of the often cited "back alley butchers." Only poor women faced the often life threatening circumstances brought about by unsanitary conditions, incompetent physicians, or the effort to do the job themselves.

In the same vein, whatever one thinks of homosexuality, it is hard to see how a decision to expand the housing and employment rights of gays, or even a decision simply to leave them alone, would threaten most Americans. There is no evidence that homosexuals are any more likely than heterosexuals to seduce young children, sexually harass coworkers, or flaunt their sexuality in ways the majority of us find offensive. Besides, in effect, we now have the Supreme Court on record as saying that what goes on in the bedroom is none of the government's business if the occupants of that bedroom are man and woman. But if two men or two women are there, all of a sudden it becomes the proper subject of government regulation.[5] Does that really make much sense?

Finally, I'm convinced that ordinary Americans have more to fear from widespread drug testing than they do from a privacy-conscious society that refuses to allow such testing. On a purely pragmatic level, there is the question of the reliability of the tests and of the laboratories that perform them. Who will "pay" for the inevitable mistakes? And who will be tested? Will it be Wall Street brokers and investment bankers? Or will it be assembly line workers and day laborers? But the real point is still privacy. If drug use interferes with performance, get rid of someone for incompetent performance. We don't need to do it for the drug use itself. Yes, there are jobs that involve responsibility for human lives. Airline pilots ought not to fly after smoking marijuana any more than they ought to fly after drinking. But what we want to know before they fly is not what they had at the party last weekend but whether or not they are now ready to fly. That's what we ought to test for.

Aren't there any individual rights whose emphasis might be harming the interests of ordinary Americans? Maybe one or two.

Thousands of Americans—most of them ordinary in most respects—are killed each year by (with) handguns. Thousands more are injured, robbed, and/or thoroughly terrorized by other Americans carrying guns. Wouldn't the ordinary citizens of New York, Chicago, Los Angeles, and Detroit be more secure if the only people in those cities carrying guns were the police? I know, to outlaw guns is not to eliminate them. Still, emphasis on the Second Amendment right to bear arms can be said to threaten the security and well-being of ordinary Americans.

In addition, a number of conservative federal judges, including Supreme Court Justice Antonin Scalia, have found in the last phrase of the Fifth Amendment a right they feel has been neglected for over half a century. The Fifth Amendment concludes with these words: "nor shall private property be taken for public use, without just compensation." It's easy enough to see that if my house is in the only viable path for a new interstate highway, that the public interest demands that I give up my house, but fairness demands that I be given a just price for it.

But government can do all sorts of things that lower property values without actually taking physical possession of the property itself. Is that a taking for which I must be compensated? In 1988 Justice Scalia convinced four of his colleagues that the state of California's demand that a couple building a new beach home give access on the beach beside that home to the general public was just such an unconstitutional taking.[6] The Supreme Court once held that the taking clause prohibited wage and hours legislation because such legislation took the right to contract for one's own labor away from average citizens.[7] There are a number of judges who want to go back to that ruling. What would that do to the economic security and well-being of ordinary Americans?

In the end, the argument boils down to this: On balance, our commitment to individual rights enhances, not threatens, the security and well-being of ordinary Americans. Yes, there are instances in which a particular exercise of his or her individual rights by one citizen does jeopardize the security or well-being of another. It is the very nature of rights that they are sometimes in conflict, and that conflict can result in tragedy. But think of the alternative. Think of a criminal justice system without the Fourth, Fifth, and Sixth amendments. Think of police knocking on your door at 3:00 A.M. Think of confessions obtained by force. Think of a government that could tell Jews to recite Christian prayers, require proof of membership in an approved religion as a condition for employment, or ban religious services altogether. Think of a government that could throw you in jail for saying that you didn't like what that government was doing. Think of those things, and I think you'll be glad that we have chosen to emphasize individual rights as much as we have.

NOTES

1. *Kelley v. Johnson*, 425 U.S. 238 (1976).
2. *Lynch v. Donnelly*, 465 U.S. 668 (1984).
3. *Engel v. Vitale*, 370 U.S. 421 (1962).
4. *West Virginia State Board of Education v. Barnette*, 319 U.S. 624 (1943).
5. The Court never said that directly, of course. But that is one not unreasonable way to read the combination of *Griswold v. Connecticut*, 381 U.S. 479 (1965), and *Bowers v. Hardwick*, the so-called Georgia sodomy case decided in 1986.
6. Daniel A. Farber, "Taking Liberties," *New Republic*, June 27, 1988, pp. 19–22.
7. *Lochner v. New York*, 198 U.S. 45 (1905).

SUGGESTED READINGS

I have been asked to suggest three additional readings. Here they are. They may not persuade you to believe what I believe, but they will give you a good idea of why I do believe it.

JOHN STUART MILL.   *On Liberty*. This will be difficult going, but it is the classic English-language defense of the rights of individuals, and anyone seriously interested in the question of why individual freedom is one of the cornerstone values of Western civilization ought to read it.

You should also read two Supreme Court opinions. The first is the classic dissent of Oliver Wendell Holmes in *Abrams v. United States*, 250 U.S. 616 (1919). The second is the opinion of Justice Robert Jackson in *West Virginia State Board of Education v. Barnette*, 319 U.S. 624 (1943). The former defends free speech, the latter religious freedom, but both speak in the most eloquent terms to the question of why we must allow people to behave in ways we don't quite understand or approve of.

Finally, to understand the reasons for our commitment to equal protection of the laws, and even our commitment to allowing people to challenge the decisions of the majority of their fellow citizens, read Martin Luther King, Jr., "Letter from a Birmingham Jail."

XI

FOREIGN POLICY

"What Major Foreign Policy Problems Will Confront the United States in the Next Thirty Years?"

Ultimately, the greatest problems confronting any nation are the problems of foreign policy: questions of war and peace, and national security. In this set of essays, as with the first, we asked the authors to speculate rather than argue a pro or con position on the nature of those problems.

There is one characteristic of the world on which we can most likely all agree: The world is constantly in flux, always changing, and that is just as true of international as of domestic politics. The rise of the fundamentalists in Iran and in much of the Islamic world, the coming to power of a Mikhail Gorbachev,

the growth of the Japanese as an economic superpower, threats to the ecological system—all of these are realities not foreseen only twenty years ago. This, of course, is by way of saying that no one can foresee the specific problems of the future with any accuracy, and none of our authors would say they could. And none can say that there will not be movements, developments, and changes that are as yet unseen and that will profoundly alter our world and demand citizens' attention.

But reasonable people must plan and policymakers must look ahead. Our essays are based on this assumption, and on the idea that by extrapolating from current trends, we can possibly gain some informed understanding as to what problems will have to be addressed and of some of the forces that are changing the world. Our three writers have chosen to emphasize quite different scenarios.

Professor Johnson in his essay "American Foreign Policy and the Challenges of a New World" sees four crucial problems. The first is the parochialism of the American people about foreign affairs, including a lack of knowledge of simple world geography. The second is disarray within and among the institutions of our government responsible for the conduct of foreign policy. He specifically means the need to involve both Congress and the presidency in the making of foreign policy and to avoid situations where members of Congress or unauthorized members of the executive branch conduct their own foreign policy initiatives. The third is our national fixation on the threat of communism, and the fourth is the tendency of our leaders to overreact to foreign policy crises and to intervene in the affairs of other nations.

Professor Mulcahy in his "Openness and Preparedness: American Foreign Policy Challenges in the 1990s" argues that the challenge posed by the Soviet Union will continue to be a predominant issue for U.S. foreign policy in the foreseeable future. The challenge will not be a simple "military challenge" but far beyond that: emphasizing the "managing" of nuclear weapons rivalry, protecting our interests in vital areas of the world (especially Europe and the Middle East), and seeking means of accommodation. All this must be done by balancing capabilities with ends and in aware-ness of a world that is changing from a bipolar one (dominated by the United States and the Soviet Union) to a multi-polar one. He argues the need for a "restructuring" of our economy (just as the Soviets have undertaken) and for an awareness that the Western alliance in the future will not be dominated by the United States, as it has been in the past. This implies an alliance based more on consensus than on simple adherence to the preferences of the United States.

José Garcia and John Neagle in their essay "Toward 2020 Vision" see a new agenda in world politics—an agenda dominated by such issues as ozone depletion, the greenhouse effect, the AIDS epidemic, and contamination of the oceans. These issues will make necessary a level of international cooperation that the nation-state, existent since the seventeenth century, is not well suited to address. The trick, they tell us, is not to abolish the nation-state system but to work around it. They point to many new international actors: the global media, organizations such as Amnesty International, church groups, and (unfortunately) terrorist organizations. They also are well aware that the nation-state is not dead and, indeed, resurgent nationalism serves to strengthen it. The nonviolent organizations, they suggest, must be able to pool enough of their resources to deal with the problems of the globe.

Little is inherently contradictory in the future as outlined by our writers, but it is clear that the emphasis of each is very different. Readers might ask themselves which emphasis seems most likely, which view of the problems we confront the most compelling.

American Foreign Policy and the Challenges of a New World

Loch K. Johnson
University of Georgia

The prominence of the United States as a world power is a relatively new phenomenon. As statesman–author George F. Kennan recalls, at the beginning of the twentieth century American diplomacy remained guided by "the concepts and methods of a small neutral nation." He remembers the Department of State in the 1920s, when he began his distinguished diplomatic career, as "a quaint old place, with its law-office atmosphere, its cool dark corridors, its swinging doors, its brass cuspidors, its black leather rocking chairs, and the grandfather's clock in the Secretary of State's office."[1]

Those simple days are gone. The Department of State is now a sprawling edifice of seemingly endless corridors, government-gray desks, and thousands of harried officials—in short, a modern bureaucracy. The life of the Foreign Service officer overseas has changed dramatically, too. Seldom in earlier times were the lives of U.S. diplomats at risk. The seventy-three who died in the first 189 years of the nation's existence were, in almost all cases, the victims of shipwrecks, natural disasters, or tropical diseases. Since 1965, in contrast, over eighty officers have died at the hands of ter-

287

rorists, including six ambassadors in the past fifteen years. In place of the once-attractive prospect of living abroad—with low rents and servants, villas with tennis courts and swimming pools, frond-trimmed verandas with lazy fans and trays of tax-free Scotch—the American diplomat now faces the constant threat of terrorism and harassment.

Yet, just as distant countries have grown more dangerous to Americans, so have they become more important. The world is increasingly difficult to ignore: the sophisticated weapons that threaten the very existence of the human species, the trading opportunities—and barriers—that so directly affect the health of the U.S. domestic economy, the need for continuing access to natural resources vital to industrial manufacturing, the reports of human rights abuses perpetrated by corrupt dictators (often with close ties to the United States) against their own people. The early American colonists also faced enormous challenges, of course, surrounded as they were on one side by an ocean dominated by powerful, hostile navies and on the other side by a vast wilderness, but today's advanced weaponry and the intricate patterns of trade interdependence have made the nuclear age an era of unparalleled risk and complexity.

At the same time, rapid advances in knowledge—from medicine and astrophysics to communications and the art of governing—encourage the hope that with every passing year the people of this planet are becoming better equipped to cope with the epic challenges before them. A number of shadows darken this optimism, however. As Americans approach the twenty-first century, they face four major foreign policy weaknesses that must be overcome if this country wishes to remain a leading world power. The first weakness is the foreign policy

parochialism of American citizens; the second, a disarray within the institutions of government that plan and implement foreign policy; the third, the nation's fixation on the threat of communism; and the fourth, a compulsion among U.S. foreign policy leaders toward an excessive, unwarranted intervention in the affairs of other countries. This essay briefly addresses each of these weaknesses in hopes of encouraging a new and more enlightened American foreign policy for the next century.

AMERICANS' PAROCHIALISM

One of the most discouraging weaknesses in this country's preparation for world leadership, and one the reader can do something about directly, is the inadequate preparation of many young Americans to assume positions of responsibility in the governing institutions of the United States—or, for that matter, even to evaluate rationally as voters the foreign policy arguments made by candidates for high office. Consider these results from recent surveys on the knowledge of American students about world geography—one index of citizen awareness of international affairs:

- 30 percent of the students at the University of Miami could not locate the Pacific Ocean on a world map;
- 25 percent of the high school students in Dallas could not name the country that lies immediately to the south of the United States;
- 50 percent of the students in Hartford could not name three countries in Africa;
- 45 percent of the high school students in Baltimore failed to shade in correctly "the United States" on a world map;
- 14 percent of the high school students

- in Washington could not name the large nation that borders the United States on the north;
- nearly 50 percent of college students in a California poll could not locate Japan on a map;
- 95 percent of the freshmen at a college in Indiana could not locate Vietnam on a map; and
- in a national sample of eighteen-year-olds to twenty-four-year-olds conducted during 1988 by the Gallup polling organization in nine Western nations, Americans finished last in geographic literacy.[2]

Americans can hardly expect to fashion a sensible foreign policy unless they are willing to learn more about the geography, culture, and politics of other lands.

Nor is this parochialism isolated to the young. The Gallup poll cited above discovered that only half of Americans above the age of eighteen realized that the Sandinistas and the U.S.-backed counterrevolutionary guerrillas (the "Contras") have been fighting one another in Nicaragua, or that Arabs and Jews were at odds in Israel. Fully one-third of the U.S. sample could not name a single member of the North Atlantic Treaty Organization (NATO), and 16 percent thought that the Soviet Union was a member of this Western defense pact, created in 1949 as a counter to potential Soviet expansion.

A report issued recently by the Southern Governors Association notes that only 1 percent of Americans have ever studied a foreign language, even though three-fourths of the people of the world do not speak English; that 10,000 Japanese, fluent in English, conduct business within the United States, while only about 900 American businessmen—few of whom know Japanese—conduct busi-

ness in Japan; that the United States is the only place in the world where scholars can earn a doctorate without any language study whatsoever; and that the U.S. Foreign Service remains the only diplomatic corps that does not require its officers to achieve fluency in another language.[3] In several American universities it is possible to earn a degree in international business without taking a single foreign language course! Little wonder the United States has fallen behind in international trade. Continued ignorance of foreign languages, geography, customs, economic practices, and politics seems a sure prescription for U.S. foreign policy failures in the future.

INSTITUTIONAL DISARRAY IN THE MAKING OF FOREIGN POLICY

A further challenge is for the officials of the U.S. government to cooperate more effectively in the making of foreign policy. Intolerable in a democracy are executive branch subterfuges epitomized by Lyndon Johnson's hidden escalation of the war in Vietnam; Richard Nixon's secret bombing in Laos; the misuse of the Central Intelligence Agency (CIA) at home and abroad (from an alliance with the Mafia in the 1960s to murder Fidel Castro to the surveillance of U.S. citizens throughout the Vietnam War era); lying to the American people (from an official distortion of events in the Gulf of Tonkin in 1964 to the illegal sale of weapons to Middle East terrorists in 1986); the improper involvement of the National Security Council (NSC) staff in efforts to bypass laws prohibiting covert action in Nicaragua; the plan (which came to light during the Iran–Contra investigations) to establish an "off-the-shelf, self-sustaining, stand-alone" invisible government led by the director of the Central Intelligence Agency and free of supervision by Congress or anyone else; and the many other horrors that have occurred in the recent annals of American foreign policy. As one astute observer of foreign policy has noted, "Three Presidents [Johnson, Nixon, and Reagan] have now brought an arrogance to power and a conviction of righteousness that allowed them to act as if they, not the American people, were sovereign."[4]

The representatives of the American people in Congress have the right, constitutionally, to participate in the making of the great decisions of war and peace, the consummation of international agreements, the use of trade sanctions and inducements, the direction and control of the secret intelligence agencies. "Contrary to popular belief, the powers are not separated in the foreign policy–national security area," comments the prominent constitutionalist Lloyd N. Cutler, "they are shared for the most part, and neither Congress nor the President can do much without the other."[5]

On its side Congress, too, must improve its level of competence and cooperation with the presidency in foreign affairs. The spectacle of junior members playing the role of secretary of state, off in some distant capital negotiating for this or that policy objective, cannot be allowed. Nor can the excessive duplication of foreign policy hearings and other forms of legislative oversight that create an unreasonable drain on the time and energies of officials in the executive branch, as well as sow confusion regarding which members of Congress have primary authority for helping to shape external relations. Both branches must continue to search for the right balance between the extremes of "micromanagement" of foreign affairs by Congress, on the one hand, and the dangers of full executive discretion over

policy making, on the other hand. "The institutional lesson to be learned . . . is not that the presidency should be diminished, but that other institutions should grow in stature," writes political scientist Aaron Wildavsky. ". . . The people need the vigor of all their institutions."[6]

A vigorous Congress and presidency working together, vital pistons in the engine of government complementing, not opposing, each other—here's the ideal. In 1988 legislators began in this spirit to revise the War Powers Resolution, calling for the establishment of a panel of eighteen congressional leaders and key committee chairmen to consult with the president before U.S. troops are sent into hostile regions. In addition, the bill would establish a "permanent consultative body" of six individuals—the speaker of the House, the president pro tempore of the Senate, and the majority and minority leaders of both chambers—with whom the president would be required to consult before the use of military force abroad.[7]

Partisan differences and institutional tensions will continue to interrupt the smooth functioning of government from time to time, even under the best of circumstances when both the executive and legislative branches are trying to act in good faith and with a spirit of comity. The proper remedy, then, is open debate before the court of public opinion, followed by votes up or down in Congress, and possible presidential vetoes. This is the framework laid out by the Constitution—not lying to congressional committees, ignoring statutory reporting requirements, dismissing legal limitations of foreign operations, or, as occurred during the Iran–Contra episode, privatizing foreign policy through secret fund-raising outside the appropriations process.

THE OBSESSION
WITH ANTICOMMUNISM

Another troubling weakness of U.S. foreign policy is the continued fixation of many decision makers on the Communist Threat (often capitalized like this to make it seem all the more dire), as if everything the United States says and does in the world has to be wrapped in a banner of anti-Sovietism. Conservative groups, in particular, keep up a steady drumbeat of exaggerated diatribe against the Soviet Union, applying loud and unrelenting political pressure against any politician who fails to march in lockstep with their cold war views.

Recently in Oklahoma, one right-wing organization filled the radio airwaves with attacks against Representative James R. Jones, a Democrat, for raising doubts about aid to the Contras in Nicaragua. Declared the ads: "President Reagan's exactly right . . . but your Congressman, Jim Jones, doesn't see the consequences of having a communist regime only two days' driving time from Texas. . . . For America's sake, call Congressman Jones right now. . . . " A 1988 fund-raising letter from the Reagan Political Victory Fund praised conservative senators as "the few who are strong enough to stand up to the threat of Communism and say 'No further!'" In contrast, the "liberals" offered only "appeasement for the Communists," and a "crippled, weakened defense." The rhetoric came straight out of the 1950s—an ongoing obsession with the dangers of Soviet world conquest, a belief that soldiers of the USSR, like Nature, abhor a vacuum and will fill every opening if the United States fails to check their aggressiveness.

This outlook is not limited to isolated groups on the fringe right; high-level public officeholders have echoed such shibboleths. You "cannot relax for a minute," warned a Reagan administration secretary of defense, Caspar W. Weinberger. The United States has to hold on tightly to every area of the world, he argued, countering Soviet imperialism wherever it raises its ugly head. "If you don't deal with it, they get a foothold."[8] A deputy assistant secretary of the air force during the Reagan years advised a forum at the National Defense University: "The most critical special operations mission we have . . . today is to persuade the American people that the communists are out to get us. . . . If we win the war of ideas, we will win everything else."[9] Troops to Lebanon, the Grenada operation, the "secret" war in Nicaragua, an armada in the Persian Gulf without strategy or timetable—practically all manifestations of interventionism abroad become justified as part of an anti-Soviet crusade.

In reality, communism is less a threat to the United States today than in earlier times. Even the most recent king of the cold warriors, President Reagan, seems to have accepted this view. In 1988 he retracted his characterization of the USSR as an "evil empire" and sought better relations between the superpowers, beginning with an agreement to eliminate intermediate-range nuclear weapons (the INF treaty). One of the candidates for president in 1988, former Arizona Governor Bruce Babbitt, accurately emphasized in his campaign speeches an important new reality of global politics: "Marxism as an economic theory has been a total, unqualified flop everywhere."[10] Aware of this, other nations are now far less drawn to the "Soviet model"—or, for that matter, to the "American model." Japan, South Korea, and Taiwan have become the economic showcases with broad appeal throughout the developing world.

Moreover, Soviet troops have experienced limited success abroad, with their most recent failure in Afghanistan, where a "pacification campaign"—the most costly Soviet military operations since World War II—was finally abandoned in 1988 after extensive losses in the field against the mujahedeen, the Afghan guerrilla force.[11] This particular defeat was aided significantly by the supply of U.S. weapons—especially sophisticated Stinger missiles—to the mujahedeen through a CIA paramilitary operation. But even without these modern weapons in the hands of its opponents, the Soviet military found war in Afghanistan a Vietnam quagmire, holding little prospect for victory. In the more than four decades since the end of World War II, the Soviet "empire" has remained relatively static. Its once firm domination of Eastern Europe collapsed with the Berlin Wall in the last weeks of 1989. Secessionist movements in the Baltics, Armenia, Azerbaijan, and throughout the non-Russian parts of the USSR sorely test the Kremlin's ability even to hold together extant territories, much less consolidate other foreign ventures. The bleak truth for the Soviet leadership is that their nation is bounded not by a Canada or a Mexico but by hostile peoples—both within and without their frontiers.

The United States urgently needs to shift its attention and foreign policy energies away from its overwhelming concentration on anticommunism and toward other global issues of importance to the prosperity of Americans alive today and generations to follow: international trade, world health and ecology, refugee migrations, food supplies, and population control, among others. The diminishing ozone layer protecting humans from dangerous ultraviolet solar rays and the rapidly mushrooming world population hold greater potential danger to citizens of the United States and the

Soviet Union than the relatively limited number of disagreements separating the two superpowers.

A shift in the focus of foreign policy does not have to—and should not—entail total abandonment of the containment doctrine. The Soviet Union, after all, does remain a powerful potential adversary with the nuclear weapons of a superpower; its capacity to destroy the United States can hardly be ignored. What a shift does entail, however, is a redefinition of containment, a redrawing of the blueprint for foreign policy. The new blueprint must retain the prudent continuation of a strong military defense but should reach out more energetically and sincerely for cordial relations with the Soviet Union and with other communist powers. It should also place higher on the national agenda the goal of improved ties with the emerging nations in joint combat against what the secretary of state in the Truman administration, George Marshall, understood to be the real enemies of international peace. In preparation for his Harvard commencement speech of 1947, announcing the European Recovery Program (the Marshall Plan), Marshall penciled out a reference in an early draft to "the Communist threat." The enemies he preferred to list were "hunger, poverty, desperation and chaos."[12]

If the United States can apply the salve of trade and cultural-educational exchange in an effort to heal the sores of past enmity and befriend the world's largest Marxist nation, the People's Republic of China, and if the United States can carry on a vigorous trading relationship with Angola at the very time our leaders criticize the presence of Cuban troops there, then surely this nation can find ways to resolve its differences with the Soviet Union. The objective of reducing the risk of World War III is at least worth a try at restoring the U.S.-Soviet friendship that blossomed during the 1930s.

The first step is for both superpowers to slough off the siege mentality that has characterized the cold war and prohibited the consideration of fresh approaches to foreign policy. Each can try harder to empathize with the historical experiences of the other. Were they to ponder the staggering loss of life suffered by Soviet citizens in World War II (over twenty-six million), Americans might appreciate more the concern of Soviets for the defense of their borders. If one minute of silence were observed for each Russian killed in that war, the silence would endure for thirty-seven years! Americans might consider, too, the effect of the harsh anti-Soviet rhetoric (of the "evil empire" strain) that so often comes out of Washington, D. C., and the peril that the Strategic Defense Initiative (SDI) might hold from the Soviet point of view as part of a potential U.S. nuclear strategy designed for a first-strike capability. Conversely, Soviet citizens and their leaders might ponder more seriously the effects on Americans of their own hostile rhetoric, arms buildup, ballistic-missile defense system, and civil defense programs.

A PREDISPOSITION TOWARD INTERVENTIONISM

Stemming from the fixation on the Soviet Union and its capacity for external aggression, the United States has abandoned its traditional strains of caution in external affairs to embrace a foolish posture of compulsive interventionism abroad. Henry A. Kissinger, secretary of state for Presidents Nixon and Ford, has outlined three questions that ought to guide the rational planning of foreign policy: (1) What international changes is the United States willing to resist? (2) What are this nation's goals? (3) What resources does the nation have to pursue these ends?[13] If anything should be clear from this nation's foreign policy experiences in this century, it is that the United States cannot shape the world to its liking. It has neither the wealth nor the will for such a mission, and appropriately so, for it does not have the right.

Yet, there are those in this country who continue to believe that it must intervene almost everywhere around the globe, especially if the Soviets have intervened—the people who see the world in black and white as an arena for mortal combat between the United States and the Soviet Union. The United States is joined in a battle "between Jesus Christ and the hammer-and-sickle," declared the chairman of the House Armed Services Committee in 1970.[14] For those who share this stark view of the world, every tremor of revolution in Chad, Grenada, or Nicaragua requires an American response—regardless how small the nation, or how large the loss of American lives or the drain on the federal treasury. Little wonder the popular West German author Günter Grass asks in anguish, "how impoverished must a country be before it is not a threat to the U.S. government?"[15]

If America is to restore its financial solvency and again become a competitor in the world's trading markets, if America is to regain the respect it once enjoyed in the early postwar period, if America is to care for its own people—with one preschool child in four now living in poverty in the United States, with its cities facing traffic gridlock, with its lakes and rivers dying from acid rain and other pollutants—surely this country must adopt a more discriminating approach toward foreign intervention. The $100 million proposed by the Reagan administration for the Contras in 1985 could have been spent in this country to enable 150,000 students to attend college or to provide 540,000 children with meals for a year.[16] "The sooner we learn to impose some reasonable restraint on our own tendency to intervene too much in other people's affairs," a member of the Senate Foreign Relations Committee once wisely urged, "the happier land we will have and the less burden we will place upon our own people to undertake sacrifices that are not really related to their own good or the good of their country."[17]

Beyond the financial costs lies the growing realization that this country can exercise only a limited influence on the affairs of other nations. The American experience in Indochina provides an illustration seared in the nation's memory. Despite an enormous commitment of U.S. blood and treasure to South Vietnam, the range of powers exercised by the United States proved unable to curb the internal corruption of the South Vietnamese government or unite its army into an effective fighting force.

This essay is not a call for a return to isolationism. Two world wars have taught Americans that they cannot escape from the world, however much they may wish to; like it or not, the United States is inextricably bound to the other nations on this globe. It is a call, though, for a more discriminating foreign policy. A secretary of defense during the Reagan years sounded an appropriate "note of caution" against the rash use of U.S. force abroad. Even though the administration often ignored his prescription, it remains a sensible checklist for future overt interventions:

- the military action had to involve vital national interests;
- the United States must intend to win;
- the operation had to have clearcut political–military objectives;
- these objectives had to be subjected to a continual reassessment;
- the American people had to be in support; and
- all alternatives to the use of overt force had to have been tried first and found wanting.[18]

As for the covert use of force (paramilitary or "special" operations), this option should be rarely used and only as a last resort when the safety of the country is at stake. Two of the nation's leading foreign policy experts have commented on the use of covert action. "The guiding criterion," advised Clark Clifford, former secretary of defense and an author of the National Security Act of 1947, "should be the test as to whether or not a certain covert project truly affects our national security."[19] Cyrus Vance, secretary of state in the Carter administration, similarly told a congressional committee that "it should be the policy of the United States to engage in covert actions only when they are absolutely essential to the national security."[20]

In agreement with these expressions of restraint becoming to a mature superpower, the argument presented in this essay calls for a more patient and tolerant United States, one that does not rush into foreign conflicts without serious thought and debate; one that realizes the world will continue to have civil wars that must be resolved by the warring factions, not by outside forces; one that honors the use of diplomacy as the first step in external relations, not the employment of force and secret operations. It calls for an America that, in a wise passage from John Quincy Adams's inaugural address, "is the friend of all the liberties in the world, [but] the guardian of only her own."

NOTES

1. George F. Kennan, *American Diplomacy, 1900–1950* (Chicago: University of Chicago Press, 1951), p. 79.
2. Reported by Lee Schwartz, "We're Failing Geography 100," *Washington Post*, December 29, 1987, p. 29; for the 1988 Gallup poll, see Connie Leslie, "Lost on the Planet Earth," *Newsweek*, August 8, 1988, p. 31.
3. *Atlanta Journal and Constitution*, November 22, 1986, p. A6.
4. William Pfaff, "If It's 'the Public Be Damned,' the Policy Is Doomed," *Los Angeles Times*, December 18, 1986, p. 11.
5. Quoted by Stuart Taylor, Jr., "Reagan's Defenders Arguing He Can Defy Congress's Ban," *New York Times*, May 17, 1987.
6. Aaron Wildavsky, "The Past and Future Presidency," *Public Interest* 41 (Fall 1975): 75.
7. Susan F. Rasky, "Senators Seeking to Overhaul War Powers Resolution," *New York Times*, May 20, 1988, p. 3.
8. An interview with John Hughes, "Lunch with Cap," *Christian Science Monitor*, September 12, 1986, p. 16.
9. Speech by J. Michael Kelly, reprinted in *Special Operations in U.S. Strategy*, ed. Frank R. Barnett, B. Hugh Tovar, and Richard H. Schultz (Washington, D.C.: National Defense University Press, 1984), p. 223.
10. Colin Campbell, "Campaign Obscured Babbitt's Expertise in Foreign Policy," *Atlanta Constitution*, February 19, 1988, p. A6. Notes Daniel Patrick Moynihan, a Democratic senator from New York and a member of the Foreign Relations Committee: ". . . The one enormous fact of the third quarter of the 20th century [is] the near complete collapse of Marxism as an ideological force in the world. Nothing quite so sudden or so complete has ever happened. Economic doctrines have faded, political canons have been discarded, but here was an extraordinary world view, thought to be irresistible, maintaining a hold on sectors of opinion in all the great metropolitan centers of the world—of a sudden, vanished." "Reagan's Doctrine and the Iran Issue," *New York Times*, December 21, 1986, p. E19.
11. See Eqbal Ahmad and Richard J. Barnet, "A Reporter at Large: Bloody Games," *New Yorker*, April 11, 1988, pp. 44–86.
12. Anthony Lewis, "When We Could Believe," *New York Times*, June 12, 1987.
13. Henry A. Kissinger, "Dealing from Reality," *Los Angeles Times*, November 22, 1987, part 5, p. 1.
14. Representative Mendel Rivers (D–South Carolina), quoted by Charles McCarry, "Ol' Man Rivers," *Esquire*, October 1970, p. 171.
15. Quoted in *Nation*, March 12, 1983, p. 301.
16. "Evening News," ABC Television, March 11, 1985.
17. Senator Frank Church, public address, Boise, Idaho, August 6, 1972.
18. The list comes from Caspar Weinberger; cited in Bernard E. Trainor, "Weinberger on Persian Gulf: Cap the Chameleon?" *New York Times*, October 9, 1987, p. A20.
19. Testimony, in Senate Select Committee to Study Governmental Operations with Respect to Intelligence Activities, *Covert Action: Hearings*, December 4, 1975.
20. Ibid.

SUGGESTED READINGS

GADDIS, JOHN LEWIS.   *The United States and the Origins of the Cold War, 1941–1974.* New York: Columbia University Press, 1972. A balanced analysis of how the United States and the Soviet Union came to be adversaries despite an earlier friendship.

KENNEDY, PAUL.   *The Rise and Fall of the Great Powers.* New York: Random House, 1987. A historian warns that the "imperial overstretch" of large powers typically exceeds their economic and military capability to defend their interests.

WHITE, RALPH K.   *Fearful Warriors: A Psychological Profile of U.S.–Soviet Relations.* New York: Free Press, 1984. An insightful argument by a psychologist for greater empathy between the superpowers—a way out of the adversarial relationship.

Openness and Preparedness: American Foreign Policy Challenges in the 1990s

Kevin V. Mulcahy
Louisiana State University

As we approach a new century, there is good news and not-so-good news about how we conduct foreign affairs. The good news is that the Soviet policy of *glasnost*, or openness, that was instituted by Mikhail Gorbachev, represents an opportunity for improved relations between the United States and the Soviet Union. The not-so-good news is that although Gorbachev's reforms represent a welcome change in how the Communist Party exercises its monopoly of power, glasnost does not automatically usher in an era of international openness. A combination of political and military preparedness must necessarily continue as the basis for U.S. foreign policy vis-à-vis the Soviet Union. The great challenge of the next generation will be how the United States can contribute to a stable world order that is both supportive of our national security interests and responsive to democratic concerns at home and abroad. This will require a foreign policy based on both openness *and* preparedness.

The post-World War II world, with the developing Cold War between the United States and the Soviet Union, confirmed what Pearl Harbor had made manifest: that national security could not be based upon isolationism, a "fortress America." American security interests were necessarily global in scope. Whatever the hopes for a peaceful world order of united nations, the realities of the international situation after 1945 dictated otherwise. The defeat of Germany and Japan and the subsequent demise of the British Empire left the United States and the Soviet Union as the great superpowers. For both nations, this was a new role. Furthermore, the resulting bipolarity, in which world dominance would be shared by only two national actors, was an unusual development in the international system. In such a situation, internation rivalry would understandably be likely, if not inevitable. On the other hand, it should be noted that for all the East–West tensions of the past forty years, the United States and the Soviet Union have never been directly engaged in hostilities with each other. However imperfect the post-War international system during the Cold War, there has been no World War III. The transformation in Soviet international behavior brought about by Gorbachev has made a superpower conflict even more unlikely.

This is not the occasion for assessing the rights and wrongs of American–Soviet relations since 1947. Moreover, the concern here is with the future of America's foreign policy and its relation to the international system. In sum, whether or not American–Soviet relations could have been more conciliatory is a moot point. What is clear is that international courtesy increased markedly as the Soviet political system moved away from domestic totalitarianism and foreign expansionism. Whether prompted by ideological reappraisal or economic bankruptcy, glasnost, with its political openness domestically and relaxation of tensions internationally, represents a complete reversal of previous Soviet behavior. In effect, the dramatic transformation of Eastern Europe is a tribute to the constancy of the American containment policy during more than forty years. From our viewpoint, better relations with the Soviet Union were always predicated upon a diminished Soviet political threat in Europe and greater freedom for the Eastern bloc nations. The mutual reduction in NATO and Warsaw Pact conventional forces and in strategic weaponry is a direct result of the changes within the Communist parties in the Soviet Union and Eastern Europe. As the Soviet Union has become more conciliatory, the United States has been more accommodating.

Since 1947, containment has been the tactical and strategic basis of U.S.–Soviet relations. Much has changed between the superpowers since George Kennan formulated the philosophical foundation of post-War American foreign policy in his "Mr. X" article on the "Sources of Soviet Conduct." Nevertheless, the principles of containment retain their basic validity. Ambassador Kennan argued that "Soviet pressure against the free institutions of the Western world is something that can be contained by the vigilant application of counter-force at a series of constantly shifting geographical and political points, corresponding to the shifts and maneuvers of Soviet policy, but which cannot be charmed or talked out of existence." In the era of glasnost, such an unflattering description of U.S.–Soviet relations may seem either quaint or unreasonably provocative. The fact remains, however, that American determination to resist Soviet efforts to dominate world affairs has been vindicated by the spectacular flowering of democratic movements in Eastern Europe and within the Soviet Union itself.

Should a future Soviet government seek to promote its geopolitical interests in ways that would threaten international stability, a containment policy might again be necessary. On the other hand, if the Soviet Union continues to suffer political and economic disarray, the United States may find itself in the curious position of propping up its historic rival to forestall a potentially destabilizing power vacuum in world affairs. As the "sick man of Europe," the Soviet Union, like the nineteenth-century Ottoman Empire, may require the help of its adversaries to keep functioning. The most curious development of the post-Cold War era may prove to be American support of the Soviet Union, to maintain the stability of the post-War international system.

There is precedent for American– Soviet cooperation, as may be seen in the reduction of the nuclear arsenal during the past few years. Paradoxically, the decreased likelihood of nuclear war is directly related to maintaining a credible deterrence. As long as nuclear weapons exist, the interrelated goal must be to create political arrangements that preclude their use and to demonstrate a capacity to respond to the threat of nuclear war. Although the likelihood of a total war involving the all-out exchange of thermonuclear weapons is remote, the development of more discriminating nuclear weapons could suggest the possibility of a "limited" nuclear war. Avoiding a suicidal nuclear escalation requires the United States to project military power in a flexible way through conventional forces. "Under these circumstances," as Zbigniew Brzezinski argues, "while retaining a residual capacity for an all-out nuclear war, to avoid being blackmailed by its threat, U.S. military power must be designed for more limited, prompt and even preemptive actions in areas clearly defined not only as vital but also as not capable of adequate self-defense."

BALANCE OF RIVALRIES

As great powers, the U.S. and the U.S.S.R. have international political interests that involve them in affairs beyond their borders. Some of these geopolitical concerns are ideological; that is, related to different world views: Communist versus liberal–democratic. Some interests are based on security considerations: on the need to protect military allies and economic resources. Prestige may also be important: being perceived as able to exert global influence in furthering the interests of one's allies. There is nothing particularly startling or amoral about such a state of international affairs. Great rivalries have characterized international relations for long periods of time, defining the world in relation to different spheres of influence. The rivalries inherent in promoting national interests should simply be recognized and managed realistically. Viewing the Soviet Union as an "evil empire" and the United States as the "city on a hill" does little to facilitate the geostrategic planning necessary to seeing this nation into the next millennium. If we accept that the U.S. and the U.S.S.R. are in a contest for dominance of world politics and that, other things being kept equal, neither side will resort to thermonuclear war, we can make certain assumptions about American foreign policy.

First, the contest between the superpowers is neither aberrational nor transitory. Rivalries between the United States and the Soviet Union are inevitable even though another cold war is highly unlikely. Second, the relative equality that keeps the rivalry at a relatively low level of intensity depends on maintaining nuclear parity. All-out war is possible only if one side either believes it has a sufficient advantage to warrant an attack or is about to experience an irreversible and unacceptable setback. Third, both the U.S. and the U.S.S.R. are strained economically by their large military establishments. A reassessment of strategic priorities is necessary to both superpowers. Fourth, the assumption of hegemonic empire that has characterized American and Soviet relations with their allies is giving way to a more pluralist system of intra-alliance. Finally, these assumptions lead to certain conclusions about how the United States should position itself for the next generation of foreign policy challenges.

REGIONAL INTERESTS

The first commitment of the United States will continue to be to Europe. In 1989, the "year of Europe," we saw dramatic changes in the political and diplomatic assumptions that had governed European affairs since World War II. With the effective dismantling of the Soviet system of Eastern European satellites and the diminution of a Warsaw Pact military threat, the *raison d'etre* for an American presence in Europe has lost its urgency. Ever since the Marshall Plan and the creation of the North Atlantic Treaty Organization, the United States has considered the security of Western Europe to be inextricably intertwined with its own. In the post-World War II period, the possibility of Soviet expansion required a substantial American military commitment; today, while such a threat is highly unlikely, the U.S.S.R. still remains the dominant continental power. Inevitably, the European nations (both Eastern and Western) will take greater responsibility for their own security. On the other hand, any plan to phase out NATO is decidedly premature. The U.S. may or may not be a European power; but as a world power it is respon-

sible for managing regional transformations. Ironically, the Soviet Union may prove to prefer the NATO alliance system to one in which a unified Germany is an international wildcard.

The second great regional interest of the United States will continue to be in the Middle East, particularly in the Persian Gulf. With the collapse of the pro-American Iranian government in 1979, a power vacuum developed in the Gulf States that had to be filled by the United States. The necessity of guaranteeing access by the United States and other Western nations to the oil supplies of the Persian Gulf is not likely to diminish in the near future. The end of the Iran–Iraq war has greatly reduced regional tensions and naval hostilities involving the American fleet. Nevertheless, a radical Iranian government and a militarily resurgent Iraq will continue to pose great problems for the moderate Gulf States allied with the United States, and for Israel. The Balkans were the tinderbox of the pre-World War I international system; the Middle East represents a similar threat to world stability today. This makes the American military presence necessary, especially a rapid deployment force and elements of the U.S. fleet.

The third area of geopolitical concern is much closer to home, in Latin America. The United States and its hemispheric neighbors have never had easy, nor particularly reciprocal, relations. What we must recognize, however, is that Latin America is a vital security interest. What might not involve the United States if it were happening in Asia or Africa must necessarily be a concern in Latin America. For example, the problem with the Sandinista regime had to do not just with the question of its faithfulness to the democratic process, but with its close relationships with Cuba and the Soviet Union. Similarly, a Marxist insurgency in

El Salvador will legitimately entail global politics quite apart from the demands of domestic social justice. However, although international security interests may affect American responses to movements hostile to those interests, the overriding interest of the United States is the promotion of stable democratic regimes in Latin America. The free elections in Nicaragua in 1990, in which the Sandinistas were defeated, clearly demonstrated the power of the democratic process and its centrality for American foreign policy.

The United States and the Soviet Union have coexisted successfully by tacit recognition of each other's security concerns. Even with the apparent eclipse of Soviet global capabilities, these concerns are certain to persist and will require keeping a credible troop presence in Western Europe, having a mixed command of naval, air, and ground forces capable of rapid deployment to trouble spots such as the Middle East, and developing a counter-insurgency program to assist hemispheric allies threatened by insurrectionary forces or drug cartels. It may seem ironic, but the decreased likelihood of nuclear war does not necessarily preclude regional and local conflicts. In fact, the very certainty of a superpower checkmate on nuclear weaponry invites more conventional tests of political and military resolve. The United States must develop a doctrine of discriminating deterrence that can manage low-intensity conflicts without disrupting the international equilibrium.

U.S. POWER: LIMITS AND PROSPECTS

Many Americans, and more than a few policymaking officials, are ambivalent about the role of power in the conduct of foreign affairs. An aversion to exercising

global power has a variety of causes, including a historic suspicion of "foreign entanglements," our post-Vietnam fear of involvement in a divisive war, and the idealistic conviction that a democratic America has a mission to transform the international political system. In contrast, there is a competing point of view, which has been termed *realpolitik*, that favors a positive exercise of power in the international arena. From a realpolitik perspective, the overriding purpose of American foreign policy is to preserve and promote U.S. geopolitical interests. These interests include maintaining the independence of Europe, preserving continued access to the Persian Gulf region, maintaining hemispheric security, and preserving good relations with Japan and allied nations along the Pacific rim. To ignore them is to invite confusion about America's role in the world and increase the danger of a global conflict based on miscalculation.

What needs to be stressed, however, is that no nation's power, even a superpower's, is omnipotent or unlimited. For too many years, the United States has been overcommitted abroad, attempting to act as the world's policeman, and lacking a sense of diplomatic priorities. If isolationism and one-worldism are to be rejected as naively unrealistic, the kind of indiscriminant approach to foreign policy that sees American interests affected by anything that might happen anywhere in the world is a recipe for diplomatic failure. In an increasingly less monolithic world order, the United States must avoid universalizing its interests and must focus on the most vital external interests. American security is not necessarily at stake in every political conflict or power change that occurs in the world. On the other hand, the results of particular conflicts and political rivalries may involve

U.S. security interests. For example, the outcomes of civil wars in Chad or Sri Lanka would not affect U.S. interests, although they are of great interest to France and India. In contrast, political developments in Nicaragua and El Salvador, Israel and Saudi Arabia, the Philippines and Thailand, as well as the relations between Western and Eastern Europe, always have major implications for American foreign policy.

To invoke a time-honored concept of international relations from the eighteenth and nineteenth centuries, American politico-military thinking should be inspired by the goal of a balance of power. An equilibrium among the nations of the international system would preclude any one nation from becoming strong enough to impose its will upon the others. Since the Second World War, the United States and the Soviet Union as the two nuclear powers have, after periods of competition for hegemony, reached a level of accommodation and mutual acceptance. This power balance was not the result of good will or identity of interest, but a recognition by both sides that any revision of the status quo by threat of force was impossible, as it would provoke a nuclear exchange. Since glasnost, a decidedly more multipolar international system is emerging. We need a new power balance among the military superpowers (the U.S. and U.S.S.R.), the economic superpowers (Japan, the European Community, a unified Germany), and China. In this post-Cold War era, the U.S. (and to a lesser degree the U.S.S.R.) will remain a great power (if not a Great Power) in a more diversified and collaborative world order.

These recent developments in the world order present new opportunities for further stabilization of international relations. Below the level of nuclear weapons, we are seeing a growing multi-

polarity in the distribution of regional power. For example, by 2010 the gross national product of the United States (about $8 trillion) will be equaled or surpassed by the member nations of the European Community (E.C.), with Japan and the People's Republic of China following (about $4 trillion), and the Soviet Union fifth in the economic hierarchy ($3 trillion). In particular, Japan has become an important international actor; it is a superpower in all but military might. Japan is overtaking the United States as the foremost contributor of international economic aid; China and South Korea both receive more than 70 percent of their development assistance from Japan. Although it is neither a nuclear nor a major military power, Japan has a defense budget that ranks sixth in the world and could soon surpass France, Britain, and Germany to rank third behind the U.S. and the U.S.S.R. What this suggests is that responsibility for maintaining world order may be devolved among a number of nonsuperpower (that is, non-nuclear) nations.

Much has been made of the relative decline in American economic power. Undeniably, U.S. primacy in the world economy that characterized the first thirty years after World War II has ended. However, it is quite another thing to argue that the U.S. is another case of *The Decline and Fall of Great Powers* (the title of Paul Kennedy's influential book) and is marked for the fate met by the British Empire. For one thing, American economic preeminence was a peculiar result of the wartime devastation of Western Europe and Japan, and the post-War revival of these nations was the result of deliberate American policy. Similarly, American economic power is declining as Japan and Western Europe gain strength because of a shift in the relations among close trading partners and political allies.

Our former enemies' resurgence proves the success of our policy of economic reconstruction and political rehabilitation. Most important, neither of the recently emergent economic superpowers represents a challenge to the military or political leadership of the United States in the international system. The E.C. lacks a national identity and Japan, for historical and pragmatic reasons, does not seek to project military force abroad.

In effect, however serious the decline in American global economy, the international standing of the United States in relation to its allies and the Soviet Union remains unchanged. This is not to say that the United States need not respond to economic challenges. A version of *perestroika*, or restructuring, is as imperative for the U.S. economy as for the Soviet Union's and, apart from considerations of domestic well-being, for other geopolitical concerns. A great power's military and diplomatic influence is only as good as its economic strength. This is a truism that is as valid argued by Henry Kissinger as by Paul Kennedy. Fortunately, the economic revitalization of the United States is decidedly likely, because of the technical accomplishment, market incentives, infrastructure development, and (perhaps especially) the kind of relationship we enjoy with our economic competitors. In an interdependent global economy, the self-interest of Europe and Japan requires a healthy American economy. Similarly, the United States must better appreciate its allies in the international system and better manage its relations with them.

A more pluralistic Western alliance need not be judged a threat to American power and national interests. U.S. interests will remain influential even if we do not dictate to our allies. A greater emphasis on alliance management and consensus building will benefit all the nations involved, as collective policies become shared responsibilities. Fundamentally, there is no realistic alternative to American influence in the world. A failure of American resolve would create an international power vacuum just as momentous changes in East–West relations make inevitable creative alternatives to the superpower rivalry of the past four decades.

SUMMING UP

Glasnost and *perestroika* represent dramatic efforts by the Gorbachev regime to reverse the ideological and economic malaise of Soviet society. Thomas Garton Ash suggests that the proper historical analogy for the decline of the Soviet Union is with the Ottoman Empire; both were "imprisoned in a rigid, archaic economic and fiscal system, incompatible with the demands of the modern industrial economy emerging around it, and incapable of competing with the West." By encouraging greater openness of intellectual, cultural, and political expression, Gorbachev hopes to inspire Soviet commitment to the economic, bureaucratic, and ideological restructuring necessary to a revitalized society. Such a society would also be better able to compete militarily and economically with the West.

From the American perspective, the Soviet Union's display of international civility is to be applauded and encouraged. The reduction in East–West tensions, the abolition of intermediate nuclear weapons and markedly reduced troop levels in Europe, the steps toward mutual reduction in strategic arsenals, and the overall normalization of diplomatic relations can work only to the advantage of the United States and its allies. The Soviet Union's stake in the survival of the existing world order will encourage its willingness to accommodate U.S. interests. Such a disposition is further likely to keep expansionist impulses contained, weapons systems controlled, regional conflicts limited, and stability preferable to revision. The constancy with which American geopolitical interests are supported will do more to guarantee the peace than ritual expressions of good will. The Cold War is over, yet rapprochement does not eliminate the differences in the world views that characterize the U.S. and the U.S.S.R. The complementary policies of openness *and* preparedness are most likely to sustain an international order that will make possible the peaceful adjustment of these differences.

SUGGESTED READINGS

JEANNE J. KIRKPATRICK, "Beyond the Cold War," *Foreign Affairs,* 69 (Winter, 1990): 1–16. A reappraisal of America's international position of power by a noted conservative scholar. Argues that the end of the Cold War will necessarily end the special status of both the U.S. and the U.S.S.R., which will remain great but no longer "super" powers.

McGEORGE BUNDY, "From Cold War Toward Trusting Peace," *Foreign Affairs,* 69 (Winter, 1990): 197–212. A liberal intellectual is cautiously optimistic about the prospect for stable and peaceful relations between the U.S. and the U.S.S.R. with the easing of Cold War tensions. Nevertheless, what this will mean in terms of strategic doctrine remains a subject of prolonged analysis.

FRANCIS FUKUYAMA, "The End of History?" *The National Interest,* 16 (Summer, 1989): 3–18. The author, a State Department official in the Bush administration, sees the end of the Cold War as the triumph of Western principles of liberal democracy and capitalist economics. At the same time, he laments the end of an era in which great ideological issues galvanized public debate and mobilized political action.

Toward 2020 Vision

José Z. Garcia and John Neagle
New Mexico State University

Nearly everyone agrees that in a startlingly brief period of time, global ecological security issues—ozone depletion, the "greenhouse" effect, the AIDS epidemic, contamination of the oceans, and so on—are beginning to crowd the agenda of world politics. Several things must be said at the outset about these issues. First, they are of a new, unprecedented, complicated, and thus far unknown urgency. We know they are serious but we don't know yet how much or exactly what kind of time we have to solve them. Second, they can be handled only through global cooperation. It is highly unlikely that one country by itself will have the resources available to eliminate these issues as major threats or to impose a solution to them. And third, at the present time the world is simply not organized well enough to assure well-informed citizens either that the urgency of the problems is being calculated accurately or that possible solutions can be implemented in the near future. Therefore, it is most likely that one of the highest priorities of national leaders during the next thirty years will be the creation of international institutions capable of monitoring the ecological health of the globe and implementing global measures designed to reduce global environmental threats.

The foregoing sentence is a cliché. Who can disagree with it? The problem seems fairly straightforward and relatively easy. It is not. To understand why it is not requires a bit of explanation about how the world is organized and how it is changing. Briefly stated, the moving of global environmental issues to the front burner of international politics is an unprecedented development, and confronts an aging world political system not designed to handle those issues.

THE NATION-STATE SYSTEM: FROM ANARCHY TO HEGEMONY AND BEYOND

For more than three hundred years global politics has been organized within a nation-state system. Ever since the Treaty of Westphalia in 1648 (marking the emergence on the world scene of the modern nation-state) world political affairs have been run by and for the interests of nation-states. The system was based in principle on equality among them, but some became more powerful than others and managed to impose their will in certain areas. But only very rarely did any one state get strong enough to impose its will in all areas, and in fact what resulted was intense international competition for power in an environment in which no state could garner enough power to make itself the ultimate authority on any given issue: a condition known as "anarchy." From 1648 until the time of the French Revolution, when the major powers in world politics were traditional European monarchies, the international system really did approach true anarchy. The distribution of wealth and power

among the prominent European nation-states was fairly even. Polarization had not yet become a noticeable feature of the world political system. The objectives of these monarchies were limited to overall national goals. And the degree of interdependence (that is, mutual forms of influence) between nations was very low. Under these conditions issues such as epidemics or regionalized economic depression that cut across national boundaries could simply not be tackled.

After 1789 and until the end of World War II, certain nations managed to rise above the pack. The European nation-states that were able to forge empires (most prominently England and France) used their foreign possessions to shape global interaction; that is, colonialism and colonial possessions (through commercial relations, the attempted transfer of domestic institutions, military deployments, and so on) became one vehicle by which certain nations could accumulate unprecedented amounts of power.

By the late nineteenth century England clearly emerged as the strongest of the imperial powers, so strong it could by itself determine the outcome of major conflicts. The anarchic character of the world diminished as England was able to establish international political and economic institutions. A polarization of the world's distribution of wealth was increasing as well, but not solely to the benefit of the European colonial powers. By the early part of the twentieth century the prominent and rising national wealth of two avowedly isolationist powers, the United States and Japan, would propel these irreversibly onto the world scene as major players.

As significant poles of international power developed out of a previously anarchic nation-state system, the goals of nation-states changed as well. Ideologies came to the fore with the American and

French revolutions. By the late nineteenth century ideologies of one kind or another came to be goals for which nations struggled against one another. Some were essentially nationalistic, such as the rising German nationalism and irredentism associated with Hitler's rise to power; some ideologies were blatantly internationalist in their appeal, such as Marxism, which came to power in Russia in 1917. Ideology as a focus of international competition would reach its zenith during this period. Polarization made possible the handling of certain transnational issues (such as establishing international mail services, and the spread of capitalist economic principles like free trade) along global lines, but ideology greatly limited the kinds of issues over which ideological competitors would cooperate with one another.

Another signpost of things to come was the increase in interdependence between nations. Although not yet close to crisis stage, the race by European nation-states to maximize their colonial possessions as quickly as possible (perhaps most dramatically noticed in the ten-year "scramble for Africa," when almost all of interior Africa was colonized at once) highlighted a world of finite resources and shorter distances. These tensions— growing interdependence, ideological conflict, and increasing inequality among nations—had much to do with igniting two major world wars in the first half of the twentieth century.

The fortunes of many great powers changed dramatically with the conclusion of World War II. Japan, which had been a feudal and agricultural power as late as the 1850s but was a major industrial and naval power by 1905 (the year in which it destroyed Russia as a naval power and occupied Korea), and which at the height of its power had controlled much of East Asia, became the only na-tion so far to suffer nuclear attack. Similarly, Germany, which at one point controlled much of continental Europe, was destroyed as an industrial power in World War II.

Many of the victors did not fare much better than Japan and Germany. Britain and France, also ravaged by the war, saw their empires unravel and experienced difficulty taking care of domestic affairs. This international vacuum was filled by the only two significant military powers extant: the United States (the only truly unscathed nation among the major participants) and the USSR. Initially, though, the United States was clearly the more dominant and powerful nation, the original superpower.

The colonial powers were falling apart, never to return. The dominance of the United States in many arenas would be manifested not on the basis of true colonialism (physical or military occupation) but by the more subtle concept of hegemony. Hegemonic control is exerted more through economic than military means; ideology would be a key component of the hegemonic system; and great emphasis would be put on norms and the need for "world order," a notion that implied only a set of rules and regulations governing (a) the interaction of states to avoid severe conflict that could escalate to nuclear war, and (b) the economic norms whereby growth and development could be fostered throughout the world. But "world order" after World War II was not designed to go beyond these two goals to resolve other issues of global management, such as ecology or human rights; ideology and bipolarity were simply too powerful to permit cooperation beyond these limited issues.

The initial postwar period, strongly bipolar and characterized by strong ideological competition between the two major camps, both striving to maintain what hegemony they had in a world of increasingly sharp interdependence, was destined to be succeeded by a multipolar world of hegemonic decline. By the mid-1970s a rough parity existed militarily between the Soviet Union and the United States. Also by this time, the ravaged former allies and enemies had recovered economically—Great Britain, France, West Germany, and Japan—so much so that U.S. economic hegemony and bipolarity were shattered. The handwriting was on the wall in 1971 when President Richard Nixon removed the gold standard backing up the U.S. dollar, yielding to increasing pressure from the growing economies of Western Europe and Japan.

What are we left with at present? Clearly the nation-state system and the anarchy that it implies have not gone away. In fact, with the decline of hegemony in both the Soviet and U.S. blocs, the world is likely to become more anarchic. This comes at a particularly bad time. The kinds of urgent ecological issues that are emerging require less anarchy, a reduction in the sovereign perquisites of powerful nations, and more global organization. Are we left with no means to handle such concerns? In spite of these trends other trends are more positive.

NONGOVERNMENTAL ACTORS

The prominence of nongovernmental actors in international politics is a recent and startling development. This is not simply the addition of more players, such as the newly independent nations of Africa, to the game, or the addition of a new type of player, such as terrorist organizations. The old "game" has been altered; the territorially defined nation-states have found it harder to maintain their norms in a world peppered with nongovernmental actors.

Much of the rise in prominence of the nongovernmental groups can be attributed to the revolution in worldwide communications. As communications technology became truly global in its scope and instantaneous as well, the informational resources of the private individual in society became a source of power. Now citizens had access to knowledge about world events once the exclusive domain of world leaders and elites. Increasing knowledge led to heightened passions. Self-confidence and interest combined in the formation of nongovernmental groups in many issue areas and their using an array of means to achieve their ends.

One set of nongovernmental actors enjoying a resurgence in today's world are terrorist groups. Terrorist groups exhibit all the complications that nongovernmental groups bring to the problem of maintaining territorial control. Many of the activities of terrorist groups within their home countries seem designed to thwart business as usual for the nation-state. Therefore, their orientation seems nonnationalist or antinationalist. In addition, they identify greatly and often coordinate their activities with like-minded brethren in other countries. We can no doubt thank global communications for this development as well.

Not only do terrorists undermine the sovereignty of nation-states by their actions but efforts to deal with terrorists have thus far been most effective when undertaken by individual nation-states rather than by international cooperative action. The triumph of the Israeli commandos at Entebbe and of the West German Grenzentruppen at Mogadishu in Somalia come to mind. Failures stick out as well, such as the tragedy at the Munich Olympics and the failed U.S. hostage rescue attempt in Iran. Some actions that are seemingly successful, such as the U.S. bombing raid on Libya, are controversial and are themselves attacked (usually by polar ideological opposites) as being terrorist in nature. But with all the successes, failures, and controversies, they represent efforts conducted by individual nation-states. An international antiterrorist institution seems a remote prospect at best.

Many nongovernmental organizations do not employ extreme means, and in fact are not very controversial and enjoy widespread respect. Most prominent among them are the human rights organizations. However, despite softer means and wider admiration for their goals and work, the human rights organizations present problems for the maintenance of the territorial norms. Indeed, they may be more of a real threat to these norms than the terrorists are.

Human rights groups such as America's Watch and Amnesty International articulate global problems in a way that does not correspond to an ideological vision, much more so than terrorist groups. For example, who among world leaders is pleased about Amnesty International when it scathingly denounces human rights abuses in both El Salvador and the Soviet Union? Both sides of the bipolar competition pretend that human rights abuses are things that occur only on the other side, or their own abuses are somehow more justified. It is not enough solace for East and West that Amnesty International criticizes their adversaries as well; both sides demand an all-or-nothing allegiance, an ideological fidelity typical of the nation-state system. Thus, human rights groups undermine the authority of the nation-state system.

Church groups, however, tend to be varied enough to enable each side in an international controversy to latch onto its own favorite organization. The modern history of Latin America displays this reality in sharp focus. Traditionally, the Roman Catholic church in Latin America was of singular importance and closely tied to the political power structure. As anticlerical movements arose in the late nineteenth century, however, this link was challenged and the church increasingly spoke out in favor of the powerless. The culmination of this process occurred at the Medellin Conference (Colombia) in 1968. There social justice was declared to be a mission of the church and, although not specified at the conference, Christian based communities sprang up around Latin America, preaching what has come to be known as liberation theology. Not all sectors of the church, however, agreed with liberation theology.

Christian based communities, supported at times by U.S. clergy, advocated social change and a reduction in the power perquisites of the rich, but often the national church hierarchies remained relatively conservative—although they often reserved for themselves the option of being sharply critical of national government policies. The new pope, John Paul II, turned out to be even more conservative, and sharply critical of some post-Medellin trends that were loved by the United States, scorned by many Marxists. In addition, evangelical Protestant groups had penetrated the Catholic monopoly in Latin America to a significant degree, gathering right-wing support. In short, there was something for everybody.

Thus, by the 1980s church groups were split into varying ideological postures, each one anxious to influence the course of international events in ways that sometimes undermine the power of governments or the bipolar organization of the world. Other institutions shared this characteristic, such as the multinational oil corporations (headquartered in the United States) whose interests coincided with the OPEC cartel's unilateral rise in prices during the early 1970s—even though the price rise caused serious political problems for the U.S. government. The international press corps, too, often shares this same characteristic with terrorist groups, human rights groups, churches, and multinational corporations; like such organizations, it often has nonnational and nonpolar goals that end up undermining the nation-state or at least competing with it.

Is there hope for a solution to global ecological problems in the emergence of these nonnational and nonpolar entities? The answer seems to lie in whether or not nonviolent nongovernmental groups will be able to pool enough of their resources, goals, and values to articulate a common response to these problems. It is clear that nation-states are the only entities with enough resources, if pooled, for resolving global ecological problems. Can nonviolent international groups influence the hearts and minds of enough citizens throughout the world to create a global culture capable of influencing the decision makers of major powers toward resolving ecological problems? There are some positive signs.

A citizen from anywhere in the world who joins Amnesty International is engaging in a mode of thought that represents at least a partial rejection of the ideological vision of both the Soviet Union and the United States. Amnesty International represents a partial criticism of both competing cold war ideologies; it transcends bipolar competition.

The success of human rights groups such as Amnesty International in mobilizing world opinion during the past decade (with targets in Uganda, the Philippines, the Soviet bloc, and several states in Latin America) suggests that we may be observing the first nonnational, nonpolar value in an emerging global culture: respect for the Universal Declaration on Human Rights.

Another emerging global norm might also be the universal acceptance of electoral democracy—not as a label but as a set of processes—as a source of governmental legitimacy. As with human rights, the upsurge for democracy does not have clear ideological boundaries. From Chile to Poland, from El Salvador to the Soviet Union, the fervor of democratization has taken hold in most societies, if not yet always in governments. This cultural imperative can even be noticed in the Soviet Union. Gorbachev's emphasis on *glasnost* (openness), including limited free elections, competing parties, and real power for the Supreme Soviet, has been coolly received by Communist party bureaucrats but much more warmly by average Soviet citizens. Whether or not he succeeds in the short run, Gorbachev leapfrogged over the power establishment and tapped into what looks like global culture.

The international news media are a likely transmission belt for global culture. Therefore, their power and prestige should grow enormously among those who share the above norms. This may seem odd in the United States, where the national press is viewed often with suspicion and derision, even in comparison with politicians. The international news media, however, are an indispensable conduit for news about global affairs, and the efforts of human rights groups, democratic groups, and others cannot succeed without enlisting their cooperation. Today virtually everyone gets into the media act. With every group erecting its own press facilities to disseminate (with increasingly sophisticated computer technology) its own version of the truth, we are left with a Tower of Babel in global communications. As groups with global capabilities increase their resources, they acquire press organs and thereby make themselves independent of official sources of information. In this sense the international press is becoming more pluralist (that is, less responsive to governments or bipolar ideologies), but an equally strong tendency toward sharing the norms of human rights, respect, and democratic procedures is also apparent. When a coalition of news media, human rights groups, and churches focuses on a particular issue, such as the regime of President Marcos in the Philippines, the regime in South Africa, or human rights in Marxist and non-Marxist Central America, recent experience suggests that these groups, acting together, wield more power than superpower governments and in fact can influence governments deeply. If global ecological issues determine primary policy goals, one can expect that the major shock troops employed to resolve them will come from those who are pressing this agenda, including representatives of organized news media, human rights pressure groups, church activists, and political coalitions designed to oust dictatorial regimes.

MILITARY POWER AND THE NEW INTERNATIONAL SYSTEM

Traditionally, threats to national power were countered by the monopoly of military force held by states. Is military power still a useful tool for nation-states? A decade ago Joseph Nye and Robert Keohane in their book *Power and Interdependence* discussed a new hierarchy of international issues, such as the distribution of oil, fishing rights, or any field of commerce with its own rules and regulations. Previously, they held, military power could have predicted the relative ranking of nations in any of these issues. But the stalemate of the modern nuclear age and the subsequent inability of the great powers to use their military power with ease or effectiveness (Vietnam, Afghanistan, the Middle East, Eastern Europe) have allowed economic strength to count more than military strength. The winners and losers in international politics cannot be predicted by looking at the military pecking order of countries. For example, Saudi Arabia and Norway, which do not have world-class militaries, nevertheless tend to win over the United States or the Soviet Union on issues that have to do with oil and fishing rights, respectively.

Today, after a decade of experimentation with military weapons—in Libya, Central America, Afghanistan, Grenada—and although the evidence is mixed, it seems clear the ultimate guarantor of the overall power of a nation-state still lies in a nation's military power. True, some states like Japan can become very powerful without military power, but their security is ensured by the military might of other nation-states, a point clearly underscored by events during the late 1980s in the Persian Gulf. What are the implications of this for the resolution of global ecological affairs in the next thirty years? First, to the extent that nation-states continue or expand the arms race, fewer resources will be available for resolving these issues. No amount of pressure by ecologically minded citizens of the world will eliminate trade-offs between the perceived military security needs of nations and ecological security issues. It seems more likely that intense competition will break out between those who favor increases in military capabilities of states (to protect nation-state goals) and those who favor increases in ecological capabilities of the emerging world culture. Second, to the extent that military and nation-state goals remain primary guarantors of national security, the anarchy of the world will almost certainly increase because the rise of secondary powers is reducing the hegemony of the United States and the Soviet Union, making the world multipolar in character. This will make international cooperation toward resolving ecological issues less likely. Whether ecological goals will be victorious in the next three decades depends in great part upon the speed with which global norms can be spread to citizens capable of neutralizing the political power of those groups most interested in protecting the military security needs of the nation-state This may well become the political battleground.

CONCLUSIONS

Originally, we were concerned about the global agenda on ecological issues, and the need for new institutions transcending national boundaries to address it. Let's consider first working with the nation-state system. Is an alliance of great powers possible whereby global issues would be addressed through international cooperation of developed countries? This would require substantial cooperation between the United States and the

Soviet Union because these two powers account for around 40 percent of global productivity each year. Is such cooperation likely? Even during the worst times of U.S.–Soviet relations, the two nations have been able to work together on issues of common vital concern, such as trying to halt nuclear proliferation. But broader cooperation would require a diminution of ideology in the relationship. This appears to be possible in the Gorbachev era, but the military threat each side represents for the other may get in the way, eventually, of substantial, long-lasting cooperation. Apart from the U.S.–Soviet concern, even allied states seem unwilling or incapable sometimes of dealing effectively with one another on global environmental issues.

We are left once again with the global culture. The trick is not to destroy the nation-state system (unnecessary and probably impossible) but to bypass it effectively. One hope is through intergovernmental organizations such as the United Nations and the World Health Organization (WHO). Clearly, the UN has a disappointing lack of power–the nation-state system proved too resilient—but perhaps the functional organizations (like the WHO) can do better. Ironically, it was once thought that the functional organizations would lead to broader intergovernmental organizations of real power. Maybe the reverse will occur: symbolic broad organizations like the UN could pave the way for functional organizations on ecology with real teeth. Thus, by the year 2020 our world could be characterized by a nation-state system that exists essentially only on paper. The real action might take place in intergovernmental organizations, such as the WHO, pressured by citizens of a rapidly expanding global culture.

SUGGESTED READINGS

STANLEY HOFFMAN, *Primacy in World Order*. New York: McGraw–Hill, 1980. One of the most influential books on international relations theory, at least until the era of glasnost.

JOSEPH NYE AND ROBERT O. KEOHANE, *Power and Interdependence*. Boston: Little, Brown Co., 1977. A very influential book that traces major changes in the international system and the impact of those changes on the use of force. Deals extensively with ecological and economic change in the world.

PAUL KENNEDY, *The Rise and Fall of the Great Powers*. New York: Random House, 1987. Popular (although scholarly) book on the dangers of overextension by the great powers.

Index